THE LIBRARY OF WORLD AFFAIRS

Editors :

GEORGE W. KEETON

AND

GEORG SCHWARZENBERGER

Number 59

THE FRONTIERS OF INTERNATIONAL LAW

WILLIAM LADD

An Examination of an American Proposal for an International Equity Tribunal (1935—Second Edition 1936).

THE LEAGUE OF NATIONS AND WORLD ORDER (1936).

MAKING INTERNATIONAL LAW WORK

(In collaboration with G. W. Keeton, 1939—Second and Revised Edition 1946).

POWER POLITICS

A Study of International Society (1941—Second and Revised Edition 1951—Translated into German, 1955 and Spanish, 1960).

INTERNATIONAL LAW AND TOTALITARIAN LAWLESS-NESS (1943).

INTERNATIONAL LAW, as applied by International Courts and Tribunals (1945—Second Edition 1949).
Third Edition: Volume 1 (1957).
                Volumes 2 and 3 (in preparation).

A MANUAL OF INTERNATIONAL LAW

(2 vols. — 1947 — Fourth Edition 1960 — Translated into German, 1951).

THE LEGALITY OF NUCLEAR WEAPONS (1958).

THE FRONTIERS

OF

INTERNATIONAL LAW

BY

GEORG SCHWARZENBERGER

Published under the auspices of
THE LONDON INSTITUTE OF WORLD AFFAIRS

LONDON
STEVENS & SONS LIMITED
1962

First published - - 1962

*Published by Stevens and
Sons Limited of 11 New
Fetter Lane in the City of
London and printed in
Great Britain by The
Eastern Press Ltd. of
London a n d Reading*

AUSTRALIA
The Law Book Co. of Australasia Pty Ltd.
Sydney : Melbourne : Brisbane

CANADA AND U.S.A.
The Carswell Company Ltd.
Toronto

INDIA
N. M. Tripathi Private Ltd.
Bombay

NEW ZEALAND
Sweet & Maxwell (N.Z.) Ltd.
Wellington

PAKISTAN
Pakistan Law House
Karachi

TO

JOHN E. READ

PREFACE

A NEW arrival from the Far East attended an introductory graduate course in Laws at a Western University and found that his learned teacher tried hard to " orientate " him and his fellow students. At one stage the newcomer considered that he had suffered more than he could be expected to bear. So he politely but firmly announced that he had come to the West not to be " orientated " but to be " occidised."

Orientation or occidisation in this sense is the first purpose this book is intended to serve, and it is meant to fulfil this function on two distinct levels. *Part One* will, it is hoped, assist potential students of international law in finding their bearings and perhaps also laymen interested in the subject in seeing international law in its wider setting. *Part Two* is intended to help the more advanced student in deciding on where to specialise in a rapidly expanding field. In this respect, any teacher in the University of London owes a special duty to the growing number of external postgraduate students who, frequently remote from any library, desire to study one or more of the increasing number of International Law options available in the examination for the degree of Master of Laws.

This book is also a long-delayed response to requests from colleagues in other Universities, and especially from abroad, where specialised work in international law is only just being contemplated, to make available to them some of these experiments in a handier form than in widely dispersed papers.

This explains both how this book came into existence, and why it was not published before. If it was to be more than a reasoned agenda of new tasks for international lawyers, the only alternative was to explore empirically over a prolonged period where the optimal frontiers of international law in our time lie and to consolidate the results of these findings later rather than sooner.

Thus, at various stages, when I contemplated—and postponed— the publication of a book on these lines, the editors and publishers of a number of publications, in which tentative and provisional versions of some of the chapters were first published, generously responded to my requests for permission to include material in this book. While more detailed references will be found in the Introduction, the names of these periodicals should head the list of acknowledgments: *Acta Scandinavica Juris Gentium; American Journal of International Law;*

Archiv für Rechts- und Wirtschaftsphilosophie; British Year Book of International Law; Current Legal Problems; Ethics; Europa-Archiv; International Law Quarterly; Nouvelle Revue de Droit International Privé; Österreichische Zeitschrift für öffentliches Recht; Review of Politics; Transactions of the Grotius Society; Virginia Quarterly Review and *Year Book of World Affairs.*

As usual, I am under a greater debt than I can tell to my colleagues associated with me in the teaching of International Law at University College London, and in the London Institute of World Affairs: Mr. E. D. Brown, Dr. B. Cheng, Mr. H. Connell and Mr. F. Parkinson. Once they became aware of the preparation of this book, they spontaneously assisted me by invaluable advice and criticism and greatly appreciated help in the reading of the proofs and the preparation of the tables and index.

Again, as in the past, the co-operation which I have received from Messrs. Stevens and The Eastern Press has been exemplary. It only remains to record my thanks to my late friend Hilary Stevens who, as on numerous occasions before, gave me the benefit of his advice in the formative stages of this book.

As a token of admiration and friendship, the book is dedicated to Judge John E. Read who, in his work as a member of the International Court of Justice, has shown so many of the qualities needed by international lawyers at all times, but never more than in an increasingly conformist age.

G. S.

UNIVERSITY COLLEGE LONDON

January 14, 1962

CONTENTS

PART TWO

THE EXPANDING FIELD

Contents   xi

TABLE OF CASES

[Cases which are referred to by title and date only are decisions of English Courts or of the Privy Council]

TABLE OF TREATIES

(The Kings of England are referred to only by name)

xv

ABBREVIATIONS

A/B - - -	Series A/B, containing the Judgments, Orders and Advisory Opinions of the Permanent Court of International Justice, 1931—1940
A.J.I.L. - -	*American Journal of International Law*
A. and P. - -	*Accounts and Papers* (United Kingdom Parliamentary Papers)
B - - -	Series B, containing the Advisory Opinions of the Permanent Court of International Justice, 1922—1930
Black Book of the Admiralty - -	Sir Travers Twiss (ed.), *The Black Book of the Admiralty* (Rolls Series), Nos. 1—3, 1871—1874
B.Y.I.L. - -	*British Yearbook of International Law*
C.L.P. - - -	*Current Legal Problems*
Cmd. - - -	Command Papers (United Kingdom) 1919—1956
Cmnd. - - -	Command Papers (United Kingdom) 1956-
COMECON -	Council of Mutual Economic Aid
Deprez-Mirot -	E. Deprez and Th. Mirot, *Les Ambassades anglaises pendant la guerre de cent ans* (1900)
Dumont - -	J. De Dumont, *Corps Universel Diplomatique du Droit des Gens* (1726—1731)
Estudios Trelles -	L. Legaz Lacambra and L. Garcia Arias (eds.), *Estudios de derecho internacional. Homenaje al Profesor Barcia Trelles*, 1958
Etudes Scelle -	*Les Techniques et les principes du droit public, Etudes en l'honneur de Georges Scelle*, 1950 (2 vols.)
European Y.B. -	*European Yearbook*
F. - - -	*Federal Reporter* (United States)
Fundamental Principles - -	Schwarzenberger, *The Fundamental Principles of International Law*, 37 Hague Recueil (1955)
GATT - - -	General Agreement on Tariffs and Trade (1947)
Grotius Transactions -	*Transactions of the Grotius Society*
Gutzwiller Festgabe - -	*Ius et Lex, Festgabe für Max Gutzwiller*, 1959
Hackworth, *Digest*	G. H. Hackworth, *A Digest of International Law*, 1940—44 (8 vols.)
Hague Recueil -	*Recueil des Cours, Académie de Droit International de la Haye*
Harv.L.R. - -	*Harvard Law Review*
Hertslet's *Commercial Treaties* -	*Collection of Treaties and Conventions between Great Britain and other Powers, so far as they relate to Commerce and Navigation, 1820–1926*
I.C.J. - - -	International Court of Justice
I.L.O. - - -	International Labour Organisation
I.L.Q. - - -	*International Law Quarterly*
I.M.T. - - -	International Military Tribunal

xxi

Lettres de Rois -	M. Champollion-Figeac, *Lettres de Rois, Reines et Autres Personnages des Cours de France et d'Angleterre*, 1839 and 1847
L.Q.R. - - -	*Law Quarterly Review*
Manual - -	Schwarzenberger, *A Manual of International Law*, 4th ed., 1960 (2 vols.)
Marsden, *Law and Custom*	R. G. Marsden, *Documents relating to Law and Custom of the Sea* (Publications of the Navy Records Society), Vol. i (1915) and Vol. ii (1916)
Marsden, *Select Pleas* -	R. G. Marsden, *Select Pleas in the Court of Admiralty* (Vols. vi and xi of the Publications of the Selden Society), Vol. i (1894) and Vol. ii (1897)
Martens, N.R.G. -	Martens, G. F. von, *Nouveau Recueil Général de Traités*, 1908—
Power Politics -	Schwarzenberger, *Power Politics*, 1951
R.G.D.I.P. - -	*Revue générale de droit international public*
R.I.A.A. - -	United Nations, *Reports of International Arbitral Awards*, 1948—
Rymer - - -	Th. Rymer's *Foedera*
S.I. - - -	Statutory Instruments
Treaty Series -	Foreign Office, *Treaty Series*, 1892—
UNESCO - -	United Nations Educational Scientific and Cultural Organisation
U.S. - - -	United States Supreme Court Reports
Vol. I - - -	Schwarzenberger, *International Law as applied by International Courts and Tribunals* (3rd ed.), Vol. I, 1957
Vol. II - -	Schwarzenberger, *International Law as applied by International Courts and Tribunals*, Vol. II (in the press)
Y.B.W.A. - -	*Yearbook of World Affairs*

INTRODUCTION

IT would be pleasant to imagine that this Introduction were to escape its generic fate of remaining unread. The reader might then acquaint himself at a glance with the theme of the book and the treatment of the material.

I—THE THEME

The theme of the book is the determination of the temporal, functional and analytical frontiers of international law in our time.[1]

Temporal Frontiers is not necessarily intended to convey the first beginnings of the law of nations. Arrested types of international law have existed since the dawn of recorded history in Asia Minor and further east, and these are of some interest to students of the history and sociology of international law.[2] Nor are Temporal Frontiers synonymous with the origins of the Doctrine of international law; for, in the initial stages, Practice usually precedes Doctrine. What, more than any other aspect of the evolution of international law, appears to call for exploration, are the points of departure of contemporary international law and the social factors of both continuity and change in the growth and expansion of international law into a universal legal system.

The term *Functional Frontiers* emphasises the purposes served by international law in its wider political and social environments. It appears that these determine the scope and effectivity of international law more decisively than vice versa.

The *Analytical Frontiers* of international law are at least as much barriers of the mind as they are limits imposed by the subject-matter. More often than not, they are laid down by a scholar's surroundings or by a lack of what Bismarck so aptly called *Zivilcourage*. Freely translated, " civic courage " may be equated with intellectual fearlessness, professional integrity, and a strong dose of non-conformism.

The extent to which these frontiers can be expanded varies from time to time and place to place. To judge by the material in the

---

1 The papers on *The Frontiers of International Law* (6 *Y.B.W.A.* (1952), p. 246 *et seq.*) and on *Neue Aufgaben für die Völkerrechtswissenschaft* (9 *Europa-Archiv* (1954), p. 6635 *et seq.*) were tentative feelers in these directions.
2 See below, p. 21 *et seq.*

1

London Record Office and similar archives on the Continent, awaiting analysis for generations, it merely requires enthusiasm and resources to widen considerably the temporal frontiers of international law as, at present, they are still largely taken for granted.

On the subject of the functional frontiers of international law, it is advisable to avoid over-generalisation. In the relations between the two world camps, these frontiers may even have shrunk in comparison with international law of the pre-1914 period. At the same time, the very decisiveness of this cleavage tends to foster closer integration within sectional agglomerations than, at present, is attainable on the global levels of either international customary law or the United Nations. Inside each of these sectors, the functional frontiers of international law—particularly in economic and social matters—are rapidly expanding. Thus, the picture is one of uneven and contradictory developments. Yet, even where the functional frontiers of international law recede, it may be possible to extend its analytical frontiers.

II—THE PARTS AND THE WHOLE

Before exploring in greater detail where, in our time, the optimal frontiers of international law should best be drawn, it is advisable to try to view the whole of its province in perspective.

It is the historical merit of the naturalist writers of the sixteenth and seventeenth centuries to have attacked this basic problem of synopsis. In undertaking this task, they may have relied too strongly on their gifts of intuitive speculation. They may also have been too prone to work from inarticulate—optimistic or pessimistic—major premises. Yet, what matters more is that they did not shirk issues which can now perhaps be investigated in ways which are more readily verifiable by rational means.[3]

Thus, in Part One, an attempt is made to view international law— as it were from the outside—from three different, but related metalegal angles. Each of the pictures of international law so obtained can be checked inductively to a greater extent than any synopsis based on deductive or eclectic methods.[4] These perspectives are related in the sense that each is intended to assist in reducing the margins of

---

[3] See further 60 *Harv.L.R.* (1947), p. 539 *et seq.*, and 9 *C.L.P.* (1956), p. 235 *et seq.*

[4] This trichotomy probably corresponds more closely to the realities of the contemporary Doctrine of international law than the antinomy of Naturalists and Positivism. See further *l.c.* above in note 3 and *Manual*, Vol. 1, p. 18 *et seq.*, and Vol. 2, pp. 396–397.

error and subjectivity inseparable from *any* interpretation and evaluation.[5]

Some of the inter-disciplinary problems raised in Part One are not limited to any one branch of law and, therefore, ought to be answered in the wider context of a Sociology of Law. It is the object of *Chapter 1* on *The Three Types of Law* [6] to provide such a legal theory at least in outline.

In *Chapter 2* on *International Law in Sociological Perspective*,[7] this theory is applied for purposes of a functional analysis of international law.

In *Chapter 3* on *International Law in Historical Perspective*,[8] an attempt is made to ascertain the temporal frontiers of international law.

In *Chapter 4* on *International Law in Ethical Perspective*,[9] the ethical element in international law is traced to the standard of civilisation. This also reveals itself as a relatively objective metalegal but normative test for the purpose of evaluating international law or any of its individual rules.

In Part Two, some of the uses of the inter-disciplinary techniques [10] applied in Part One are further illustrated. The main burden of this Part is, however, to show how largely neglected material can be systematically co-ordinated in new special branches of international law and may then yield insights, not necessarily limited to the special branch directly concerned.

Chapter 5 on *International Law in Early English Practice* [11] is one of the case studies on which some of the generalisations in earlier Chapters are based.

5 The opportunity offered by the publication of this book will enable me to limit myself in the contemplated treatise on *International Law in Perspective* to the purely legal issues sketched provisionally in *The Fundamental Principles of International Law* (87 *Hague Recueil* (1955), p. 195 *et seq., q.v.* at p. 198).
   At the same time, the further treatment in Part One of these inter-disciplinary problems has made it possible to clarify and develop views expressed on some of these issues in Chapters 1 and 13 of *Power Politics.*
6 First published in 53 *Ethics* (1943), p. 89 *et seq.*
7 First published under the title *International Law and Society* in 20 *Virginia Quarterly Review* (1944), p. 566 *et seq.*
8 Based on papers published under the titles *The Rule of Law and the Disintegration of International Society* in 33 *A.J.I.L.* (1939), p. 56 *et seq., The Growth and Expansion of International Society* in 3 *Oesterreichische Zeitschrift für öffentliches Recht* (1950), p. 89 *et seq.,* and *The Frontiers of International Law* in 6 *Y.B.W.A.* (1952), p. 251 *et seq.*
9 First published under the title *The Standard of Civilisation in International Law* in 8 *C.L.P.* (1955), p. 212 *et seq.*
10 See also 9 *C.L.P.* (1956), p. 250 *et seq.*
11 First published in 25 *B.Y.I.L.* (1948), p. 52 *et seq.*

Chapter 6 on *The Protection of Human Rights in British Practice* [12] is intended to show the conditions on which, in a heterogeneous international society, effective protection of human rights depends. At the same time, this paper, like the preceding one, is one of a series of " pilot " studies on international law as applied in British practice.[13]

In *Chapter 7* on the *Impact of the East-West Rift on International Law*,[14] the weakest link in the chain of post-1945 international law is examined as it presented itself during the impasse of 1950. At the time, diplomatic relations between the two world camps had reached their nadir. This is probably still as good a point of departure as any for understanding the relatively subordinate place of law in the relations between the two antagonistic groups of Powers, uneasily co-existing in a state of nuclear stalemate.[15]

In *Chapter 8* on *The Problem of an International Criminal Law* [16] and in *Chapter 9* on *The Principles and Standards of International Economic Law*,[17] the claims of two candidates for admission to the rank of specialised branches of international law are examined.

In *Chapter 10* on *Jus Pacis ac Belli?* [18] the inadequacy of the traditional system of international law with its dichotomy into the laws of peace and war is considered. Attention is drawn to the need for recognising a *status mixtus* or state of intermediacy between peace and war in order to obtain a more realistic picture, especially on the level of international customary law. In studies subsequently published and constituting valuable corroborating evidence, other scholars have arrived at similar conclusions.[19] It, therefore, is probably fairest to republish the relevant sections of this paper in the original form in which they were published in 1943.

In *Chapter 11* on *Functions and Foundations of the Law of War*,[20] the major formative influence on the rules of warfare are examined. To assist in reassessing the present-day significance of this branch of international law, these rules are classified into four types.

---

[12] First published in 10 *Review of Politics* (1948), p. 174 *et seq.*
[13] See further *Vol. I*, p. XVII, and 9 *C.L.P.* (1956), p. 244 *et seq.*
[14] First published in 36 *Transactions of the Grotius Society* (1950), p. 229 *et seq.*
[15] See below, p. 279.
[16] First published in 3 *C.L.P.* (1950), p. 263 *et seq.*
[17] First published in 2 *International Law Quarterly* (1948), p. 402 *et seq.*
[18] First published under the title *Jus Pacis ac Belli?* in 37 *A.J.I.L.* (1943), p. 460 *et seq.*
[19] See, for instance, F. Grob, *The Relativity of War and Peace* (1949), and P. C. Jessup, *Should International Law Recognise an Intermediate Status between War and Peace?* 48 *A.J.I.L.* (1954), p. 98 *et seq. Cf.* also M. S. McDougal, *Peace and War*, 49 *A.J.I.L.* (1955), p. 63 *et seq.*, and *Manual*, Vol. 2, pp. 580–581.
[20] First published in 44 *Archiv für Rechts- und Wirtschaftsphilosophie* (1958), p. 351 *et seq.*

Chapter 12 is concerned with *Reflections on the Law of International Institutions*,[21] another specialised branch of international law which has come to stay.

In *Chapter 13* on *Scope and Limits of International Legislation*,[22] an attempt is made to put the discussion of problems *de lege ferenda* on a rationally verifiable basis.

In the concluding *Chapter 14* on *The Prospects for International Law*,[23] a forecast of the fortunes of international law made in the late autumn of 1945 is reproduced unaltered so as to enable readers to judge for themselves the methods on which it was based.[24]

I have considered myself free to cut, expand, or rewrite the papers included in the book. In every case, however, the exact place where the essay was first published has been given. In a few instances, the texts of papers are intentionally left unaltered. Then, the reasons for this decision are given.

Such overlapping between some of the chapters as has not been ironed out is also intentional. Although this has its advantages, the various chapters of *The Frontiers of International Law* need not be read in their systematic order. Some readers may wish to read merely one or other chapter. They may then find it helpful if each chapter is, if not self-contained, at least more or less self-explanatory. To the extent to which this has proved impossible, the cross-references inserted will assist in guiding readers to closely related chapters.

To avoid overloading the book with bibliographical references, cross-references to Vol. 2 of the 4th edition of the *Manual* have been added where this has been thought helpful.

---

21 First published in 13 *C.L.P.* (1960), p. 276 *et seq.*
22 First published in 22 *Acta Scandinavica Juris Gentium* (1952), p. 6 *et seq.*
23 First published in 8 *Review of Politics* (April 1946), p. 168 *et seq.*, and, under the title *L'avenir du droit international*, in 13 *Nouvelle Revue de Droit International Privé* (1946), p. 17 *et seq.*
24 For subsequent evaluations, *cf. Manual*, Vol. 1, p. 359 *et seq.*, and Vol. 2, pp. 661–662, and *Fundamental Principles*, p. 372 *et seq.*

PART ONE

PERSPECTIVES

CHAPTER 1

THE THREE TYPES OF LAW

As distinct from every one of the multitude of legal systems of all ages, Law as such exists only in the realm of concepts. It is an abstraction from the realities of past and existing legal systems.

If a definition of Law is to be what it sets out to be, it should be catholic in the sense of embracing any system of norms which, at any time or place, men have accepted as law, be it natural or positive; primitive, archaic or mature; unitary or federal; democratic, authoritarian or totalitarian; municipal or international.

Because of the fragmentary character of the reality from which they have been abstracted, most definitions of law offered by jurists fail to live up to this test of universality. Thus, they tend to suffer from a noticeable degree of subjectivity and arbitrariness.

It is not difficult to understand why this should be so. On the basis of abstraction from the known legal systems, law would appear to be a system of rational rules of human conduct which, if required, can be authoritatively determined on a basis of consent or compulsion and enforced by the application of external sanctions.

A definition on so high a level of abstraction is relatively meaningless. At the most, it has limited uses for didactic purposes. If, however, we want to understand differences such as those between primitive and mature law, between the laws of democratic, authoritarian and totalitarian States and between municipal and international law, definitions of law which are applicable to all forms of human association are of little help.

For such purposes, it is preferable to descend to more earthbound levels of abstraction and to concentrate on the social functions fulfilled by law. Once law is related to its social environment—or, more accurately, its varying social environments—the contours of the various legal systems which it may be desirable to distinguish stand out in greater clarity.

I—THE SOCIAL ENVIRONMENTS OF LAW

Naturalist writers groped their way instinctively to this Archimedian point. Vitoria and Hobbes mark extremes in the appraisal of the

9

state of nature, the hypothetical starting point of all these deductive thinkers. While to Vitoria the state of nature is one of " natural society and fellowship," [1] to Hobbes it means the exact opposite : " The estate of men in this natural liberty is the estate of war." [2]

In the Europe of the sixteenth and seventeenth centuries, it was remarkable to have merely attempted to assess intuitively the character of the social background of law. Speculation, even if coloured by individual inclinations towards optimistic or pessimistic world pictures, is preferable to obliviousness of a problem of this calibre.

In the mid-twentieth century, however, the alternative is no longer one between uncontrolled subjectivism and virtuous self-denying ordinances. By now, political scientists and sociologists should have taught us to work with " ideal " or, rather, " pure " types and to measure any particular social environment in terms of approxima- tion to one or the other extreme of the basic dichotomy between Society and Community.[3]

To use a simile of Schopenhauer, who applied it to human society as such, a society in the pure sense may be compared to an assem- blage of hedgehogs. These hedgehogs may be thought to live in a climate in which they are compelled to huddle together in order to keep warm. Nevertheless, they remain subject to an instinct of repul- sion which is based on their characteristic anatomical structure. Similarly, Spinoza, visualising the state of nature in terms of a society, arrived at the conclusion that " the natural right of every individual is only determined by his power." [4]

A community calls for different forms of action and behaviour. The way of life which corresponds to this pattern has found its classic expression in the Sermon on the Mount and the Meditations of Marcus Aurelius.[5] This spirit is just as much at home in the *Analects* of Confucius [6] and in the writings of the optimistic variant of Euro- pean naturalists. Thus, Pufendorf held it to be " one of the first principles of natural law that no one unjustly do another hurt or

---

1 *De Indis Noviter Inventis* (1532), Section III, 386.
2 *De Corpore Politico*, Ch. 1, Sect. 11, in *Tripos* (1684), p. 101. See also below, p. 234.
3 See, for instance, Sir Henry Sumner Maine, *Ancient Law* (1861); F. Tönnies, *Gemeinschaft und Gesellschaft* (1887); M. Weber, *Wirtschaft und Gesellschaft* (1922); J. MacMurray, *Freedom in the Personal Nexus* in R. N. Anshen (ed.), *Freedom: Its Meaning* (1942) and R. G. Collingwood, *The New Leviathan* (1942).
4 *Tractatus Theologico-Politicus* (1670), Chap. 16.
5 11, 18.
6 Vol. I, Bk. 3, Ch. 7.

damage. as well as that men should perform for each other the duties of humanity." [7]

The criterion by which a society is distinguishable from a community can be formulated in a variety of ways. While a society is a means to an end, a community is an end in itself. Whereas a society is based on interest and fear, a community requires self-sacrifice and love. The one is founded on distrust, and the other presupposes mutual trust. Or, in the words of Tönnies, the members of a society remain isolated in spite of their association. The members of a community are united in spite of their separate existence.

It is imperative to realise that these patterns are "ideal" or "pure" types. In actual life none of these groups exists in undiluted form ; they all are hybrids. Communities such as the family, nation or church are tainted by greater or smaller admixtures of society elements. Conversely, at least in their internal relations, societies such as a limited company, a cartel or even a gang of bandits must accept a minimum of moral standards. Yet community aspirations remain necessarily dwarfed in such uncongenial surroundings.

Whether any particular group approximates one rather than the other extreme or maintains an equipoise between them can only be determined inductively in each particular case. Moreover, at one and the same time, man belongs to a number of social groups and, therefore, may display simultaneously the vastly different attitudes associated with society and community relations.

The key to the understanding of the functions fulfilled by any legal system lies in the structure of its social environment. Admittedly, such a relation is not one-sided. Yet primarily it is the specific character of the social group which impresses itself on the law. In its turn, the law affects the character of the group whose ends it serves, but merely in a secondary way. Thus, the next step must be to explore the functions of law in the nexus of societies and communities.

II—THE FUNCTIONS OF SOCIETY LAW : THE LAW OF POWER

To illustrate the functions of society law, a hypothetical example may be chosen. What would a group of well-armed gangsters do who had resolved to establish their sway over a powerless people and themselves as the ruling class in that country?

[7] *De Jure Naturae et Gentium* (1688), Bk 8, Ch. 6, s. 2.

In the first place, they would accumulate overwhelming military power in their hands and attempt to create a legal monopoly of such power. They would reserve to themselves all important political decisions and, at the most, grant sham representation to their subjects if they thought this an advisable screen for their real designs. They would jealously insist on their exclusive right to all key positions in the administration and judiciary.

Through an appropriate State agency, they would expropriate previous owners of the land, take possession of the best parts and leave to the subjects only as much as secured them a bare minimum. Any part of their income beyond starvation point would be taken from these helots by way of taxation, and their wages and salaries would be fixed in such a manner that all taxation would lie exclusively on their shoulders.

The Government would control education as well as freedom of opinion and political association. It would constitute an important governmental task to inculcate the belief both at home and abroad that the indigenous population was backward and incapable of any development toward real self-government and that, therefore, it was in their own best interest to be ruled by the master race.

Although it was left to Hitler's " New Order " to develop to its logical conclusions such a system of wholesale exploitation, the treatment in the past of conquered peoples and the deeds of early Western colonialism and imperialism prove that this pattern of society relations is not as hypothetical as the above illustration appears to suggest. In this type of social environment Bentham's definition of the functions of law would sound like bitter sarcasm : " All the functions of law may be referred to one or other of these four headings : to provide subsistence, to aim at abundance, to encourage equality and to maintain security." [8]

Although power is the overriding element in an extreme society, it tends to harden into law. Arbitrariness and extravagance on the part of individual members of a ruling clique are antagonistic to the interests of the group as a whole. In its own interest, therefore, every slave-holding society has to give a minimum of protection to its slaves. As it is in the interest of the masters not to drive their slaves to despair and, for this reason, to impose upon themselves a certain amount of self-restraint, so, from the point of view of the oppressed,

[8] *Introduction to Principles of Morals and Legislation* (1789) in *The Theory of Legislation* (ed. L. G. K. Ogden—1931), p. 96.

the harshest law of power is preferable to the blind play of brute force.

The history of early Roman law and the struggle between plebeians and patricians prove that the first consideration and strategic objective of inferior orders are not mitigation and reform of the law, but its clear formulation and participation in its interpretation and application.

The overriding function of a society law which is characterised by gross disparities in rights and duties may be defined as the stabilisation of relations of power. Society law provides one of the three fundamental types of law : *the Law of Power.*

A law such as this best serves its purpose if its real character and function are well disguised behind façades of technicalities and quasi-ethical doctrines. It necessarily tends to fulfil the concomitant function of an ideology by which the vested interests it serves to protect are disguised and made to appear identical with the interests of all.[9]

This is what Pascal meant when he wrote [10] : " It is right that what is just, should be obeyed ; it is necessary that what is strongest, should be obeyed. Justice without might is helpless ; might without justice is tyrannical. Justice without might is gainsaid, because there are always offenders ; might without justice is condemned. We must then combine justice and might, and for this end make what is just strong, or what is strong just. Justice is subject to dispute ; might is easily recognised and is not disputed. So we cannot give might to justice, because might has gainsaid justice, and has declared that it is she herself who is just. And thus being unable to make what is just strong, we have made what is strong just."

III—THE FUNCTIONS OF COMMUNITY LAW :
THE LAW OF CO-ORDINATION

It is conceivable that a small community is able to dispense with law altogether. Thus, it could be imagined that groups such as a family, blood-brotherhood or church were capable of regulating their affairs without organs whose duty it is to interpret authoritatively the standards of conduct demanded by these relations and without any need for external sanctions by which such obligations are enforced.

[9] *Cf.* the speech of Thrasymachus in Plato's *Republic*, 1. 3.
[10] *Pensées,* No. 298.

Even in intimate groups of this kind, situations may arise in which, in the absence of legal norms and institutions, man will not necessarily " both discern what is good for mankind as a community and invariably be both able and willing to put the good into practice when he has perceived it." [11] In such contingencies, common moral standards require to be supplemented and supported by law. Moreover, in communities which comprise more than a small number of members, agencies are needed which give visible expression to common values and, whenever necessary, adapt them to changing circumstances.

It would be hasty to assume that sanctions were entirely lacking in groups of this kind. The sanctions which are at the disposal of a highly integrated community are more refined and often differ in kind from those available in a more crudely organised society. The members of a community may value so highly membership in it and approval of their conduct by the other members that the mere possibility of disapproval by, and exclusion from, the community acts as a deterrent and a guide for the actual behaviour of its members. Thus, even a community law has its own system of inherent and congenial sanctions.

The law of the community serves the purpose of assisting in the maintenance and continuous integration of the community and the protection of the group against exceptional aberrations of its members. Its main function consists in promoting the co-ordination of activities in the interest of the community by the rationalisation of customary rules of behaviour. Spheres of work must be delimited. Duties and responsibilities have to be assigned. If rights are granted, this is done because it is in the interest of all, and not because a member so desires.

In the early Roman community the maintenance of the family *sacra*—a religious duty incumbent upon the *pater familias*—was considered of the highest importance. In the absence of a son who would succeed his father in the fulfilment of this sacred duty, a substitute had to be found. Thus, the institution of adoption and a limited freedom of testation developed in order to enable Roman citizens to fulfil their duties to the gods and the community.

In a medieval monastery life was sufficiently complex to require government and the assignment of tasks. Rules had, therefore, to be devised how best to assure the achievement of the common purpose —the glorification of God and the maintenance of the community.

[11] Plato, *The Laws* (trans. A. E. Taylor, 1934), p. 265.

It was assumed that every member was anxious to contribute his share, and the more onerous and burdensome the work, the higher was the honour it conferred.

The primary function of a community law is the co-ordination of efforts. This feature is the decisive characteristic of a law which is diametrically opposed to an extreme society law. The Law of Power and the Law of Co-ordination form the two antipodes which legal genius has devised. The one embodies strong ideological elements. The other, because of the shortcomings of human nature, remains largely an unfulfilled aspiration and, to this extent, Utopian.

IV—THE FUNCTIONS OF LAW IN HYBRID GROUPS : THE LAW OF RECIPROCITY

In actual reality, both societies and communities show traits which blur the border line between the two groups. Correspondingly, the Law of Power partakes of the characteristics of the Law of Co-ordination, and the Law of Co-ordination borrows from its opposite. Even in a typical society, such an ambivalent stage may arise if the members of the society happen to be of approximately equal strength.

In such a situation, a third type of law, the Law of Reciprocity, comes into its own. In Aristotle's words, " among equals whatever is fair and just ought to be reciprocal, for this is equal and right ; but that equals should not partake of what is equal, or like to like, is contrary to nature." [12]

A state of affairs in which the equilibrium of power makes it possible for power to be ignored corresponds to the typical nature of man. It has produced barter, the earliest form of legal transaction. Both parties to such a bargain are content if they are convinced that they have received more than, or at least as much as, they have given.

This implies that man is not predominantly altruistic but is prepared to act on the basis of the maxim *do ut des*, to consider the application of this rule to his own affairs as just and fair, and to come to an understanding with his fellow men on the standards by which the *quid pro quo* is to be determined.

In exceptional circumstances *homo juridicus* appears willing to give more than he takes. This may be due to inferiority of power,

[12] *Politics*, 7. 3.

mistake or fraud. In such situations, merely formal reciprocity is attained.

In the case of inferiority of power, the lack of equilibrium is compensated for by a realisation of what might have happened if agreement had not been reached or the Law of Power had been disobeyed. In cases of mistake and fraud, reciprocity is assumed, but in reality does not exist, and has to be restored by special remedies. These two examples represent typical society constellations.

Willingness to forgo actual reciprocity may also be due to voluntary self-limitation and self-denial. In this case, reciprocity in a spiritual sense is achieved by the consciousness of such sacrifice and its acknowledgment by the community. Such attitudes are typical of the Law of Co-ordination.

The Law of Reciprocity constitutes a compromise between the Laws of Power and of Co-ordination, between the extremes of brutal domination and saintly self-negation. While it is characteristic of groups which themselves are hybrids between societies and communities, it may be used intentionally by a community for the regulation of affairs which, from the point of view of the group as a whole, are considered peripheral. As becomes manifest from systems of private law which require *causa* or *consideration*, or discourage gratuitous contracts, even highly integrated groups make use of egotistic levers of social action : " Every one has his special interest in view, no one thinks of the purpose, and yet this purpose is perhaps furthered in this way more surely and quickly than if it had been pursued by the Government directly." [13]

Thus, mankind has developed three basic patterns of law, and the working principles behind these three types of law are power, co-ordination and reciprocity. Such value as this typology may claim depends on a simple test. Does it provide any additional insight into the phenomenon of law? It would surpass the scope of this Chapter to attempt more than to sketch the potentialities inherent in this approach to a few selected problems of Jurisprudence.

V—THE THREE TYPES OF LAW AND SELECTED PROBLEMS OF JURISPRUDENCE

This theory of law is not put forward in any spirit of exclusiveness. On some problems of legal theory more light is likely to be thrown

---

[13] R. von Jhering, *Law as a Means to an End* (1877 and 1883—transl. 1913), p. 32.

by the use of analytical, comparative, or historical methods than by a sociological treatment. Yet the investigation of law as a social phenomenon may assist in the fuller understanding of some jurisprudential problems.[14]

The Definition of Law

The position has not essentially changed since Kant wrote : " The jurists still seek a definition of their concept of law." They have defined law by reference to its substance : as truth, reason, or authority. They have tried to comprehend it as an aggregate of laws : as rules of conduct, as the sum total of decisions, or as the prophecy of official action. They have conceived it as synonymous with the legal order or in terms of canons of value ; and finally they have identified it with the judicial process.

It is possible to find definitions of law which apply to society and community laws alike. Yet, of necessity, such definitions must remain rather abstract.[15] Nevertheless, they indicate something real : the elements common to law in every human association.

In so far as the definitions are concerned according to which law is identified with *auctoritas* or *veritas,* it might pay to investigate the closer relation between the former and society types of social association and between the latter and highly integrated communities. It appears that the more a group is organised on the pattern of a society, the more law may rightly be defined as " the word of him that by right hath command over others," [16] and the more a group may claim to be a community, the truer it is to call its law " the force or tendency which makes for righteousness." [17]

Contents of the " Law " of Nature

Expositions of the law of nature tend to be limited to statements of vague characteristics of natural " law " : that it is unwritten, that it has actual validity, that it postulates an idea of law which can be used as a measuring rod of positive law, and that it comprises " natural " norms in accordance with which social behaviour should obviously be regulated.

---

[14] I hesitate to apply the three types of law to primitive law if by this is understood law before its separation—at least in part—from basically pre-rational group life, especially religion. Pending further research on the subject, I tend to limit the attribution of rational forms of behaviour to periods of legal evolution in which law may be equated without undue artificiality with either *veritas* or *voluntas.*
[15] See above, p. 9.
[16] Hobbes, *Leviathan* (1651), Part I, Chap. 15.
[17] E. Jenks, *The New Jurisprudence* (1933), p. 1.

Once writers attempt to express their ideas in more concrete terms, their statements are flatly contradictory. Two instances may illustrate this point.

According to Hobbes, " seeing then to the offensiveness of man's nature one to another, there is added a right of every man to everything, whereby one man invadeth with right, and another with right resisteth ; and men live thereby in perpetual diffidence, and study how to preoccupate each other ; the estate of men in this natural liberty is the estate of war." [18]

According to Pufendorf, however, " it is one of the first principles of natural law that no one unjustly do another hurt or damage, as well as that men should perform for each other the duties of humanity, and show especial zeal to fulfil the matters upon which they have entered into particular agreements." [19]

While Hobbes pictures the state of nature in terms of a society, if not anarchy, Pufendorf conceives it in those of a community. Thus, their conclusions on *ordo rerum* are diametrically opposed to each other. In order to do justice to these doctrines, it is necessary to distinguish between theories of natural law appertaining to a society and others based on the assumption of a community proper. Then the apparent discrepancies disappear, and it emerges that these theories contain valuable insights in ethical garbs into the purposes and functions of community and society laws.

The Meanings of Justice

The treatment of Justice as the central value in any system of natural " law "—or, more correctly, ethics—has suffered from the same methodological shortcomings as the exposition of natural law doctrines in general.

If the essence of Justice is defined as *jus suum cuique tribuendi* or as the equal treatment of equals, it depends entirely on the structure of the human association in which it is to be meted out, what is due to every one, and which members of a group should be treated as equal.

The decisive problem is the desirable degree of disregard for any actual inequality. Thus, what is just in a society may be a travesty of justice in a community. It appears futile to discuss Justice in the abstract without reference to the purpose and structure of a given

18 *L.c.* in note 2 above.
19 *De Jure Naturae et Gentium* (1672), Bk. 8, Ch. 6, s. 2.

group. There was wisdom in the name which Jaroslav the Just (A.D. 1015–1050) gave to his code. He called it *Pravda Russkaya* —" Russian Truth."

As natural Equity is nothing but the application of principles of Justice to concrete cases, similar considerations apply to discussions on the meaning and functions of natural Equity.

The Controversy on the Autonomous or Heteronomous Character of Moral and Legal Norms

In the perennial discussions on the difference between Morality and Law it is frequently asserted that, whereas moral rules are auto-nomous, legal norms are heteronomous. In other words, while Morality appeals to the individual's own conscience (*forum inter-num*), Law relies in the last resort on compulsion from outside (*forum externum*). Reference to the social background of both sets of rules suggests that the criterion which divides Law from Morality cannot be found in this alleged difference. Actually, both Law and Morality are autonomous *and* heteronomous.

Morality is not entirely autonomous ; for the *forum internum* is more strongly conditioned by its social environment than lawyers have commonly imagined. Conversely, Law is not entirely hetero-nomous and requires more than blind obedience. The degree of law obedience cannot be measured by the relatively few cases which lead to litigation but must be gauged from the untold number of cases which do not arise in the law courts, because both the fairness and effectivity of the law are widely accepted.

Here again a connection exists between the three types of Law and its autonomous *and* heteronomous character. The more a legal system is a community law, the stronger is its autonomous character and *vice versa*.

The Legal Character of Law in Totalitarian States

For the extreme positivist the problem of the legal character of Law in totalitarian States does not arise. Their laws emanate from law-givers, they are applied by the courts, they are normally obeyed and, if not, sanctions are put in operation. From the point of view of an extreme doctrine of natural law, however, some portions of the law of totalitarian States may be no more than *corruptelae legis* and, therefore, null and void. Although sociological Jurisprudence cannot answer the question in the terms put by the naturalists, it can draw attention to specific features of totalitarian law which, otherwise, may be in danger of being overlooked.

It appears essential to distinguish between the various types of law which totalitarian rulers apply in a mixture peculiar to these legal systems. They make use of principles pertaining to the law of co-ordination. They give it, however, an arbitrary and exclusive twist which may subject certain groups within their sway to an undisguised law of power or sheer arbitrariness. The ruling élite may also consider itself free to suspend the community law in relation to members of the *Herrenvolk* itself, and expose them to a law of power which is incompatible even with the maintenance of a closed community limited to the chosen people.

The Legal Character of International Law

Is international law law or is it merely positive morality? How can a system claim legal character if it lacks all or some of the customary attributes of municipal law : legislative organs, courts and sanctions? Questions of this kind uncritically take it for granted that there is only *one* type of law—law as it is known within the State.

The sterile discussions which centre around this problem ignore the vital difference between the social background of municipal and international law. They lead to euphemistic and unrealistic assertions of the identical character of municipal and international law or to a resigned admission of inexplicable differences which deprive international law of its legal character. Actually, like other legal systems international law comprises all three types of law, but in a blend of its own.[20]

The fact that this typology may be applied with ease to problems of both national and international Jurisprudence indicates that the three types of the laws of power, reciprocity and co-ordination are generally applicable in the realm of legal theory.

[20] See below, p. 25 *et seq*.

CHAPTER 2

INTERNATIONAL LAW IN SOCIOLOGICAL PERSPECTIVE

IF the place of law is as precarious as it is in international society, apprehension regarding sociological inquiries may be voiced in the " best interest " of international law.[1] It is not—so the argument runs—one of the purposes of scholarship to make more apparent than can be helped the forces conditioning a normative system still so tender.

Anybody is entitled to deny himself such insight as the view of international law in sociological perspective may give. Adherents of this school will, however, find that the scope of their work is then narrowly circumscribed.

Unless they are willing to resort to questionable *ad hoc* sociologies, they prevent themselves from considering basic problems of international law such as its limitations and peculiarities, and from making suggestions for the development or improvement of international law ; for every one of these problems presupposes views on the place of law in international society and on the likely repercussions of proposals *de lege ferenda* on the social environment of international law.

Actually, most scholars who object to the sociological interpretation of international law would be astonished at the number of unchecked statements—more often implied than articulately voiced—of sociological content that abound in their own contributions to international law.[2]

If such pre-scientific subjectivity is to be avoided, it is necessary to deal consciously with international law in its social context and, in this way, to put the discussion on a rationally verifiable level.

I—THE SOCIAL ENVIRONMENT OF INTERNATIONAL LAW

Law is primarily conditioned by its social environment.[3] The analysis of international law in its historical perspective reveals how strongly

---

[1] For encouraging signs that, in this respect, the attitude of international lawyers is changing, see the bibliography in *Manual*, Vol. 2, p. 395 *et seq.*

[2] See further 9 *C.L.P.* (1956), p. 250 *et seq.*

[3] See further above, p. 9 *et seq.*

the character of international society has impressed itself on international law.[4] The primary task is, therefore, to clarify our minds on the essential characteristics of this environment. To provide this analysis is the task of another branch of Sociology, the academic discipline of International Relations.[5] It must suffice to present here in a concentrated form the conclusions of inductive research on this related subject.

The international nexus is best understood as an extreme type of society. As a result of a threefold process, which will be discussed in the next Chapter,[6] international society has been transformed into a world society. The reason why this environment is described as a society, as distinct from a community, is that the bond that, ultimately, holds world society together is not any overriding common purpose or spiritual values, but power. The essence of power is the ability to exercise compelling pressure irrespective of its reasonableness.[7]

In a society of this type, groups wielding maximum political, economic and military power have the best chance of survival. Compared with the individual, or with other less potent types of association, compulsory territorial organisations, endowed with overwhelming physical force, are like giants in relation to dwarfs. This explains the pre-eminent position of States in international society.

Compared with earlier types of State, the twentieth-century State can claim one distinct asset. Allied with strong sentiments, such as nationalism or other ideologies of comparable impetus, it is capable of attaining a degree of cohesion that any mere apparatus of physical force could never hope to achieve. This makes intelligible the paradox that a world which is objectively one both in a political and technical sense is, nonetheless, split into separate and antagonistic loyalty areas. The concept of sovereignty in its various forms makes this reality articulate in terms of legal and political theory.[8]

The *ensemble* of sovereign States forms the international aristocracy. Yet, within this select circle, the principle of power operates with no less force than between sovereign States and the minor

---

4 See below, p. 43 *et seq.*
5 See further, *Power Politics*, p. 3 *et seq.*
6 See below, p. 43 *et seq.*
7 See further *l.c.* in note 5 above, p. 14.
8 See further 10 *C.L.P.* (1957), p. 264 *et seq.*

players on the international stage. Power is the test which deter-
mines the place of sovereign States in the hierarchy of the international aristocracy. Thus, States have come to be graded into
world Powers, middle Powers and small States.

The world Powers form the oligarchy inside the international
aristocracy. It entirely depends on circumstances whether conflicts
between members of the international oligarchy are settled at the
expense of the lower ranks or whether the danger of one of the world
Powers coming within reach of world domination has the effect of
rallying the other members of the international oligarchy to the
defence of the weaker members of the international aristocracy.

In such an environment, the primary object of every member of
the international aristocracy is its own self-preservation. Every means
by which this object can be secured is prima facie justified in the
eyes of those who guide the policies of sovereign States. As none
of them can be sure that other members of the international aristocracy do not give a more aggressive and expansionist interpretation
than it does itself to their own requirements of self-preservation,
inter-State relations are permeated by an atmosphere of mutual
suspicion and never-absent fear of the real intentions of others.

The objects of foreign policy and the motives behind it determine
the choice of instruments, strategies and tactics of foreign policy.

Diplomacy and armaments are the traditional weapons of the
sovereign State. Corresponding to the increasing importance of
public opinion in present-day mass society, States have found it
necessary to seek closer contact with this elusive phenomenon. Thus,
propaganda has become a junior branch of the foreign service.
Although despised by some, the new art is practised by all.

The patterns of international strategy leave little choice to the
imagination of Foreign Offices. Isolationism and neutralism are
cherished dreams for inoffensive members of the international aristocracy. Yet, in a world in which the trend towards the centralisation of
power is at work with continuously increasing force,[9] it is hard for
the majority of States to base their foreign policy on this pattern.[10]
Most States are thrown back on policies of alignment for at least
some purposes. Alliances, however, beget counter-alliances.
Guarantees by one greater Power are answered by guarantees to small
States within the orbit of other greater Powers, or both sides compete

---

[9] See further below, p. 58 *et seq.*
[10] See further 15 *Y.B.W.A.* (1961), p. 233 *et seq.*

for the privilege of guaranteeing the integrity of such States. Alliances and counter-alliances tend to coalesce into systems of balance of power.

Corresponding to the expansion of international society into a world society, such balance of power systems have come to span the whole of the globe. At this stage, a point is easily reached when, in addition to the factors of instability inherent in any balance of power system, such a system loses even the pretence of its usefulness by depriving itself of the balancer. World society is left divided into armed and potentially hostile camps.[11]

For short, relations on such footing may be described as power politics. The term signifies a type of relations between States in which certain types of behaviour predominate : armaments, isolationism, power diplomacy, power economics, regional or universal imperialism, alliances, balance of power and war.

Additional elements of a definition are furnished by the assumption on which a system of power politics is based and by the criterion by which the hierarchy between the members in any such society is determined. Each group considers itself not merely as a means to a common end, but as an end in itself. At least for purposes of self-preservation, any measure which is required to achieve this object is deemed to be justified. Law and morality within this social environment are limited to relatively subordinate positions. The hierarchy between groups is measured by their weight in a potential or actual conflict.

Thus, *power politics* may be defined as a system of international relations in which groups consider themselves to be ultimate ends ; use, at least for vital purposes, the most effective means at their disposal and are graded according to their weight in case of conflict.

If a system of power politics is not actually replaced by an international community proper but continues on the same basis as before under the cloak of a community, such a state of affairs may be described as a system of *power politics in disguise*.

The sceptic may be forgiven for doubting whether in a sphere so permeated by power as international society, any scope is left for law. Yet the very States which, since time immemorial, have been immersed in the vortex of power politics, themselves attest to the reality of international law. In diplomatic notes of their Foreign Offices, they regularly complain of the alleged violation of

11 See below, pp. 146 and 280 *et seq*.

their rights under international customary law and international treaties ; they demand, and make, reparation for breaches of international law ; they conclude agreements for the settlement of disputes on the basis of international law, appear before international courts and tribunals, and, as a rule, comply ungrudgingly and punctiliously, with international decisions and awards. In their practice, international judicial institutions, particularly the World Court, have built up a considerable body of case law, ranging over the whole field of international law.

What, then, are the functions of law in international society?

II—THE INTERNATIONAL LAW OF POWER

In a society in which power is the overriding consideration, the primary function of law is to assist in maintaining the supremacy of force and the hierarchies established on the basis of power and to give to such an overriding system the respectability and sanctity of law. International law serves these purposes in a variety of ways.

The independence of States is one of the corner-stones of international law.[12] To the extent to which the exercise of sovereignty is not limited by rules of international customary law, treaties or general principles of law recognised by civilised nations, international society is prevented from interfering with any matter in the domestic jurisdiction of any State. Topics such as armaments, access to raw materials and markets, and questions of migration are in principle reserved subjects which every sovereign State may treat as it sees fit. Similarly, any change in the internal structure of independent States belongs to this category.

It follows from the absence of any superior international authority that the participation of a State in an international congress or conference depends on its own free will. Moreover, in the absence of agreement to the contrary, unanimity is required for any decision reached in the plenum of any such international gathering. Finally, any binding third-party settlement of a dispute on the planes of either law or equity depends on the consent of the States concerned.

In a society as dynamic as international society, such a state of affairs is tolerable on one condition alone, that is to say, that States are willing to compromise and agree voluntarily to make concessions which, in justice and fairness, they may be asked to make. If they

[12] See further *Fundamental Principles*, p. 214 *et seq.*, and Vol. I, p. 114 *et seq.*

should refuse to do so, other States must either let matters rest at
this or contemplate the use of the only available alternative pattern,
that is to say, means of unilateral pressure, including, in the last
resort, war.

By building international customary law on the foundation of
State sovereignty, States make sure of leaving open to themselves
the choice between the basic alternative patterns of international
tactics, that is to say, between peace and war.[13]

Actually, by putting compulsory measures short of war at the
disposal of States, international customary law enables States lawfully
to increase pressure by stages against one another and, thus, to introduce further refinements into an otherwise even cruder game of
power politics.[14] Having endowed war with the dignity of a legal
status and devised rules, however slender, in accordance with which
war should be conducted, international law is but consistent in going
a step further. If war ends with the complete breakdown of one of
the belligerents (*debellatio*), the legal personality of such a State is
destroyed. The victor may annex the territory of the defeated State,
treat it as *territorium nullius* or establish a new subject of international law in the territory of its former enemy.[15]

If the defeated State survives as an international person, the
usual way of terminating war is by way of a peace treaty. In the
absence of a peace treaty, the victor would be forced to continue
war until *debellatio* or keep the enemy territory indefinitely occupied.
It saves strenuous exertions, if the vanquished can be persuaded to
accept more limited forms of control which may serve as well the
purpose of maintaining the victor's supremacy.

In this case, the settlement is no longer based on mere force.
The signature of the defeated and the consensual character of the obligations undertaken by him endow the peace treaty with the sanctity
of law. While in probably any mature system of municipal law
the free consent of the parties to a contract is a condition of its
validity, in international customary law nothing short of actual
physical threat to, or coercion of, the actual plenipotentiaries
responsible for the signature or ratification invalidates a treaty.[16]

Peace treaties are not necessarily limited to the settlement of

[13] See further *l.c.* in note 5 above, p. 191 *et seq.*
[14] See below, p. 234 *et seq.*
[15] On modifications of this position by way of multilateral treaties and the
significance of these changes, see below, pp. 60, 253, 270, 301 and 311.
[16] See further *Fundamental Principles*, p. 264 *et seq.*

issues between former belligerents. Especially in the case of multi-lateral peace treaties the whole balance of power system established in the preceding major war is put on a consensual basis.[17] Other types of political treaties—treaties of alliance, guarantee and neutra-lisation—give such legal precision as may be desired to the strategies of international politics on which Powers may be agreed. Yet this is not the sole reason why governments embody such understandings in formal treaties.

Statesmen know that as a rule, they can expect such obligations to be honoured only if the fulfilment of treaty obligations is in harmony with the vital interests of the contracting parties. According to Bismarck, " the contracting parties must trust one another that when the case arises, the question will be loyally weighed and decided by the other party."

What is the value of couching such understandings in legal terms? Even if governments themselves should not be unduly impressed by such " scraps of paper," it is still of political signifi-cance whether a State goes back on an obligation solemnly under-taken in legal form. In the eye of public opinion, the other contracting party is then likely to score by having relied on the pledged word of the treaty-breaker. Conversely, the government of the latter is put in an embarrassing position both at home and in the world at large.

In order to avoid or mitigate such unpleasantness, international law offers a number of devices. On the level of auto-interpretation of international law by every sovereign State, it is their common pur-pose to provide convenient excuses of a quasi-legal character. The principles of self-preservation and self-defence and the *clausula rebus sic stantibus* are favourites in this game.[18]

Admittedly, it is a sound legal proposition that a treaty should not be considered to cover situations which, at the time of the con-clusion of the treaty, neither party could possibly have contemplated. Thus, in countries in which the currency had lost practically all its value, municipal courts rightly held that a serious inflation affected the very basis of contracts, and that a party could not be asked to perform a contract merely in order to receive valueless paper in exchange.

[17] See below, p. 59 *et seq.*
[18] See further *l.c.* in note 16 above, pp. 273 and 327 *et seq.*

There is, however, all the difference between a situation in which independent courts judge the submissions of the parties directly concerned and either pronounce the contract to be terminated or adjust it to changed circumstances, and the position under international customary law. Failing their consent, States are not bound to submit any dispute to any court or tribunal, and every one of them remains judge in its own cause. Thus, allegation stands against allegation, and it is ultimately a question of influencing public opinion both at home and abroad whether any particular unilateral action is regarded as a breach of treaty or as well justified.

The measures taken by Russia in 1871 regarding the Black Sea clauses in the Paris Peace Treaty of 1856, by Austria-Hungary in 1908 regarding the annexation of Bosnia-Herzegovina, or the denunciation by the Third *Reich* of the Locarno Treaties and of the Non-Aggression Pact with Poland fall into this category.

Another field in which international law has been employed as a pure law of power is that of the imperialist and colonial expansion of the Western nations.[19] If coveted territories were inhabited by groups outside the pale of international law, any of their lands might be treated as *territorium nullius*. Queen Elizabeth, for instance, in 1578 granted a charter to Sir Humphrey Gilbert to " inhabit and possess at his choice all remote and heathen lands not in the actual possession of any Christian prince."

Where the status of non-European tribes or nations as subjects of international law was recognised, treaties of cession would produce the same result. If native chieftains and princes showed undue reluctance to part with any of their territories, war and conquest, followed by cession, would achieve the same end.[20]

In cases in which the application of any of these techniques proved inopportune, domination by more indirect means might be obtained with the apparent consent of those passively concerned. International and colonial protectorates as well as leaseholds provided suitable devices for this purpose. In other cases, the sovereignty of African or Asian States was formally respected. Yet their fate was settled over their heads by the conclusion of treaties by which third States agreed that parts of a country such as Ethiopia or Persia should be treated as spheres of exclusive influence.

19 See below, p. 51 *et seq.*
20 See below, p. 54 *et seq.*

Beyond sustaining the supremacy of force in international relations and serving practically any of the strategies and tactics of individual States, international customary law is well suited to fulfil a further function. It helps to maintain the key position of the aristocracy of sovereign States in international society.

It depends on each of the existing subjects of international law whether, in relation to itself, any aspirant to the status of international personality should be granted such recognition. Inroads on the practice that sovereign States alone are considered to be eligible as subjects of international law have been made merely within a narrow compass. These exceptions hardly affect the general picture of international law as an exclusive legal system that applies primarily between the members of the international aristocracy.[21]

To the extent to which international customary law is a law of power, it fulfils the functions of an extreme society law. It gives authority and sanctity of law to power and force, without seriously restraining the freedom of action of its " subjects " in the word's dual meaning.

This description of the international law of power may be conceded as a correct analysis of some of the practices fulfilled by international law in the " bad old days " of the pre-1914 period. Yet is it equally true for the brave new worlds of the post-1919 and post-1945 eras? An adequate answer to these questions depends on a sociological interpretation of these systems of power politics in disguise [22] and the detailed analysis of the impact of these superstructures on the basic principles of classical international law.[23]

III—THE INTERNATIONAL LAW OF RECIPROCITY

Is international customary law merely a pious fraud, at which the augurs smile? To rest content with an unqualified answer in the affirmative would be as unrealistic as it would be to ignore the ideological functions fulfilled by international law. So long as world society is engulfed in a system of power politics, international law will have to serve its purpose. Yet, international law

21 See further below, p. 57 *et seq.*, *Fundamental Principles*, p. 228 *et seq.*, and Vol. I, p. 127 *et seq.*
22 See above, p. 24. and further *Power Politics*, p. 259 *et seq.*
23 See further below, p. 146 *et seq.*, and *Manual*, Vol. 1, p. 265 *et seq.*

is not only a law of power, but also a law of reciprocity,[24] and even traces of the law of co-ordination [25] can be diagnosed.

In rules of which those governing diplomatic immunity are typical, the influence of the principle of reciprocity becomes apparent. At a time when, in this sphere, international law was still in a formative stage, States were free to choose whether to interpret restrictively the rights of immunity granted to the representatives of foreign States or to give them a liberal construction. If, in the interest of their own untrammelled sovereignty, they preferred the former course, there was nothing to prevent them from taking such a line. In this case, they could not, however, expect any more generous treatment for their own representatives in foreign countries than they themselves were prepared to grant to those of other States.

Actually, States did not act in so short-sighted a manner. Thus, on the basis of innumerable treaties of a reciprocal character, a set of rules of international customary law concerning diplomatic immunity grew up. It derived its strength and authority from the automatic working of the principle of reciprocity.[26] In most civilised countries, the international law of diplomatic immunity received added support from national statutes, codifying the rules of international customary law, and from national courts, sustaining international law by a liberal construction of these statutes.

Or, to turn to the question of the maritime frontier, States found it advisable to subject to their exclusive control a belt of the high seas next to their own coast lines. If they made exaggerated claims regarding the width of their own territorial sea, they were bound to be met by similar arguments whenever they demanded the benefits of the freedom of the seas in waters bordering on the coasts of other States. Thus, at a time when the range of shore batteries extended to about three miles and roughly coincided with the range of visibility in good weather of land from the sea and vice versa, a widely accepted rule of international customary law crystallised,[27] fixing at this distance the minimum breadth of the territorial sea.

Although peace treaties offer examples *par excellence* of treaties likely to be used in the interest of the law of power, the typical

---

24 See above, p. 15 *et seq.*
25 See above, p. 13 *et seq.*
26 See below, p. 92 *et seq.*
27 See further W. L. Walker, *Territorial Waters: The Cannon Shot Rule*, 22 *B.Y.I.L.* (1945), p. 210 *et seq.*, H. S. Kent, *The Historical Origins of the Three-Mile Limit*, 48 *A.J.I.L.* (1954), p. 537 *et seq.*, and *Vol. I*, p. 317 *et seq.*

function of international treaties consists in giving concrete expression to the principle of reciprocity in fields in which, on a basis of mutuality, States desire to limit the exercise of their unfettered national sovereignty. States are likely to do so only when, in their view, the benefits to be derived from restrictions of the domestic jurisdiction of other States appear to outweigh or, at least, balance the disadvantages resulting from corresponding restrictions of their own freedom.

Thus, crime constitutes a menace to any human society. If, by leaving the country in which punishment threatens them, criminals could manage to escape punishment or if, without appreciable risk, they could operate on an international scale, criminal justices would be outwitted by the most dangerous types of lawbreaker. Extradition treaties provide a means of solving the problem.[28]

Similarly, in the spheres of transit, transport, communications on land, sea, and in the air, the protection of copyright and trade marks, or international trade, treaties on a basis of reciprocity assist in making more bearable the life of the individual in a world of sovereign States.[29]

It is not by accident that these illustrations of the operation of the principle of reciprocity are taken from activities which, from the point of view of power politics, are either peripheral or irrelevant. If, however, States desire to behave rationally even on matters they treat as " political," the principle of reciprocity provides a sensible common denominator.

This proposition may be illustrated by a comparison between the Minorities Treaties of the post-1919 period and the Geneva Convention of 1922 between Germany and Poland regarding Upper Silesia.[30] The States which had been unilaterally burdened in 1919 and after with obligations in favour of national, ethnical and religious minorities, considered these restrictions as an affront to their newly gained national sovereignties.

After the division of Upper Silesia between Germany and Poland, both States agreed to accept far-reaching restrictions of their national jurisdiction on both sides of an artificial frontier. This complicated experiment, codified in over 600 articles of the Geneva Convention, worked exceedingly well. Each of the Parties soon found that, if, under the Convention, it demanded a liberal interpretation of its

[28] See below, p. 188 *et seq.*
[29] See below, pp. 130 and 210 *et seq.*
[30] See further *l.c.* in note 5 above, p. 617 *et seq.*

own rights, the same construction would in due course be asked for by the other side. In accordance with the principle of reciprocity and the assistance of the international organs entrusted with the task of supervising the interpretation and application of the Convention, an equilibrium was soon established which secured a reasonable continuation of social and economic life in the divided area.

While it may sound paradoxical, it is no more than logical that the principle of reciprocity may be found at work in the spheres of the laws of war and neutrality. Once the trump cards of power politics have been played, and the issue is left to be decided in terms of force, even for the purpose of attaining the objects of war, unlimited application of the means of destruction may prove unnecessary. Thus, on a basis of mutuality even in these fields, a limited scope for humanitarian considerations exists.[31] Similarly, in the relations between belligerents and neutrals, an equilibrium tends to be reached when the advantages to be derived from interference with neutral rights are outbalanced by the risk of an outraged neutral allying himself with a more scrupulous belligerent.

Nevertheless, a reservation is necessary. This analysis of the effectivity of the laws of war and neutrality applies to wars fought for limited purposes, such as the Crimean War or the Franco-German War of 1870–71, that is to say, duel wars. In wars such as the Napoleonic Wars, however, or the First and Second World Wars, that is to say, wars to the finish, the weaker side has a tendency to ignore the limitations imposed by international customary and treaty law and to seek short-range advantages by breaches of the laws of war and neutrality.

Even less scope exists for the application of the principle of reciprocity if, as in the Second World War, aggressor States not only challenge a specific system of power politics, but world civilisation as such, and, intentionally and indiscriminately, flout international law with the object of widening still further the gulf between their nations and the rest of the world.[32]

It is apposite here to consider the degree of homogeneity of States which is essential for the survival and development of international law. International law was originally applicable only between Christian nations. It was later extended to non-European

[31] See further below, p. 256 *et seq.*
[32] See further the writer's *International Law and Totalitarian Lawlessness* (1943), p. 30 *et seq.*

States on the assumption that the standards of value underlying the Christian law of nations were accepted by the Near and Far Eastern States at least in a modified form, that is to say, as standards of conduct common to civilised nations. But even this element of homogeneity was thrown overboard when the last barrier to heterogeneity was broken down in favour of an international law that was applicable between all sovereign States.[33]

Has this position been substantially affected by the rise of authoritarian and totalitarian régimes in the post-1919 period? Prior to the First World War, Czarist Russia, Imperial Germany, monarchical Britain and republican France existed side by side in international society and, in principle, nothing prevents democratic, authoritarian and totalitarian States from adopting similar attitudes of mutual tolerance and co-existence—be it active or competitive—towards one another.

The real problem is to decide whether the fact that a State is democratic, authoritarian or totalitarian makes any perceptible difference in its readiness to honour its international obligations. In the political sphere, the difference appears one of degree rather than of kind and, on the non-political side, the principle of reciprocity appears to have a stronger pull than ideological sympathies or antipathies arising from homogeneity or disparity of internal State structure. However, unless the internal structure of States is roughly similar, the principle of reciprocity may in some instances be applicable merely in a formal sense.

Thus, in the economic field a wide diversity exists between capitalist and socialist economies, to mention merely the two extreme forms of present-day economic organisation. The importance of this difference should not, however, be exaggerated. During the transitional period from the mercantile system to industrialism and free trade, comparable differences existed between the members of international society in their division of functions between the State and the individual. Yet they did not result in the breakdown of international law. A similar process of assimilation is now noticeable even in States which value highly the freedom of the individual. In spite of remaining differences, this development may in the long run restore a state of substantial reciprocity which depends on a roughly equal division of the functions allotted to the State and to the individual.

[33] See further below, pp. 57 and 75 *et seq.*

Another aspect of the issue is perhaps more significant. This is the general increase of State control in spheres which, prior to the First World War, were reserved to the initiative of the individual and which are increasingly encroached upon in democratic as well as authoritarian and totalitarian States.[34] Economic and social international relations, as well as education and culture, are becoming increasingly involved in the turmoil of power politics, where law serves predominantly as an ideology. On a world scale, this development tends to circumscribe more narrowly than in the past the scope for the international law of reciprocity.

IV—THE INTERNATIONAL LAW OF CO-ORDINATION

In spheres remote from power politics, international law even shows some traces of a community law.[35]

Perhaps the most substantial contribution to the international law of co-ordination is the gradual limitation and abolition of the slave trade. This important step in the development of international law can be traced back to the example given to the world by Great Britain in the nineteenth century.[36]

At the Congress of Vienna, Great Britain induced the other greater Powers of Europe to agree in principle to the abolition of the slave trade. A clause to this effect was incorporated into the Peace Treaty of Paris of November 20, 1815. Thus, as it was formulated in the Additional Article on the Abolition of the Slave Trade, the ground was prepared " for the entire and definitive abolition of a Commerce so odious, and so strongly condemned by the laws of Religion and of Nature."

To make the campaign against the slave traders more effective, it still required the patient work of a number of British Foreign Secretaries to make more retrograde States enter into bilateral anti-slavery treaties with Great Britain. On a basis of reciprocity, Great Britain even granted to contracting parties the right of visit and search of British merchant ships which were suspect of engaging in the slave trade. The final stage in this humanitarian battle was reached when most civilised States agreed to the outlawry of the slave trade by multilateral treaties.[37]

---

[34] See further *l.c.* in note 32 above, p. 42 *et seq.*
[35] See above, p. 13 *et seq.*
[36] See also below, pp. 135 and 198 *et seq.*
[37] See further *Manual*, Vol. 2, pp. 533–534.

Conventions on the status of refugees, the white slave traffic, international opium and drug control and the suppression of the traffic in obscene publications offer further illustrations of the international law of co-ordination.

So far, the concept of an international community has taken its most concrete form in the sphere of the law of international rivers. On the basis of treaties, by which, in the interest of the freedom of navigation and commerce, States have limited their sovereignty, State practice and courts have developed the idea of an international river community and elaborated the legal duties inherent in such relations.

Thus, in the case of the *Donauversickerung* (1927)[38] of Württemberg and Prussia *versus* Baden, the German *Staatsgerichtshof* held that " the exercise of sovereign rights by every State in regard to international rivers traversing its territory is limited by the duty not to injure the interests of other members of the international community. Due consideration must be given to one another by States through whose territories an international river flows. No State may substantially impair the natural use of the flow of such a river by its neighbour. This principle has gained increased recognition in international relations, in particular in modern times when the increased exploitation of the natural power of flowing water has led to a contractual regulation of the interests of States connected by international rivers. . . . The application of this principle is governed by the circumstances of each particular case. The interests of the States in question must be weighed in an equitable manner against one another."

Another intrusion of the law of co-ordination into international economic law is furnished by the General Agreement on Tariffs and Trade of 1947. The parties to this Convention have added a new standard to the traditional standards of international economic law— the standard of economic good neighbourliness.[39] The infusion of this type of community ethics into international law enables the members of GATT to apply towards one another the principle of reciprocity in a more generalised form than was possible by using merely the classical standards of international economic law.

---

[38] *Entscheidungen des Reichsgerichts in Zivilsachen,* Vol. 116, Appendix, p. 18 *et seq.,* at pp. 31–32. See also *Vol. I,* p. 220, and, on the reservations subject to which decisions of federal courts on matters of international law can be legitimately used, *Fundamental Principles,* pp. 291–293.

[39] See further below, p. 228 *et seq.*

In its Advisory Opinion on *Reservations to the Genocide Convention*,[40] the World Court formulated some essential features of the international law of co-ordination: " The Convention was manifestly adopted for a purely humanitarian and civilising purpose. It is indeed difficult to imagine a convention that might have this dual character to a greater degree, since its object, on the one hand, is to safeguard the very existence of certain human groups and, on the other, to confirm and endorse the most elementary principles of morality. In such a convention the contracting States do not have any interests of their own ; they merely have, one and all, a common interest, namely, the accomplishment of those high purposes which are the *raison d'être* of the convention. Consequently, in a convention of this type one cannot speak of individual advantages or disadvantages to States, or of the maintenance of a perfect contractual balance between rights and duties. The high ideals which inspired the Convention provide, by virtue of the common will of the parties, the foundation and measure of all its provisions." [41]

V—LIMITATIONS AND PECULIARITIES OF INTERNATIONAL LAW

The relatively small number of groups which are bearers of rights and duties under international law accounts for some of the special features of this legal system. Yet the most essential differences between international law and mature systems of municipal law are due to the fact that the emphasis in international customary law is so strongly on the law of power.

The Growth of International Law

International law cannot grow in the way of municipal law because of the need for obtaining the consent of all concerned to any change in the law. Treaties are, therefore, the chief vehicle of the development of international law.[42]

In its origins, even the existing body of international customary law is the product of treaty law to a much greater extent than is generally realised, or the result of parallel national practices.[43] Similarly, the position regarding new rules of international customary

[40] *I.C.J. Reports, 1951*, p. 23.
[41] See further below, p. 203 *et seq.*, and *Vol. I*, pp. 271–272.
[42] See further *Fundamental Principles*, p. 262 *et seq.*, and *Vol. I*, p. 421 *et seq.*
[43] See below, pp. 85 and 256 *et seq.*

law is not very different from that in the field of treaties. A rule is only considered as one of general international customary law if it has been accepted by most, if not all, subjects of international law.[44] It is widely taken as implied in this proposition that all the greater Powers have accepted such a rule.[45]

The principle of consent imposes no less severe restrictions on international courts and tribunals in the development of international law by means of decided cases. This is not so much because international law does not admit of the principle of binding precedents but because international arbitration and the judicial settlement of international disputes are purely optional devices.

The modest place occupied by international courts and tribunals in international society is thus directly attributable to the rules governing the principles of State sovereignty and consent. As the Permanent Court of International Justice emphasised in the *Eastern Carelia* case,[46] " it is well established in international law that no State can, without its consent, be compelled to submit its disputes with other States either to mediation or to arbitration, or to any other kind of pacific settlement."

A not uncommon attitude among governments, and especially those of greater Powers in their relations with other potentially hostile major Powers,[47] is aptly described in a statement made at the time of the First Hague Peace Conference by Baron von Holstein,[48] the *éminence grise* of the German Foreign Office under William II : " Small disinterested States as subjects, small questions as objects of arbitral decision, are conceivable, great States and great questions are not. For the State, the more so the bigger it is, regards itself as an end, not as a means towards the attainment of higher aims lying outside it. There is no higher aim for the State than the protection of its own interests. But the latter, in the case of the great Powers, are not necessarily identical with the maintenance of peace but rather with the subjugation of an enemy and rival by a well-constructed stronger group."

The techniques which States and, in particular, major Powers, have employed in the past to maintain their practically complete

---

[44] See further *Vol. I,* pp. 20, 27 and 39 *et seq.*
[45] See also 60 *Harv.L.R.* (1947), at pp. 558–559.
[46] (1923), Series B 5, p. 27.
[47] See below, p. 146 *et seq.*
[48] *Die Grosse Politik der Europäischen Kabinette 1871–1914,* Vol. 15 (1924), p. 189.

freedom of action from international courts and tribunals in politically vital matters have changed, but not their basic attitudes.[49] This may still be expressed in the reversal of the legal maxim *de minimis non curat praetor.*

The Monopoly of Armed Force

Municipal law in developed communities rests securely on the organised power of the State. The government insists on the monopoly of the use of legitimate force, puts its overwhelming strength behind the law and, if it acts wisely, forestalls revolution by timely adaptation of the law to changing circumstances. By way of contrast, international law is not only dependent for change on the consent of every State concerned but also lacks any central authority capable of imposing its will on recalcitrant members of the international aristocracy.

States still cling to their monopolies of armed force and, in particular, of the super-weapons of any age. In 546 B.C. the representatives of fourteen Chinese States assembled to discuss the subject of disarmament, but failed to reach agreement.

Since then, the position has little changed. It is well summed up in the official French Report [50] on the First Hague Peace Conference of 1899 : " From the first meeting it was easy to see that the delegates of every Power, while appearing animated by the desire to respond to the humanitarian intentions of H.M. the Emperor of Russia, derived either from their own convictions or from the instructions of their governments a resolve not to accept any measure which might result in really diminishing the defensive or offensive forces of their countries, or even in limiting the increase of those forces."

The Sanctions Behind International Law

So long as every State is its own policeman, the position regarding sanctions under international customary law is necessarily peculiar. If a State refuses to comply with the demands of another State—not backed as a rule by any judicial decision—to live up to its duties under international law, the latter can enforce its own

---

[49] See, for instance, C. H. M. Waldock, *The Decline of the Optional Clause,* 32 *B.Y.I.L.* (1955–56), p. 244 *et seq.,* and S. Rosenne, *The International Court of Justice* (1957), p. 302 *et seq.*

[50] *L.c.* in note 48 above, p. 203, note.

interpretation of international law only by compulsory measures short of war or by resort to war.[51]

" Self-help " of this kind has little in common with self-help in mature systems of municipal law.[52] Within the State, the scope of self-help is strictly limited by legal rules. Moreover, the community itself supervises the methods by which this extraordinary procedure is applied, and the object of such measures may invoke the assistance of the courts if in his opinion his opponent has overstepped the bounds of his rights. Thus, in the municipal sphere sufficient safeguards exist for keeping the exercise of the right of self-help within narrow bounds and preventing any serious abuse of this right. International customary law provides none of these guarantees.

Although action of a State amounting to self-help may be within the law, no certainty exists on the level of international customary law that it will keep within such limits. In these circumstances, the classification of intervention, reprisals and war as measures of self-help or sanctions of international customary law is a euphemism. It provides a convenient legal cloak for action which more often than not belongs to the sphere of the rule of force. The institution of self-help is a model illustration of situations in which legal terminology is prone to be abused for ideological purposes. What in such circumstances is likely to be applied is the higher " law " of international society, but it is not law and remains decorously hidden behind the seemly façade of international customary law.

The position is different in those fields of international law in which the principle of reciprocity has free play. Here, the advantages of compliance with international law are so great that it would not be worth while even for a powerful State to break the law. Law abidance could hardly be more irksome than the inconvenience of the non-existence of such rules or exclusion from their benefits. Hence a legal order based on mutuality and reciprocity can safely rely on the penalties inherent in its social machinery, that is to say, on the unwillingness of participants to jeopardise the enjoyment of the benefits they derive from the legal régime in question.

Moreover, powerful pressure groups inside the State which are anxious to preserve stability in the international society, such as banks, export industries, transport and trade establishments, can be depended upon to exert their influence to maintain and extend these

[51] See below, p. 234 *et seq.*
[52] See further *Fundamental Principles*, pp. 342 and 353 *et seq.*

reciprocal relations. Yet, this is true only subject to the overall reservation of the overriding exigencies of power politics.

The Legal Character of International Law

Finally, what is the answer to the time-honoured question persistently raised since the days of Austin's *Lectures on Jurisprudence* : Is International Law law? [53]

If the issue is raised against the unstated premise that, in order to be regarded as law, a legal system must live up to the standards of a mature system of municipal law, the answer is a foregone conclusion. To put the question in this way is, however, unscientific because arbitrary.

Why should only systems in which the character of a community law or of hybrids between community and society laws predominates be regarded as law? To make this assumption would mean to exclude from the realm of law all legal systems in the category of society laws and treat them as " non-law." Actually, international law is not the only instance of a society law, though admittedly it presents an extreme case. It has essential features in common with the laws of absolutist and totalitarian States.

Lettres de cachet and other forms of tyranny are as inseparably connected with the law in absolutist States as concentration camps and mass executions are the necessary accompaniment of totalitarian law. Nevertheless, the France of Louis XIV and the Germany of Hitler were based upon detailed and complicated legal systems regulating the everyday lives of their citizens. It needed, however, merely a sign from the one man above the law or powerful leaders in his entourage to override the law whenever this was deemed expedient.

The legality of this procedure is based on the handy fiction that, in such cases, nobody actually stands above the law, since the supreme lawgiver—the king or *Führer*—modifies the law for particular purposes and in particular instances. Nevertheless, such an explanation does not amount to more than a polite statement of the hard fact that, in these cases, the legal system is allowed to function only subject to its compatibility with the " law" of expediency. The relation between power and law in these systems

---

[53] (1832)—5th ed., ed. by R. Campbell (1885), pp. 173 and 183 *et seq.* For further literature, see *Manual*, Vol. 2, p. 387.

of municipal law is not unlike that between power politics and international customary law.

In the spheres of the laws of reciprocity and of co-ordination, and especially on the level of international institutions,[54] international law may claim to be law even when measured by orthodox standards. Here a body of mutually advantageous rules of social conduct with a more precise legal content is applied, and the sanctions which are inherent in the laws of reciprocity and co-ordination secure the observance of international law in these fields by greater Powers and small States alike.

VI—SOCIOLOGICAL WORKING HYPOTHESES

It appears possible to formulate tentatively a number of sociological working hypotheses which are relevant for purposes of international law[55]:

(1) The practice of States and the case law of international courts and tribunals prove that international law is not identical with international morality.

(2) Prima facie, international law is the exclusive law of the aristocracy of sovereign States and such other entities as, for general or limited purposes, the existing subjects of international law choose to treat on this footing.

(3) Power, and not Law, is the overriding consideration in world affairs, especially in the relations between States which regard themselves as potential enemies.

(4) In such a nexus, the primary, but certainly not the exclusive, function of international law is that of a law of power and, in matters which States, especially world Powers, consider as vital, they tend to reserve to themselves complete freedom of action.

(5) Changes in any particular legal *status quo* depend on consent[56] or the successful application of unilateral pressure unless this is limited or excluded by treaty.

(6) In any system of power politics or power politics in disguise, the border line between peace and war remains necessarily fluid.

---

54 See further *Manual,* Vol. 1, p. 227 *et seq.*

55 For, partly, confirmatory and, partly, complementary historical working hypotheses, see below, p. 64 *et seq.*

56 The term is used in its widest sense, including Acquiescence and Recognition. See further *Fundamental Principles,* p. 229 *et seq.*

(7) In view of the reservations and escape clauses in multilateral treaties of the post-1919 and post-1945 periods, the special position granted in the Charter of the United Nations to the world Powers and the difficulties inherent in the attempts at the outlawry of aggressive war, it would require convincing evidence to the effect that, in any material respect, these working hypotheses have ceased to be relevant.[57]

(8) In many fields of international law, especially those remote from central political issues, international law is able to fulfil the functions of a law of reciprocity [58] and it has been considerably strengthened by the creation of functional international institutions.[59]

(9) On a basis of reciprocity, laws and customs of war and neutrality have developed.[60] They are, however, subject to the risk of being discarded in favour of a system of negative reciprocity by way of reprisals and counter-reprisals. In the nuclear age, they are further strained by powerful trends towards total war.[61]

(10) The international law of reciprocity is not necessarily affected by the absence of constitutional homogeneity between States, but requires an indispensable minimum of an ethical common denominator.[62]

(11) Within, so far, narrow limits and, in particular, between States which rule out the possibility of any future war between themselves, international law can fulfil even the functions of a community law as distinct from a society law.

---

[57] See further *Power Politics*, p. 261 *et seq.*, and *Manual*, Vol. 1, p 265 *et seq.*
[58] See further below, p. 210 *et seq.*
[59] See further below, p. 274 *et seq.*
[60] See further below, p. 256 *et seq.*, and *Manual*, Vol. 1, p. 170 *et seq.*, and Vol. 2, p. 579 *et seq.*
[61] See further below, p. 79 *et seq.*
[62] See further below, p. 294 *et seq.*

CHAPTER 3

INTERNATIONAL LAW IN HISTORICAL PERSPECTIVE

IN order to see international law in its proper historical perspective, it is necessary to be aware of two obstacles.

The first difficulty is that the widely practised identification of the history of the Doctrine of international law with that of international law distorts, rather than mirrors, the growth of international law; for the Doctrine of international law tends either to lag behind practice or, if not subject to stringent self-criticism, to anticipate developments which may, or may not, come true.[1] Moreover, the deductive and eclectic treatment of international law is prone to suffer from a rationally unverifiable subjectivism which appears inseparable from both these methods. Thus, any presentation of international law based on either of these techniques is always in danger of failing to do justice to relevant aspects of reality which do not happen to fit into such preconceived systems.[2] Viewed in isolation, the history of the Doctrine of international law is, therefore, unlikely to reflect accurately the genesis of contemporary international law.[3]

The second difficulty is to find the best starting point. It is occasionally suggested that medieval international law did not exist because it could not exist. Reasoning on these lines is based on the hierarchical structure of the medieval Christian community. It may claim a measure of support from the theory of the Holy Roman Empire. It leaves, however, out of account the very different story of the reality of this conglomeration, the opportunities which the increasing weakness of its apex provided for a kind of quasi-international law to grow inside this constitutional monstrosity, as Pufendorf termed the Holy Roman Empire of the German Nation, and, even more significant, the existence on its fringes of States which never formed part of the Holy Roman Empire.

Others, who are dimly aware of the existence of some medieval

---

1 See further 6 *Y.B.W.A.* (1952), p. 252 *et seq.*

2 See further 9 *C.L.P.* (1956), p. 235 *et seq.*, and 60 *Harv.L.R.* (1947), p. 550 *et seq.*

3 For an exemplary treatment of the dialectic relation between the history of the Doctrine and practice of international law, *cf.* E. Reibstein, *Völkerrecht*, Vol. I (1958).

international law summarily dismiss it as too rudimentary to be relevant for understanding present-day international law. Yet, study of the material proves how much continuity exists between medieval and contemporary international law, and how much the simplicity of medieval international law can assist in a better comprehension of the basic structure of twentieth-century international law.[4]

Thus, it appears that the starting point should certainly not be placed later than early medieval international law. The only remaining question is whether it should be earlier. Such evidence as is available does not suggest that any earlier or separate system of international law co-existing with medieval European international law has exercised any appreciable influence on early medieval law.[5] Even so, these systems are important from a sociological point of view.[6] They do not, however, appear to throw much light on the genesis of present-day international law.

I—THE EVOLUTION OF INTERNATIONAL SOCIETY

In our time, the whole world forms, at least for some purposes, one international society. For others, the Western Hemisphere, Europe, Africa, the Near East, the Russian orbit, Communist China, and the regions of the Indian Ocean and of the Pacific still represent separate, but overlapping magnetic fields of their own.

This world society is the result of a threefold process of disintegration, expansion and centralisation. The community of medieval Europe is probably the most significant point of departure. To consider Europe as the nucleus of this evolution is more than an egocentric whim. It means putting the emphasis on the active agent in a course of events of which, on the whole, the rest of the world was merely the passive object.

The Medieval European Community

There is room for disagreement on whether to consider medieval times as a " dark " or " progressive " period in the history of Europe. Irrespective of such value-judgments, much is to be said—at

---

[4] See below, pp. 59 and 85 *et seq.*

[5] *Cf.*, for instance, I. R. Moreno, *El Derecho Internacional Público antes de la Era Cristiana* (1946); R. Numelin, *The Beginnings of Diplomacy* (1950); G. Stadtmüller, *Geschichte des Völkerrechts*, Vol. I (1951) and A. Nussbaum, *A Concise History of the Law of Nations* (1954).

[6] See above, p. 21 *et seq.*

least in terms of relativity—for classifying the *unum Corpus Christianum* as a community.[7]

The diarchy of Pope and Emperor provided a common framework for Christendom, however shaken it may have been by the interminable struggles between its spiritual and temporal heads and the political feuds between its members. The social structure of the Holy Roman Empire rested on the triarchy of State (*imperium*), Church (*sacerdotium*) and University (*studium*). This scheme served as a model for the other Christian communities. The Christian world was rent apart by devastating wars, but common codes of honour and chivalry created generally accepted standards, at least in the relations between members of the European nobility.

In spite of all excesses, a minimum of decency was observed even in the hostile relations between the Christian and Islamic worlds.

The Christian Church set limits to freedom of thought, but the wandering scholar had the benefits of a member of a lodge in every university of Europe. In spite of bitter feuds between different schools, members of all universities shared a basic philosophical and scientific outlook. The common use of Latin constituted an additional bond between scholars. Medieval art and architecture were the outward symbols of the spiritual unity of medieval Europe.

The Disintegration of the Medieval European Community

The Christian commonwealth of the Middle Ages succumbed to the combined onslaught of diverse forces. Capitalist enterprise undermined the relatively static economic system of feudalism. New classes of manufacturers, merchants and labourers arose with attitudes to life more dynamic and less hide-bound by tradition. Cannon, at the disposal of anybody who could afford them, made castles and city walls redundant. Standing armies of mercenaries proved themselves superior to temporary and cumbrous feudal levies. The urge of individual freedom and self-expression found scientific, philosophical and religious outlets in the movement of the Renaissance and Reformation. Disintegration of an age dying from within was hastened by the discovery of the New World and of the sea passages to India. Their gold and riches contributed in full measure to the transformation of medieval Europe into a turbulent society.

[7] See above, p. 10.

Bellum omnium contra omnes appeared inevitable. As Hobbes put it,[8] the problem of the age was to find a working alternative to "that miserable condition of Warre which is necessarily consequent . . . to the natural passions of men when there is no visible Power to keep them in awe, and tye them by feare of punishment to the performance of their Covenants."

The territorial princes of Europe, the most stable remnants of the pyramidal structure of the Holy Roman Empire, used their opportunities and transformed themselves into absolutist rulers within their domains. They furnished one of the few remaining rallying points. Internecine struggles between them and a period of chaos brought to the surface those monarchs who, by reason of power, astuteness and location of their territories, were best fitted to survive the turmoils of a revolutionary age.

The Expansion and Centralisation of International Society

The forces released by the decay of medieval Europe were too vigorous and dynamic to allow themselves to be compressed within the compass of medieval Europe. The world was their field.

In the process of the colonial and imperial expansion of the European Powers, the European society of nations gradually engulfed the New World, Asia and Africa. Though divided in their religious allegiances, the European States still shared a vast fund of values, cherished by Roman Catholics and Protestants alike and ultimately derived both from Christianity and the rediscovery of Antiquity.

This tradition could be passed on to the newly discovered continents in which emigrants from Europe settled in considerable numbers. Although Europe was strong enough to open up and subjugate other parts of the world, it could not force the rest of mankind to accept the Western way of life. At the most, the old civilisations of Asia were prepared to bide their time and, meanwhile, to study the means by which the West so successfully had defeated what they still considered to be their own superior ways of life.

Thus, not much more than the overwhelming power of the Western States, the common technological devices and mutual commercial interests held together the emerging world society, ruled by the Western civilised nations,[9] as they, at least, viewed themselves.

In the course of their continuous struggle for survival, European States and empires grew and decayed, but some of them succeeded

---

[8] *The Leviathan* (1651), Part II, Ch. 17.
[9] See further below, p. 51 *et seq.*

in stabilising themselves and in drawing additional strength from a newly emerging emotional force : modern nationalism. The sovereign States of Europe became the aristocracy of the new international society. This aristocracy was ruled by the oligarchy of the greater Powers.

With the expansion of European society into a world society, the original aristocracy and oligarchy correspondingly expanded and, increasingly, came to include non-European States. The status of greater Powers came to be determined on a world scale, and the cradle of this global society sank back into the position of one of a number of fields of world politics and world wars.[10]

II—MEDIEVAL INTERNATIONAL LAW

The historical premises of medieval international law were of brutal simplicity.[11] In the first place, in the absence of an agreed state of truce or peace, war was the basic state of international relations even between independent Christian communities. Secondly, unless an exception was made by means of individual safe-conduct or by way of treaty, rulers considered themselves entitled to treat foreigners at their absolute discretion. Thirdly, the high seas were no man's " land " and anyone might do as he pleased.

The Points of Departure

The conditions on which the transformation of this state of anarchy into relations on the basis of law depended were first fulfilled in the political and economic environment of the Italian City States and the independent States on the fringes of the Holy Roman Empire.

The rivalries for supremacy between Popes and Emperors enabled the Italian City States to achieve independence in all but name within the loose framework of the Holy Roman Empire.

---

10 See further *Power Politics*, p. 102 *et seq.*
11 These, and the following, generalisations are primarily based on the inductive study of some of the relevant material of State practice in North-Western Europe, especially English and Scottish practice (see below, p. 85 *et seq.*) and, regarding the practice of the Italian City States, on A. P. Sereni, *The Italian Conception of International Law* (1943). Any of these findings are necessarily subject to correction by further inductive research into the practice of other medieval States.

For a welcome change in emphasis from the history of Doctrine to regard for State practice, compare the first and second editions of A. Nussbaum, *A Concise History of the Law of Nations* (1947 and 1954). See also the same writer's *Forms and Observance of Treaties in the Middle Ages and the Early Sixteenth Century* in G. A. Lipsky (ed.), *Law and Politics in the World Community* (1953), p. 191 *et seq.*

Owing to their proximity to one another, the foreign policies of any
one of these cities affected all the others, forcing them to be continuously on guard against the hegemonical designs of the most powerful in their midst. Their response to the continuous danger of
obliteration as self-governing communities was the creation of an
intricate system of balance of power.

City States such as Milan, Venice and Florence were compact
and powerful units in a political, economic and military sense. They
exercised effective control over their citizens and subjects, and their
frontiers were clearly defined. Their wide-flung political and economic interests demanded binding commitments between one another
and between these City States and the Powers of Europe as well as
the Christian and Muslim rulers on the fringes of Africa and Asia.

From the twelfth century onwards, the treaty system of the Italian
City States extended to the Byzantine emperors, the Christian kings
of Cyprus, Syria and Armenia, Sultans, Beys and Tartar princes. A
century later, they established permanent residential embassies among
one another.

A common fund of legal concepts, derived from Roman Law,
and stereotyped forms of treaties facilitated the growth of rules of
international customary law, especially in the field of maritime law.
Mediation and arbitration were used in forms, and within limits,
basically akin to the practices of subsequent periods.

In North-Western Europe, a relatively close international nexus
existed between England, Scotland, France and powerful princes
such as the Count of Flanders and the Duke of Normandy. It very
much depended on circumstances whether the latter, and other
princes, who were still under feudal obligations towards their liege
lords, felt themselves restrained in their freedom of action or behaved
as, in fact, independent rulers.

In this respect, the kings of England were in an especially
favourable position. England never had formed part of the Holy
Roman Empire, and its island character provided at least some
natural frontiers for the nucleus of the possessions of the English
kings. Although, for a time, the Pope insisted on claiming Scotland
as a fief of the Holy See, in fact, the position of Scotland was very
similar to that of England.

As early as the twelfth century, the net of diplomatic and treaty
relations between the kings of England and foreign powers extended
beyond the original triangle formed by England, Scotland and France.

It included the Emperor, the City of Cologne and the kings of Portugal and Sicily.

By the end of the fourteenth century the map of English treaty relations showed remarkable changes. Relations in the original diplomatic field had become much more complex, and the field itself had greatly expanded. It comprised the whole of South-Western and Western Europe, the most powerful princes within the Holy Roman Empire, and the Italian City States. In the North and North-East, it extended to Norway and Poland, and in the South-East to Constantinople, the Black Sea and Asia Minor.[12]

The Predominance of Treaty Law

Medieval treaty practice proves that little was taken for granted even between Christian princes. Diplomatic immunity—one of the conditions of regular diplomatic relations—rested for centuries on the issue of individual safe-conducts. These were gradually replaced by treaties generalising the conditions on which diplomatic immunity would be granted. It took until the seventeenth century for these treaty clauses to be regarded as merely declaratory of international customary law and, therefore, as redundant.[13]

Similarly, a state of peace was far from being considered as normal between the princes of Christendom. Peace was conceived as an agreed state of international affairs. Frequently Christian princes were content to establish between one another a state of truce for shorter or longer periods. If their relations were on a footing of amity, there were various incentives to establish still closer legal ties between themselves. They all were anxious to obtain and strengthen their monopolies in the conduct of foreign affairs. Prevailing practices of piracy and private reprisals constituted a continuous challenge to this claim and were detrimental to peaceful commerce. Treaties provided the tools with which to lay the foundations of an international quasi-order of truce or peace. On this basis—again by way of treaty—more ambitious superstructures were erected in the fields of politics and commerce.[14]

Subsidies and alliances, neutrality and mutual insurance of princes against internal rebellion were the typical objects of medieval political treaties. Occasionally, they included provisions for the

---

12 See further below, p. 85 *et seq.*
13 See further below, p. 92 *et seq.*
14 See further below, p. 108 *et seq.*

pacific settlement of international disputes and foreshadowed even contemporary power politics in disguise.[15]

The Italian League, which was directed against France, and to which Henry VII acceded, showed a curious affinity to the League of Nations. Similarly, the League of Cambray was first aimed at Venice and then at France, and the object of the Treaty of General Peace and Concord of 1518 was neither peace nor concord, but war against the Ottoman Empire.

Equally direct was the interest of princes, who were steeped in bullionist conceptions of international trade, in the conclusion of commercial treaties with foreign Powers. The typical object of these treaties was to achieve an appreciable measure of freedom of commerce. Although the standards employed to secure this object varied according to circumstances, the patterns of customary, reciprocal, national and most-favoured-nation treatment which emerged proved reasonably stable.[16]

Rules of international law on subjects such as the validity, interpretation, duration and breach of international treaties were first cautiously elaborated in some of these early treaties. Subsequently, these rules were taken for granted and treated as rules of international customary law. A similar process took place in fields as wide apart as State responsibility for torts committed against foreigners, reprisals, shipwreck and neutrality.[17]

The Binding Character of Medieval International Law

What gave to medieval international law its binding force? There were glaring cases in which obligations solemnly undertaken were unscrupulously broken. In others, reciprocal interest and expediency were the reasons why international pledges were kept and carried out.

Contracting parties tried to safeguard themselves by multiple sanctions which might be incorporated side by side into treaties between Christian princes. They might consist in the exchange of hostages, in the pledging of towns, castles and territories, in mortgaging the movable and immovable properties of kings or their subjects, or in the appointment of powerful nobles of the contracting parties or of foreign princes as guardians and guarantors of such treaties.

[15] See further above, p. 122, and *Power Politics*, p. 695 *et seq.*
[16] See further below, pp. 123 and 219 *et seq.*
[17] See further below, p. 96 *et seq.*

Sometimes, the signatures of princes were strengthened by adding those of powerful representatives of the three estates of their realms ; or else the need for confirmation of a treaty by the parliaments of the countries concerned was expressly stipulated.

Supernatural sanctions might be added. Sovereigns or their ambassadors might have to take solemn oaths to observe faithfully such treaties, or treaties might provide for the excommunication of a guilty party.

Ultimately, however, these treaties rested on the word and good faith of the princes concerned. A common Christian religion and a common moral code derived from it allowed contracting parties to assume that, power, reciprocity and expediency apart, the rule of *pacta sunt servanda* would be respected. The fact that, in many cases, this expectation was disappointed is less significant than the constant and recurrent attempts of princes to settle matters on this basis of trust and order.

III—INTERNATIONAL LAW AND THE EXPANSION OF INTERNATIONAL SOCIETY

When the medieval State system broke up, the spiritual basis of international law was weakened but not eliminated. In proclaiming the principle of *Fides non est habenda cum infidelibus* and, by infidels, meaning Christian heretics, the Council of Constance (1414–1418) came dangerously near to a complete split between Roman Catholics and Protestants.

The Rational Basis of the European Law of Nations

In spite of such extremism and the religious wars, the Christian nations of Europe remained aware of the fact that they might have lost a common creed, but still shared a considerable fund of basic Christian values (*conjunctio hominum cum Deo, conjunctio hominum inter sese*).

Naturalist writers rationalised these values into systems of rights and duties of princes under divine and human—obligatory and voluntary—natural law. Others, in a more rationalist manner, preferred to go back to classical philosophy, rediscovered by the scholars of the Renaissance, and to imagine international society in terms of humanity at large, a society of human beings endowed with reason.

In *De Jure Belli ac Pacis Libri Tres*,[18] Grotius used this formulation.
In choosing this basis, he was on common ground with the naturalists
of the Italian and Spanish schools and also with Gentili, all distinguished ancestors of the "Father" of international law.

Legal Relations between Christian and Non-Christian States

The universalist spirit which imbued the naturalist Doctrine of
international law greatly assisted the law of nations. It gave to
international law the elasticity to weather the storms of the transition
of Europe from a community into an international society and to
adapt itself to a constantly widening international environment.

The issue of legal relations between the Christian and non-
Christian worlds had already arisen in a variety of ways during the
Middle Ages. Was it lawful to conclude treaties of alliance or
commerce with Muslim Powers? Could there be peace treaties
between Christian princes and the infidels? Was it permissible for
Christian communities to remain neutral in wars between Christian
and non-Christian Powers?

Islamic law as then interpreted denied the possibility of peace
with unbelievers and, at the most, conceded the lawfulness of temporary armistices with Christian princes. The Christian Church, in
her turn, equally discouraged peaceful relations with the Muslim
world. In 1179, the Third Lateran Council forbade trade with
infidels in ships and war material. Pope Clement V prohibited all
trade with them, but to little effect.

In the Age of Discovery, new legal problems arose from the
Spanish and Portuguese conquests in the New World. Was the
doctrine of just war applicable to wars with American aborigines?
Was it lawful to reduce them to slavery and to deprive them of their
territories? Were there any legal limitations to colonial exploitation?

Spanish scholars, especially Vitoria, struggled manfully with these
problems. Their idealistic teachings did at least prick the conscience
of the government at home, although they did not essentially modify
the practice of the *conquistadores* and the majority of the colonial
administrators on the spot.[19] The naturalists contributed, however,
to a remarkable sophistication in the execution of Spain's and
Portugal's colonial designs.

---

[18] (1646—*Editio Nova*), Bk. 1, Ch. 1.
[19] See, for instance, L. Hanke, *The Spanish Struggle for Justice in the Conquest of
America* (1949) and *Aristotle and the American Indians* (1959).

The *conquistadores* were accompanied not only by chaplains and missionaries, but also by learned notaries. Their task consisted in making sure that due legal form was given to all transactions during such expeditions. The *Requirimiento*, a Spanish Royal Proclamation drafted by Palacios Rubios in 1513, illustrates what this meant in practice.

The document had to be read in full by a notary and translated to the Indians. It consisted of a fantastic saga of Papal and Spanish claims to the New World and left the Indians with the alternative of acknowledging the supremacy of the Pope and of the Spanish Crown or enslavement and confiscation of their property. When the ceremony was completed, and the Indians were still proving recalcitrant, the way was free to war or annexation of their territories.

In any case, nothing was easier than retrospectively to fit the facts into the generously wide categories provided by naturalist moralists and writers. Indian rulers might have rights over territory just as Christian princes, and their subjects might be entitled to undisturbed enjoyment of their property rights. Yet were not the Spaniards assured by Vitoria of their equally undisputed right to travel innocently through—and to stay in—Indian empires? If then, contrary to expectations of innocent travellers, Indian princes unreasonably refused access to their lands or shadowed these strangers with their own forces, was the natural right of self-defence to be denied to a Pizarro in Peru or a Cortez in Mexico?

If, without good reason, Indians refused to trade with the Spaniards, was this not a just cause of war? If Indian rulers or their subjects prevented Spaniards from converting Indians to Christianity, was this not a just cause of war? If they attacked converted Indian princes, who had allied themselves with the Spaniards, who could deny that these were excellent grounds of war expressly mentioned by Vitoria himself? However idealistic the intentions of the Spanish naturalists were, in fact, their doctrines provided highly convenient ideologies for the empire-builders of the sixteenth century.

When the separation of international law from Christian morality had progressed further still, the application of doctrines derived from Roman law led to similar results which were required by the expansion of European society. Unless recognised as subjects of international law, colonial rulers were not *sui juris*. They were mere objects of international law, and their territories *res nullius*, owner-less possessions, which any subject of international law was entitled to appropriate to himself.

In other cases, it proved more convenient to acknowledge the binding force of international law in relation to non-European communities and to treat in a simplified form, the scope of international law as being universal. As was affirmed by Sir William Scott in the case of *The Hurtige Hane*,[20] non-Christian rulers might " on some points of the law of nations, be entitled to a very relaxed application of the principles, established by long usage between the States of Europe, holding an intimate and constant intercourse with each other."

One of the rules of international law not restricted to use in Europe was that every State was free to alienate its territories by cession or to renounce all or some of its sovereign rights to other subjects of international law. Thus, on a liberal scale, treaties were concluded by which territories situated in Africa, Asia and the Pacific were ceded to European Powers.

In other cases treaties provided the means of establishing international protectorates of European Powers over areas such as Morocco, Tunis and Zanzibar. Frequently, international dependency was merely the prelude to the establishment of a colonial protectorate, that is to say, a protectorate under municipal law, over the territory in question. In such a case, the protected State was deprived of even the shadow of its former international personality. This was what happened in the cases of many of the British protectorates in India and of the Dutch protectorates in the East Indies.

In other cases mutual jealousies of the Powers or local susceptibilities made it advisable to avoid the open dismemberment of a country or the outright cession of its territories. Strategic or economic requirements of Western Powers could then be satisfied in substance by the lease of such territories for a long term of years. Such leases, as were granted by the Sultan of Zanzibar to the British and German East Africa Companies, by China to the European Powers or by Cuba to the United States, form, however, part of a relatively late stage of imperialist expansion.

---

[20] (1801) 3 C.Rob. 324. *Cf.* also below, p. 70 *et seq.*

International Law as the Law of Civilised Nations

In the initial stages of contact between the West and the Far East, different techniques had to be employed. Much to their surprise Western Powers found Chinese officials looking down on them as "immature and uncivilised" people. The Middle Kingdom refused to treat with European Powers on a footing of equality and international law. It confronted them with its own claim to potential universality. In spite of their overwhelming superiority, the Western Powers were content to assert their equality of status, to force China to deal with them on the footing of the Western law of nations and to secure by treaties their right of trade with China. Japan and Tibet were incorporated into international society on a similar basis.

In the Far East, as well as in the Islamic countries of the Near and Middle East and of East Africa, the symbiosis of East and West raised additional problems. The civil and, still more so, the criminal laws of these non-European countries were based on the principle of collective responsibility, and this was entirely unsuited to the requirements of a capitalist world.

The discrepancies in the evolution of Western and Eastern legal systems were bridged by means of capitulation treaties. Citizens of Western Powers were treated as extraterritorial, that is to say, they remained subject to the laws and jurisdiction of their home States.

Law was administered to them either in consular courts on the spot or in colonial possessions of the Western Powers in the vicinity. Consular and mixed courts were granted jurisdiction in civil disputes between Europeans and subjects of States which had granted such extraterritorial rights, and even in cases of criminal offences against foreigners.

Thus, by means of capitulation treaties the conditions were created which, in the formulation of Protocol 13 of the Paris Peace Conference of 1856, were "essential to the peaceful residence of Christians within these countries, and the successful prosecution of commerce with their people."

In the beginning, the apparent lack of reciprocity in these treaties roused little resentment, especially in Islamic countries. For a long time, the Ottoman Porte considered it below its dignity to concern itself with the squabbles between "Christian dogs." When, however, Western nationalism invaded Asia, and Asian countries imitated Western ways and, in particular, assimilated their judicial systems to those of the West, they increasingly resented these treaties as symbols of Western domination and their own inferiority in Western eyes. In their view these treaties had lost their *raison d'être*, and they claimed to be treated on the same footing as other sovereign and civilised States.

Once this test was accepted—as it increasingly was since the end of the nineteenth century—the law of nations entered a new phase. The standards of value, on which international law had been originally based, were affected by this development in two ways. The non-European States, which had maintained some measure of independence during the imperialist expansion of the occidental world, submitted to the new state of affairs as an unavoidable necessity. They accepted their obligations under international law in a spirit of prudent outward conformity rather than moral conviction of the inherent righteousness of these rules.

This process had its repercussions on the attitude which the Western Powers themselves took towards international law. They themselves became increasingly indifferent to the religious and moral values on which the European law of nations had originally been based. In their own eyes, the Christian law of nations had changed into the law that was applicable between all sovereign and civilised States.

How was it to be determined whether a State belonged to the " civilised and commercial nations of the world," as, in *The Prometheus*,[21] they were described by the Supreme Court of Hong Kong?

The governing tests were elaborated in diplomatic notes of the Western Powers to States in South and Central America and on the colonial fringes of international society, in treaties of commerce with countries thought to be ignorant, or faltering in their observance, of the minimum standards of international law, and in decisions of international tribunals, especially various United States–Mexican Mixed Claims Commissions.

It was expected from a civilised State that it should protect the life, liberty and property of foreigners on a footing commensurable with the standards applied by western Powers in their own countries. Due process of law as understood in the United States, the rule of law as interpreted in England, the *bürgerliche Rechtsstaat*, as

---

21 (1906) 2 *Hong Kong Law Reports* 207.

developed in the political and legal thinking of Continental liberalism, were the criteria which were taken for granted.

So long as States furnished evidence of a certain minimum of efficiency in running the machinery of their governments and administration and of a reasonable measure of consideration for the rights of foreigners, they qualified as civilised nations.

The primary interest of the western Powers consisted in the protection of their own nationals, and they willingly granted the complementary implication that the nationals of the non-European States were the exclusive concern of these States. Exceptional cases of humanitarian intervention and isolated treaties in favour of minorities merely confirmed the general rule.[22] Thus, international law exchanged its Christian basis for that of a liberal civilisation of the nineteenth-century type.[23]

International Law as the Law of Sovereign States

From international law as the law of primarily sovereign and civilised States, it was merely one further step to make sovereignty itself the exclusive measuring rod of international personality. Thus, when Italy adopted a Fascist system, the practices of Mussolini's followers were regarded as matters solely within Italy's domestic jurisdiction. The problem of whether such a basic change was compatible with the standard of civilisation was not considered. Similarly, recognition of the Soviet Union was made dependent on changes in Soviet policy regarding her repudiation of pre-war foreign loans and concessions and on promises regarding Communist propaganda abroad, but not on discontinuation of the liquidation of whole classes of her own population or the extensive use of forced labour in the Soviet Union. Is it necessary to elaborate this point by reference to the Third *Reich* or Japan before and during 'the Second World War?

The sum total of this development was that, between 1919 and 1939, the subjects of international law even jettisoned the standard of civilisation as a test of international personality.[24] Whether a State was civilised or barbarian ceased to be relevant. What mattered was that a State was independent. International law had become the law of sovereign States.

---

[22] See further below, p. 130 *et seq*.
[23] See further below, p. 67 *et seq*
[24] See further below, p. 75 *et seq*.

IV—International Law and the Centralisation of Power

In the limited sense in which the principle of the equality of
States applies in international law, it is the complementary aspect
of State sovereignty.[25] Prima facie, it is, therefore, unlikely that
the trend towards centralisation of power in international society
should have been able to leave its imprint on international law.
The violent and, in retrospect, slightly comical disputes over rank
and precedence between sixteenth- and seventeenth-century monarchs and ambassadors form part of the history of diplomacy rather
than of international law. The practice that ambassadors should
be exchanged exclusively between greater Powers, and that smaller
States had to be content with ministers, was observed during the
nineteenth century and in the pre-1914 period, but, since then, has
given way to an inflationary movement in which ministers tend to be
levelled up to an egalitarian ambassadorial status.

Perhaps more significant is the hesitation of States to recognise
the assumption of the more exalted titles of emperor and king by
heads other than those of greater Powers. Still more relevant is the
weighting of votes according to the financial interest taken by members of international institutions as, for instance, in the International
Bank for Reconstruction and Development and the International
Monetary Fund. Similarly, the representation of the governments of
the eight States of chief industrial importance on the Governing Body
of the International Labour Organisation may be explained on functional grounds. At the same time, such a place offers evidence of
economic strength and, indirectly, political power.[26]

The most direct acknowledgment of the effect of superior power
on legal status—again on a basis of formal consent on the part of
middle Powers and small States—is to be found in the Covenant of
the League of Nations and in the Charter of the United Nations.

The Principal Allied and Associated Powers—France, Great
Britain, Italy, Japan and the United States of America—had reserved
to themselves permanent seats on the Council of the League of
Nations. In the United Nations their place was taken by China,
France, the Soviet Union, the United Kingdom and the United States
of America.

In both cases, the permanent character of representation meant

---

[25] See further, *Fundamental Principles*, p. 214 *et seq.*, and *Vol. I*, p. 114
et seq.
[26] See further, *Manual*, Vol. I, p. 322 *et seq.*

that none of these Powers had to concern itself with winning the sympathies of the electorate in the League Assembly or the General Assembly of the United Nations. In the former case, no special privileges accrued to the permanent members of the League Council. Owing to the wide acceptance of majority vote in the organs of the United Nations, this was to be very different in the United Nations.

In other than procedural matters, the concurrence of each of the Big Five is required to carry majority decisions of the Security Council. Each one of the five permanent members can stultify by its veto any enforcement action even in disputes to which it is a party. It is in the power of each of them to exercise a negative control over the admission of new members. The permanent members are automatically represented on the Trusteeship Council, and by refusing to ratify an amendment to the Charter, any of them may prevent such an amendment from coming into force. Finally, under Article 106 of the Charter, the five permanent members of the Security Council occupy a special position for an indefinite period in matters concerned with the maintenance of international peace and security.[27]

Thus, the evolution of international law faithfully reflects the major forces which have come to shape contemporary world society : the disintegration of the Christian commonwealth of Europe and its transformation into a European society, the worldwide expansion of European society, and the centralisation of power in the hands of a rapidly decreasing number of world Powers.

V—THE PREMISES OF INTERNATIONAL LAW
IN HISTORICAL PERSPECTIVE

Are the historical premises of international law [28] so dated that they may safely be ignored or replaced by more advanced " logical " premises of " modern " international law? [29]

War as the state of Normalcy

As concerns the first premise of medieval international law, peace has remained an agreed state of international law. Yet three changes have taken place. First, treaties of peace are no longer primarily of a bilateral character. Secondly, in modern international law, the

[27] See further, *Manual*, Vol. I, p. 278 *et seq.*
[28] See above, p. 49.
[29] See further 6 *Y.B.W.A.* (1952), p. 259 *et seq.*

presumption is in favour of a state of peace between nations which
are not actually at war with one another. Thirdly, the trend towards
the concentration of power has made possible in each of the two
halves of the world further integration under the aegis of a *Pax
Sovietica* or *Pax Americana.*

Instead of resting mainly on bilateral treaties, peace since the
seventeenth century has been founded increasingly on the great peace
settlements made after every major war. The international law of
peace in every inter-war period came to rest on one of these multilateral treaties until war once more cast every one of them into the
melting pot.

This aspect of the matter has been obscured by the fact that the
Wars of the Spanish Succession, the Napoleonic Wars and the First
and Second World Wars were won by coalitions primarily aiming
at the restoration of the *status quo ante bellum.* Thus, these fortui-
tous results of the resort to armed force strengthened the illusion of
a continuity in the international law of peace which, actually, was
fictitious.

The Covenant of the League of Nations, the Kellogg Pact and
the Charter of the United Nations themselves are reminders of the
fact that, even in our time, peace still rests on a treaty basis. The
" cold war " between East and West further underlines the relativity
of peace and war in any system of power politics or power politics in
disguise.[30] In the microcosm of the Near East, the rise of Israel out
of a short but sharp war and the still precarious state of armistice
between Israel and each of her neighbours are a belated repetition of
a process which, in the past, was common experience.

Is this to deny the growth of trends in international society which
point to the development of an international community? Are there
not many nations among which, with or without treaty obligation to
this effect, war has become unthinkable? Do we not witness day
by day in the non-Communist world acts which betoken the rise of
a new spirit of international co-operation? Are there not the International Monetary Fund, the International Bank, the International
Development Association, the Organisation for Economic Co-operation and Development, the European Economic Community, the
European Free Trade Association and other encouraging signs of

[30] See below, pp. 146 and 279 *et seq.*

international integration? While all this may be admitted, what does it mean?

The States among which war has become a matter of past history are within the orbit of either the Kremlin or the Capitol. There has been growing international integration, but primarily within each of the two segments of world society, the one controlled by Moscow and the other by Washington. While the contingency of war between the Soviet Union and Poland, or between the United States and France, may be dismissed as remote, who would make bold to suggest that a war between the Eastern and Western camps is unthinkable?

In our time, power politics in the grand style is played foremost, if not exclusively, between the world's two super-Powers. The relations between the two world camps provide a commensurate test whether the first of the three historical premises of international law still corresponds to reality.

The Rightlessness of Foreigners

To turn to the second premise, an historical and sociological analysis of the development of international law elucidates the real influences which brought about improvements in the lot of the individual whose misfortune it was to be abroad. Even in the early days of international law, self-interest, reasonably interpreted, and religious scruples frequently mitigated the extreme application of the principle of the rightlessness of foreigners. The reason why in this field international law developed, was, however, hardly the potency of the ideal of *Civitas Maxima*. This was little more than a naturalist rationalisation and idealisation of a more earthbound, though highly fertile, working principle behind international law: that of reciprocity.[31]

Whatever the prevalent economic theories of the day—medieval bullionism, mercantilism or liberalism—most princes, as well as their successors in the role of representatives of *raison d'État*, considered it to their advantage to encourage at least a modicum of international trade. If for no other reason, they recognised the need for such a policy because international trade added to their revenues, and this meant political independence from meddlesome estates of the realm.

So that foreign merchants might be induced to come with their wares, they had to be granted a minimum of security of person and

[31] See above, p. 29 *et seq.*

property. Starting with individual safe-conducts, these rights were gradually incorporated into formal treaties and, on a footing of reciprocity, extended to all subjects of contracting parties.[32]

During the nineteenth century and in the pre-1914 period, Great Britain, as the leading political and economic nation, insisted on these rights of foreigners being treated as based on a minimum standard of international customary law and, thus, as being binding irrespective of their incorporation into treaties.[33]

This policy corresponded to the general interests of investors and was increasingly followed by other creditor nations, especially the United States. Debtor States, more or less gracefully, accepted these standards. Attempts to whittle down their obligations under international law by devices such as the Calvo Clause or Drago Doctrine remained ineffective counter-moves, but served notice of the existence of a latent protest movement against rules of international law primarily shaped by capital-exporting countries. So long as debtor countries required capital on practically any terms, a broad reciprocity of interests existed. When this need diminished, the minimum standard of international law, especially regarding the protection of private property abroad, no longer went unchallenged.[34]

Matters came to a head when, with the growing success of the Soviet experiment, a socialist and totalitarian State challenged by its very existence the assumptions of a capitalist and liberal world. With the establishment of the Soviet monopoly of foreign trade, the reciprocity of economic interests, on which the protection of foreigners by the minimum standard of international law had essentially rested, appeared to have vanished.

While the Soviet Union was weak, she was forced to accept, within limits, the traditional standards. However, most States trading with her in the post-1919 period did not think it advisable to take Soviet compliance with these standards for granted. As of old, they insisted on the incorporation of these rules of international law in their treaties of commerce and residence with the Soviet Union. In the post-1945 era, foreigners in parts of the world controlled by Russia and China are hardly better protected than the populations of these countries or their own forefathers had been protected abroad in the early stages of international law.[35]

---

[32] See below, p. 123 *et seq.*
[33] See below, p. 139 *et seq.*
[34] See further 5 *C.L.P.* (1952), p. 295 *et seq.*, and 13 *ibid.* (1961), p. 213 *et seq.*
[35] See below, p. 174 *et seq.*

The High Seas as No Man's " Land "

Finally, is the third initial premise, that is to say, anarchy on the high seas, still of present-day significance? On the basis of numerous treaties, piracy was outlawed, and the jurisdiction of States on the high seas to proceed at their will against pirates *jure gentium* gradually grew into a rule of international customary law.

In the sense of exclusive jurisdiction of the flag State over its ships on the high seas, the principle of the freedom of the seas came to be acknowledged in time of peace. Today, this freedom is again indirectly challenged by extravagant claims of States to exclusive jurisdiction over the continental shelf and regarding the width of the territorial sea.[36]

Similarly, by way of treaty, rules of neutrality were developed and consolidated into a body of rules which, since the middle of the nineteenth century, rested primarily on the Declaration of Paris of 1856. In the duel type of war, the greater Powers insisted on these rules being observed. In major wars, these principles were largely ignored. Policies of reprisals and counter-reprisals, based on alleged breaches of established rules of maritime warfare, the advent of the submarine, the use of aircraft against merchant ships and the disappearance of the " innocent " merchant in the wartime economies of belligerents again reduced the freedom of the seas in time of war to the pristine rule of hardly restricted force.[37]

In our present world, the " terrestrial " emphasis in international law is even more serious than with regard to the high seas in respect to the third dimension : the air space and outer space.[38] In time of peace, the rule of unlimited sovereignty of States over the air space above their territories serves as a rule of thumb. In time of war, saturation bombing and, in United Nations parlance, " unconventional " means of warfare, such as nuclear weapons,[39] give a new and sinister meaning to the third initial premise of contemporary international law.

Thus, on a world scale, the initial premises of international law, which inductive research into the history of the law of nations reveals, are still as valid as ever. Where, in the relations between East and

---

[36] See further *Fundamental Principles*, p. 358 *et seq.*
[37] See further the writer's *International Law and Totalitarian Lawlessness* (1943), p. 30 *et seq.*
[38] On the rudimentary character of such rules of *lex lata* as apply to outer space, *cf. Manual*, Vol. 1, p. 110 *et seq.*, and Vol. 2, p. 512 *et seq.*
[39] See further the writer's *The Legality of Nuclear Weapons* (1958).

West, strong mutual and complementary interests make advisable
limitations of the exercise of untrammelled sovereignty, there may be
room for the further development of universal international law.[40]

VI—Historical Working Hypotheses

Five historical working hypotheses which are partly confirmatory of,
and partly supplementary to, the sociological working hypotheses
outlined in the previous Chapter [41] may be regarded as fairly well
established :

(1) The efforts made over more than eight centuries to reverse the
    historical premises of international law have been attained
    primarily by means of treaty.

(2) The parties to such treaties have come to take for granted certain
    moral assumptions without which the legal validity of any of
    these treaties would have been inconceivable.

(3) International customary law, as distinct from rules relating to any
    assumed or inherent legal order or quasi-order, amounts to little
    more than a residue of treaty clauses of past ages which are
    generally taken for granted as embodying self-understood legal
    obligations or, in some spheres, give expression to roughly
    parallel national practices.

(4) The growth of international law mirrors so accurately every
    essential change in its social environment that, prima facie, the
    rules of international law appear to reflect, rather than condition,
    the structure of international society at any particular time.

(5) On the level of universal international law, the historical premises
    of international law are as valid as ever. Arguments to the con-
    trary, which are drawn from higher degrees of integration attained
    in each of the two camps of a divided world may be valid within
    these limits. They hardly affect, however, the place of law in the
    vital overall relations between the two major power blocs.

---

40 See below, pp. 274 and 288 *et seq.*
41 See above, p. 41 *et seq.*

CHAPTER 4

INTERNATIONAL LAW IN ETHICAL PERSPECTIVE

ANTICIPATION of a sociological interpretation of law in general, and international law in particular, is not the only debt we owe to naturalist writers.[1] They have done equally valuable spade work in performing another of the main tasks of legal science : censorial criticism of *lex lata* by the application of external standards of a normative character. It matters little whether we accept any of their varying—and often contradictory—measuring rods ; for we share with them the shortcoming of human fallibility, and even the best among us will never catch more than a glimpse of *the* truth.

From this point of view, it is equally irrelevant that, at one time or another, every one of these doctrines has enabled vested interests and revolutionary claims to be based on such a " higher law," and that natural law has served equally well the ends of papists, imperialists and conciliarists in the Middle Ages ; of slaveholders and abolitionists in the American Civil War, or of democracy, authoritarianism and totalitarianism in our own time.[2] In this context, we may ignore that natural law has been praised as the " vindication of the rights of man "[3] and condemned as an ever-reviving fallacy which merely satisfies man's constant " need for justification."[4]

Be all this as it may, natural law has exercised some influence on the formation of international law, although less on its Practice than its Doctrine.[5] Moreover—and, in an analysis of international law in

---

[1] See above, p. 9 *et seq.*
[2] See, for instance, Ch. G. Haines, *The Revival of Natural Law Concepts* (1930), p. 65 *et seq.*; R. McKeon, *The Philosophical Bases and Material Circumstances of the Rights of Man*, 58 *Ethics* (1948), p. 180 *et seq.*; C. L. Becker, *The Declaration of Independence* (1948), p. 242 *et seq.*; E. Wolf, *Das Problem der Naturrechtslehre* (1955); A. Ross, *On Law and Justice* (1958); C. W. Jenks, *The Laws of Nature and International Law* in *Liber Amicorum François* (1959), p. 160 *et seq.*; D. Lloyd, *Introduction to Jurisprudence* (1959), p. 53 *et seq.*; A. Verdross, *Primäres Naturrecht*, etc., in *Gutzwiller Festgabe* (1959), p. 447 *et seq.*; W. Friedmann, *Legal Theory* (1960), p. 43 *et seq.*; and the writer's *International Law and Totalitarian Lawlessness* (1943), p. 18 *et seq.*
[3] H. Lauterpacht, *International Law and Human Rights* (1950), p. 111.
[4] H. Kelsen, *What is Justice?* (1957), p. 159, and further *Reine Rechtslehre* (1960), p. 60 *et seq.*
[5] That is to say, as norms guiding a State's *own* behaviour as distinct from ideological uses to which natural law has been frequently put in advancement of political claims or denunciation of legal claims of opponents. See further A. P. Sereni, *The Italian Conception of International Law* (1943), pp. 57 and 122; E. Reibstein, *Die Anfänge des neueren Natur- und Völkerrechts* (1949), and below, p. 85 *et seq.*

65

ethical perspective, this is the essential point—natural law has provided normative tests by reference to which international law can be critically evaluated.

Yet, in a doubting, if not faithless, age natural law is hardly any longer a universal or generally acceptable ethical foundation of law. We also are too conscious of the fact that " *le droit naturel suppose une tête non pas critique . . . mais spéculative.*" [6] Thus, lawyers who, in our time, draw on natural law as an article of faith, cannot expect more than the tolerance due to any metaphysical belief. Thus, we are still in search of an ethical standard of less subjectivity and with a better chance of commanding general acceptance. [7]

This is readily available in the standard of civilisation. To apply this test to international law appears far from arbitrary. Historically, at least as close a connection exists between Western civilisation and international law as between natural and international law. [8] Moreover, the general principles of law recognised by civilised nations are one of the three law-creating processes which, in applying international law, the World Court is enjoined to take into account. [9] Thus, even at this preliminary stage, it is apparent that, to this extent at least, the standard of civilisation has been incorporated into international law. [10] Finally, it may be surmised that only few nations, or their leaders, would deign to refuse being considered as civilised, however much they may find others wanting by this standard.

Civilisation is a many-sided phenomenon. To understand its real nature and to avoid dangerous pitfalls, it will be necessary to attempt to comprehend its essence and to pay attention to the historical nexus between Civilisation and international law.

[6] J. Haesaert, *Théorie Générale du Droit* (1948), p. 283.
[7] For a different attempt at finding a commensurate standard of extraneous criticism of existing international law, *cf.* M. S. McDougal, *International Law, Power and Policy, Hague Recueil*, Vol. 82 (1953), p. 188 *et seq.*
The " goal value " of human dignity in a " policy-oriented " international law bears a certain affinity to the standard of civilisation. This approach appears, however, to suffer from over-emphasis on one aspect of a " civilised " international law, that is to say, the advancement of the protection of the individual, as compared with the other purposes which an inter-group law such as international law must necessarily serve. Moreover, it appears essential to emphasise that whatever standard is chosen, it is acceptable only as an extraneous standard of criticism for purposes *de lege ferenda*. It must not, however, be allowed to blur the border-line between *lex lata* and *lex ferenda*.
[8] See above, p. 43 *et seq*
[9] See below, p. 77 *et seq.*, and further *Vol. 1*, p. 25 *et seq.*
[10] See further below, p. 73 *et seq.*

I—THE MEANING OF CIVILISATION

A group is frequently called civilised if it has acquired a mature apparatus of thought and action and is characterised by the extensive use of rational behaviour patterns.[11] Terms such as "civilised country," "civilised system of law," "civilised community" or other synonyms in dicta of English and United States courts,[12] or "advanced nations" in Article 22 of the Covenant of the League of Nations bear this meaning.

Civilisation in this sense implies a contrast with groups of a rationally less predictable character. Emphasis on reason and organisation is certainly one of the distinctive features of civilised life. Any definition of civilisation which relies on this as the only or decisive criterion remains, however, on the surface of the phenomenon of Civilisation. It does not appear to convey its full meaning.

It will assist in our further analysis if, from the outset, a distinction is made between the two main aspects of Civilisation. It affects the relation of man to nature and of man to man.[13] In the main, we shall be concerned only with this second facet of Civilisation. It may safely be left to Equity lawyers authoritatively to settle whether a school which does not provide hot-water baths for its pupils should be considered a barbarous place.[14]

Further insight into the nature of Civilisation is gained by awareness of the plurality and multiplicity of this phenomenon. In our time when we have the works of pioneers such as Spengler,[15]

---

11 *Cf.*, for instance, John Stuart Mill, *Civilisation* in *Dissertations and Discussions* (1875), Vol. 1, p. 160 *et seq.*; L. Oppenheim (ed.), *The Collected Papers of John Westlake on Public International Law* (1914), p. 139; W. A. Robson, *Civilisation and the Growth of Law* (1935), p. 15; and Qu. Wright, *A Study of War* (1942), Vol. 1, p. 152.

12 See, for instance, *Re Don's Estate* (1857) 4 Drew. 194 at 197 (*per* Sir Richard Kindersley V.-C.); *Simonin* v. *Mallac* (1860) 2 Sw. & Tr. 67; *Cammell* v. *Sewell* (1860) 5 H. & N. 728; *Brook* v. *Brook* (1861) 9 H.L.C. 193 at 212 (*per* Lord Campbell); *Lloyd* v. *Guibert* (1865) L.R. 1 Q.B. 115; *Udny* v. *Udny* (1869) L.R. 1 Sc. & Div. 441 (*per* Lord Westbury); *R.* v. *Keyn* (1876) L.R. 2 Ex.D. 63; *Re Queensland Mercantile and Agency Ltd.* [1892] 1 Ch. 219 at 226 (*per* Lindley L.J.); *West Rand Central Gold Mining Co., Ltd.* v. *R.* [1905] 2 K.B. 391 at 407 (*per* Lord Alverstone C.J.); *Fibrosa Case* [1943] A.C. 32 at 61 (*per* Lord Wright); *Bendall* v. *McWhirter* [1952] 1 All E.R. 1307 at 1315 (*per* Denning L.J.); *R.* v. *Secker & Warburg* [1954] 2 All E.R. 683 at 685 (*per* Stable J.); *Bamgbose* v. *Daniel* [1954] 3 All E.R. 263 at 267 (*per* Lord Keith); *The Paquete Habana* (1900) 175 U.S. 677; *Louis Dreyfus* v. *Paterson Steamships Ltd.* (1930) 43 F. (2d) 824 (*per* Judge Learned Hand).

13 See further R. G. Collingwood, *The New Leviathan* (1942), p. 291.

14 *Re Geere's Will Trusts, The Times* newspaper, May 18, 1954.

15 *Der Untergang des Abendlandes* (1918–22). For pertinent criticism of Spengler's naturalist conception of civilisation, *cf.* R. Niebuhr, *The Nature and Destiny of Man* (1943), Vol. 2, p. 313.

Toynbee,[16] and Alfred Weber [17] at our elbow, this aspect of the matter hardly requires further explanation. It is, however, of real relevance for our purposes. Already in his Essay on *Caniballes* (1580),[18] Montaigne had warned his readers against calling barbarous or savage that " which is not common to them." Awareness of the multitude of civilisations, their co-existence and impact on each other will assist in avoiding the fallacy of egocentricity and identification of any particular civilisation with Civilisation as such.

A further element which is characteristic of Civilisation is its constitutional fragility and relativity. It never is more than an approximation to an ideal. In Jaquetta Hawkes' telling words,[19] it is " like a skin of ice above bottomless waters." It is an ever continuing, but always precarious effort.

It is true that this deficiency is not one peculiar to civilisation, but is inherent in any human effort.[20] Nevertheless, it appears advisable to stress this point. Too often, the relativity of every civilisation and the elements of barbarism in it [21] are ignored and states of civilisation and non-civilisation contrasted as if they were absolutes. In Toynbee's apt terminology,[22] civilisation is a movement and not a condition. It is a voyage and not a harbour.

Even if we are aware of the preponderance of the rational and organisational elements in Civilisation, of the multiplicity of civilisations and of the relativity of their achievements, we are still on the fringes of the problem. We shall not grasp the elusive essence of Civilisation until we ignore the unimportant trappings of material advance which are incidentals of any civilising process and realise that the ultimate basis of any civilisation is religious and ethical.[23] It is this flame of the spirit which gives its impetus and driving power to Civilisation as an historical process.

As with the functions fulfilled by Law and Morality,[24] it is possible to be still more specific regarding this spiritual kernel of

---

16 *A Study of History* (1933–1961); *Civilisation on Trial* (1948).
17 *Kulturgeschichte als Kultursoziologie* (1935). *Cf.* also N. Elias, *Über den Prozess der Zivilisation* (1939—2 vols.).
18 Transl. by J. Florio (ed. H. Morley—1886), p. 94.
19 *Man on Earth* (1954), p. 149.
20 *Cf.*, for instance, N. Berdyaev, *Slavery and Freedom* (1948), p. 117 *et seq.*
21 *Cf.* for instance, the facts, in *Gregson* v. *Gilbert* (1783) 3 Dougl. 232, or the observations of Story J. in *U.S.* v. *The Schooner La Jeune Eugenie* (1822) 2 Mason's Reports 409, at p. 446, on the change in the attitude of " enlightened and civilised nations " to slavery.
22 *Cf.* for instance, *loc. cit.* in note 16 above, 1948, p. 55.
23 See further A. Schweitzer, *The Philosophy of Civilisation* (1929–1932), and *ibid.*, Part 1 (1932), pp. 38–39, on the misleading antithesis of civilisation and *Kultur*.
24 See above, p. 9 *et seq.*

civilisation if we make use of the basic sociological distinction between the pure, or ideal, types of community and society.[25]

In relation to nature, civilisation means intelligent exploitation. In the relations between men, the position is reversed. Human association is the more civilised the less it has to rely on the exploitation of man by man or of one group by another, and the more it is based on consent and voluntary co-operation.

By way of contrast, exploitation is ultimately based on force. No human group has yet succeeded in dispensing altogether with coercion. It appears, however, a safe test of Civilisation to measure its achievement by the degree to which it is able to dispense with this crudest of all driving forces and replace it by reliance on the principles of reciprocity and voluntary co-ordination of effort. In other words, the less a group has a society character and the more it approximates the pure state of a community,[26] the more any individual civilisation approximates Civilisation.

Once Civilisation is related to the basic types of human association, it is no longer necessary to be content with the mere enumeration and description of a bewildering number of civilisations. It becomes possible to evaluate and measure individual civilisations in the light of a universally applicable test of the degree of civilisation which any such particular endeavour has attained.[27]

The criterion of Civilisation provides the key to understanding whether, and to what extent, democratic States may claim to be more civilised than authoritarian or totalitarian systems. It explains why it is useful to distinguish between groups which are called savage, because they have not yet reached any appreciable stage of civilisation, and groups which may be termed barbarian because they have forsaken civilisation.[28]

More important still, groups whose members, in their internal relations, may claim to be civilised frequently base their relations with other groups on different standards. It may also happen that, whether

[25] See above, pp. 10–11.
[26] See above, p. 11 *et seq.*
[27] It is implied in these statements that human relations based on agreement are superior to those based on force or coercion of a less visible character. The ultimate justification why the degree of civilisation attained at any time or place should be linked with the acknowledgment of the absolute value of human beings and the refusal to treat them merely as means to worldly ends can only be metaphysical. Thus, anyone dissenting from this assumption which, in the last resort, is unverifiable, is fully entitled to reject this test.

    On the conditions on which value-judgments may legitimately be used in research work, see further *Power Politics*, p. 22.
[28] See further Collingwood, *loc. cit.* in note 13 above, p. 342 *et seq.*

they like it or not, they are engulfed in an overriding society nexus which imposes severe limitations on the best of intentions. Then, even the paradox of civilised States advancing to barbarism on the high road to nuclear co-extermination becomes explicable, although not necessarily more attractive.

II—THE COALESCENCE OF INTERNATIONAL LAW AND CIVILISATION

The existence of law [29] in savage and barbarous groups, in the Trobriand Islands [30] no less than in the Third *Reich*,[31] proves that Law and Civilisation are not inseparable companions. Law can exist without Civilisation. It is, however, hard to imagine Civilisation without Law, especially civilisations which aim at the attainment of community standards in the relations between their members.[32]

This proposition applies as much to international law as to municipal law. International law is possible whenever, first, two parties recognise each other as equal in status and neither of them recognises a third party as its superior, secondly, they desire to treat each other on the footing of law and, thirdly, they consider themselves bound by their mutual obligations. Historical evidence bears out that international law on the basis of such an ethical minimum is more than a mere hypothesis. Relations on the footing of international law have actually existed over prolonged periods between savage and barbarous groups.[33]

Nonetheless, it is true that, under the influence of Christianity, chivalry and trade, the harshness of early medieval international law was considerably mitigated.[34] It underwent a civilising process of some magnitude. In its turn, it came to fulfil the function of an additional guardian of the Christian civilisation of Europe. However precarious the observance of medieval international law was, it incorporated an appreciable minimum of the values cherished by the members of this *una Christiana res publica*.

---

[29] See further above, p. 9 *et seq.*
[30] The object of one of Malinowski's suggestive field studies. See *Crime and Custom in Savage Society* (1932). *Cf.* also A. S. Diamond, *Primitive Law* (1950), and W. Seagle, *The Quest for Law* (1941), p. 27 *et seq.*
[31] If evidence were required for the retrogression from civilisation to barbarism in the Third *Reich*, it would suffice to refer to G. Reitlinger, *The Final Solution* (1953).
[32] See further *loc. cit.* in note 13 above, p. 327 *et seq. Cf.* also J. Stone, *The Province and Function of Law* (1947), p. 331 *et seq.*
[33] See the literature mentioned above, p. 44, note 5, *Manual*, Vol. 2, p. 395, and R. Numelin, *The Beginnings of Diplomacy* (1950), pp. 238 and 242.
[34] See above, pp. 29 and 47 *et seq.*, below, p. 85 *et seq.*, and further R. Ward, *The Foundation and History of the Law of Nations in Europe* (1795), Vol. 2.

Under the triple impact of the disintegration of the European community of nations, the expansion of the European society into a world
society and the ever continuing process of the concentration of political and economic power, the coalescence of international law and
European civilisation began to show visible signs of strain.[35] The
price which the European law of nations had to pay for universality
was to be, first, increasingly separated from its Christian foundation
and, subsequently, drained of most of its ethical contents. It underwent a process of formalisation to become a law congenial to the needs
of the industrial pioneer and capitalist investor.

The test whether a State was civilised and, thus, entitled to full
recognition as an international personality was, as a rule, merely
whether its government was sufficiently stable to undertake binding
commitments under international law, and whether it was able and
willing to protect adequately the life, liberty and property of
foreigners. In a multitude of treaties these minimum standards were
codified in meticulous detail and gradually grew into rules of
international customary law.[36]

At the same time, the distinction between civilised and non-
civilised communities served less disinterested purposes of Western
colonialism and imperialism whenever it was opportune to treat communities on the fringes of the expanding Western world on a footing
other than that of sovereign States.[37]

On a number of occasions, Christian conscience, allied with
powerful radical and rationalist humanitarian movements, asserted
itself. Notable examples are the British lead in the abolition of the
slave trade,[38] and the more complex instances of intervention, sometimes humanitarian and sometimes so misnamed.[39]

---

[35] See further above, p. 44 *et seq.*, and 33 *A.J.I.L.* (1939), p. 56 *et seq.*
[36] See also above, p. 49, and below, p. 219 *et seq.*
[37] See above, p. 25 *et seq.*
   Cf. also John Stuart Mill, " A Few Words on Non-Intervention " in *Dissertations and Discussions*, Vol. 3 (1875), p. 152 *et seq.* One sample must suffice:
" To characterise any conduct whatever towards a barbarous people as a violation of the law of nations, only shows that he who so speaks has never considered
the subject " (p. 168).
   More tolerant voices were not, however, lacking. *Cf. The Hurtige Hane*
(1801) 3 C.Rob. 324; *The Madonna del Burso* (1802) 4 C.Rob. 169; Sir Robert
Phillimore, *Commentaries upon International Law* (1879), Vol. 1, p. 22 *et seq.*,
and H. A. Smith, *Great Britain and the Law of Nations* (1932), Vol. 1, p. 14
et seq.
[38] See above, p. 34 *et seq.*, and below, p. 135 *et seq.*
[39] See pp. 130 and 234 *et seq.*
   On the reserved attitude of Lord Salisbury towards humanitarian intervention,
cf. the note by Sir P. Currie of May 19, 1891, and the draft circular letter on
British Protected Persons of July, 1891 (F.O. 83/1723).

Comparable trends in the humanisation of the laws of war have often been traced. What is less known is how little, within medieval Christendom, obligations of Christian ethics and chivalry counted in actual warfare against heretics [40] or in the practice of hostile contacts between the Christian crusaders and the Saracens.[41] Still less restraint was shown in the course of the overseas expansion of the European Powers down to the nineteenth century.[42]

Nevertheless, the revulsion against the unlimited character of seventeenth-century warfare, the rational strategy of eighteenth-century military thinking and the formation of professional armies assisted in encouraging the idea that war could be reduced to a game that was played in accordance with fixed rules or, at least, to a technique of civilised if violent settlement of international conflicts.

This movement suffered a serious setback in the course of the Napoleonic Wars when the warfare of the French mass *levées* provided the first forebodings of the effects of emotion-laden nationalism on the precarious restraints which, in the preceding century, had been imposed on the god of war.

In the post-1815 era it appeared as if Progress were again on the march. A relatively stable system of balance of power, the unchallenged rule of the British Navy on the world's seven seas and the paternal eye kept by an all-powerful City of London on countries in need of British capital permitted war to be regarded as a remote contingency. This atmosphere encouraged further humanising efforts by way of multilateral conventions, culminating in the work of the Hague Peace Conferences of 1899 and 1907.

The results attained, and their limitations, may be summed up in

---

[40] See, for instance, on the sack of Béziers in 1209 in the war against the Albingenses, a letter of the Papal Legate to Pope Innocent III (*Innocent III. epist.* (1682), Vol. 2, p. 373 *et seq.*): " *Capta est civitas Bitterensis, nostrique non parcentes ordini, sexui vel aetati, fere viginti milia hominum in ore gladii peremerunt . . . spoliata est tota civitas succensa.*" Still more illuminating is another, if slightly imaginative, account of the same event in Heisterbacensis's *Dialogus Miraculorum (Distinctio V, cap.* 21): " *Cognoscentes ex confessionibus illorum Catholicos cum haereticis esse permixtos, dixertunt abbati: Quid faciemus, domine? Non possumus discernere inter bonos et malos. Timeno tam abbas quam reliqui, ne tantum timore mortis se catholicos simularent, et post ipsorum abcessum iterum ad perfidiam redirent, fertur dixisse: Caedite eos; novit enim dominus qui sunt eius.*"

[41] See above, p. 51, and further Ward, *loc. cit.* in note 34 above, Vol. 2, pp. 81 *et seq.* and 362 *et seq.*, and S. Runciman, *A History of the Crusades* (1951–1954 —3 vols.).

[42] See, for instance, L. Curtis, *The Commonwealth of Nations* (1916), Vol. 1, p. 131 *et seq.*, or F. J. P. Veale, *Advance to Barbarism* (1953), p. 85 *et seq.*

the words of the British *Manual of Military Law* [43] : " The development of the laws and usages of war is determined by three principles. There is firstly, the principle that a belligerent is justified in applying any amount and any kind of force which is necessary for the purpose of war : that is, the complete submission of the enemy at the earliest possible moment with the least possible expenditure of men and money. There is, secondly, the principle of humanity which says that all such kinds and degrees of violence as are not necessary for the purpose of war are not permitted to a belligerent. And there is, thirdly, the principle of chivalry, which demands a certain amount of fairness in offence and defence, and a certain mutual respect between the opposing forces."

Thus, the pre-1914 generation of international lawyers was fully justified in regarding international law as a powerful civilising agency. In a spirit of self-assured optimism, they could point to undeniable evidence of a far-reaching incorporation of the minimum standards of Western civilisation in the international law of peace and war.

III—THE STANDARD OF CIVILISATION
IN CURRENT INTERNATIONAL LAW

In order to present a balanced picture, it is advisable to put proper emphasis on the advances made since the First World War in a number of relevant fields.

By and large, the minorities treaties of the post-1919 period constituted a valuable complement [44] to the traditional minimum standards of international law in favour of foreign nationals. With few exceptions,[45] however, States in the post-1945 period refused to undertake any comparable legal commitments.

Instead, the members of the United Nations freely professed their adherence to the Universal Declaration of Human Rights. It was then also avowed that, in this way, the individual as such was duly protected, and the need for the protection of minorities had passed. Yet, at the very moment when the General Assembly unanimously accepted the Declaration, speaker after speaker carefully added his *caveat* on the merely moral character of the new *Magna Carta*.

[43] *Amendments (No. 12), 1929* (1936), pp. 2–3, reproduced with minor verbal changes in Part Three of the 1958 ed. (pp. 1–2).
[44] See further above, p. 31, *Vol. I*, p. 273 *et seq.*, *Power Politics*, p. 617 *et seq.*, and J. Robinson and Others, *Were the Minorities Treaties a Failure?* (1943).
[45] See, for instance, the Delhi Pact between India and Pakistan of April 18, 1950. See further *Power Politics*, p. 637.

Inside the Western camp, the movement towards the effective international protection of human rights was more successful. In particular, this is true of the relations between those members of the Council of Europe between which the European Convention on Human Rights of 1950 is in force.[46]

Similarly, the establishment of mandates and trust territories has imposed some international restraints which may be listed on the credit side of the balance sheet.[47] Moreover, a representative collection of multilateral treaties, ranging from assistance to refugees *via* the suppression of traffic in women and children to the protection of wild birds and plants,[48] deserves to be noted.

The *International Labour Code, 1951*,[49] although still least implemented by those members of the International Labour Organisation most in need of living up to the standards proclaimed in this " Code," should also be remembered. Similarly, other specialised agencies of the United Nations and regional organisations do valuable work in direct furtherance of worthy objects of civilisation.[50]

Yet, the decisive point is not the progress made, and the integration attained, on either side of a divided world. It is the East-West rift, the basic cleavage of our age.[51]

In a bipolarised world, it is a relatively minor matter whether, for instance, countries in Western Europe recognise the standard of civilisation in their relations with one another or succeed in intensifying these relations by in themselves highly beneficial treaties. What is vital is whether in the relations between the United States and the Soviet Union, or between partners, allies or satellites on opposite sides of the world fence, the standard of civilisation maintains its traditional place or is in danger of becoming evanescent.

[46] See further *Power Politics*, p. 633 *et seq.* and p. 793. On the equally symptomatic Genocide Convention of 1948, see the Advisory Opinion of the International Court of Justice on *Reservations to the Convention on the Prevention and Punishment of the Crime of Genocide* (1951), *I. C. J. Reports* 1951, p. 20 *et seq.*, above, p. 36, and below, p. 205 *et seq.*
　　Cf. also the revealing Report of the *ad hoc* I.L.O. Committee on *Forced Labour* (1953) and H. Bülck, *Die Zwangsarbeit im Völkerrecht* (1953).
[47] See further *Power Politics*, p. 648 *et seq.*
[48] *Cf.* M. O. Hudson, *International Legislation* (1919–1945) and *Manual*, Vol. 2, pp. 500 *et seq.* and 533–534.
[49] Published by the International Labour Office (1952).
[50] " *Dans le champ du droit positif, c'est en elles (les institutions internationales) que se dessinent le plus visiblement les tendances de l'évolution* " (M. Bourquin, " *L'Humanisation du droit des gens* " in *La Technique et les Principes du Droit Public* (1950), Vol. 1, p. 21, at p. 54). See also C. W. Jenks, *The Common Law of Mankind* (1958), p. 255 *et seq.*, and *Power Politics*, p. 232 *et seq.*
[51] See further below, p. 146 *et seq.*, and *Power Politics*, p. 398 *et seq.*
　　See also Sir Winston Churchill's speech in the House of Commons, *Hansard*, March 1, 1955, Vol. 537, col. 1897.

It must suffice to explore this problem in relation to three basic issues : Recognition, the General Principles of Law Recognised by Civilised Nations, and the Law of War.

Recognition

In the period between 1815 and 1914, State practice regarded the recognition of new States, and still more so that of new governments, as, in principle, a matter within the exclusive jurisdiction of every foreign State. Prohibition of premature recognition was the only restriction imposed by international law on these discretionary powers. Governments such as those of the United States and Great Britain used their freedom of action to obtain express guarantees that States and governments in quest of recognition would live up to their international obligations and, in particular, to the minimum standard of civilisation regarding the protection of foreign nationals and their property.[52]

In the post-1919 period, discretion was exercised as of old. Yet, compliance with the standard of civilisation was not treated as an essential condition of recognition any longer. Although, for a prolonged period, some States held back on mixed grounds over the grant of recognition to the Soviet government,[53] the United Kingdom granted it recognition as the *de facto* government of Russia as early as 1921 and *de jure* recognition in 1924.

In *Luther* v. *Sagor*, the Court of Appeal even bestowed on Russia the designation of being a " civilised country." [54] Scrutton L.J. absolved his own conscience and squarely placed the responsibility where it belonged : " This immunity follows from recognition as a sovereign State. Should there be any government which appropriates other people's property without compensation, the remedy appears to be to refuse to recognise it as a sovereign State." [55]

When the Fascist régime was installed in Italy, it did not appear to have occurred to other governments that to establish diplomatic

---

[52] See above, p. 55 *et seq.*, and below, p. 219 *et seq.* On British practice during the relevant period, *cf.* Smith, *loc. cit.* in note 37 above, p. 77 *et seq.*; the writer's Letter to the Editor of *The Times* newspaper on " The Recognition of Governments," January 9, 1950, and H. W. Kaufmann, *British Policy and the Independence of Latin America, 1804–1828,* 1951. See also *Fundamental Principles*, p. 228 *et seq.*, and *Vol. I*, p. 127 *et seq.*

[53] See H. A. Smith, *The Crisis in the Law of Nations,* 1947, p. 19; H. Lauterpacht, *Recognition in International Law*, p. 110; T. C. Chen, *The International Law of Recognition*, 1951, pp. 126–127, and T. Charpentier, *La Reconnaissance Internationale* (1956), p. 281 *et seq.*

[54] [1921] 3 K.B. 532, at 546 (*per* Bankes L.J.).

[55] *Ibid.*, at p. 556.

relations with it involved at least the question whether such totalitarianism within the very core of the Western world was compatible
with the minimum standards of civilisation.

By way of mitigating circumstances, the statesmen of that period
could probably plead that, in the beginning, they did not realise the
full implications of Fascism. Yet when, subsequently, Fascism
revealed its true nature beyond any possibility of doubt, nothing was
farther from the minds of the governments of the period between the
First and Second World Wars than to contemplate the withdrawal of
recognition from this régime.

It was, therefore, hardly surprising that the government of the
Third *Reich* was treated on the same footing as that of any other
State. Similar to the development in the League of Nations which,
for purposes of the admission of new members contented itself with
identifying self-government with sovereignty,[56] independence as such
came to be a sufficient title-deed for the recognition of a new State,
and effective control of the State machinery the test for the recognition of a new government. It became fashionable to describe as an
inescapable " fact " that which it was deemed inopportune to
evaluate.[57]

The only safeguard that remained was the discretionary character
of Recognition. The United Kingdom threw even this overboard
when, at the time of the recognition of the Communist government of
China, the doctrine of recognition as a legal duty received official
approbation.[58]

Admittedly, this argument softened the blow dealt by this action
to the United States. It would probably also have been inadvisable
to allow a split on this issue to occur between the " white " and
" non-white " members of the British Commonwealth. Still, was it
wise to elevate apparent considerations of expediency into a hard and
fast legal rule and, at that, one so much out of step with a well-tried
tradition of British recognition policy?

---

[56] See further the writer's *The League of Nations and World Order* (1936), pp. 32
    et seq. and 87 *et seq.*
[57] On the fallacy that recognition of a fact does not involve value-judgments, see
    Power Politics, p. 22.
[58] Observations of H.M. Government in the United Kingdom on the Draft Declara-
    tion with regard to the Rights and Duties of States, August 24, 1948 (United
    Nations, *Preparatory Study concerning a Draft Declaration on the Rights and
    Duties of States* (1948), p. 186). *Cf.* also H. Lauterpacht, *Recognition of
    Governments* (*The Times* newspaper, January 6, 1950); *loc. cit.* in note 52 above,
    January 9, 1950, and Sir Gerald Fitzmaurice, *Chinese Representation in the
    United Nations*, 6 *Y.B.W.A.* (1952), p. 36 *et seq.*

The General Principles of Law Recognised by Civilised Nations

In the course of the coalescence of international law and civilisation, the term *civilised nation* acquired a meaning which, by and large, was identical with the maintenance of the rule of law, in the Anglo-Saxon meaning of the term, in favour of foreign nationals. A State which protected the life, liberty and property of foreigners in accordance with the rule on the minimum standard of international law complied with its international obligations and was entitled to be regarded as civilised.[59]

Sufficient evidence existed for claiming that the rule on the minimum standard had become embodied in international customary law. In any case, it could be regarded as a general principle of law recognised by civilised States. When occasion offered itself, international courts and tribunals, foremost among them the Permanent Court of International Justice, reaffirmed the rule on the minimum standard.[60]

The first sign of a breach in this rampart was the growing hesitation in the post-1919 period to uphold the sanctity of foreign private property. Since then, the position of property abroad has become precarious even in a large belt not subject to Communist control.[61]

In many parts of the world, even the minimum standard regarding the protection of the life and liberty of foreign nationals can no longer be taken for granted. Nationals of Western States in the orbits of Russia and Communist China [62] have found to their cost that their home governments cannot any longer give them effective protection under international law.[63]

Attention must also be drawn to the tendencies in the current Doctrine of international law to refrain from any analysis of the words " recognised by civilised nations " in the treatment of the general principles of law or to treat these words as redundant.[64] From this point of view, the twilight of this subsidiary law-creating process of international law in the Soviet Doctrine of international law is especially significant.[65] This may explain the curious reformulation

---

[59] See above, p. 55 *et seq.*

[60] See further *Vol I*, p. 200 *et seq.*

[61] See further 5 *C.L.P.* (1952), p. 295 *et seq.*, and 14 *ibid.* (1961), p. 213 *et seq.*

[62] A recent judicial description of this type of régime may be found in the Judgment by Cassels J., *Ex p. Kolczynski* [1955] 1 Q.B. 540, at p. 547.

[63] See further below, p. 174 *et seq.*

[64] See, for instance, E. Ruck, *Grundsätze im Völkerrecht* (1946), p. 13.

[65] See further I. Lapenna, *Conceptions soviétiques de droit international public* (1954), p. 161 *et seq.*, and *International Law Viewed through Soviet Eyes*, 15 *Y.B.W.A.* (1961), p. 204 *et seq.*

of Article 38 (1) (c) of the Statute of the World Court by Judge Krylov
as general principles of law " recognised by the nations." [66]

The process of flouting traditional concepts of international law
by States in the Russian and Chinese orbits does not necessarily stop
at the point of a divorce of international law from civilisation. It has
reached the crucial point where serious doubts have arisen in Western
minds—probably reciprocated in Russian and Chinese quarters—
whether, in the relations with these States, that minimum of good faith
can still be taken for granted without which even treaty relations on
any major topic can hardly be contemplated. While this issue raises
still more fundamental problems than are within the scope of this
Chapter,[67] little doubt remains that, in so far as these countries are
concerned, international law has ceased to be an effective safeguard
of the minimum standard of international law regarding the protection
of foreign nationals as, hitherto, applied between civilised States.

The Law of War

In the pre-1914 era, it was still possible to envisage that, in fields
not codified at the Hague Peace Conferences of 1899 and 1907, " the
inhabitants and the belligerents remain under the protection and the
rule of the principles of the law of nations, as they result from the
usages established among civilised peoples, from the laws of
humanity, and the dictates of the public conscience." [68]

The First World War soon taught three hard lessons. First, public

---

[66] Dissenting Opinion in *Reparation for Injuries suffered in the Service of the United Nations, I.C.J. Reports 1949*, p. 219. *Cf.* also S. B. Krylov, *Les Notions Principales du Droit des Gens*, Hague *Recueil*, Vol. 70 (1947), p. 449, and Vol. I, p. 43 *et seq.*

[67] See below, pp. 146 and 288 *et seq.*, Ann van Wynen Thomas, *Communism versus International Law* (1953), and *Fundamental Principles*, p. 295 *et seq.*

    A similar view underlines the judgments in *Ex p. Kolczynski (loc. cit.* in note 62 above). After paying formal tribute to the principle that " the Court must not assume that the foreign State will not observe the terms of the (extradition) treaty," Lord Goddard C.J. considered it necessary, " if only for reasons of humanity, to give a wider and more generous meaning to the words we are now construing " than in the case of a country which could be relied on not to institute criminal proceedings for non-extraditable offences (at pp. 35–36), and Cassels J. expressly held that if the applicants were extradited for non-political offences under the Extradition Treaty between Poland and the United Kingdom of January 11, 1932, they might well only be tried for such offences, but, in fact, punished for an offence of a political character (*ibid.*, at p. 34). See also E. Hambro, *New Trends in the Law of Extradition and Asylum*, 5 *Western Political Quarterly*, p. 1 *et seq.*, and L. C. Green, *Recent Practice in the Law of Extradition*, 6 *C.L.P.* (1953), p. 283 *et seq.*

[68] Para. 9 of the Preamble of Hague Convention IV, October 18, 1907 (J. B. Scott (ed.), *The Hague Convention and Declarations of 1899 and 1907* (1915), pp. 101–102).

    On this so-called de Martens Clause, see further the writer's *The Legality of Nuclear Weapons* (1958), pp. 10–11.

opinion in neutral countries counts more in wars in which powerful nations stand aside than in world wars in which all greater Powers are involved.[69] Secondly, once the principle of negative reciprocity by way of reprisals and counter-reprisals is at work, as has happened, in particular in the field of maritime warfare, the law tends to be modified in a manner which happens to suit the convenience of the Powers applying such measures. Thirdly, when one side, especially the one in danger of otherwise losing the war, hopes to avert this fate by the use of "miracle" weapons—as, for instance, Imperial Germany imagined unrestricted submarine warfare—the temptation to break established rules of warfare and neutrality tends to become irresistible.

The First World War also foreshadowed other disintegrating trends which, in the Second World War, became more clearly visible : the growing unreality of the distinction between combatants and non-combatants, the increasingly impersonal character of warfare and the transformation of two-dimensional into three-dimensional war.[70]

In so far as war crimes *stricto sensu* were concerned, the war crimes tribunals established in the wake of the Second World War limited themselves to the punishment of acts which had not been essentially affected by these developments. Thus, they could avoid coming to grips with the major problems presented by the unparalleled advances of twentieth-century technology. In the absence of more than embryonic rules of air warfare, mechanisation could celebrate its orgies of destruction. Words such as carpet bombing or saturation bombing became technical terms. Hitler's V-weapons indicated the potentialities of long-range guided missiles, and the competitive hunt by the Allies of a war only just ended for the German experts in V-weapons was an augury of things to come.[71]

Well founded anxiety that, at last, technology had reached the point when total war and civilisation had become incompatible became deadly certainty with the advent of nuclear weapons.

It has been suggested that it may be possible to limit the use of such weapons to tactical military purposes. The military experts on

---

[69] See further the writer's *International Law and Totalitarian Lawlessness* (1943), p. 30 *et seq.*
[70] See further J. M. Spaight, *Blockade by Air* (1942); *Bombing Vindicated* (1944); *Legitimate Objectives in Air Warfare*, 21 *B.Y.I.L.* (1944), p. 158 *et seq.*; Sir Arthur Harris, *Bomber Offensive* (1947); H. A. Smith, *loc. cit.* in note 53 above, p. 67 *et seq.*, and Stone, *Legal Controls of International Conflict* (1959), p. 335 *et seq.*
[71] See further the writer's *The Law of Air Warfare and the Trend towards Total War*, 1 *University of Malaya L.R.* (1959), p. 120 *et seq.*

the Commission of Experts, summoned by the International Red Cross Committee, and the International Red Cross Committee itself rightly failed to be impressed by such arguments.[72]

A variant of this school of thought draws comforting analogies from the absence of gas warfare in the Second World War. It is, however, perhaps not entirely irrelevant that the development of nuclear weapons has been accompanied by the discovery of the strategy of the " first crippling blow."

Actually, the illegality of nuclear weapons rests on the prohibition under international customary law of the use of poison and poisoned weapons. In this respect, the Geneva Poison Gas Protocol of 1925 is merely declaratory of international customary law. Yet, the observance of these two rules is as precarious as that of any rules subject to being rendered inoperative by way of reprisal.[73]

In fact, it appears to matter little whether the use of nuclear weapons is contrary to international law. Some of the foremost political and military leaders of the North Atlantic Treaty Organisation make no secret of it that Western strategy is based on the " philosophy of massive retaliation " and the use of nuclear weapons. At the same time, they affirm and re-affirm that, in no circumstances, will they resort to preventive war. Their counterparts in the Soviet camp reciprocate with corresponding protestations. Yet, likewise, they do not fail to supplement the declarations of their peaceful intentions by minatory references to their own abundant stocks of nuclear weapons. However, it matters little whether we believe the spokesman of either or both blocs. What does matter is whether they believe each other, and this is a matter of doubt.

If the contingency of a Third World War were ever to arise, the experiences of past wars, and the express statements made by responsible spokesmen in both camps, suggest that both sides would use nuclear weapons. Moreover, if any other but an artificial line could be drawn between tactical and strategic nuclear weapons, such a distinction would sooner or later tend to break down. If such action

---

72 International Red Cross Committee, *Summary of the Opinions expressed by the Experts* (1954), p. 2, and *Collection of Constitutional Texts and Documents concerning the Legal Protection of Populations and War Victims from the Dangers of Aerial Warfare and Blind Weapons* (1954), p. 84. *Cf.* also Sir Winston Churchill's Speech in the House of Commons, *loc. cit.* in note 51 above, cols. 1901 and 1905, and H. Kahn, *On Thermonuclear War* (1960).

73 See further *l.c.* in note 68 above (1958), p. 25 *et seq.*, and, for further literature, the Report on *The Principle of Self-Defence under the Charter of the United Nations and the Use of Prohibited Weapons* in *Report of the Brussels (1962) Conference of the International Law Association.*

were admitted to be contrary to international law, then international law would be broken in the interest of what the side actually breaking international law would advertise as the "ultimate vindication of the law of nations." [74] If the use of such weapons were legal, this would merely underline the supreme irrelevance of international law from the point of view of civilisation in a crisis of such magnitude. In either case, the result would be mechanised barbarism.

Here the crucial point is reached. Lapses from the standard of civilisation regarding relatively minor, though by no means unimportant matters, such as Recognition or the Minimum Standard of International Law, can be remedied. Isolated breaches of the rules of warfare also hardly constitute any novel problem, nor the fact that, *de lege lata*, certain aspects of warfare are not subject to generally accepted rules of international law.

What is new is this : each of the two sides in any world war to come cherishes certain values in its own way of life higher than peace and is resolved, in such a contingency, to risk co-extermination and the breakdown of civilised life in large portions of the world rather than defeat or surrender.

IV—THE OUTLOOK

In Collingwood's pregnant terminology,[75] every social problem can be treated in an eristic or dialectic manner. The one permits settling disagreement by imposition of one's own will on the opponent. The other is a "constant endeavour to convert every occasion of non-agreement into an occasion of agreement." [76]

Admittedly, in group relations as well as in personal relations, it takes two to arrive at a constructive solution of any issue. The contribution which the international lawyer can make to this end is limited. He must rest content to point out the ominous character of a movement which has first led to a coalescence of international law and civilisation, but, on a global level, appears now to point towards the evanescence of the standard of civilisation from international law.

If any particular international lawyer also happens to be a student

---

[74] Oppenheim's *International Law* (ed. by H. Lauterpacht—1952), Vol. 2, p. 351, note 2. *Cf.* also *l.c.* in note 68 above (1958), p. 42, and 13 *Europa-Archiv* (1958), p. 10686, note 67.
[75] See *l.c.* in note 13 above, pp. 225 *et seq.* and 326 *et seq.*
[76] *Ibid.*, p. 326.

of international relations, he may be able to explain the reasons for this disturbing degeneration or even suggest available remedies.[77]

If a persistent questioner should ask how such dialectic agreement could possibly be attained in a world rent apart by another Babylonian confusion of tongues, the reply might well be that the picture of the Tower of Babel itself is the answer. It is not only the symbol of human *hybris*, but also carries a positive message for those with eyes to see, and, probably, the only one which is commensurate to this overriding problem of the nuclear and space age.

[77] See further below, p. 288 *et seq.*

PART TWO

THE EXPANDING FIELD

CHAPTER 5

INTERNATIONAL LAW IN EARLY ENGLISH PRACTICE

EMPHASIS on State practice in the field of international law—as distinct from the Doctrine of the law of nations—enables us to push back by centuries the frontiers in time of international law.

The rise of international law depends on two conditions being fulfilled. It requires the symbiosis of independent States. Such States must be sufficiently in contact with each other to become conscious of a choice: continuous uncertainty and possibly war of all against all, or regulated peaceful relations if only for certain periods of time.[1] If there happens to be a certain amount of international trade between such communities, political considerations in favour of the emergence of international law are reinforced by fiscal and economic factors working towards the same end.[2] Recent research by American and Soviet international lawyers into the history of international law in ancient times and within the nexus of the Italian City States bears out this proposition.[3] It may draw additional support from the study of early English State practice. The State practice of England—and Scotland—shares with that of the Italian City States the distinction of dating back to the dawn of the European law of nations. Yet it may claim a feature of its own. This is its unbroken continuity over more than eight hundred years.

I—THE INTERNATIONAL ENVIRONMENT OF MEDIEVAL ENGLAND

The co-existence over a prolonged period of the independent kingdoms of England and Scotland within " this Nobill Ile, callit Gret Britanee " [4] made acute the need for a choice between the alternatives outlined above. In view of the traditional enmity between the Crowns of England and France, and the continuous friction on the English-Scottish border, which predestined Scotland to become for centuries

[1] See above, p. 59 et seq.
[2] See above, p. 61 et seq.
[3] See above, pp. 44 and 47.
[4] In the confirmation by James III of Scotland of Confederations and Truces between England and Scotland, October 26, 1474 (11 Th. Rymer's *Foedera* (subsequently abbreviated to *Rymer*), 1704–1735, p. 825).

the natural ally of France, the seriousness of the issue was underlined. This situation offered to each of the three parties scope for manoeuvring with any one of the two others against the third. In spite of intermittent attempts on the part of England to assert supremacy over Scotland,[5] the normal relationship between the two Crowns until the ultimate union between the two countries was well formulated in the Truce of 1381 between King Richard II and King Robert of Scotland as one of equality in the absence of a common superior.[6]

The scope of England's international relations during the twelfth century will become apparent from the following catalogue of treaties and other legal documents bearing upon foreign affairs :

> Treaty of Subsidy between King Henry I and Count Robert of Flanders (March 10, 1101).[7]
> Treaty of Alliance between the same (1103).[8]
> Treaty of Succession between King Stephen and Duke Henry of Normandy (1153).[9]
> Treaty of Commerce between King Henry II and Cologne (1154).[10]
> Grant of the right to conquer Ireland by Pope Adrian to King Henry II (1155).[11]
> Letter of Pope Alexander to King Henry II on the Peace between the Kings of England and France (1162).[12]
> Treaty of Alliance between King Henry II and Count Theodore of Flanders (March 19, 1163).[13]
> Letter of King Henry II on the Right of Wreck (May 26, 1174).[14]
> Peace Treaty between King Henry II, on the one hand, and the King of France and the Sons of King Henry, on the other (October 11, 1174).[15]

---

5 See, for instance, the trial of Sir William Wallace in 1305 (1 W. Stubbs, *Chronicles of the Reigns of Edward I and Edward II* (Rolls Series, 1882), p. 137 *et seq.*).
6 " Quoniam ex quo Reges Angliae et Scotiae non habent ipsis Superiorem, qui possit Quaestionem hujusmodi terminare, justum est et aequum quod in alium compromittant " (Art. 1 of the Truce of June 18, 1381, between England and Scotland: 11 *Rymer*, p. 313).
7 1 *ibid.*, p. 1. The Record Edition of vol. 1 of *Rymer* (1816) does not contain any earlier document which is relevant for the period between the Conquest and the year 1101. Thus the choice of this year by Rymer is less accidental than has been assumed. See further T. D. Hardy, *Syllabus of Rymer's Foedera*, vol. i (1869), p. li, n. 1, and D. C. Douglas, *English Scholars* (1939), p. 285 *et seq.*
8 1 *Rymer*, p. 4.
9 *Ibid.*, p. 13.
10 Sartorius Freyherr von Waltershausen, *Urkundliche Geschichte des Ursprungs der deutschen Hanse*, vol. ii (1830), p. 3.
11 1 *Rymer*, p. 15. The date of the much-disputed Bull *Laudabiliter* mentioned in Rymer is 1154, but should be 1155. On the whole controversial issue, see further R. Foreville, *L'Église et la Royauté en Angleterre sous Henri II Plantagenet* (1943), p. 83 *et seq.*
12 1 *Rymer*, p. 21.
13 *Ibid.*, p. 23.
14 *Ibid.*, p. 36.
15 1 J. De Dumont, *Corps Universel Diplomatique du Droit des Gens* (1726-1731) (hereinafter abbreviated to *Dumont*), Part 1, p. 92.

Treaty of Allegiance to the King of England between King Henry II and King William of Scotland (December 8, 1174).[16]

Treaty of Allegiance to the King of England between King Henry II and King Rodericus of Connacta, Ireland (1175).[17]

Letter of King William of Sicily to King Henry II, confirming the obligations undertaken by oath on his behalf by his Ambassadors (August 23, 1176).[18]

Compromis between King Alfonso of Castille and King Garcia of Navarra, by which they submit all their disputes to arbitration by King Henry II (September 24, 1176).[19]

Judgment of King Henry II in the above Dispute (1177).[20]

Convention between King Henry II and King Louis VII of France regarding their Crusade (September 25, 1177).[21]

Treaty of Friendship and Alliance between King Henry II and King Philip of France (June 28, 1180).[22]

Letter of Emperor Cursaeus Angelus on the Right of Transit granted to King Henry II and his Army in the War against the Saracens (1188).[23]

Letter by King Richard I on the restitution of the independence of Scotland (December 5, 1189).[24]

Treaty between King Richard I and King Philip of France regarding their Crusade (December 30, 1189).[25]

Agreement between King Richard I and King Philip of France on the rules to be observed during the Crusade by their Armies (1190).[26]

Charter of Peace between King Richard I and King Tancred of Sicily (1190).[27]

Convention of Peace and Liberation from promise of marriage between King Richard I and King Philip of France (March 1191).[28]

Announcement by Emperor Henry VI to King Philip of France of the Capture of King Richard I (January 5, 1192).[29]

Convention between Emperor Henry VI and King Richard I for the latter's liberation (1193).[30]

Convention between Prince John and King Philip of France (January 1193).[31]

Treaty of Peace between King Richard I and King Philip of France (1195).[32]

Treaty of Alliance between King Richard I and Count Baldwin of Flanders (1196).[33]

Treaty of Perpetual Alliance between the same (1197).[34]

Letters of King John regarding the Treatment to be accorded to the Ambassadors of the King of Portugal (June 30, 1199).[35]

Treaty of Alliance between King John and the Count of Flanders (1199).[35a]

[16] 1 *Rymer*, p. 39.
[18] *Ibid.*, p. 42.
[20] 1 *ibid.*, p. 48.
[22] *Ibid.*, p. 53.
[24] *Ibid.*, p. 112.
[26] 1 *Dumont*, Part 1, p. 112.
[28] *Ibid.*, p. 69.
[30] *Ibid.*, p. 84.
[32] *Ibid.*, p. 91.
[34] 1 *Rymer*, p. 94.
[35a] *Ibid.*, p. 114.

[17] *Ibid.*, p. 41.
[19] *Ibid.*, p. 43.
[21] *Ibid.*, p. 50.
[23] 1 *Dumont*, Part 1, p. 112.
[25] 1 *Rymer*, p. 63.
[27] 1 *Rymer*, p. 66.
[29] *Ibid.*, p. 70.
[31] *Ibid.*, p. 85.
[33] 1 *Dumont*, Part 1, p. 120.
[35] *Ibid.*, p. 113.

The diplomatic correspondence of King Richard II with foreign princes bears witness to the expansion and intensification of England's international relations which took place between the twelfth century and the last quarter of the fourteenth century.[36] By then, the Kings of England had established regular contacts with the heads of many countries situated *in partibus longinquis*.[37] Those with whom King Richard II maintained diplomatic relations and with whom, during the period between 1377 and 1399, cases of English subjects were taken up and treaties concluded comprised on the Continent and in the eastern Mediterranean the following :

The King of France and the Dukes of Brittany and Burgundy ;
the Duke of Holland, the Count of Flanders, and the Towns of Ghent and Utrecht ;
the Emperor (until his coronation as Emperor, the King of the Romans), the King of Bohemia and Hungary, the Dukes of Austria, Bavaria, Gelders, Lorraine, Luxembourg and Brabant, Mecklenburg, Stettin, Teschen and Wolgast-Pommern, the Count Palatine of the Rhine, the Archbishop of Cologne, and numerous Hanse Towns;
the Kings of Norway and Poland and the General Master of the Teutonic Order ;
the Kings of Portugal, Aragon, Castille, and Navarre ;
the Doges of Genoa and Venice, the Lords of Milan and Mantua, and the Marquess of Ferrara ;
the Emperor of Constantinople and the Kings of Armenia, Cyprus, and Jerusalem.[88]

Political and economic interests combined in shaping the pattern of early English State practice in international law. First, however, the legal foundations for the growth of treaty and customary international law had to be laid : the status of the Kings of England as

[36] On thirteenth-century English diplomacy, *cf.* F. M. Powicke, *King Henry III and the Lord Edward*, vol. i (1947), p. 156 *et seq.*
[37] Letter of King Henry III of July 7, 1225, " de instructionibus et pecunia missis ad Nuncios Regis longinquis partibus agentes " (1 *Rymer*, p. 280).
[88] See 11 and 12 *Rymer*, and E. Perroy (ed.), *The Diplomatic Correspondence of Richard II* (Camden Third Series), vol. xlviii (1933).
 It also deserves to be mentioned that, in the Treaty of Alliance of October 14, 1201 between King John and King Sancius of Navarre, there is an express reference to the King of Morocco, who alone is exempted from the princes against whom their alliance might become operative (1 *Rymer*, p. 127).
 The bundles in the Exchequer Accounts containing the expense accounts of English diplomats regarding their missions abroad give a good idea of the scope and intensity of England's international contacts during the period between 1327 and 1450. *Cf.* E. Deprez and L. Mirot, *Les Ambassades anglaises pendant la guerre de cent ans* (1900) (subsequently abbreviated to *Deprez-Mirot*).

sovereign princes had to be established, the position of diplomatic envoys clarified, and an attempt made to distinguish states of peace and truce from those of war and mere absence of fighting.

II—The Sovereignty of the Kings of England

In a Treaty of 1474 between King Edward IV and Duke Charles of Burgundy the status of the latter's territories was defined as the possession of territories, " in which he does not recognise—nor can be held to recognise—any superior." [39] Sovereignty is used in this sense in English documentary material at least since the thirteenth century [40] and well describes the status of the Kings of England.

As has often been said, the very island character of England emphasises the fact of her independence. This aspect of the matter is relevant in a more concrete sense than is usually connected with this statement. The frontiers of most medieval States—apart from those

[39] " In quibus nec superiorem recognoscit nec recognoscere tenetur." The document continues as follows: " Proinde quoque, tanquam Princeps suis in Dominiis Suppremus, et nemini astrictus, liberius potest quascumque Confoederationes inire " (11 *Rymer*, p. 805). A similar clause will be found in another treaty between the same parties of the following day, July 26, 1474 (*ibid.*, p. 811).

See also the Letter of King John of France of July 27, 1361, by which he ceded to King Edward III the County of Rouergue save, for the time being, " la souveraineté et le derrenier ressort "; or the Letter of King Edward III of July 19, 1362 (*ibid.*, p. 152), by which he reserved to himself the sovereignty over the principality of Aquitania, granted on the same day to the Prince of Wales, and the acknowledgment of this position in Prince Edward's Letter of July 20, 1362 (*ibid.*, p. 154).

The legal and political significance of the conception of kingship by the grace of God is clearly brought out in a Letter from King Henry V written in 1419 to King Charles VI of France:

" Eidem nostrae protestationi pariter hunc adjecto quod, nulli-umquam hominum in temporalibus subjiceremur nec quicquam bonorum, quae tunc habuimus aut essemus imposterum habituri, teneremus nisi a solo Deo." M. Champollion-Figeac, *Lettres de Rois, Reines et Autres Personnages des Cours de France et d'Angleterre*, 1839 and 1847 (hereinafter abbreviated to *Lettres de Rois*), vol. ii, p. 370.

" Item totus ducatus Normanniae et alia quaecumque per nos in regno nostro Ffranciae adquisita, cum eorum omnia supradictorum juribus et pertinentiis universis, quae pro expressis haberentur, etiam si talia forent quae expressionem requirerent, nec sub generalitate transirent, habenda nobis et haeredibus ac successoribus nostris, tanquam domino supremo, a nullo hominum, sed a solo Deo, ita libere ab omni subjectione et obedientia cujuscumque viventis, et ita secure, sicut nos et consilium nostrum sciremus avisare, parati fuimus et essemus vobiscum componere pacem finalem " (*ibid.*, pp. 370-371).

Cf. also O. Gierke, *Political Theories of the Middle Ages* (transl. by F. W. Maitland, 1927), pp. 16-17, and 2 *Lettres de Rois*, p. 136, at p. 141.

[40] See, for instance, the renunciation by Edward III of his *superioritas Regni Scotiae* on March 1, 1328 (4 *Rymer*, p. 337), or the Peace Treaty of May 8, 1360, between King Edward III and the Regent of France, according to which the King of England was to hold the ceded French territories on the same footing as the King of France had held them: " Ce que en sovereinete en souvereinete, ce que en demaine en demaine " (6 *ibid.*, p. 178). See also *Carta Donationis Regis Castellae Terrarum Principi Walliae Concessarum*, September 23, 1366 (6 *ibid.*, p. 521).

of the Italian City States [41]—were ill defined and fluid over prolonged periods. The same applied to the frontier on the English-Scottish border, to the maritime frontiers of England, and to those of England's continental possessions.

Yet there always was a clearly defined nucleus of territory in which, since time immemorial, the Kings of England exercised personal and territorial jurisdiction, and the uncontested exercise of such jurisdiction is the surest evidence of sovereignty. By the middle of the fifteenth century the King of England exercised such jurisdiction " pour son Royaume d'Angleterre, ses Paiis d'Irlande, Guienne, et Normandie, les Villes et Places de Calaiz, Crotoy, et pour tous autres ses Paiis, Seigneuries, Hommes, Vassaulx, Feodaulx, Serviteurs, et Subjectz quelzconques et de son Obeissance tant deca comme dela la Mer." [42]

As England did not form part of the Holy Roman Empire, arguments in favour of England's dependence could not be drawn from membership of this feudal hierarchy.[43] Apart from duties of fealty

[41] P. de La Pradelle, *La Frontière* (1928), p. 13 *et seq.* and Sereni, *op. cit.*, p. 12.

[42] *De Appunctuatis per Ducissam Burgundiae Confirmatio Ducis*, May 12, 1446 (11 *Rymer*, p. 129). See also *ibid.*, pp. 133–134.

From the early days of the Doctrine of international law onwards, the inference of sovereignty from the exercise of jurisdiction in a territory has been a favourite way of arguing. See, for instance, Selden, *Mare Clausum* (1635), Book II, chap. 14. The argument obviously gains in strength if the exercise of jurisdiction is unchallenged or recognised by other sovereigns (*cf. ibid.*, chap. 20 *et seq.*). *Cf.* also A. Justice, *A General Treatise of the Dominion and Laws of the Sea* (1705), p. 222 *et seq.*, and E. Jenks, *Law and Politics in the Middle Ages* (1905), pp. 32–36.

It would be unsafe to draw any conclusions regarding the scope of sovereignty from the titles and " scuchions of armes " of the Kings of England, or any other sovereign. If not merely lingering memories, they are in the early stages of international law more often than not visible symptoms of territorial aspirations. See, for instance, the Letter of December 30, 1369, from King Edward III to the Grand Seigneurs of Aquitania (2 *Dumont*, Part 1, pp. 75–76); the counter-charges by King Charles V of France of May 14, 1370 (*ibid.*, p. 75); Art. 26 of the Treaty of May 21, 1420, between King Henry V and King Charles VI of France (2 *ibid.*, Part 2, p. 147), the Act of Parliament of December 2, 1421, reserving the independence of England in the case of a union of the two Crowns in the person of the King of England (2 *Lettres de Rois*, p. 393) and, to give an example from Elizabethan times, Sir Nicholas Throckmorton's correspondence on the use by Queen Mary of Scotland of the titles and arms of the Queen of England. In his negotiations in France, Throckmorton justified Queen Elizabeth's use of those of France by long usage and sufferance (1 P. Forbes's *Papers* (1740), pp. 134, 139, 238, 240, and 339–340), this practice dating back to 1340, in which year King Edward III assumed the title and arms of the King of France.

There are also treaties by which sovereigns guarantee to each other that " nec jus aut titulum ad Regna, Terras, et Dominia sua hujusmodi quovismodo usurpabunt, dampnumque ipsorum impedient fideliter pari modo " (Treaty of Friendship and Confederation of August 6, 1466, between King Edward IV and King Henry IV of Castille: 3 *Dumont*, Part 1, p. 589).

[43] A curious letter of King Henry II to the Emperor Frederick Barbarossa, in which the Emperor's pre-eminence appears to be recognised, is explained by Selden as

of a strictly localised character regarding some of the English possessions on the Continent,[44] the only effective challenge to the complete
independence of the English Crown came from the Holy See.

King John had surrendered " the whole Kingdom of England and
Ireland into the vassalage of the Holy Roman Church," and the Pope
regranted him his kingdom as that of a feudatory of the Church of
Rome.[45] Henry III accepted the position created by his predecessor.

But already King Henry I had warned Pope Paschal II that even
if he, the king, were willing to accept any encroachments upon England's independence, his nobles, " nay the whole people of England
would not tolerate such a state of affairs." [46] This " shadow of a
feudal relation " [47] was removed by the parliaments of Edward I and
Edward III who repudiated the last vestiges of England's vassalage
to Rome.[48]

being merely of a complimentary character (*Titles of Honour* (1672), Part I,
chap. 2).

On King Richard's acknowledgment—if so, then probably under duress—of
the Emperor as *Universorum Dominus* and on the pretensions of the Emperor
to have sole power to create notaries public anywhere in Christendom, see *ibid.*
and 4 Coke's *Institutes*, chap. 74. In 1320 King Edward II prohibited their
admission into England (3 *Rymer*, p. 829). *Cf.* also Lord Bryce, *The Holy
Roman Empire* (1918), pp. 183 *et seq.* and 240–241.

[44] Thus, Edward I consented to fealty to the King of France as Duke of Aquitania
and Peer of France (Treaty of Perpetual Peace and Friendship, May 20, 1303:
2 *Rymer*, p. 924).

Evidence of how formal the fulfilment of these feudal duties had become by
then is furnished by the letter of King Edward to King Jacob of Aragon of
September 13, 1324 (1 *Dumont*, Part 2, p. 73).

On the influence of feudalism on the early law of nations, see R. Ward,
An Enquiry into the Foundation and History of the Law of Nations in Europe,
vol. i (1795), p. 202 *et seq.* *Cf.* also G. P. Cuttino, *English Diplomatic
Administration, 1259–1339* (1940), p. 2 *et seq.*

[45] In 1208 (1 *Dumont*, Part 1, p. 60) and again in 1213 (*ibid.*, p. 147). See also
J. Ch. Luenig, 4 *Codex Italiae Diplomaticus* (1732), cols. 79–82, and the strange
admission in the letter of Henry II to the Pope in 1173: " Vestrae jurisdictionis
est Regnum Angliae, et quantum ad feudatarii juris obligationem, vobis duntaxat
obnoxius teneor, et astringor " (1 *Rymer*, p. 35).

[46] In a Letter written in 1103 (1 *Dumont*, Part 1, p. 60). See also the Letter of
King Henry III to the Pope on the state of the kingdom of December 10, 1223
(1 *Rymer*, p. 263) and the Papal Bull of April 17, 1244 confirming the immunities
and rights of England (*ibid.*, p. 425).

[47] W. Stubbs, *The Constitutional History of England*, vol. iii (1903), p. 300.

[48] In 1298 King Edward I and King Philip of France agreed to submit all their
disputes for arbitral settlement to the Pope, but only *tamquam in privatam
personam* (Leibniz, 1 *Codex Juris Gentium Diplomaticus* (1693), p. 21). On the
other hand, it was held in the sentence of June 27, 1298 that the Pope held the
territories of both kings in their respective names, but without prejudice to
the legal position as it existed before the judgment (*ibid.*, p. 22. See also 2
Rymer, p. 821).

On February 12, 1301 the English Parliament drew up an energetic protest
against the Pope's claim to overlordship over the King of England (*ibid.*, pp.
874–875). The letter was, however, never sent to the Pope. In the words of
Th. P. Taswell-Langmead, " Edward I, like many other monarchs, discovered
that public protests could be combined with private compromises according to

There might be squabbles over rank and precedence with other sovereign princes,[49] yet what really mattered was the substantial independence and equality of status flowing from it which made princes —and, subsequently, their countries—eligible to become bearers of rights and duties under international law. As it would be called in the State papers of a later period, for all practical purposes the kings of England were *sui juris*. Other terms employed were *sibi princeps* and *imperator regni sui*.[50]

The position of the Kings of England in relation to foreign princes was considerably strengthened by the plenitude of the powers of the English Crown which practically amounted to a monopoly in the conduct of foreign affairs. Four of the privileges inherent in the royal prerogative were to prove pregnant with constructive possibilities for the future development of international law : the authority to grant safe-conducts, the right to make peace and war, the treaty-making power, and the Droit of Prize.[51]

III—STATUS AND POWERS OF DIPLOMATIC ENVOYS

The conclusion of treaties of truce and peace as well as of the various types of treaties which were concluded within this framework was usually preceded by prolonged negotiations. It appears, therefore, apposite to deal at this stage with those aspects of the status of diplomatic envoys which are of special relevance from the legal point of view : their personal safety and their power to act on behalf of their sovereign.

Safe-conducts

The status of *vir religiosus* was in itself a protection if, as it often happened, priests and monks were used by sovereigns on

the requirements of the diplomacy of the moment " (*English Constitutional History* (ed. by T. F. T. Plucknett, 1946), p. 289).

Cf. also 2 Stubbs, *op. cit.* (1896), pp. 159 and 435, and 4 Coke's *Institutes*, chap. 1. On the felony of bringing from abroad Bulls of Excommunication, cf. 3 *ibid.*, chap. 36.

49 *Cf.* Sir Robert Cotton, *A Briefe Abstract of the Question of Precedency between England and Spaine* (Harleian MSS); Sir George Mackenzie, *Observations upon the Laws and Customs of Nations as to Precedency* (1680); J. Howell, *Discourse concerning the Presidency of Kings* (1664); and 4 Coke's *Institutes*, chap. 74.

50 See for early evidence of relations with the Emperor on a footing of equality the Letter of April 13, 1227 from King Henry III to the Emperor on the latter's proposal for a treaty of *amicitia et mutuum foedus* (1 *Rymer*, p. 292). *Cf.* also *ibid.*, p. 407.

The title " Majesty " was, however, conceded to the Kings of England by the Imperial Chancellery only in 1633 (Lord Bryce, *op. cit.*, p. 259, note *j*).

51 See Jenks, *op. cit.*, p. 93, Taswell-Langmead, *op. cit.*, p. 38, and below under III, IV, and V.

diplomatic missions.[52] Yet the problem would become acute in the case of visits by one sovereign to another, or if a prince preferred to rely on the services of a layman. Then, as in the case of merchants who did not come to England under the protection of a treaty, the issue of a safe-conduct would be the means of guaranteeing safety to a foreign sovereign or envoy. Thus, the letters patent granted in 1200 to the King of Scotland provided for him and his suite a " safe-conduct to come to us, to stay at our Court and to return safely and securely to your own country." [53]

The issue of safe-conducts was a complicated affair. In each individual case application had to be made for them, and a messenger —not protected by a safe-conduct—had to be sent abroad in order to deliver the letter containing the request to the foreign sovereign for the safe-conduct and to bring home the required letters patent.[54] In the early stages, safe-conducts might be limited in time.[55] They might be restricted to the achievement of the particular objects of a mission.[56]

Subsequently, they would be issued more frequently without time-limit [57] or might be completely dispensed with under treaties. In the Treaty of September 30, 1471 between King Edward IV and Duke François of Brittany, for instance, it was stipulated that, for the duration of the truce between the two contracting parties, ambassadors and messengers from one court to the other should not require any other safe-conduct than to be able to show the letters or messages which they carried with them from their prince to the

---

[52] See, for instance, the Letters of January 4, 1220, " De forma Treugae Regi Franciae mittenda " (1 *Rymer*, p. 236), and of March 22, 1226, " De Tractato Pacis cum Rege Franciae resumendo " (*ibid.*, p. 285), and Cuttino, *op. cit.*, p. 90.
  According to Gratian, those who maltreated envoys were to be excommunicated (E. Nys, *Les origines du droit international* (1894), p. 339).

[53] October 30, 1200 (1 *Rymer*, p. 121). See also the safe-conduct granted on August 25, 1242 by King Henry III to the eldest son of the King of Navarre (1 *Lettres de Rois*, p. 72).

[54] See, for instance, the Letter of July 20, 1212 of King John to the Count of Flanders (1 *Rymer*, pp. 161–162), the Letter of July 24 of King Henry III to the King of France (*ibid.*, p. 232), or the expense account of John Pretewell for his journey to France from January 25 to April 14, 1396, in order to obtain safe-conducts for the Ambassadors of King Richard II (*Deprez-Mirot*, No. DXXIII).

[55] See, for instance, the Letter of King Henry III of June 12, 1217 regarding the safe-conduct granted to the Ambassadors of Louis, Dauphin of France (1 *Rymer*, p. 219).

[56] " ita tamen, quod in itinere illo, non tractet de aliis negotiis, quam de negotio quod inter nos et Dominum suum Regem Castellae tractatur " (safe-conduct granted by King John to the Chancellor of the King of Castille, March 8, 1208: *ibid.*, p. 149).

[57] Thus the Ambassador of the King of Norway to King Henry III was furnished in 1238 with " litterae Regis de protectione patentes sine termino " (*ibid.*, p. 382).

other sovereign.[58] Special safe-conducts, however, were still necessary for envoys travelling to third countries, unless special provision to the contrary was made in the treaty.[59]

It becomes evident from this practice that the customary inviolability which attached to heralds or ambassadors of war[60] did not automatically extend to diplomatic envoys in times of truce or peace. Their safety entirely depended on the unilateral promises contained in safe-conducts or on treaty provisions. The underlying idea was that, for this reason, they were under the king's special protection.[61]

The fiction that their immunity derived from their extraterritoriality belongs to a later period when jurists attempted to rationalise rules of international customary law which, by then, had grown on the subsoil of defunct safe-conducts and treaty clauses dispensing with safe-conducts. In some of these safe-conducts another kind of fiction was actually used. It underlies the conception behind this

[58] 3 *Dumont*, Part 1, p. 438.

[59] See, for instance, the Letter of King Richard II to King Robert II of Scotland, written between 1382 and 1389, for a safe-conduct for Landgraf Johannes, who was on his way to Norway on business for the King of the Romans and of Bohemia (Perroy, *op. cit.*, p. 20). The favour was asked on a basis of reciprocity: " ut proinde ad consimilia vestre excellencie concedenda decetero nos constituatis propensius inclinatos."

A clause providing for *transitus innoxius* of their ambassadors, messengers, or posts to third countries, provided they are not at war with one of the contracting parties, is contained in the Anglo-Russian Treaty of June 16, 1623 (17 *Rymer*, pp. 506–507).

See further Gentili, *De Legationibus Libri Tres* (1594), Bk. II, chap. 3; Ch. de Martens, *Manuel Diplomatique* (1822), p. 41; A. R. Adair, *The Exterritoriality of Ambassadors in the Sixteenth and Seventeenth Centuries* (1929), pp. 110–114.

[60] Their immunity was based on *armorum honesta consuetudo*, to use the language of a document of the early fifteenth century (2 *Dumont*, Part 2, p. 93). See also Gentili, *op. cit.*, Book I, chap. vi; 4 Coke's *Institutes*, chap. 17, and Ward, *op. cit.*, vol. i, p. 171.

How much the recollection of the distinction between ambassadors and heralds was still alive in the sixteenth century is shown by Queen Elizabeth's exclamation in response to the insolence of an ambassador of the King of Poland: " How have I been deceived: I looked for an ambassador; I have found a herald " (Zouche, *Juris et Judicii Fecialis sive Juris inter Gentes Explicatio* (1650), Section VIII, No. 7).

Cf. also G. W. Keeton, *Shakespeare and His Legal Problems* (1930), pp. 70–71.

[61] In the words of a safe-conduct granted by King John in 1202, the ambassador was taken " in manu, conductu et protectione nostra " (1 *Rymer*, p. 128). The telling term *assecuratio* was also sometimes used. *Cf.* the safe-conduct for the King of Navarre of June 2, 1235 (*ibid.*, p. 340).

The same conception applied in the case of a safe-conduct granted to a foreign sovereign. Thus, King Edward III " suscepit in salvum et securum Conductum suum, ac in Protectionem et Defensionem suam specialem " the King of Navarre (January 12, 1377: 7 *Rymer*, p. 133).

What might happen to an ambassador, who was found to have ventured on his errand without a safe-conduct, is illustrated by the treatment meted out to the ambassadors of King Charles V at Bordeaux by the Black Prince, known as the " flower of chivalry " (*cf.* Ward, *op. cit.*, vol. i, p. 168).

institution. Accordingly, "anything that you may do to him or his suite, shall be deemed to be done to us."[62]

Full Powers

The hazards of travelling in foreign parts in general, the dangers to the persons of sovereigns in particular, and the risks of rebellions in the absence of the sovereign from his homeland probably account for the fact that, from the earliest times, ambassadors were freely entrusted with full powers to negotiate and conclude treaties and to commit their sovereigns in other ways.

While subsequent full powers are more elaborate and explicit, the early full powers from 1202 onwards already contain all the essentials. They authorise the ambassador to negotiate and conclude on behalf of his sovereign whatever business he may have on hand.[63] Full Powers granted in 1213 expressly mention that the king will ratify whatever his ambassadors may agree on his behalf.[64] In the following year the formula *ratum et gratum habebimus* makes its appearance.[65]

In Full Powers issued in 1235, King Henry III asked the Count of Provence to conclude a marriage contract on his behalf of his daughter with the king's ambassadors as if it were concluded with the king in person.[66] Ambassadors are even authorised to swear oaths on behalf of their sovereign *in animam nostram*,[67] and, by 1254, fully fledged plenary powers are in use in which ambassadors may not only bind their king but also his heirs if they should deem this expedient.[68]

---

[62] Letter regarding a safe-conduct to Louis, Dauphin of France, September 14, 1217 (1 *Rymer*, p. 222). See also the Letter of King Edward I to the Earl of Lincoln, November 17, 1295 (1 *Lettres de Rois*, p. 421).

On the origin of the fiction of extraterritoriality in the Doctrine of the sixteenth century, *cf.* Adair, *op. cit.*, p. 15 *et seq.*

[63] Full Powers regarding the Truce to be concluded between King John and King Philip of France, December 26, 1202 (1 *Rymer*, p. 132) or those issued to the Ambassadors to Emperor Otho, 1212 (*ibid.*, p. 156).

[64] Full Powers to the Ambassadors to the Count of Flanders, June 27, 1213 (*ibid.*, p. 173). See also *ibid.*, p. 175.

[65] Full Powers to the Ambassadors to the King of France, September 13, 1214 (*ibid.*, p. 191). See also *ibid.*, p. 199.

[66] *Ibid.*, p. 345, at 346.

[67] *Potestas de Treuga cum Francia juranda*, October 2, 1249 (*ibid.*, p. 448).

See for a *Recognitio* on the part of the English ambassadors that they had sworn peace *procuratorio nomine* that of June 1, 1258 (1 *Dumont*, Part 1, p. 208).

[68] Full Powers for the Conclusion of Peace between King Henry III and the King of Castille, February 8, 1254 (*ibid.*, pp. 498–499). *Cf.* also Cuttino, *op. cit.*, p. 108 *et seq.*, and, for the discussion of an instance of fourteenth-century full powers, J. Mervyn Jones, *Full Powers and Ratification* (1946), pp. 1–2.

IV—LAYING THE FOUNDATIONS

Since the Peace Treaties of Westphalia, peace as a state of international relations has rested on multilateral treaties which provided a relatively stable framework for the following inter-war periods. Duel wars, as distinct from major wars, which again threw into the melting-pot the whole quasi-international order resting on these foundations, were fought with limited objectives within the setting of these settlements.[69]

The multilateral character of these treaties has obscured the fact of the contractual character of the state of peace in international relations which is such a striking feature of early international law. If, at the time, anything was " normal," it was the state of complete anarchy and licentiousness in the absence of express agreement between princes to the contrary.

The position as it then was in the absence of treaties is well illustrated by the fateful chain of events which began with a quarrel between two sailors in the neighbourhood of Bayonne or on the coast of Brittany.[70] Ward describes the incident as follows :

" In 1292 two sailors, the one Norman, the other English, quarrelled in the port of Bayonne, and began to fight with their fists. The Englishman being the weaker, is said to have stabbed the other with his knife. It was an affair which challenged the intervention of the civil tribunal, but being neglected by the Magistrates the Normans applied to their King, (Philip le Bel) who with neglect still more unpardonable, desired them to take their own revenge. They instantly put to sea, and seizing the first English ship they could find, hung up several of the crew, and some dogs at the same time, at the mast head. The English retaliated without applying to their Government, and things arose to that height of irregularity, that, with the same indifference on the part of their kings, the one nation made alliance with the Irish and Dutch ; the other with the Flemings and Genoese. Two hundred Norman vessels scoured the English seas, and hanged all the seamen they could find. Their enemies in return fitted out a strong fleet, destroyed or took the greater part of the Normans, and giving no quarter, massacred them, to the amount of fifteen thousand men. The affair then became too big for private hands, and the Governments interposing in form, it terminated in that unfortunate war, which by the loss of Guienne entailed upon the two nations an endless train of hostilities, till it was recovered." [71]

---

69 On the relevance for international law of the distinction between duel and major wars, see, further, above, p. 32 ; H. A. Smith, *The Crisis in the Law of Nations* (1947), pp. 57–58, the present writer's *International Law and Totalitarian Lawlessness* (1943), p. 30 *et seq.* and 14 *Y.B.W.A.* (1960), p. 374, n. 21.

70 According to more recent research, the incident happened in Brittany. See Sir James Henry Ramsay, *The Dawn of the Constitution* (1908), p. 402.

71 Ward, *op. cit.*, vol. i, pp. 176–177. A fuller account will be found in D. Hume, *The History of England*, vol. ii (1810), p. 486 *et seq.*
    For a similar private battle which took place between English and French

The factors which caused a change are of a complex character. The role played by religion and the Church has received due recognition.[72] The political and economic interests which worked in the same direction deserve to be more strongly emphasised. Foreign affairs become more calculable if, in a world full of potential and actual enemies, the position of allies and neutrals can be fixed with a certain amount of reliability.[73] It then becomes also possible—on the basis of mutual insurance between princes—to stabilise the internal position of sovereigns against rebellious nobles and dissidents [73] and, by the outlawry of all but public and just wars, to strengthen the king's monopoly in the conduct of foreign relations.[74] Finally, a minimum of international security is required in the interest of foreign trade and, in the mercantilist systems of pre-liberal economy, trade with other countries is rather consciously recognised to be the king's very direct concern.[75]

Thus, interests of very different kinds contribute to the choice of sovereign princes in favour of a limitation of their unbounded discretion, and they freely use treaties in order to create a foundation for a more rational type of international relations. Treaties providing for the establishment of truce or peace, for the limitation of reprisals, and for a check on piracy are the favourite means for the achievement of this end. On this basis it becomes possible to distinguish, at least to some extent, the state of war from those of truce and peace.

Treaties of Truce

The frequency of truces in early English State practice is in itself an indication of the precariousness of peace in those days. Their primary purpose is to put an end to open violence and to secure for

---

ships in 1351 see J. Hosack, *On the Rise and Growth of the Law of Nations* (1882), p. 108. *Cf.* also D. Hume, *History of England*, Vol. II (1810), p. 486.

[72] See, for instance, Ward, *op. cit.*, vol. ii, p. 1 *et seq.*; Hume, *op. cit.*, p. 2; C. M. Kennedy, *The Influence of Christianity upon International Law* (1856); or Sir Thomas Erskine Holland, *Studies in International Law* (1898), p. 40 *et seq.*

[73] See further below, p. 108 *et seq.*

[74] On the connection between public and just wars and the monopoly of foreign politics, see below, p. 234 *et seq.*

During the reign of King Edward III and subsequently, Parliament was frequently consulted on questions of war and peace. This, however, was not done as " a requirement of constitutional law, but as a dictate of political prudence," owing to the increasing financial liabilities involved in the conduct of war. See Taswell-Langmead, *op. cit.*, pp. 185–187.

[75] See further below, p. 123 *et seq.*

a limited period the territorial *status quo*.[76] It entirely depends on the contracting parties whether all or only some of their territories are included in the truce, whether it is limited to exclude spoliation on land or also extends to the high seas,[77] or whether the treaty is open for adhesion by third parties.[78] The truce may last for a few months or for a prolonged period.[79] Especially at a later stage it is likely to contain clauses on the administration of justice to each other's subjects or on freedom of commerce.[80] While it lasts, a state of truce may completely assimilate the relations between the contracting parties to those in a state of peace or become a transitional stage to a state of peace.[81]

It becomes apparent from the wording of even fairly early specimens of treaties of this type how quickly a settled States practice developed in this field,[82] and how standard precautions were taken against the breach of such treaties. In the absence of a clause to the contrary, any breach of the truce by a contracting party or any of his subjects entitled the other side to denounce the truce.[83] Yet should the infraction of the truce have been committed without the

---

[76] *Treuga inter Regem Angliae et Vicecomitem de Thoarcio*, November 2, 1202: " Ita quod nos, durante tempore treugarum, ipsi Vicecomiti, vel terrae suae malum, per nos, vel nostros non faciemus; nec Vicecomes per ipsum, vel per alium malum nobis vel terrae nostrae interim faciet, vel perquiret, vel fieri procurabit " (1 *Rymer*, p. 131).
Truce between King Henry III and Louis of France, February 3, 1236: " Insuper nos, et praedictus Rex Franciae, pro nobis, et hominibus, et inprisiis nostris manifestis, toto tempore treugarum istarum, erimus in eadem saisina, in qua eramus illa die qua treugae istae captae fuerunt " (1 *ibid.*, p. 350).
Cf. also 4 Coke's *Institutes*, chap. 26.

[77] Compare the Truce on land and sea of April 7, 1243 between King Henry III and the King of France (1 *Rymer*, p. 416) with the geographically limited Truce of June 15, 1528 between King Henry VIII and others, and Marguerite of Austria (4 *Dumont*, Part 1, p. 517).
The difference between general and territorially limited treaties of this kind is brought out by a clause in the Treaty of Peace of December 14, 1528 between King Henry VIII and King James V of Scotland: " Non dicentur nec reputabuntur omnino generalis sive generales (Pax, treugae sive Guerrarum abstinentiae), nec se extendent ad Dominium de Lorne in Regno Scotiae, nec ad Insulam de Lundey in Regno Angliae; sed Dominium et Insula praedicta intelligentur nullo modo in hac Pace et hiis Guerrarum abstinentiis comprehensa " (*ibid.*, p. 521).

[78] Jean de Bailleul of Scotland was included—though with reservations—in the Truce of January 26, 1301 between the Kings of England and France (1 *ibid.*, Part 1, pp. 328–329).

[79] Compare the truces mentioned above (n. 76) with that of June 12, 1468 between King Edward IV and the Duke of Bretagne (3 *ibid.*, Part 1, p. 438).

[80] Prolongation of Truce between King Henry VI and King Charles VII of France, March 11, 1447 (*ibid.*, p. 564) or Truce and Treaty of Commerce of July 22, 1486 between King Henry VII and Duke François of Bretagne (12 *Rymer*, p. 303).

[81] *Cf.* the Letter of King Henry III of July 17, 1227 on the successful conclusion of the mission of the English ambassadors to France (1 *ibid.*, p. 294).

[82] " Talis est autem forma treugarum," etc. (Truce of July 1255 between King Henry III and the King of France; 1 *Rymer*, p. 555).

[83] See, for instance, the letter of King Henry III to the English Barons, June 7, 1242 (*ibid.*, p. 405).

king's knowledge or in the face of his disapprobation, it is frequently stipulated that the truce shall remain in force.[84] Then it is for the sovereign concerned or for the keepers of the truce [85] to bring the offenders to punishment or, within more or less clearly defined limits, the injured party may have recourse to measures of self-help.[86]

If a truce is terminated or denounced, the relations between the parties revert to their pristine state of lawlessness and violence.[87] Even then there is still a device left by which *ad hoc* protection can be granted to individual merchants who are not covered by treaties of truce or peace : the issue of safe-conducts, the ultimate basis in the European law of nations of both diplomatic immunity and freedom of commerce.[88]

Peace Treaties

A truce, such as the Treaty concluded on February 13, 1478, between King Edward IV and King Louis XI of France for their lifetime and a hundred years after the death of either of them, differs merely in emphasis from a peace treaty. The essential feature of treaties of truce is their primarily negative and prohibitory character. The status created by such a truce is well described in the above-mentioned Treaty as *praesentes guerrarum abstinentiae.*[89]

Something more positive and solemn is required if sovereigns wish to settle territorial issues with an air of finality and to establish closer bonds with other States—usually on the solid foundation of common enmity to a third Power.[90] Frequently, treaties of peace

---

[84] *Cf.* Prolongation of the Truce between the Kings of England and France, March 31, 1324 (1 *Dumont*, Part 2, p. 66).

[85] See below, p. 125 *et seq.*

[86] Truce of June 1228 between King Henry III and King Louis IX of France (*ibid.*, Part 1, p. 165).

[87] See, for instance, the notification to the Barons of the Cinque Ports of the termination of the Truce with France, May 15, 1224 (1 *Rymer*, p. 272).

    The Letter of King John of France of July 27, 1361 contains a vivid description of the misery caused to the civil population by the previous Anglo-French wars (2 *Lettres de Rois*, p. 136, at 137).

[88] See further below, p. 123 *et seq.*

    Thus, for instance, after the termination of the Truce with France, a safe-conduct was issued to French ships: " Concessimus quod naves, de potestate ejusdem Regis, carcatae blado, vinis et victualibus, salvo et secure veniant in Angliam " (November 5, 1226: 1 *Rymer*, p. 287).

    Cf. also the Letter of King Henry III of September 20, 1242 (1 *Lettres de Rois*, p. 64); Sir Travers Twiss (ed.), *The Black Book of the Admiralty* (Rolls Series, Nos. 1–3), 1871–1874 (hereinafter abbreviated to *Black Book of the Admiralty*), Appendix, p. 380 *et seq.*, and 20 Hen. VI, c. 1 (1444), which expressly provided for the enrolment of safe-conducts granted to enemies.

[89] 3 *Dumont*, Part 2, p. 20.

[90] See, for instance, the Treaty of Alliance of June 16, 1373 between King Edward III and King Ferdinand and Queen Eleanor of Portugal: *Amicis Amici et Inimicis Inimici* (7 *Rymer*, p. 17) or the Truce, to be followed by a final peace treaty,

provide simultaneously for a confederation and alliance,[91] and, opportunity permitting, the union is cemented by suitable political marriages.[92] Peace treaties may be concluded for limited periods,[93] but more often than not the intention of the parties is to establish a state of peace in perpetuity between their countries for themselves, their heirs and successors.[94] Even the object of universal peace is incorporated into some of these treaties.[95] Reciprocal political and economic advantages are granted more freely and comprehensively than in treaties of truce,[96] and these positive contents of treaties intended to be valid over a prolonged period give greater substance to peace treaties as compared with treaties of truce. Their real value, however, depends on the willingness of the contracting parties to prevent a relapse into indiscriminate violence and private war. For this reason, the contractual obligations undertaken by the parties

of February 16, 1471 between King Edward IV and King Louis XI of France: " Les dites Seigneurs Roys de France et d'Angleterre . . . se monstreront et declaireront, l'un pour l'autre, Amy de ses Amys, et Ennemy de ses Ennemy; Reserve toujours leurs dites confederez et Alliez " (11 *Rymer*, p. 687). The Powers referred to, who if they wished were to be comprised in the Truce, were enumerated (*ibid*., p. 685).

[91] *Cf.* Alliance of March 31, 1254 between King Henry III and King Alfonso of Castille (1 *Rymer*, p. 503); Peace Treaty of May 20, 1259 between King Henry III and King Louis IX of France (*ibid*., p. 675); or the Treaty of Peace and Friendship of October 20, 1468 between King Edward IV and King John of Aragon (3 *Dumont*, Part 1, p. 599).

[92] " Cum igitur nullo competentiori modo inter Principes amicitia mutua contrahatur, quam per vinculum foederis conjugalis . . ." (Full Powers issued by King Henry III for the conclusion of a contract of marriage with the King of Castille, May 15, 1253: 1 *Rymer*, p. 490).

" In omnibus hujus Seculi Negotiis quod magis in animo nostro fixum semper habuimus atque illud proculdubio est, non solum Amicitiam et Foedera, quae inter Nos sunt et Serenissimum Enricum Angliae Regem . . . conservare, verum illa eadem omnibus Amoris et Consanguinitatis Vinculis roborare atque augere, ita ut nihil addi ulterius possit " (Confirmation of the Marriage Contract between the Prince of Wales and Infanta Katerina of Castille, June 23, 1503—13 *ibid*., p. 76).

See also the Powers granted by King Edward II for Negotiations with the King of Aragon, March 13, 1324 (4 *ibid*., p. 45).

[93] Treaty of April 9, 1450 between King Henry VI and Christiernus I of Denmark (3 *Dumont*, Part 1, p. 571).

[94] Peace Treaty of October 1259 between King Henry III and King Louis of France (1 *Rymer*, p. 691); Confederation between King Henry III and King Magnus IV of Norway, August 1269 (1 *Dumont*, Part 1, p. 408); Treaty of Peace, Friendship, League, and Confederation of August 5, 1529 between Henry VIII and Emperor Charles V (4 *ibid*., Part 2, p. 42).

Art. 1 of the Peace Treaty of April 2, 1559 between Queen Elizabeth I and King Henry II of France contains the following fulsome formulation of the object which the contracting parties had in mind: " Vera, firma, solida, sincera, perpetua, et inviolabilis pax, amicitia, unio, confoederatio, ligua, mutua intelligentia, et vera concordia, perpetuis futuris temporibus duratura " (1 Forbes's *Papers* (1740), p. 70).

[95] " *Pacis universalis Propagationem* " *cupientes* (Treaty and Confederation of General Peace and Concord of October 2, 1518 between King Henry VIII and King Francis of France (13 *Rymer*, p. 624)). See further below, p. 108 *et seq*.

[96] See below, p. 123 *et seq*.

to treaties of peace and truce alike for the limitation of reprisals and the repression of piracy are of signal importance.

Reprisals

Treaties of peace and truce in themselves provided only the weakest barrier against a return to wholesale anarchy. If one side alleged a breach committed by the other contracting party or his subjects, and no redress could be expected—or there was no duty first to seek redress—reprisals, authorised and unauthorised, would follow and be answered in their turn by counter-reprisals.

Liberty to take general or special reprisals would be granted, as happened in 1295 under a letter of reprisal against Portugal which was issued to a citizen and merchant of Bayonne in order to enable him " to take reprisals against people of the Kingdom of Portugal and especially those of the City of Lisbon and their goods, wherever he may find them, within the jurisdiction of our lord the King and Duke, or without, to seize, retain and appropriate them, until Bernardus and his heirs or successor shall receive full restitution, including reasonable expenses incurred on that occasion, for the spoil of his goods or their value as declared above." [97]

Self-help of this kind was bound to disturb friendly political relations between the States concerned, and to increase considerably the natural hazards of medieval trade. *Raison d'état* and commercial interests [98] alike, therefore, combined in attempts to make more secure the *securus status*,[99] established by treaties of truce and peace. The general precautions taken for securing observance of treaties by the sovereigns themselves,[1] a general reparation clause,[2] or provision for arbitration [3] would go some way to achieve this object.

---

[97] Letter of October 3, 1295 (2 *Rymer*, p. 692). See also 1 *Lettres de Rois*, p. 418.

[98] " A fin de a dez Entretenir, Multiplier, et Accroistre la Marchandise en noz Paiis et Seigneuries " (*De Appunctuatis per Ducissimam Burgundiae Confirmatio Ducis*, May 12, 1446: 11 *Rymer*, p 129).

[99] Term used in the Letter of the Duchess of Burgundy on the Renewal of the Truce between England and Burgundy, July 12, 1446 (*ibid.*, p. 133).

[1] See below, p. 125 *et seq.*

[2] See, for instance, the Treaties between King Henry IV and Jean *sans peur*, Duke of Burgundy and Count of Flanders, March 10, 1406 (2 *Dumont*, Part 1, p. 304), between King Henry IV and the General Master of the Teutonic Order, December 4, 1409 (*ibid.*, p 330), or between King Henry VI and the Duke of Burgundy of August 4, 1446: in case of infraction of the treaty, " sera le fait Repare par les Seigneurs de l'une et de l'autre Partie, et mis en son premier Estat et den " (11 *Rymer*, p. 145).

[3] See the Convention of Mutual Peace and Friendship of December 30, 1505 between King Henry VII and Duke George of Saxony (4 *Dumont*, Part 1, p. 75). See also below, under V, and E. S. Colbert, *Retaliation in International Law* (1948), pp. 11 *et seq.*

The most difficult hurdle, however, consisted in infractions of treaties by subjects of the contracting parties, and in delay or denial of justice to foreign merchants who had claims in contract or tort or were in need of protection by local criminal justice. Unless a constructive solution of this problem could be found, peace and truce would become merely nominal, and recourse would be had again to reprisals.

The answer was found in a combination of various devices. There was to be a separation between responsibility for breach of treaty which was attributable to the sovereigns themselves, and acts of their subjects. In the latter case, the treaty itself was not affected in its validity,[4] but the contracting party had to make available proper organs of justice for the investigation of claims,[5] to secure restitution,[6] and frequently to make such acts punishable offences under his own municipal law.[7]

Self-help might still be permitted by some treaties as an alternative or cumulative remedy,[8] but the issue of letters of reprisal was increasingly limited to the grant of special as distinct from general reprisals,[9] and made dependent on the fulfilment of prior

[4] A typical clause to this effect is that contained in the Truce of March 23, 1357 between England and France: " Ne ne serra reputee ceste Treue pur Rompue pur Attemptaz, qui se facent par ascun d'une Partie ou d'autre s'il n'estoit fait du commandement des Rois, ou des Lieuxtenans Generaus d'yceux Rois; mes se sera Restitucion et Reparacion come dit est, la Trieue tous jours durans en sa vertue " (6 *Rymer*, p. 9).

[5] See, for instance, the Truce of March 31, 1438 between King Henry VI and King James II of Scotland (3 *Dumont*, Part 1, pp. 540–541).

[6] See, for instance, the Truce cited in n. 4, above, or the Peace Treaty of August 6, 1489 between King Henry VII and King Johannes of Denmark and Sweden (3 *Dumont*, Part 2, p. 240).

[7] " Nous les Punirons, come Violateurs de la Paix, par Peine de Corps et de Biens, sicome le cas le requerra, et qui raison voudra " (Confirmation by King Edward III of the Treaty of May 8, 1360 with France, October 24, 1360: 6 *Rymer*, p. 230). In the Proclamation of King Henry VI of July 17, 1426 on the General Peace with the Duke of Burgundy and Count of Flanders the intention is expressed " illos, qui culpabiles et Delinquentes invenientur, taliter Punire et Puniri facere, quod caeteris cedet in Exemplum " (10 *ibid.*, p. 362).
   The Truce of January 28, 1414 between King Henry V and King Johannes of Castille (9 *ibid.*, p. 105), providing for the punishment of offenders against the Treaty, is of special interest, as it led to the passing of a statute in the same year (2 Hen. V, st. 1, c. 6) by which the breaking of truces was made treason. As the Act met with strong opposition, it was suspended in 1436 and 1442 and, when re-enacted in 1450, the provision on treason was omitted. See further R. G. Marsden, *Documents relating to Law and Custom of the Sea* (Publications of the Navy Records Society), vol. i (1915), and vol. ii (1916) (subsequently abbreviated to *Law and Custom*), vol. i, pp. 116–117.

[8] See, for instance, the Truce of June 1228 between King Henry III and King Lewis IX of France (1 *Dumont*, Part 1, p. 166) or the Truce of March 31, 1438 between King Henry VI and King James II of Scotland (3 *ibid.*, Part 1, p. 541).

[9] The principle of individual responsibility was also emphasised by another type of treaty clause by which it was provided that individual merchants should only be responsible for contractual obligations and torts or crimes committed by such

requirements. There had to be evidence of delay or denial of justice.[10] The contracting party whose subject had suffered injury must first appeal to the other side, under whose jurisdiction such a delay or denial of justice had occurred, and redress must have been refused.[11] Only then might letters of reprisal be granted.

The exercise of this right might be restricted to the person and goods of the wrongdoer [12] or those living in his vicinity.[13] Vessels putting to sea might have to give guarantees for the observance of such restrictions.[14] Merchants might have to produce evidence that they were subjects of a foreign prince with whom a state of truce or peace existed.[15]

Similarly, ships might have to carry flags and letters patent issued by the authorities provided for in the treaty in order to show that they were entitled to peaceful treatment.[16] Finally, in order to determine whether prizes were taken within the framework of a treaty, and that self-help did not overstep the limits of due reparation, proceedings for the adjudication of prizes taken by way of reprisals

merchants. See, for instance, the Treaty of Alliance and Friendship of December 4, 1409 between King Henry V and the General Master of the Teutonic Order (2 *ibid.*, Part 1, pp. 329–330).

[10] See, for instance, the Treaty of March 8, 1297 between King Edward I and Count Guy of Flanders (2 *Rymer*, p. 759), the Peace Treaty of November 3, 1492 between King Henry VII and King Charles VIII of France (3 *Dumont*, Part 2, p. 293), or the Decree of the High Court of Admiralty in *Reyman* v. *Bona Hispanica* (1586): R. G. Marsden, *Select Pleas in the Court of Admiralty* (vols. vi and xi of the Publications of the Selden Society), vol. i (1894) and vol. ii (1897) (subsequently abbreviated to *Select Pleas*), vol. ii, p. 161, at 162.

[11] See, for instance, the pleadings in the trial of the Mayor of Lynn in 1306 (1 Marsden, *Select Pleas*, p. 57), the reply of July 18, 1369 of the King's Council to a petition on behalf of the masters and merchants of Castille and Biscay, J. F. Baldwin, *The King's Council in England during the Middle Ages* (1913), Appendix I, p. 486, the Letter of Reprisals of May 14, 1414 (9 *Rymer*, p. 125), or the Conventions of March 27, 1489 between King Henry VII and King Ferdinand and Queen Elizabeth of Castille (3 *Dumont*, Part 2, p. 223).

[12] See, for instance, the Truce of March 31, 1438 between King Henry VI and King James II of Scotland (*ibid.*, Part 1, p. 540), or Art. 18 of the Treaty of 1559 between Queen Elizabeth and King Henry of France (1 Forbes's *Papers*, p. 76).

[13] *Cf.* the Treaty of Peace and Friendship of January 24, 1501 between King Henry VII and King James IV of Scotland (4 *Dumont*, Part 1, p. 25).

[14] See, for instance, the Truce of January 3, 1414 between King Henry V and Duke Johan of Brittany (9 *Rymer*, p. 84).

An instance of a commission of inquiry into alleged depredations at sea in violation of the Truces with Flanders and Brittany is furnished by that of February 12, 1414 (*ibid.*, p. 116).

Cf. also *Officium Domini* v. *Sadler; The Fortune*, decided by the High Court of Admiralty, 1602 (2 Marsden, *Select Pleas*, p. 203, at 204), or *Officium Domini* v. *Reynolds; The Diamond*, 1602 (*ibid.*, p. 204, at 205).

[15] Thus, for instance, subjects of the Duke of Brunswick to whom letters of safe-conduct had been issued by King Henry III were announced as carrying also letters patent from the Duke in which it was testified " quod sint homines ipsius Ducis de Bruneswick " (Letter of King Henry III of November 10, 1230: 1 *Rymer*, p. 317).

[16] *Cf.*, for instance, the Treaty of 1297 with Flanders (2 *ibid.*, p. 759).

became more frequent [17] and, in the end, proceedings in prize became obligatory.[18]

Within limits, this policy succeeded in establishing a consensual law of peace, and in subjecting reprisals to effective State control. The distinction introduced by these treaties between international torts committed by sovereigns and their subjects, and the elaboration of rules regarding denial of justice and the necessity for seeking redress by diplomatic means prior to recourse to self-help, is, however, of wider significance. They are milestones on the road to the contemporary international customary law of tort which has grown in the fertile soil of these early treaties. Equally, it was due to these necessities that, on a considerable scale, municipal law, and especially criminal law, was put to the service of the law of nations, and the latter provided with exogenous sanctions for its enforcement.[19]

Piracy

A further obstacle to the observance of treaties of peace and truce and to freedom of commerce consisted in the existence until the fourteenth century of considerable pirate forces in western Europe. They did not acknowledge allegiance to any of the sovereign princes, but might use the territories of these princes as bases of operation or enlist the support of the local population in the disposal of pirate goods. Their ranks would be swelled at times by the subjects of such princes, or mariners might engage on their own account in piratical ventures.[20]

From early times onwards, English law treated piracy as a capital crime and, if committed by English subjects, at times assimilated it to treason.[21] The Statute of the Staple of 1353 provided that if pirate goods were brought to England, merchants, foreign as well as

---

[17] See, for instance, the Truce cited in n. 14 above.

[18] *Cf.* the Statutes of 1536 and 1537 (27 Hen. VIII, c. 4, and 28 Hen. VIII, c. 15) and the Order of Council of 1589 that all ships and goods " taken by virtue of any commission of reprisall . . . shal be kepte savely . . . till judgement hath first passed in the high courte of the Admiralty that the said goodes are a lawful prize " (1 Marsden, *Law and Custom*, p. 252).

[19] See further below, p. 125 *et seq.*, and p. 183 *et seq.*

[20] *Cf.* Sir Nicholas Harris Nicolas, *A History of the Royal Navy*, vol. i (1847), p. 241.
    On piracy during the latter part of the fifteenth century, see A. Spout, *La Marine Française sous le Règne de Charles VIII* (1894).

[21] See the Statutes of 2 Hen. V, Stat. 1, c. 6 (1414), and 28 Hen. VIII, c. 15 (1536); 3 Coke's *Institutes*, chaps. 1 and 49; Zouche, *The Jurisdiction of the Admiralty of England* (1663), pp. 89–90; Sir Leoline Jenkins' charge given at a session of Admiralty within the Cinque Ports, September 2, 1668 (Wynne, *The Life of Sir Leoline Jenkins*, vol. i (1724), pp. lxxxvi–lxxxvii); Ch. Molloy, *De Jure Maritimo et Navali* (1744), p. 61; 1 Marsden, *Select Pleas*, p. xxxviii, n. 1.

English, should be admitted to prove their ownership, and upon proof the goods were to be restored to them without the necessity of a previous suit at common law.[22]

In order to avoid situations in which pirates might play off one sovereign against another, and secure a more effective suppression of this scourge, its was, however, found that unilateral measures were not enough. Again treaties on a basis of reciprocity provided the answer, and clauses on piracy found their place side by side with those already discussed. This appeared the natural solution ; for only by treaties of truce and peace was it possible to distinguish friend from enemy and, for a long time, only a thin border-line existed between *piratae et alii inimici nostri*.[23]

In the Treaty of February 24, 1495, between King Henry VII and Archduke Philip of Austria pirates were linked with " others who, without authority from their princes, make war on sea." They were not to be given shelter in the territories of the contracting parties, nor be supplied with provisions or shown any other favours. The Treaty contained detailed regulations regarding the procedure for the restitution of pirate goods to their owners. The contracting parties undertook to issue in their ports *edicto publico prohibitiones poenales* against the receiving and purchase of pirate goods.[24]

The Treaty of Depredations of October 4, 1518, between King Henry VIII and King Louis of France dealt exclusively with these questions. It constituted a determined attempt to shorten proceedings for the recovery of piratically seized property through various devices : the establishment of central tribunals—in London the Admiral, Vice-Admiral, or their deputies [25]—the imposition of fines on inferior judges who might be recalcitrant in transferring

---

22 27 Edw. III, Stat. 2, c. 13. For the position under the common law regarding the sale in a market overt of goods seized piratically from foreigners, though in league with England, see Molloy, *op. cit.*, p. 67.

23 Letter of King Edward III of August 18, 1353 (2 *Lettres de Rois*, p. 105, at 106), or *Black Book of the Admiralty*, p. 248.

In the Treaty with Burgundy of 1446 (11 *Rymer*, p. 143) pirates were still described as " escumeurs, ou autres gens labourans sur la Guerre."

The change in the estimation of pirates is symbolised by the changed meaning of the term which " in former times was used in a better sense, being attributed to such persons to whose care the Mole or Peer of a Haven was intrusted " (see Dr. Cowel's *Interpreter* (ed. by Th. Manley, 1672), *sub nomine Pirata*). See also 3 Coke's *Institutes*, chap. 49.

24 12 *Rymer*, p. 583. See also the Treaty of Commerce of July 12, 1478, between King Edward IV and Maximilian and Maria, Dukes of Austria and Burgundy (*ibid.*, pp. 72–73), and B. A. Wortley, *Pirata non mutat dominium*, 24 *B.Y.I.L.* (1947), p. 258 *et seq.*

25 The Commission of the Court which included the Judge of the Admiralty of May 29, 1519, will be found in 13 *Rymer*, p. 700.

cases from their courts to the courts stipulated in the Treaty ; provision for speedy procedure: " summarie et de plano, sine strepitu et figura Judicii, et sola facti veritate inspecta, procedentes " ; the fixing of time-limits and provision for the execution—subject to bail given—of sentences pending appeal to the King's Council. Instead of execution of the sentence, the party who had obtained judgment for restitution might ask the King from whose subject he had suffered damage to make such restitution himself, provided that the claimant ceded to the sovereign concerned all actions and claims against the delinquent.[26] It was probably due to this Treaty that the Admiralty Court, whose records commence about 1520, was resuscitated[27] and a new tribunal subsequently created for the trial of piracy as a criminal offence.[28]

Open and Just War

The analysis of the material examined so far yields two clear results. Sovereigns were anxious to eliminate private war and attempted to do so by bringing reprisals under their control and by taking severe measures against piracy. Thus, there is a noticeable trend from private war to public war. Equally, the disadvantages of indiscriminate violence or *procès de fait* [29] were such as to lead to the establishment of states of truce and peace on a treaty basis between parties to such treaties and third Powers for whose adhesion provision was made.

If a sovereign resorted to war in breach of treaties of truce or peace, such breach of treaty might be considered by the other side as illegal.[30] Similarly, the opening of hostilities without formal *diffidatio* was regarded as a breach of custom, though not necessarily

---

[26] 13 *Rymer*, pp. 649–653.

[27] 1 Marsden, *Law and Custom*, p. 149. On the origin of the Admiralty Court in the fourteenth century owing to difficulties experienced in connection with foreign claims regarding piratical spoliation, see 1 Marsden, *Select Pleas*, pp. xiv and xxxv–xxxvi.

[28] Statutes of 1536 and 1537 (27 Hen. VIII, c. 4, and 28 Hen. VIII, c. 15). See also *State Papers (Domestic)*, *Eliz.*, vol. 135, which is a mine of information on piracy and the *status mixtus* between peace and war of that period.

[29] Term used in the Renunciation of War by the Sons and Magnates of the King of France, October 24, 1360 (6 *Rymer*, p. 270).

In other documents, such *de facto* war is called *via facti* or *omnis facti actus*. See, for instance, the powers granted by King Henry VI for the conclusion of a truce with King Charles VII of France, June 27, 1444 (3 *Dumont*, Part 1, p. 554).

[30] See, for instance, the announcement by King Henry III regarding the commencement of war with the King of France, June 8, 1242 (3 *Dumont*, Part 1, p. 404); the Letters of May 28 and July 28, 1324, of King Edward II to Pope Johannes XXII (4 *Rymer*, pp. 55 and 75); or the Letter of February 25, 1235, of King Henry III to the Pope (1 *ibid.*, p. 336).

of customary law.[31] Sovereigns during the period under review did not, however, show undue hesitation to lay down in treaties of alliance their respective obligations in case of attack by one of the contracting parties on a third prince.[32]

This circumstance alone suggests caution regarding any inferences from the available material on the illegality of unjust war as distinct from illegal war in breach of treaty obligations. Considering the rather hypocritical use made of this requirement in the State practice of subsequent centuries and the " liberality " of even naturalist Doctrine in this respect,[33] it would be surprising if the result had been otherwise. Then—as subsequently—decisions on policy were made first, and suitable excuses and ideologies were manufactured afterwards. In a letter to the Duke of Buckingham, King Charles I expressed himself with few inhibitions on the subject :

" I have seen a draught of a manifest which ye have sent my Lord Conway, which, if ye have not published, I would wish you to alter one point in it, that whereas ye seem to make the cause of religion the only reason that made me take arms, I would only have you declare it the chief cause, you having no need to name any other ; so that you may leave those of the religion to think what they will ; but think it much inconvenient by a manifest, to be tied only to that cause, of this war ; for cases may happen that may force me to go against my declaration (being penned so) which I should be loth should fall out." [34]

[31] See the above Letter of July 28, 1324 (4 *Ibid.*, p. 75), and above, p. 94, n. 60.
Details regarding the ceremonies to be complied with will be found in 2 *Lettres de Rois*, pp. 495–496.
[32] See, for instance, the exchange of letters between King Edward IV and Duke Charles of Burgundy in 1474 in which they defined in great detail the mutual obligations under their Treaty of Alliance. Accordingly, in the case of a defensive war on the part of one of the contracting parties, the other was bound to give part of the stipulated assistance at his own expense, whereas, " si Bellum non suscipiatur Defensionis Causa, sed alias inferatur, Pars, rogata seu requisita de Auxilio praestando, debebit praebere Parti illud roganti seu requirenti Sex Milia dumtaxat Armatorum sine ullo sumpto suo; et stipiendiabuntur Armati ipsis Expensis illius Partis quae Auxilio uti volet " (11 *Rymer*, p. 809).
[33] See further below, p. 234 *et seq.* and W. Ullmann, *The Medieval Idea of Law as represented by Lucas de Penna* (1946), p. 193.
[34] Letter of August 13, 1627 (Lord Hardwicke's *Miscellaneous State Papers from 1591–1726*, vol. ii (1778), p. 14).
See also the draft of the Letter prepared by the King's Council in 1419 and intended to be sent to the King of France in case of failure of negotiations which were concluded by the Treaties of May 1419 (2 *Lettres de Rois*, p. 359, at 360): " Bellorum remedia ad quae, ob continuatam injuriam atque justitiam denegatam ultimate oportuit in hoc casu habere recursum. . . . Et quia, post tantas et tales instantias ac requisitiones, nullum congruum poterat habere responsum, tunc primum bellum justum suum et praemissorum occasione causatum, indixit et prosecutus est, et prosecutione ejusdem omnipotens Dominus suam justiciam ostendit."
The Letter in which King Henry V notified King Charles VI of France that he considered himself free from the above Treaties unless the King of France executed the Treaties within eight days from the receipt of this Letter, was written in a similar vein: " Sedulo nostrae mentis revolventes intuitu, non sine visceribus compassivis, quod innumeris malis originem et fomentum diutina

V—THE POLITICAL SUPERSTRUCTURE

The primary object of sovereigns in a continuously shifting and inherently dangerous international environment is to strengthen their position both internally and externally. International law could be made to serve both these ends. Treaties of alliance would fulfil the function of defining relations with the enemy's enemies.[35] Allies could be expected to show an interest in one another's internal stability and, on a basis of reciprocity, might be inclined to refuse shelter to rebels or even to extradite them. Other sovereigns might at least be kept out of the enemy's camp, and causes of friction with them could be reduced by defining their position with respect to a war between the other contracting party and a third State. Thus the law of neutrality emerges. Even the law of international political institutions makes its appearance with mediation and arbitration, and the concept of a collective system against the aggressor is used —not for the last time—in order to give ideological cover to a grand alliance.

Treaties of Subsidy and Alliance

It is perhaps symbolic for the place of international law in a system of power politics that the first treaty recorded in Rymer's *Foedera* should be a treaty of subsidy. It was concluded in May 1101 between King Henry I and Count Robert of Flanders and only thinly veiled in a feudal garb. Accordingly, on forty days' notice either by ambassador or letter, the Count would send 500 knights to his ports for transport in the King's ships to England or he would also send them into Normandy or Main if so summoned by the King. In return, the Count was to receive an annual subsidy of 400 marks. The Treaty applied against any enemy of the King of England— " contra omnes homines, qui vivere et mori possint "—with the

ministrat guerrarum tempestas, quas inter inclita Franciae et Angliae regna, ob defectum justitiae, maxima pacis solitae proscriptio suscitavit, ad ipsius reformationem, qua nichil posset in creatis delectabilius concupisci, et pro sedanda clade intestina fidelium, in quantum nostrarum virium se extendit facultas, operas adhibere sategimus efficaces. Ad hoc enim propositi nostri continua in hanc horam anclavit sinceritas, praesertim ex quo, volente Deo, ad regalis fastigii diadema conscendimus; ad hanc nostra in dies sitivit intentio, nam pacis obtentu bella gessimus, hujus desiderio gladio nos accingere curavimus militari, cum ad guerrarum vobiscum ineunda certamina legatis atque licita necessitas nos coegit, non libido dominandi aut ultrix impiaque voluntas " (*ibid.*, pp. 368–369).

35 Though treaties of guarantee were not yet such a prominent feature in early international law as they became subsequently, they were not entirely lacking. See, for instance, the Treaty of Friendship of September 25, 1177, between King Henry II and King Louis VII of France (1 *Dumont*, Part 1, p. 102).

exception of King Louis of France, the Count's liege lord. The Count's duties towards the King of England were also defined for the contingency of an invasion of England by the King of France. If Louis was to plan such a war, the Count would do everything in his power in order to persuade him not to undertake such an enterprise. If, however, Louis was to invade England and bring the Count with him, the latter would supply only as small a contingent as he could afford without forfeiting his fief.[36]

If there is a mutual interest in military assistance, and especially if the contracting parties are about equally matched, alliances on a reciprocal basis meet the need. They may be of a purely defensive character [37] or extend to offensive war [38]; they may be limited to assistance against external enemies [39] or involve assistance also against rebels [40]; they may be bilateral or multilateral.[41]

The centre of interest is the definition of *casus foederis*. From the earliest times onwards,[42] it is realised by the draftsmen of such treaties that, ultimately, the contracting parties have to rely on each other's good faith to carry out their obligations as circumstances may permit. Thus, according to the Treaty of Alliance of May 5, 1367 between King Edward III and the Count of Flanders, each side

[36] 1 *Rymer*, pp. 1–3. In form, this treaty should be classified as a *fief de bourse*, that is to say, as a *fief* with an incorporeal object or, as French theorists sometimes aptly described it, as a *fief en l'air*. On the sublimation of the conception of the *fief* in the *fief de bourse*, see further F. L. Ganshof, *Qu'est-ce que la Féodalité?* (1947), pp. 131–133.

[37] See, for instance, the Defensive League of May 20, 1303, between King Edward I and King Philip IV of France (2 *Rymer*, p. 927).

[38] See, for instance, the Treaty of Confederation of March 31, 1254, between King Henry III and King Alfonso of Castille (1 *Dumont*, Part 1, p. 393), or the Offensive and Defensive League of July 19, 1372 (2 *ibid.*, Part 1, p. 84). See also above, p. 107, note 32.

[39] See, for instance, the Alliances of May 5, 1367, between King Edward III and Count Louis of Flanders (6 *Rymer*, p. 561).

[40] See, for instance, the Treaty of Alliance of June 16, 1373, between King Edward III and King Ferdinand and Queen Eleanor of Portugal (7 *ibid.*, p. 17).

A diplomatic correspondence took place in 1829 between Lord Aberdeen and the Portuguese Foreign Minister on the *casus foederis* under the above and subsequent treaties between England (Great Britain) and Portugal. In it the validity of the above Treaty was recognised to the extent to which it had not been modified by such subsequent treaties. It was, however, maintained by Lord Aberdeen that, whatever might have been the original meaning of these treaties, a practice of long standing had developed, in accordance with which the *casus foederis* had been limited to cases of foreign invasion (16 *British and Foreign State Papers*, p. 424 *et seq.*).

[41] See, for instance, the Alliance of December 7, 1527, between Pope Clement VII, the Kings of France and England and others against the Emperor (4 *Dumont*, Part 1, p. 510); and see below, p. 120 *et seq.*

[42] See the Treaty of Subsidy of 1101 (1 *Rymer*, pp. 1–3): " per fidem, absque malo ingenio " (Art. 2). The bona fide reasons which might have prevented the Count of Flanders from accompanying his contingent to England or to Normandy are enumerated in Arts. 6 and 17 of the Treaty.

undertook to carry out his obligations " come il pourra bonement, en bon foi et conscience, sanz fraude et malengin, despourter en regarde a la distance et prochainetee de Lieu, et Terme ou quiel la Guerre se ferra, et aussi en regard a l'estat du Paiis de Nous qui requis serra." [43]

Sometimes, treaties of this type contain additional clauses by which the parties promise each other not to conclude any separate armistice or peace treaties,[44] or to refuse the right of passage to the enemies of the other party,[45] or they contain stipulations regarding jurisdiction over forces sent in fulfilment of the treaty [46] or regarding the spoils of common victory.[47]

As it appeared to an historian of the law of nations by the end of the eighteenth century, these treaties were far from being merely of antiquarian interest. Ward saw, however, one great difference between the old treaties of alliance and those of his own time : " All the distinction . . . is that our downright ancestors named the very persons against whom the alliance was made, while the modern refinements have confined it chiefly to quotas, and wrapt up the object in general terms." [48]

Treaties of Mutual Insurance

The continuous danger to sovereigns from " overmighty sub- jects " [49] and the risks involved in the alignment of powerful rebels with foreign powers made it advisable for princes to restrict by treaty their right of asylum and, on a basis of reciprocity, to reinsure them- selves against their enemies from within by co-operation with other sovereigns. The need for provision against such contingencies was

---

[43] 6 *Rymer*, p. 561. See also below, p. 125.

[44] See, for instance, the Alliance of July 12, 1337, between King Edward III and Count William *Le Bon* of Holland (1 *Dumont*, Part 2, p. 161).

[45] See, for instance, the Alliance of May 5, 1367, between King Henry III and Count Louis of Flanders (6 *Rymer*, p. 560).

[46] See the Treaty cited on p. 109, n. 36, above, or the Offensive and Defensive Alliance of May 14, 1596, between Queen Elizabeth and King Henry IV of France (5 *Dumont*, Part 1, 526).

[47] See, for instance, the Alliance of August 1, 1351, between King Edward III and King Charles of Navarre (1 *ibid.*, Part 2, p. 265).

[48] 2 Ward, *op. cit.*, vol. ii, p. 190.

[49] This position found its ideological reflection in the medieval doctrine of the right of resistance to a *rex injustus*. The risks resulting from such claims were increased by the interest that, in time of conflict between State and Church, might be taken by the Pope in the causes of such rebels and the claim of the Church to be entitled in certain contingencies to discharge the king's subjects from their oath of fealty. See further Gierke, *op. cit.*, p. 15, n. 34, and p. 117; and F. Kern, *Kingship and Law in the Middle Ages* (transl. by S. B. Chrimes) (1939), pp. 81 *et seq.* and 194 *et seq.*

especially pressing when sovereigns expected to be absent for pro-longed periods from their realms.

Thus, the Treaty of September 25, 1177 between King Henry II and King Louis of France, in which they bound themselves to take the Cross, contains a clause to this effect. Both sides undertook to banish on request each other's enemies from their dominions.[50] Another treaty concluded twelve years later between King Richard I and King Philip of France—again with a crusade in view—provided for the mutual extradition of wrongdoers.[51]

It becomes, however, apparent from other treaties that sovereigns desired to have at their disposal an alternative to a possibly highly embarrassing extradition. This was either banishment [52] or punishment of the offender in the country where he had found refuge.[53] Persons assisting fugitive rebels might be liable to the same treatment as the rebels themselves,[54] and sovereigns might agree to furnish each other with information regarding the plans of rebels which would come to their ears.[55]

Probably the most far-reaching attempt at mutual insurance between sovereigns was the Treaty of Friendship of August 29, 1475 between King Edward IV and King Louis XI of France. The agreement provided for mutual assistance against each other's rebels and then dealt with the obligations of the two parties in case—*quod Deus avertat*—one of them should be expelled from his country owing to the " disobedience of his subjects." Then it became the duty of the other contracting party to receive the exiled sovereign *omni cum humanitate* and to assist him by all means in his power to achieve restoration.[56]

---

[50] 1 *Rymer*, p. 50. On the medieval attitude to rebellion as the most practicable means of redress, see Taswell-Langmead, *op. cit.*, p. 98 (*c*).

[51] December 30, 1189 (1 *Dumont*, Part 1, p. 379).

[52] See, for instance, the Treaty of 1373 with Portugal (7 *Rymer*, pp. 20–21).

[53] " Inimicos et Rebelles alterius eorumdem, ut eorum proprios et Capitales Inimicos, Vitare, Persequi et Destruere totis Viribus teneantur " (Treaty of March 11, 1471, between King Edward IV and King Alfonso V of Portugal: 11 *Rymer*, p. 742).

[54] Treaty of September 28, 1473, between King Edward IV and King James III of Scotland (3 *Dumont*, Part 1, p. 462).

[55] Treaty of Truce and Commerce of February 16, 1471, between King Edward IV and King Louis XI of France (11 *Rymer*, p. 688).
    The Truce of March 31, 1438, between King Henry VI and King James II of Scotland contains an interesting clause on the revocation of safe-conducts of fugitives and the postponement of acceptance of allegiance on their part at the request of the other contracting party (10 *ibid.*, p. 693), and provides further that " non admittentur nec recipientur ad Officia, nec super Assisas, nec ad perhibendum Testimonium Personae Infames, Rebelles, Fugitivi, Proditores unius Partis vel alterius, aut Convicti per Assisam; sed boni, fideles, justi, fidedigni, et insuspectae Personae " (*ibid.*, p. 694).

[56] 12 *ibid.*, pp. 19–20.

Neutrality

The early law in this field was based on a simple major premise. It was that, unless the contrary was established by treaty, all foreign princes and their subjects might be treated as enemies.[57] Whether met on land or sea, they were fair prey. If a foreign prince or his subjects were to expect any different treatment, they had to show that they were in a state of amity with the other Power concerned or at least protected by a treaty of truce or special safe-conducts.

If foreign merchants entrusted their goods to enemy ships, such cargo would be treated as being infected with enemy character. If enemy property was found in neutral ships, it was already considered a concession if such neutral ships and the neutral cargo on board were not made to share the fate of enemy goods. If neutrals carried their own goods to the enemy, they brought comfort to the enemy. The most they could hope for was that a distinction would be made between goods which were more directly useful for the prosecution of war and others which might escape being treated as contraband.

In order to avoid the pitfalls of anachronism, it is equally essential to recall the peculiar structure of medieval trade, which was very different from that of the subsequent liberal era, during which the classical conception of neutrality flourished. The medieval trader worked within a mercantilist system in which the direct advantages of foreign trade to princes and their realms were very consciously perceived. There was, therefore, little inclination—or reason—to distinguish between the rights and duties of neutral princes and those of " innocent " merchants.

It has often been asserted that, in those days, there was no scope for neutrality. The character of the Holy Roman Empire, the division of the world between believers and unbelievers, and other more or less convincing arguments have been put forward in favour of this thesis.[58] It may be admitted that the term " neutrality " dates back only to the fifteenth century.[59] The substance of the problem, however, existed long before. This could hardly have been otherwise; for the conditions of neutrality were pre-eminently fulfilled by the system of medieval power politics. A sufficient number of at least *de facto* sovereign States existed. While some of these were linked by a network of alliances, others held themselves

---

[57] See above, p. 59 *et seq.*
[58] See above, p. 43.
[59] *Cf.* E. Nys, *Études de Droit International et de Droit Politique*, 2e série (1901), p. 58.

free to side with one or the other camp or to remain friends with both.

This situation is well described in the first English Proclamation of Neutrality. It was issued in 1536 by King Henry VIII during the war between the Emperor and the King of France, and by it English subjects were enjoined on pain of forfeiture of goods and imprisonment no longer to cloak the goods of either French or Flemish as their own to the detriment of either belligerent. The explanation given for such detachment deserves to be quoted in full :

"His Highnes is knit in league and amity with either of the said Princes, not entending without honest and just occasions to violate the same, but so to order and direct himself and his subjects in all his proceedings that no manner of suspicion of the leaneing more to the one parte than to the other shall appear in anie time in his grace, but that alwayes he may declare himself in this poynt of neutrality upright and indifferent, as to a Prince of honour, troth, and virtue, apperteyneth." [60]

Owing to their particular position in the system of medieval international relations, the kings of England were more often belligerents than neutrals. Their sea-power made them more inclined to stress the rights of belligerents at sea than the interests of neutral commerce. Yet the use of their power had to be tempered by consideration for the interests of other Powers which they could ignore only at their peril. Thus, the medieval law of neutrality developed according to a logic of its own and on lines which link it organically with subsequent phases in the legal relations between belligerents and neutrals.

In the nature of things, England was primarily concerned with the rights and duties of neutrals in sea warfare. What was the position of neutral goods on enemy ships and vice versa? Might neutrals carry their own goods in their own ships to belligerents? Had belligerents the right of visit and search? By what procedure was the enemy character of ships and cargo or their classification as contraband to be determined?

Each of these questions arose and had to be answered. In the first instance, such issues were treated as questions within the king's discretion,[61] and not as questions of international rights and duties. Yet, out of the customary treatment of typical cases and recurrent

[60] 1 Marsden, *Law and Custom*, pp. 149–150.
   For the refinements introduced by auxiliary treaties concluded since the thirteenth century in accordance with which princes could be at war with each other in certain territories, while remaining at peace with one another regarding others, *cf.* Ward, *op. cit.*, vol. ii, p. 174 *et seq.*
[61] See further below, p. 118 *et seq.*

diplomatic controversies, patterns of a rather stereotyped character developed. The rules of the *Consolato del Mare* recommended themselves widely to princes and merchants alike. Again, treaties provided the most convenient means of guaranteeing that such treatment would be granted as a matter of right, of defining precisely the rights and duties of the contracting parties, and of departing from the regular procedure in favour of Powers who could expect and, in return, would be willing to offer, preferential treatment.

Neutral Goods on Enemy Ships

In English practice, the position of neutral cargo on enemy ships was regulated by the simple rule that, like the enemy ship itself, it was good prize of war.[62] In the Grant of the Custody of the Sea to the Earl of Salisbury of 1445 it was expressly mentioned that the same treatment also applied to English goods found on enemy vessels.[63] The fact that the rule " The enemy flag covers friends' goods " was embodied in the *Consolato del Mare* offers evidence of the realistic character of the " Good Customs of the Sea " ; for this rule would naturally recommend itself to any strong sea Power. In a sixteenth-century Order in Council, the resort to this principle was further justified on the ground that " the Frenchemen have lawes and doo putt the same in execution against the subjects of this realme whiche the counsell think convenient to be kepte lykewise towardes them." [64] On the other hand, it might be agreed on a reciprocal basis to exempt from capture the goods on enemy ships of subjects of the other contracting party.[65]

---

[62] It has been held that, in this respect, English practice was less liberal than the general medieval rule. See, for instance, F. R. Sanborn, *Origins of the Early English Maritime and Commercial Law* (1930), p. 323.

Chap. 231 of the *Consolato del Mare*, however, merely suggests the advisability of a compact in such cases between the admiral and the neutral merchants " for a suitable price according as they may be able " (3 *Rolls Series*, p. 543).

An instance of a more liberal English practice regarding an enemy ship chartered by neutrals deserves to be mentioned. The *Seint Alphines*, a Castilian (enemy) ship, had been chartered by Aragonese (friendly) merchants and in Aragon " ad usum et commodum dictorum Mercatorum Arragoniae onerata et carcata fuerit." The case was reviewed by the King's Council on December 5, 1386. Held that the goods, or their true value, be restored to the claimants, but the ship " quia fuit de parte adversa remaneat forisfacta et quod pro fretto bonorum et mercandisarum predictorum satisfiat." Baldwin, *op. cit.*, Appendix III, p. 510. See also Perroy, *op. cit.*, pp. 41 and 199.

[63] 1 Marsden, *Law and Custom*, p. 117.

The same principle was laid down in the Act of 1441 (20 Hen. VI, c. 1).

[64] Marsden, *Law and Custom*, pp. 165–166.

[65] See, for instance, the Treaty of Truce of August 1, 1351, between King Edward III and the King of Castille (5 *Rymer*, p. 719).

Enemy Goods on Neutral Ships

There is a fair number of treaties concluded by the kings of England since the thirteenth century, in which the parties promised each other to prohibit their subjects from carrying enemy goods in their ships. Merchants might then have to be furnished with official papers issued by their home authorities stating that ship, crew, and cargo were of a friendly character.[66] Sometimes it was expressly provided that the testimony under oath of the master or merchants should be regarded as sufficient evidence of the friendly nature of the cargo.[67]

From the manner in which this type of clause was formulated, namely, that masters and merchants were to admit honestly, if asked, the presence on board of enemy goods, it may be concluded that though such carriage was in contravention of treaty obligations, in such a case, neutral merchants had not to fear more than condemnation as good prize of such enemy cargo and not condemnation of the ships as well. This milder practice avoided the inconveniences of the more extreme solution introduced by France in the sixteenth century,[68] and adopted by way of reciprocity in an English Order in Council of 1557.[69] That this compromise between the interests of belligerents and neutrals met with general approval is proved by the fact that it was incorporated in the *Consolato del Mare*.[70] In accordance with these " Good Customs of the Sea," the managing owner of the ship even received his freight charges to the place where he intended to discharge his cargo.

Since the fourteenth century English practice adopted this equitable principle.[71] It becomes evident, however, from the cases of *The*

[66] See, for instance, the Treaty of August 4, 1370, between King Edward III and the Count of Flanders (6 *ibid.*, p. 660).

[67] See, for instance, the Treaty of Truce and Commerce of February 13, 1460, between King Henry VI and the Republic of Genoa (3 *Dumont*, Part 1, p. 583).

[68] *Edit* of King Francis I of 1543. *Cf.* Sir Robert Phillimore, *Commentaries upon International Law*, vol. iii (1885), p. 310. For the text of the French Ordinance of 1560 see 2 Marsden, *Select Pleas*, p. 119.

[69] " In case that enemy goods are found in friends' ships or friends' goods in enemy ships, then the whole shal be judged to be of goode prise " (1 Marsden, *Law and Custom*, pp. 165–166).

[70] 3 *Rolls Series*, p. 539. On a relevant case which arose in 1164 in the war between Genoa and Pisa and in which an Egyptian ship was involved, see J. M. Pardessus, *Lois Maritimes Antérieurs au Dix-Huitième Siècle*, vol. ii (1828), p. 122, and Sereni, *op. cit.*, pp. 53–55.

[71] *Cf.* the cases of *The St. Anne* (1375) and *The Ships of Flanders* (1378), 1 Marsden, *Law and Custom*, pp. 102 and 106, and on the subsequent practice until the Declaration of Paris of 1856 see Phillimore, *op. cit.*, vol. iii, pp. 753–755.

Two Ships of Bruges (1327) [72] and *The Matye Sterlyng* (1373) [73] that, first, the condemnation of enemy cargo on neutral ships was considered to be the exercise of a well-established right,[74] secondly, the release of the neutral ship and cargo, and payment of freight for the condemned enemy goods could only be expected by subjects of princes linked with the kings of England by treaties of truce or peace,[75] and thirdly, as was emphasised in the second case, rather as a matter of grace than of right.[76]

Exceptionally, treaties embodied the rule of " Free Ship, Free Goods." Thus, in the Treaty of August 5, 1357, between King Edward III and the King of Castille, it was agreed that Castilian ships should be entitled to carry goods belonging to subjects of the King of France who then was at war with the King of England. As was explained in the Treaty, reciprocity was achieved by a corresponding treaty between the Kings of Castille and France, according to which the King of France undertook to leave English goods in Castilian ships unmolested.[77]

Contraband

A major problem still to be settled in connection with neutral trade to belligerent countries was the question of neutral cargoes in neutral ships destined for belligerent countries. The only basis of demands for the restriction of such trade was self-interest, backed by compelling sea-power. The sole equivalent that, apart from increased trade with the State making such a request, could be held out to neutral princes was reciprocal treatment in a similar contingency.

Thus, when King Edward III asked the Count of Holland not to supply his Scottish enemies with ships, he concluded his letter with the invitation that " whenever it is in our power to gratify you in a

---

[72] The ships belonged to citizens of Bruges and were arrested in the course of the war between England and Scotland on the charge of carrying goods belonging to Scotsmen. The Order of King Edward III of December 22, 1337, for the release of the ships with payment of freight for any Scottish goods found aboard will be found in 4 *Rymer*, p. 328.

[73] A Portuguese ship arrested during the war against Henry, the Bastard of Spain. For the Order of King Edward III for the release of the ship on the same terms as above of February 20, 1373, see 7 *ibid.*, p. 3.

[74] According to Chap. 231 of the *Consolato del Mare*, in this case the admiral of the armed ship might force and constrain the master of the captured ship to " carry *as a matter of obligation* the enemy's property and to keep it safe on board his ship or vessel until it is in a place of safety " (3 *Rolls Series*, p. 539).

[75] *Cf.* for a much more strictly formulated safe-conduct for the Catalan galley *St. Mary*, issued in 1374, 1 Marsden, *Law and Custom*, p. 97.

[76] " Volentes cum eisdem agere gratiose " (7 *Rymer*, p. 3).

[77] 6 *ibid.*, p. 29.

like case, may you write to us as we are now writing to you." [78] In isolated cases, it might be agreed, as was done in the Treaty of May 20, 1303, between King Edward I and the King of France, that they would not give, nor suffer to be given, any assistance to each other's enemies, and arms and victuals were merely mentioned as especially important classes of contraband.[79] Yet, as a rule, neutrals could not be induced to forgo altogether trade with belligerents.

An equilibrium—albeit rather unstable—was reached between the interest in curtailing such trade when England was at war, and those of neutrals in its maintenance by singling out trade in goods which were of most direct assistance to the enemy in the prosecution of war. As is shown by an Order of 1293 for the arrest of German and Frisian ships, suspected of contraband trade with France, the then prevailing view treated as contraband "horses, boards, arms, and divers merchandises, which they were intending to carry to Flanders and elsewhere in the Kingdom of France, for the use of our enemies." [8c] The Treaty of August 4, 1370, between King Edward III and the Count of Flanders provides an instance of a rather narrow definition of contraband goods. They were limited to *armures, artilliers, ou vitailles*.[81] The practice and treaties of this period did not differ in kind from subsequent unilateral proclamations regarding contraband or treaties on the subject,[82] and, in common with them, they failed to solve the clash of antagonistic interests on any other than a purely pragmatic basis. Yet the Treaty of 1357 between King Edward III and the King of Castille, already referred to in another connection,[83] shows that the possibility of permitting completely unrestricted trade relations between neutrals and belligerents was not beyond the grasp of the early draftsmen. Nevertheless, this pattern imposed restraints on the use of sea-power to an extent which did not recommend itself for general adoption. In times to come, less liberal practices would be based on "that supreme lawe of government ingrafted by nature in the hart of every souverain Prince,

[78] Letter of November 3, 1336 (1 Marsden, *Law and Custom*, p. 65).
[79] 2 *Rymer*, p. 927.
[80] 1 Marsden, *Law and Custom*, p. 22. See *ibid.*, at p. 21, for a detailed enumeration of the " divers merchandises."
[81] 6 *Rymer*, p. 660.
[82] See, for instance, on the English practice since Queen Elizabeth I's Proclamation of 1589 until the beginning of the seventeenth century, the Certificate by the Lord High Admiral of 1601 (1 Marsden, *Law and Custom*, pp. 317–318), and on seventeenth-century practice in general, R. Lee, *A Treatise of Captures in War* (1759), p. 154 *et seq.*
[83] See 6 *Rymer*, p. 660.

warranted by the lawe of God, and confirmed by the continuall practice of her neighbour nations in these latter times." [84]

Right of Visit and Search

Doctrines on the freedom of the sea since the seventeenth century are based on the assumption that any restriction of such freedom is the exception rather than the rule. Thus, the right of visit and search is explained as one of the limitations which a neutral merchant ship has to suffer under international customary law. Such rationalisations became justified when war was no longer the initial hypothesis of all argument. In the age of medieval international law there was no need for any special justification of the right of visit and search. It was implied in the right of capture of any ship that was not expressly exempted from such treatment.

Thus, the right of examination of ships on the high seas was rather a safeguard for ships partaking of privileged treatment under treaties or safe-conducts. In the case of *The Seint Alphines* before the King's Council (1386), this right was taken for granted as well established [85] and it was equally so treated in the war-time instructions to the Lord Admiral which are to be found in the *Black Book of the Admiralty*.[86] If a ship should offer resistance, then, in the words of the instructions issued by King Henry VIII in 1512,[87] it was lawful to capture such ship " with strong hand " and to bring her " holy and entierly to the said Admiral without dispoyllyng, rifelying, or embeselyng of the goods, or doing harme to the parties, ther t'abyde th' ordinance of the lawe as the saide Admirall shall awarde."

Prize Courts

According to English constitutional doctrine, which dates back to the thirteenth century, all prize is a *Droit* of the Crown and can

---

[84] Proclamation by Queen Elizabeth of about 1601, prohibiting trade with Spain and Portugal, justified, *inter alia*, by the " dishonourable and unworthie " practices of the late King of Spain of seeking the assistance of " traiterous and disloyall subjects " of hers (1 Marsden, *Law and Custom*, p. 313, at 315).

See also E. P. Cheyney, " International Law under Queen Elizabeth," in *English Historical Review*, 20 (1905), p. 659 *et seq.*, and Ph. C. Jessup and F. Déak *Neutrality*, vol. i : *The Origins* (1935), p. 52 *et seq.*

On the relatively late development of blockade in the technical sense, see Jessup and Déak, *op. cit.*, vol. i, p. 105 *et seq.*

[85] Baldwin, *op. cit.*, p. 508. See also above, p. 114.
[86] Rule 7 (*Black Book of the Admiralty*, p. 29).
[87] 13 *Rymer*, p. 331.

become the property of the captors only by royal grant.[88]   Already in order to secure the king's own rights, it became necessary to establish some sort of procedure by which it could be established whether a prize was good and lawful.   Until the sixteenth century there was not, however, any prize court of a permanent character, and matters were dealt with on an *ad hoc* basis.   Thus, in 1373, King Edward III charged Andreas de Tyndale with an inquiry regarding several ships captured on the high seas.[89]   Such improvisation was sufficient as long as the questions at issue were primarily those between king and captors.

The situation changed when foreign merchants could increasingly demand as of right exemption of their ships and cargoes from capture. Such claims might be based on individual safe-conducts or on treaties of truce, peace, alliance, or neutrality.[90]   If the rights of foreign subjects were ignored, the matter might be raised on a diplomatic level and referred by the king to his council.[91]   Or, as happened in the case of the Treaty of 1414 between King Henry V and the Duke of Brittany, the contracting parties might provide in the treaties themselves for the judicial settlement of prize cases,[92] or for their examination by the Admiral or his deputies.[93]

The growing number of such treaties establishing standards for the treatment of foreign merchants, and the convenience which resulted from the possibility of answering diplomatic protests by reference to the existence of competent judicial organs, finally led to the recognition of the High Court of Admiralty in the sixteenth century as the proper court for proceedings in prize.   The High Court would primarily apply the law maritime, which meant civil law, and international law only to the extent to which safe-conducts and treaties

---

[88] See, for instance, the grant in 1205 by King John to a captor of half of his prizes (1 Marsden, *Law and Custom*, p. 1); the right granted by King Henry III on August 4, 1242, to the citizens of Bayonne to keep half of the prizes made during the war with France (1 *Rymer*, p. 408); or the case of *The Cog of Flanders* (1337), in which King Edward III granted to the captors " the aforesaid ship and all her apparel, which, as a capture from our enemies aforesaid, belongs to us " (1 Marsden, *Law and Custom*, p. 66). According to Rule 19 of the *Black Book of the Admiralty*, the King's share in prize was one quarter (1 *Rolls Series*, p. 21).

[89] 7 *Rymer*, p. 29.

[90] See, for instance, the Reply of the King's Council to the masters and merchants of Castille and Biscay of July 18, 1369 (Baldwin, *op. cit.*, pp. 487–488), and the Proclamation of King Henry VI of 1426 (10 *Rymer*, p. 368).

[91] *Cf.* the case of *The Seint Alphines* (1386), referred to above, pp. 114 and 118.

[92] 9 *Rymer*, p. 84.

[93] Art. 14 of the Treaty of Peace and Commerce of May 24, 1497, between King Henry VII and King Charles VIII of France (3 *Dumont*, Part 2, p. 377). See also the case of *The Saint Salvador* (1357), 6 *Rymer*, p. 14.

imposed limitations on municipal law. Its procedure was the general procedure in use in ecclesiastical courts. It was supplemented gradually by specific rules made necessary by the technical character of prize cases and treaty undertakings for the speeding up of—and other improvements in—prize court proceedings.[94]

Pacific Settlement of International Disputes

In the course of the negotiations between England and France for the settlement of the French piracy claims, Richard de Graveshende set out in 1297 four possibilities for the peaceful settlement of these claims. The " apésement " could be achieved " par voie trétié, ou de ordenance, ou de amiable composicion, ou de arbitre." [95] English State practice shows that all these methods were tried at times, and proved as effective as in any system of power politics. That is to say that, whenever reasons of a dynastic character or other considerations made a peaceful solution advisable, there was no difficulty in finding the appropriate legal forms for the pacific settlement of disputes.

Apart from the interest of the Church in peaceful relations between Christian sovereigns—especially at times when the Holy See wished to see all their efforts concentrated on Crusades against the infidels— two other circumstances favoured mediation and abitration during this period. Most of the princes of Christendom were related to one another by birth or marriage. Furthermore, there was not then that difference between sovereign princes and other mortals which made the pacific settlement of disputes between them a problem different in kind from that of other quarrels between medieval nobles.[96] It required the rise of the Renaissance State to throw doubt on the possibility whether suitable judges could be found for the settlement of disputes between " supreme princes." [97]

Three instances of mediation in the time of Edward I may be mentioned. King Edward I offered his mediation to King Philip le Hardi of France in the latter's dispute with the King of Castille. It

---

94 See above, p. 104 *et seq.*, and further, R. G. Marsden, " Early Prize Jurisdiction and Prize Law in England," in *English Historical Review*, 24 (1909), p. 675 *et seq.*, and E. S. Roscoe, " Prize Court Procedure," in 2 *B.Y.I.L.* (1921), p. 90 *et seq.*

95 1 *Lettres de Rois*, pp. 427–428.

96 See, for instance, the *Compromis* between King Edward I and the Bishop and Chapter of Bazas for arbitration on the jurisdiction over Bazadois of August 26, 1283 (*ibid.*, p. 320) and the judgment rendered in the same year (*ibid.*, p. 324).

97 Letter of Queen Elizabeth to Emperor Rudolph, April 21, 1593 (16 *Rymer*, p. 206).

was refused on the ground that the Pope had already offered mediation.[98] Edward I also mediated in the dispute over Sicily between
the Houses of Anjou and Aragon, and, through his mediation, a truce
was concluded in the year 1286.[99] In 1396 King Richard II accepted
the offer of the Duke of Bavaria to act as " médiatour et moieu entre
nous et notre adversaire de France." [1]

Arbitration was not essentially different from the *ad hoc* tribunals
of subsequent periods. It might be entrusted to the Pope,[2] to a king
in amity with both disputants,[3] to an equal number of arbitrators
appointed by each side,[4] or to the ambassadors of the contestants
with a possible reference, in case of disagreement between the
ambassadors, to umpires selected by neutral princes.[5]

The *compromis* concluded in 1176 between the Kings of Castille
and Navarre may serve as an illustration of this type of treaty. The
contracting parties submitted their disputes to the arbitration of King
Henry II. The King of Castille was the son-in-law of Henry II, and
the King of Navarre was his uncle. Each of the parties was to give
four named castles as security that he would comply with the judgment. The parties undertook to send within a specified time ambassadors to England to argue their cases before Henry II and to receive
judgment.

The *compromis* contained detailed provisions for contingencies
such as delay on the part of the ambassadors owing to illness or
captivity. While, in such cases, the castles would not be forfeited,
it would be otherwise if, without good reason, the ambassadors failed
to make their appearance before the English Court. In the case of
the death of the arbitrator, the King of France was to be his substitute. Furthermore, the parties agreed to a seven years' truce, made
provision against its infringement, stipulated to settle by arbitration
any new dispute that might arise between them, and agreed to carry
out the treaty in good faith and without bad intentions.[6]

[98] Letter of King Philip le Hardi to King Edward I, December 6, 1281 (1 *Lettres
de Rois*, p. 286).
[99] 2 *Rymer*, p. 330. See also *ibid*., p. 501.
[1] 2 *Lettres de Rois*, p. 288.
[2] See, for instance, the arbitration between King Edward I and King Philip of
France of 1298 (1 *Dumont*, Part 1, p. 308 *et seq.*)
[3] See, for instance, the Treaty of September 24, 1176, between the Kings of Castille
and Navarre, to accept judgment from King Henry II of England (1 *Rymer*,
p. 43).
[4] See, for instance, the Treaty of April 23, 1294, between King Edward I and the
King of Portugal (2 *ibid*., p. 632).
[5] See, for instance, the Treaty of March 16, 1474, between King Edward IV and
King Christiernus of Denmark (3 *Dumont*, Part 1, p. 528).
[6] 1 *Rymer*, pp. 43–44.

This Treaty is typical of the numerous arbitration treaties which were subsequently concluded. They have in common a very wide formulation of the issues which were considered to be justiciable and a tendency to settle matters *in amicitia aut jure* rather than on the basis of strict law.[7] This will explain why, frequently, the *compromis* was not followed by a judgment, or such a decision was superseded by the turmoil of war between the parties to such treaties.

The offers of various kings of England to settle their disputes with foreign princes by ordeal of battle—either alone or accompanied by a number of their knights—may be mentioned as *curiosa* of merely tactical significance. They were never accepted, and were not meant to be taken too seriously.[8]

The attempts at power politics in ideological disguise in the later part of the medieval period are of greater interest. Fifteenth-century diplomacy was fully alive to these possibilities, and this approach to international affairs was well formulated in a letter sent in 1419 by King Henry V to King Charles VI of France. It put the matter in a nutshell : " Aliud agitur et aliud agi simulatur." [9] This might well have been the motto of the Italian League, promoted by the Pope and adhered to by several of the most powerful European princes, including King Henry VII.

In Henry VII's letter of accession of 1496 the League's purposes were described as being to serve peace, maintain the dignity and authority of the Holy See, and to promote the Christian religion. The union was to last for a minimum period of twenty-five years. The members guaranteed to each other their territorial possessions against any disturbance. The Covenant provided for peaceful settlement of disputes, for assistance to the victim of aggression, and for support from the Pope with his " spiritual weapons." Members of the League were not to conclude separate peace treaties, and any

---

[7] See, for instance, the Treaty cited above on p. 121, n. 5, and Cuttino, *op. cit.*, p. 49 *et seq.*

[8] See, for instance, the Letter of King Edward III to King Philip of France, July 26, 1340 (1 *Dumont*, part 2, p. 189), and the latter's reply (*ibid.*, p. 196). See also Selden, *Jani Anglorum Facies Altera* (1683), Book I, Chap. 19.

[9] 2 *Lettres de Rois*, p. 371.

Probably the earliest attempt made in English practice to enlist academic support for purposes of foreign policy was Edward I's invitation to the Universities of Oxford and Cambridge to refute the Pope's claim to the Kingdom of Scotland as a fief of the Roman Church, as set out in the Pope's Bull of 1299. Edward's reply of the following year which was never sent, but served its purpose as an appeal to public opinion at home, commenced with a description of " how Brutus of Troj after her distruction came to Albion " and proceeded from this solid basis to a demonstration of the superior English claims to Scotland (1 *Dumont*, Part 1, p. 322).

territories of a member which had been invaded were to be restored to the victim of aggression.[10]

In spite of its noble language, the Treaty was nothing but a grand alliance in disguise against France. In the following year, however, King Henry VII thought it wise to reinsure himself by a treaty of peace and commerce with King Charles VIII of France.[11] The League of Cambray, to which Henry VIII adhered in the year 1512,[12] and the Treaty of General Peace and Concord of 1518 against the Turks [13] were conceived in the same spirit. The possibilities inherent in the use of the political superstructure of international law for ideological purposes had become fully apparent.

VI—THE ECONOMIC SUPERSTRUCTURE

As in the political field war must be considered as the initial hypothesis, so in the economic field we must start from the basic assumption that the individual is rightless abroad. However, just as there were good reasons why there should be a minimum of stability and calculability in political affairs, there were corresponding tendencies in the economic field. They received strong support from the doctrines of medieval bullionism, as this type of mercantilism is aptly described.

Thus, it was ordained in the Statute of the Staple that foreign merchants should be under the king's protection and only pay the ancient customs in order " to replenish the said Realm and Lands with Money and Plate, Gold and Silver, and Merchandises of other Lands, and to give Courage to Merchant Strangers to come with their Wares and Merchandises into the Realm and Lands aforesaid." [14]

As becomes apparent from Letters of Marque and Reprisals issued against the Genoese in 1413, equal attention was paid for the same reasons to the export trade, and the merchandises mentioned in these Letters had been sent " to Western parts, there to be sold for the advantage and increase of Our Realm." [15]

The more far-sighted among the medieval princes furthered these objects of commercial policy by unilateral enactments under their own systems of municipal law and guaranteed to foreign merchants safe

[10] 12 *Rymer*, p. 638.
[11] 3 *Dumont*, Part 2, p. 376.
[12] 13 *Rymer*, pp. 305 and 323.
[13] *Ibid.*, pp. 621 and 623.
[14] 1353 (27 Edw. III, Stat. 2, c. 2).
[15] 8 *Rymer*, p. 773.

entry and stay in their realms and unhindered exit from them. As
becomes evident from Article 41 of Magna Carta, provided that
English merchants received reciprocal treatment, even enemy merchants could expect to continue their trade in England during war
as in time of peace.[16]

Within the compass of this Chapter, it is not possible to describe
in detail the growth of international economic law as applied in early
English practice.[17] The general trend, however, can be sketched
in brief.

The first stage in the evolution was characterised by an increasingly liberal grant of safe-conducts to individual foreign merchants.[18]
The mutual interests of princes in foreign trade secured as a rule a
de facto reciprocity in the grant and scope of such safe-conducts.

It was, however, soon found convenient to secure the right of
safe-conducts for each other's merchants on a treaty basis and, thus,
to establish *de jure* reciprocity of treatment in this field. Princes
might consent only to deal with each individual application for a safe-
conduct on its merits[19] or agree to grant safe-conducts if, and when,
required.[20] If trade relations between two countries became sufficiently close they might stipulate that, by virtue of the treaty, their
merchants should be considered for the duration of the treaty to be
under their safe-conduct[21] and not to require any general or special
safe-conduct beyond the treaty itself.[22]

From this second phase, it was only one further step to provide
positively for mutual freedom of commerce between all subjects of
contracting parties. It was usual both to stipulate general standards
of treatment and the enjoyment of especially important rights.
Among the general standards, those of national and most-favoured-
nation treatment were of particular importance.[23] Individual rights
which for a long time were enumerated in detail in commercial

---

16 See further below, p. 133 *et seq.*
    For the case of the arrest of French merchants in England in 1242, following
    the arrest of English merchants in France, see Nicolas, *op. cit.*, vol. i, pp. 198–
    199.
17 See also below, pp. 133 and 210 *et seq.*
18 See, for instance, the Letter of September 13, 1215, of King John to King Philip
    of France (1 *Rymer*, p. 207).
19 Treaty of Peace and Friendship of January 24, 1501, between King Henry VII
    and King Jacob IV of Scotland (4 *Dumont*, Part 1, p. 24).
20 Treaty of February 12, 1479, between King Edward IV and King Christiernus
    of Denmark (3 *ibid.*, Part 2, p. 66).
21 Treaty of Peace and Friendship of October 20, 1468, between King Edward IV
    and King Johan of Aragon (*ibid.*, Part 1, p. 600).
22 Treaty of Perpetual Friendship of July 25, 1474, between King Edward IV and
    the Duke of Burgundy (*ibid.*, p. 485).
23 See further below, p. 219 *et seq.*, and 22 *B.Y.I.L.* (1945), p. 96 *et seq.*

treaties, were those of the protection of the person, liberty, and property of foreign merchants and their free access to local courts.[24] From the point of view of the general development of international law, this latter type of treaty clause is of special significance. It consists in the fact that most of these rights found general acceptance in the course of centuries of constant treaty practice and became gradually embodied in international customary law.

In order to see the picture of the economic superstructure of medieval international law in its proper perspective, it is necessary to remember the security which commerce received indirectly from some of the treaties in the political field. Apart from the basic treaties of truce and peace, those limiting reprisals, providing against denial and delay of justice, stipulating for effective measures against piracy, and determining the rights of neutral merchants should be recalled.[25]

VII—THE CHARACTER AND BINDING FORCE OF MEDIEVAL INTERNATIONAL LAW

The examination of early English practice in international law permits tentative generalisations on the character of medieval international law. Even in so far as English practice is concerned, these results are very provisional and require to be tested especially in the light of the manuscript material which it has not yet been possible to use for this paper. Equally essential are parallel investigations regarding the practice of other countries and the comparative analysis of such case studies. Only then will it be possible to arrive at conclusions of more finality than is possible at this stage.

The Predominance of Treaties

The overriding feature is the predominance of treaties as compared with international customary law. At first sight, it might be suspected that this is merely due to the greater difficulties in preserving the knowledge of the unwritten law. That this is not the real answer can be shown in several ways.

Records of customary maritime law such as the *Consolato del Mare*, the Laws of Oléron, or the Black Book of the Admiralty present a wealth of rules of customary law in fields where such customs existed, that is to say between merchants and merchants.

---

[24] See, for instance, the Treaty cited below on p. 126, n. 27.
[25] See above, p. 96 *et seq.*

The very fact that these compilations contain a few references to the law of neutrality, and attempt to state whatever little law appeared to exist in the field of inter-State relations, indicates the vacuum existing in the absence of treaties.

This conclusion is borne out by the records of relevant decisions of English courts. In matters of spoliation, prize, or piracy, they primarily applied the common law, general principles of equity, or civil law as the case might be. International law would only come in as an overriding limitation if there was a treaty. In such an event a foreign merchant could claim this privilege in the same way as he might produce an individual safe-conduct granted to him by the king.

Thus, in the case of the *Masters and Mariners of Castille and Biscay* (1369), who complained of unjustified reprisals and denial of justice, the King's Council dealt with the question of restitution of their properties by reference to treaties, good faith, and *droit et equite*.[26]

There does not, however, appear to be evidence for the proposition that the law maritime was conceived as anything but a branch of municipal law in the sense of a law applicable between the subjects of princes, and which some maritime Powers might have in common.[27]

A further test is provided by the diplomatic correspondence in disputes between the kings of England and foreign princes. If there had been generally accepted rules of international customary law, it is likely that appeal would have been made to such law with the same frequency as reference was made to treaties, principles of justice and equity, and the mutual interest of princes in reciprocally favourable treatment of each other and their subjects.[28]

If it is remembered that states of truce and peace between medieval rulers rested on a consensual basis, the paucity of rules of international customary law is not surprising. In addition, there was less opportunity in the field of international law than within municipal law to define such rules by means of judicial decisions. Even so, the vagueness of medieval customary law was such that, even within the State, the quest for certainty led to a perfect obsession with charters,

---

26 Baldwin, *op. cit.*, pp. 487–488. See further 1 Marsden, *Select Pleas*, pp. xxv–xxix, and 2 *ibid.*, p. 92.

27 See, for instance, the Treaty of Peace, Confederation, and Friendship of June 30, 1523, between King Henry VIII and King Christiernus of Denmark (4 *Dumont*, Part 1, p. 388).

28 See, for instance, Perroy, *op. cit.*, Nos. 46–49, 103–105, or 144–148, or 2 *Lettres de Rois*, p. 195.

" the solitary firm pillar of legal tradition." [29] This aspect of the matter, which further explains the emphasis on treaties during this period, becomes quite explicit in some of the earlier treaties. Thus, in the marriage contract of 1173 between King Henry II and the Count of Mauriana, the reason for this document is stated as follows: " Quam in dubium venit, quod a memoria recedit, repertum est, in rei gestae testimonium, perhennis rescripti remedium." [30]

Owing to the frequent use made of treaties, the technique of draftsmanship became highly developed from an early stage onwards, and most of the clauses found in modern treaties, or meanwhile transformed into rules of international customary law, can be traced back to these early treaties. They contained elaborate provisions regarding duration, interpretation, participation of third parties, relations between treaties, and consequences of breach of treaty by one of the contracting parties.

The civilist and canonist background, against which these treaties were drafted, is unmistakable. The way, however, in which the customary exceptions of the civil and canon law were frequently declared to be inapplicable, is of significance. It shows that the draftsmen of these treaties worked on the assumption of a practically complete freedom of contract on the part of sovereign princes, and that they freely adapted the legal forms as applied between individuals so as to meet the requirements of relations ultimately based on the rule of force. [31]

Natural law does not appear to have decisively influenced this treaty practice. Like references in preambles of treaties to the precepts of Christian religion and to Augustine, natural law made a rather belated appearance in treaty clauses from the middle of the fifteenth century onwards. In these cases it served ornamental rather than other purposes. [32] In others it was used—in diplomatic practice even earlier—either as a spurious title-deed, whenever more solid foundations for political claims were lacking, or as a means of denouncing one's opponents. [36] In this respect, too, there appears

[29] Kern, *op. cit.*, p. 174.
[30] 1 *Rymer*, p. 33. See also *ibid.*, p. 281.
[31] See, for instance, the Treaty of Peace, Friendship, and Confederation of August 30, 1525 between King Henry VIII and King Francis I of France (4 *Dumont*, Part 1, 439), and the valuable introduction by Mr. H. Jenkinson to the catalogue of an Exhibition of Treaties at the Public Record Office, 1948.
[32] See, for instance, the Convention of April 9, 1450 between King Henry VI and King Christiernus I of Denmark (3 *ibid.*, Part 1, p. 569).
[33] See, for instance, the Letter of King Edward II to Pope Johannes XXII, March 8, 1325 (1 *Dumont*, Part 2, pp. 73–74).

to exist a remarkable continuity in the evolution of international law.

Sanctions of Treaties

Medieval draftsmen tried to secure the observance of treaties on the part of their masters by means of a variety of devices. Frequently these were employed cumulatively in one and the same treaty.[34]

In the first place, particular credibility was attached to the " word of Princes." In order to strengthen the signatures of sovereigns, it was frequently stipulated that the treaty was to be confirmed and ratified by the three estates of the realms concerned. This was not due to any limitation of the king's treaty-making power. At least in so far as England was concerned, the king's prerogative in this respect was unchallenged. Naturally, this did not rule out that the king might find it prudent to assure himself of the support of Parliament, and this was frequently done.[35] As it was put by King Henry III in a letter of 1220 to the King of France, he was prepared to " strengthen " in this way the truce between the two princes.[36]

Material pledges might be added to the signature and ratification of treaties with or without the consent of Parliament. They would range from giving hostages to the hypothecation of all the movable and immovable possessions of the contracting parties, sometimes including also the private property of their subjects.[37] Supernatural sanctions might be added in the form of an oath and, with the co-operation of the Pope, breach of treaty might be threatened with the penalty of excommunication.[38]

Conservatores or *Dictatores* might be appointed from among powerful nobles of the contracting parties to watch over the observance of the treaty, or foreign princes in amity with both sides might be asked to discharge this function.[39] Yet, in substance, the situation would be very much as it was to be in times to come. In the case

---

34 See, for instance, the Treaty of Peace of May 8, 1360 between Edward, Prince of Wales, and Charles, Dauphin of France (2 *ibid.*, Part 1 pp. 12 and 15–16).
35 See n. 51 on p. 92 above.
36 1 *Rymer*, p. 237.
37 See, for instance, the Convention of March 27, 1489 between King Henry VII and the King and Queen of Castille (3 *Dumont*, Part 2, p. 224).
38 In a letter sent in 1209 to some German Princes, King John referred to the alliance with them, " de scriptis et sacramentis firmata, quae de jure rumpi non poterit, nec debebit " (1 *Rymer*, p. 154).
39 King Henry VIII was one of the conservators of the Treaty concluded in 1521 between the Emperor Charles V and King Francis I of France (4 *Dumont*, Part 1, p. 353).

of political treaties, they lasted as long as the underlying power position remained unaltered. Their strength lay in the reciprocal interest
of the parties to such treaties in observing them. If this basis
vanished, they would be broken under the flimsiest of pretexts, as in
fact frequently happened.

Within this rather unstable quasi-order—and as long as it lasted
—treaties of a primarily economic character flourished ; for here the
sanctions inherent in any system of reciprocity could work with less
hindrance than in the field of high politics. The frequency with which
this element of reciprocity was expressly mentioned both in diplomatic correspondence and treaties proves the awareness of the draftsmen of the value of the law of reciprocity. The principle was
expressed in a classic form in the letter of King Edward VI which
Sir Hugh Willoughby and Richard Chancellor took with them in
1553, in their attempt to discover Cathay. The king authorised them
to

" goe to countries, to them heretofore unknown, as well as to seeke sitch
things as we lacke, as also to carry unto them from our regions, sitch
things as they lacke. So that hereby not only commoditie may ensue both
to them and us, but also an indissoluble and perpetual league and friendship. . . . We therefore desire you Kings and Princes, and all other to
whom there is any power on Earth, to permit unto these our servants, free
passage by your regions and dominions ; for they shall not touch any thing
of yours unwilling unto you.—Consider you, that they also are men. If,
therefore, they shall stand in need of any thing, we desire you of all
humanitie, and for the nobilitie which is in you, to aide and help them
with such things as they lacke.—Shewe yourselves towards them, as you
would that we and our subjects should shewe ourselves towards your
servants, if at anie time they shall passe by our regions." [40]

[40] 2 Ward, *op. cit.*, p. 212.

CHAPTER 6

THE PROTECTION OF HUMAN RIGHTS
IN BRITISH PRACTICE

IN the post-1945 era, the international protection of human rights has become a prominent topic both in the literature on international law and on the agenda of organs of the United Nations.

The experiences of two world wars and the " oppression of dictators " [1] would in themselves provide sufficient reasons for such interest. Reassertion of the inalienable rights of man serves as a reminder of the truth that man is not merely a means for the attainment of transient ends.

Although, in a divided world, the remoteness from reality of drafts for universal bills and covenants of human rights is apparent,[2] they evoke sympathy; for they voice widely-felt anxiety over the ever-increasing pressure of organised groups upon the individual, the ultimate basis of life in national and international group relations.

Beyond that, charters of human rights, suitably formulated in the abstract, have their utility value in war and peace. They provide a convenient common denominator for allies primarily united in negatives, that is to say, by common enmity to their adversaries. Once, however, victory has eliminated the unifying element, the functions of such wartime ideologies change. They become " artillery of popular excitation " [3] in the peacetime struggles of world power politics and, like religion in former times, a " cloak to shadow divers factious designes." [4]

It is not the purpose of this chapter either to produce yet another blueprint for an international bill of the rights of man or to assess such greater scope as exists for the more effective protection of human

---

[1] *United Kingdom Draft of an International Bill of Human Rights* (1947), p. 3.
[2] For instructive changes in emphasis, *cf.* H. Lauterpacht's *International Bill of the Rights of Man* (1945) and *International Law and Human Rights* (1950).
    For cogent criticism at an early stage, see J. L. Brierly, *Outlook for International Law* (1944), p. 109 *et seq.*, and A. N. Holcombe, *Human Rights in the Modern World* (1948). See further below, p. 160 *et seq.*, and *Power Politics*, pp. 613 *et seq.* and 793.
[3] Speech by Canning, December 12, 1826 (H. Temperley, *The Foreign Policy of Canning* (1925), p. 579, at p. 581).
[4] Instructions of Queen Elizabeth I to the English Ambassadors to Denmark, 1602 (16 Rymer's *Foedera*, p. 430).

rights in the relations between like-minded nations assembled in one of the world camps. The Rome Convention on Human Rights of 1950 offers an illustration of the constructive potentialities of a relatively homogeneous political and social environment.[5] It is rather the object of this essay to emphasise that traditional international law has been fully seised of this perennial problem, that it has its own ways of facing the challenge of the State making increasing inroads on human rights, and, finally, that British practice throughout the centuries has coped with the issue in a manner which, short of a basic transformation of world society, is the best that, in the foreseeable future, is likely to be attainable on a world scale.

I—INTERNATIONAL LAW
AND THE PROTECTION OF HUMAN RIGHTS

Sovereign States, the predominant type of bearers of rights and duties under international law, have so far succeeded in maintaining a monopoly of exclusive or concurrent jurisdiction over the individual that has barely been challenged.

The position under international customary law is trenchantly stated in a British Memorandum in the case of the *Finnish Shipping Claims* : " International law is a law regulating the rights and duties of States *inter se* and creating no rights and imposing no duties on individuals—a view which the Permanent Court of International Justice appears to have definitely adopted." [6] This is not meant to deny the possibility that if the existing subjects of international law choose to transform the status of the individual from that of an object to that of a subject of international law, they are free to do so. Yet, on any global scale, they have shown considerable reluctance to take so far-reaching a step, and if romantic pirates or ignoble war criminals are adduced as evidence to the contrary, they leave the reader with the uneasy feeling of being treated to singularly weak specimens of special pleading.[7]

---

5 Cmds. 8969 (1953) and 9221 (1954). *Cf.* for instance, A. H. Robertson, *The Law of International Institutions in Europe* (1961), H. Wiebringhaus, *Die Rom-Konvention für Menschenrechte* (1959) and R. Cassin, *La Cour Européenne des Droits de l'Homme*, 7 *European Yearbook* (1959), p. 75 *et seq.*

For constructive possibilities as may exist in multi-racial communities, see the proposals for the changes in the Southern Rhodesia Constitution (Cmnd. 1400–1961) or are offered by functional international institutions, see C. W. Jenks, *Human Rights and International Labour Standards* (1960).

6 League of Nations, *Official Journal* (1932), pp. 816–817.

7 See further *Vol. I*, 137 *et seq.*, and *Fundamental Principles*, p. 288 *et seq.*

In principle, the individual remains under the domestic jurisdiction of the existing subjects of international law. Whoever desires
to take up the case of an individual against a subject of international
law has to prove the exception to the rule by producing evidence of
his *locus standi*.[8]

British practice in this field—as in others—may claim to be of
special interest. It offers evidence of an unrivalled continuity. For
centuries, the security of Britain's island position enabled her statesmen to take a less opportunist view of their duties towards individuals
committed to their charge than most States on the Continent. The
growing strength of Great Britain in the formative period of international law made it possible for British Foreign Secretaries not only
to stand up for British interests, but also to offer guidance on the
treatment of individuals as human beings to States anxious to be in the
good books of Great Britain.

British governments were powerfully aided in this task—and often
urged on to shoulder the burden—by a virile and vigilant public
opinion which felt that it behoved Great Britain to make her voice
heard on behalf of freedom and human rights anywhere within the
orbit of *Pax Britannica*. Thus British diplomats all over the world at
various times fulfilled the task of keeping the countries to which they
were accredited " on the lines which reasonable people in England
will think reasonable." [9]

II—THE BRITISH EXAMPLE

In international as in personal relations nothing is more persuasive
than one's own example. This aspect of the matter is brought out
well in Lord Granville's General Statement of Foreign Policy : " In
the opinion of the present Cabinet, it is the duty and the interest of
this country, having possessions scattered over the whole globe, and
priding itself on its advanced state of civilisation, to encourage moral,
intellectual and physical progress among all other nations. For this
purpose the foreign policy of Great Britain should be marked by

[8] See further *Vol. I*, p. 584 *et seq.*
[9] Mr. Leeper (Athens) to Mr. Eden, January 15, 1945 (Cmd. 6592 (1945), p. 2).
　For an instance of the sensitiveness of a British Foreign Secretary to public
opinion at home, see Castlereagh's State Paper of May 5, 1820 (A. and P. (1823),
XIX, pp. 69–71).
　Other notable examples are furnished by the consistent policies adopted by
successive British Governments regarding the suppression of the Slave Trade.
See above, p. 34, and below, p. 135 *et seq.*

justice, moderation and self-respect, and this country should in its relations with other States do by others as it would be done by." [10]

That Great Britain claimed from other countries no greater protection of human rights than she was herself prepared to grant is worth illustrating by a few examples.

Freedom of Commerce and the Rule of Law

It is fitting to introduce this survey by a reference to *Magna Carta* which granted freedom of commerce to foreign merchants. Admittedly, this right was seriously limited by the confirmation in the same Charter of the liberties and customs of the English boroughs.[11] It must, however, be recalled that, from the twelfth century onwards, treaties of commerce provided the means by which, on a basis of reciprocity, foreigners could obtain national and most-favoured-nation treatment.[12]

The position reached in the second half of the nineteenth century is well described in a British State Paper of the time : " By the existing law of Great Britain all foreigners have the unrestricted right of entrance into and residence in this country and, while they remain in it, are, equally with British subjects, under the protection of the law; nor can they be punished except for an offence against the law, and under the sentence of the ordinary Tribunals of Justice, after a public trial, and on a conviction founded on evidence given in open Court. No foreigners, as such, can be sent out of this country by the executive government, except persons removed by virtue of treaties with other States, confirmed by Act of Parliament, for the mutual surrender of criminal offenders." [13]

Toleration

British Foreign Secretaries willing to take up cases of religious intolerance and persecution can draw on a tradition of long standing.

---

10 January 12, 1852 (H. Temperley and William M. Penson, *Foundations of British Foreign Policy* (1938), pp. 183–184).
11 Sir Frederick Pollock and F. W. Maitland, *The History of English Law*, Vol. I (1923), pp. 464–465.
   See also Chapter 28 of the Statute of the Staple of 1353 (27 Edw. 3, Stat. 2) and on the trial of aliens *per medietatem*, Ch. Molloy, *De Jure Maritimo et Navali* (1744), p. 488 *et seq.*
12 See above, p. 123 *et seq.*, and further 22 *B.Y.I.L.* (1945), p. 96 *et seq.*
13 Lord Granville to Mr. Mayard (Madrid), March 8, 1872 (*Parliamentary Papers* 1872, LXX, 715 (C. 502), No. 2, p. 4).
   The position of the Executive regarding the expulsion of aliens has since been strengthened on the basis of statutory enactments. See, for instance, the Aliens Order, 1960 (S.I. 1960, No. 2214) and further Lord McNair, *International Law Opinions*, Vol. II (1956), p. 40 *et seq.*, J. Mervyn Jones, *British Nationality Law* (1956), p. 65 *et seq.*, and C. Parry, *Nationality and Citizenship Laws of the Commonwealth* (1957), p. 28 *et seq.*

It must suffice to quote here from a dispatch by Lord Aberdeen to Sir Stafford Canning in which Lord Aberdeen referred with justifiable pride to the " justice and to the favour with which the vast body of Mohamedans subject to the British rule are treated in India, in support of their demand that all persons, subjects of the Porte and professing Christianity, shall be exempt from cruel and arbitrary persecution on account of their religion, and shall not be made the victims of a barbarous law, which it may be sought to enforce for their destruction." [14]

Reception of Refugees

The treatment of Gentili, a Protestant refugee from Italy, in Elizabethan England, where he became Regius Professor of Civil Law in Oxford and a famous practitioner in civil law and the law of nations, is symbolic of the proud record of Great Britain in its attitude to refugees from oppression abroad.[15]

On numerous occasions, the British Navy fulfilled the self-imposed duties which were set out in a letter from the Foreign Office to the Admiralty : " A British man-of-war has always and everywhere been considered a safe place of refuge for persons of whatever country or party who have sought shelter under the British flag from persecution on account of their political conduct or opinions ; and this protection has been equally afforded, whether the refugee was escaping from the arbitrary acts of a monarchial government or from the lawless violence of a Revolutionary Committee." [16]

Colonial Trusteeship

Long before President Theodore Roosevelt, during the Conference of Algeciras in 1906, raised the possibility of an international mandate

[14] January 16, 1844 (32 *British and Foreign State Papers*, pp. 915–916).
    The dispatch dealt with cases in which former Mohamedans who had become converts to Christianity were on this ground condemned to death and executed. Lord Aberdeen considered this " barbarous practice " an abuse of sovereignty which justified the intervention of any Christian government in the interest of such Christian subjects of the Porte : " Her Majesty's Government require the Porte to abandon, once and for all, so revolting a principle. They have no wish to humble the Porte by imposing upon it an unreasonable obligation ; but as a Christian Government, the protection of those who profess a common belief with themselves, from persecution and oppression, on that account alone, by their Mohamedan rulers, is a paramount duty with them, and one from which they cannot recede " (*ibid.*, p. 916).
[15] On the multilateral treaties relating to refugees to which the United Kingdom is a party, see *Manual*, Vol. 2, pp. 436 and 503 *et seq.*
[16] August 4, 1849 (50 *British and Foreign State Papers*, p. 804). See also 2 Moore's *Digest of International Law* (1906), p. 847, and Lord McNair, *op. cit.*, Vol. II, p. 67 *et seq.*

for Morocco, Locke's conception of government as a trust was applied by British statesmen to the administration of British colonial possessions.

A line may be traced from Burke's speech of December 1, 1783, on Fox's India Bill *via* the work of the Select Committee of the House of Commons, appointed in 1835 under the pressure of the Aborigines' Protection Society, to the present position.[17]

The spirit behind this policy of devolution and decolonisation is well summed up in a speech made by a British representative in the Assembly of the League of Nations : " The only thing that holds the British Empire together is equality of status and freedom. . . . The British Empire does not conceive of itself in terms of racial solidarity, but in terms of the free association of free people, encouraged to develop their national consciousness within the greater unit, and, above all, bound together by what is the real guarantee for all minorities all over the world—free self-governing institutions." [18]

The transformation, almost complete, from Empire into Commonwealth, offers the best evidence available of good intentions not merely proclaimed, but also generously—and realistically—implemented.[19]

Anti-Slavery Policy

The most impressive contribution to the protection of human rights made by any single country in recent history is the abolition of slavery and the slave trade in the British colonial empire and the stigmatisation of the slave trade as piracy under British criminal law.[20]

---

[17] See further *Power Politics*, p. 648 *et seq.*

[18] Mr. Ormsby-Gore in the 14th Assembly of the League of Nations (*Official Journal*, Spec. Suppl. No. 120, p. 35).

See also J. M. Ward, *British Policy in the South Pacific* (1948) and G. R. Mellor, *British Imperial Trusteeship 1783-1850* (1951).

[19] As Sir Patrick Dean reminded the Security Council, whereas, since 1939, 22 million people were incorporated in the Soviet Union, since the end of the Second World War, 550 million people formerly belonging to the British Empire became citizens of independent countries (United Nations, *Records of the Security Council*, June 9, 1961, S/PV 956).

The remaining British colonies for which either complete independence or varying forms of wider self-government is contemplated comprise about 20 million inhabitants. See further the *Guide to the Remaining British Colonies*, *The Times* newspaper, June 16, 1961, and *Power Politics*, p. 71 *et seq.*

[20] In England, *habeas corpus* proceedings served to prevent any revival of slavery as had existed until the twelfth century (*Somersett's Case* (1772) 20 St.T. 1). See further Pollock-Maitland, *op. cit.*, Vol. I, p. 35 *et seq.*

On the abolition of slave trading and slavery in British colonies, *cf.* Th. Clarkson, *The History of the Abolition of the African Slave Trade by the British Parliament*, 2 vols. (1808) and the Act of 1824 to amend and consolidate the Laws relating to the Abolition of the Slave Trade (5 Geo. 4, c. 113).

Since the days of the first Stuart kings, the activities of English chartered companies engaged in the slave trade had been " sustained by all the power and patronage of the British government, both in legislative measures and diplomatic acts," [21] and in the *Asiento* of 1713 with Spain it was expressly recorded how " desirous of coming into this commerce " with the Spanish colonies was the Britain of Queen Anne's days.[22] As a result of this treaty, the monopoly of the slave trade to the Spanish colonial empire was transferred from French to British merchants, and by 1770 more than half of the one hundred thousand slaves annually exported from Western Africa were transported in British ships. In the face of all the formidable vested interests arrayed against the reformers, British public opinion gradually froced reluctant Parliaments into action, and secured the " establishment of a Magna Carta for Africa in Britain." [23]

There could be no more telling tribute to the British example in setting her own house in order than is to be found in a contemporary Spanish State paper, in which the Council of the Indies recommended in vain to the King of Spain the immediate abolition of the slave trade :

" Twenty years of important and luminous discussions, in the Parliament of Great Britain, have exhausted every variety of argument ; and England, which, in a less enlightened Age, had been amongst the most forward in engaging in a commerce against nature, merely because it encouraged the cupidity and avarice of her merchants, has the glory of having been the first likewise, of all the civilised nations of Europe, in promoting and sanctioning its entire abolition. Justice thereby triumphed. The lamentations of the African slaves, this wretched portion of the human species, were listened to and insulted humanity reasserted its rights. The name of the illustrious William Pitt, the first mover of those discussions, and that of the pious and indefatigable Wilberforce, the author of the

21 H. Wheaton, *History of the Law of Nations* (1845), p. 586.
22 E. O'Bryan, *The Compleat History of the Treaty of Utrecht*, Vol. I, Part 2 (1715), p. 155. *Cf.* also G. Scelle, *La Traite Négrière aux Indes de Castille*, 2 vols. (1906).
23 Clarkson, *l.c.* in note 20 above, Vol. 2, p. 580. *Cf.* also Sir Reginald Coupland, *Wilberforce* (1923) and *The British Anti-Slavery Movement* (1933), Ch. Lloyd, *The Navy and the Slave Trade* (1949), Lord McNair, *op. cit.*, Vol. II, p. 77 *et seq.* and C. W. W. Greenidge, *Slavery* (1958) above, p. 34, and below, p. 198.
    For a critical survey of British anti-slavery policy, see H. Wheaton, *Enquiry into the Validity of the British Claim to a Right of Visitation and Search of American Vessels suspected to be engaged in the African Slave Trade* (1842).

Abolition Bill, will be for ever respected by all who feel and can appreciate the high dignity of man." [24]

III—THE BRITISH WAY

Traditional international law offers abundant scope for the protection of human rights. Powers must be prepared, however, to make use for this purpose of their freedoms and rights under international law.

Recognition

British practice in granting recognition to new States and governments and in maintaining or breaking diplomatic relations with foreign Powers, offers instructive evidence of how the discretion granted in matters of recognition to subjects of international law may be exercised in the interest of the effective protection of human rights.

British recognition of new States might be made dependent on the latter granting freedom of commerce to British nationals [25] and religious liberty to their own nationals [26] or on the conclusion of treaties for the abolition of the slave trade.

Thus Palmerston informed the representative of Texas who had come to London to obtain the recognition of Texas that Great Britain " would not be willing to conclude a Treaty of acknowledgment with any new State possessing a naval flag, unless such State were to consent to conclude at the same time with Great Britain a Treaty for the suppression of the African Slave Trade." [27]

It would, however, be an oversimplification to maintain that

---

[24] Report of February 16, 1816 (4 *British and Foreign State Papers*, p. 517).

[25] *Cf.*, for instance, Canning to Sir W. à Court (Madrid), January 30, 1824 (11 *British and Foreign State Papers*, p. 61).

See on this dispatch also H. Lauterpacht, *Recognition in International Law* (1947), pp. 13–14, and further the Memorandum of a Conference between the Prince de Polignac (France) and Canning, held on October 9, 1823 (11 *British and Foreign State Papers*, p. 50) and the Treaty between the Argentine Confederation and Great Britain of February 2, 1825 (3 Hertslet's *Commercial Treaties*, p. 44).

The Conference of Ambassadors made *de jure* recognition of Lithuania dependent on acceptance by Lithuania of the provisions of the Peace Treaty of Versailles of 1919 regarding freedom of navigation on the Niemen (1 Hackworth's *Digest of International Law* (1940), pp. 201–202).

[26] See, for instance, the modalities accompanying the recognition of Serbia and Rumania by the Powers represented at the Congress of Berlin (*Parliamentary Papers*, 1878, LXXXIII, 391 (C. 2083), Enclosures in No. 20, pp. 106–107 and in No. 26, p. 144).

[27] Palmerston to General Hamilton (Texas), October 18, 1840 (29 *British and Foreign State Papers*, p. 617).

British practice regarding the recognition of new governments— especially of new governments brought into power by revolution— at all times required more than effectiveness and willingness to fulfil their international obligations.[28] There are, however, frequent instances in which such stability was considered to consist in the subsequent legitimation of the government by more or less convincing evidence of popular support,[29] and others in which " free elections " [30] were required as an indication of the independence of governments from outside domination.

In some of these cases, insistence on support of governments by the greater part of the population may have had the indirect effect of strengthening the cause of political freedom in countries with weak— or without—democratic traditions. Developments in Eastern Europe since the Second World War have, however, proved that stipulations of this kind at the time of recognition in themselves offer no effective guarantee against subsequent constitutional changes towards autho- ritarian or totalitarian forms of government or against promises made by such governments being broken at a future date.[31]

Recognition of a government is granted on the assumption that the latter will fulfil its obligations under international law. A dispatch from Lord Russell to the British representative in Mexico may serve as an illustration of the way British State practice linked recognition with the protection of legitimate private interests. In it Lord Russell explained that instructions issued, both before and since the victory of the Liberal Party in Mexico, " made the recognition by Great Britain of the Constitutional Government contingent upon the acknowledg- ment by that Government of the liability of Mexico for the claims of British subjects, who, either in their persons or in their property, for a

---

[28] Palmerston to Bloomfield (St. Petersburg), March 28, 1848 : " The Government of Great Britain is in the habit of acknowledging any government established in a foreign State when such government shall appear to be firmly and permanently established " (*l.c.* in note 10 above, p. 159). See above, p. 75, and further, H. A. Smith, *Great Britain and the Law of Nations*, Vol. I (1932) p. 106 *et seq.*, H. Lauterpacht, *Recognition in International Law* (1947), T. Chen, *The International Law of Recognition* (1951), and T. Charpentier, *La Reconnaissance internationale et l'évolution du droit des gens* (1956).

[29] See, for instance, Lord Derby's speech on Spain in the House of Lords on March 8, 1875 (*Hansard*, 3rd series, Vol. 222, Col. 1382).

[30] Protocol of the Proceedings of the Crimea Conference, February 11, 1945 (Cmd. 7088 [1947], p. 4).

In the case of Finland, Great Britain considered in 1918 the holding of elections as proof of Finland's independence and held out hopes that recognition would follow such elections (*Foreign Relations*, 1918 [Russia], Vol. 2, p. 739 *et seq.*).

[31] See further below, p. 177 *et seq.*

long series of years, can be proved to have suffered wrong at the hands of successive Governments in Mexico." [32]

Finally, reference must be made to cases in which Great Britain threatened to break off diplomatic relations or had recourse to this measure in order to induce foreign Powers to show greater respect for the rights of British nationals [33] or even their own subjects.

Thus, in 1856, the Earl of Clarendon informed the Government of the Two Sicilies that Great Britain was not in a position to maintain diplomatic relations with a government which upheld as inhumane a régime as that practised in Naples, and which was determined to persevere in a course condemned by all civilised nations. [34]

In words which have not lost their significance, Lord Russell expressed himself in another dispatch on the subject of the police State : " You will press strongly on the Principal Minister of the Crown the necessity of abolishing, as soon as possible, the despotism of the police. Men may differ about the merits of Representative Constitutions, and the form and time in which they should be put in force ; but there can be no difference of opinion among enlightened men about the necessity of a due, impartial, and speedy administration of justice. To keep men in prison without trial ; to place them under zealous and suspicious police, thus embarrassing all their actions—even the most innocent—is contrary to every principle of justice. . . . It was the open, systematic, and continued violation of justice which induced Her Majesty's Government to suspend friendly relations with Naples." [35]

Treaty Practice

Peace treaties and treaties of commerce provide a vast mine of information on the ways in which, since the twelfth century, England attempted to secure fair treatment for her subjects abroad.

[32] March 30, 1861 (52 *British and Foreign State Papers*, p. 237).
See further *Fundamental Principles*, p. 228 *et seq.*
[33] See, for instance, the dispatch from the Earl of Malmesbury to Sir H. Bulwer (Florence), May 29, 1852 (42 *ibid.*, p. 531).
[34] Dispatch from the Earl of Clarendon to G. G. Petrie (Naples), October 10, 1856 (46 *ibid.*, p. 773).
On the rupture of diplomatic relations with Serbia, following the murder of the King and Queen of Serbia in 1903, see *British Documents on the Origins of the World War, 1898–1914*, Vol. 4, p. 124 *et seq.*, and Smith, *l.c.* in note 28 above, p. 229 *et seq.*
[35] Lord Russell to the Hon. H. Elliott (Naples), July 6, 1859 (51 *British and Foreign State Papers*, pp. 1336–1337).
It was made clear in the same dispatch that Great Britain did not intend to interfere with the internal affairs of the Two Sicilies, but merely wished to make clear the indispensable conditions on which British " moral " and " material " support to the reigning dynasty depended (*ibid.*, p. 1339).

Since the Treaty of 1154 with Cologne, it has been one of the set purposes of English—and, subsequently, British—treaty practice to obtain freedom of commerce on a basis of mutuality and reciprocity.

At a time when generally recognised minimum standards of international law regarding the treatment of foreigners did not yet exist, English draftsmen performed pioneer work in the formulation of treaty clauses by which reprisals against individual traders were reasonably limited, the personal and property rights of foreign merchants liberally defined, and their rights of free movement and free access to the local law courts established beyond doubt.[36]   By way of ancillary rights, even freedom of conscience and of religion was obtained in countries in which, otherwise, the grant of freedom of commerce would have been merely of nominal value.[37]

In addition, England took the lead in the elaboration of other standards of international economic law, of which those of most-favoured-nation and national treatment are the most important. These treaties were concluded in the interest of her own nationals. The effect of these treaties was, however, of a more general character. A good many of the minimum standards fixed in these treaties grew into rules of international customary law, thus becoming available to other States and their nationals.[38]   In addition, other States increasingly participated in the nexus of most-favoured-nation treaties and, on this basis, automatically partook of the rights which Great Britain secured for her own nationals.[39]

Seen in historical perspective, British practice in this field was building on the rudimentary foundations of international customary law an elaborate superstructure of treaties in which the rights of individuals abroad were firmly and liberally established. It was not only the " public law of Europe " which was enriched in this way. Great Britain's wide overseas interests enabled her to spread the canons of Western civilisation all over the world.

Near and Far Eastern communities which remained independent were made to accept minimum conditions without which relations on

[36] See above, p. 85 *et seq.*
[37] See, for instance, Article 14 of the Treaty of Peace and Alliance between the Commonwealth and Portugal, July 10, 1654 : " Forasmuch as the Rights of Commerce and Peace would be null and void, if the People of the Republick of England should be disturbed for Conscience sake, while they pass to and from the Kingdoms and Dominions of the said King of Portugal, or reside there for the sake of exchanging their wares," therefore, within the limits of the Article, freedom of religion was granted to English merchants.
[38] See below, p. 210 *et seq.*
[39] See above, pp. 123 *et seq.* and 130.

a footing of equality were hardly feasible. If their structure and habits were separated by too wide a gulf from those of European States, exterritoriality treaties provided the means of peaceful symbiosis during a transitional period.[40]

African kingdoms had to learn that friendly terms with Great Britain depended on their abandoning uncivilised habits of warfare among themselves and barbarous rites resulting in the slaughter of innocent men and women at the feasts and funerals of tribal chiefs.[41]

The newly established republics of South and Central America were induced by way of treaties of commerce to accept minimum requirements of effective State organisation and fair administration of justice without which it was vain for them to expect the flow to their countries of British capital and skilled labour.[42] Thus, British treaty practice throughout the centuries served as an effective means of, and remains a telling witness to, the civilising mission performed by the British Empire in most of the independent States bordering on, or near to, the seven seas.

It is not possible within the compass of this Chapter to pay more than passing attention to the many multilateral treaties in the humanitarian field which were either initiated by Great Britain or in which she participated.[43] Two types of bilateral treaties must, however, be mentioned. The Treaty in favour of the Waldenses of 1690 between England, the United Provinces of the Netherlands and Savoy is a hallmark in the international protection of minorities.[44] Similarly, the Anglo-Chinese Treaty of Peace, Friendship and Commerce of 1858 is memorable, as it embodies the first international arrangement on questions of labour.[45]

The Enforcement of International Customary Law

By the middle of the nineteenth century, standards regarding the treatment of individuals considered normal in Western countries were taken so generally for granted that British practice increasingly tended

[40] See above, p. 55 *et seq.*
[41] *Cf.*, for instance, Article 18 of the Treaty with the Chiefs of the Timmanees, February 13, 1841 (40 *British and Foreign State Papers*, p. 894).
[42] See, for instance, the Treaty of Friendship, Commerce and Navigation between Colombia and the United Kingdom, February 16, 1866 (Foreign Office, *Handbook of Commercial Treaties* (1931), p. 118 *et seq.*).
[43] See further, *Manual*, Vol. 2, p. 500 *et seq.*
[44] 18 *British and Foreign State Papers*, p. 670.
[45] Article 13 (11 Hertslet's *Commercial Treaties*, p. 86).

to claim their observance as due to British nationals under international customary law or as general principles of law recognised by
civilised nations.

Thus, in 1872, the consuls in Bucharest of Austria-Hungary,
France, Germany, Great Britain, Greece, Italy and the United States
of America sent a collective note to the Government of the Princi-
palities of Moldavia and Wallachia in which it was maintained that
" a civilised country . . . as such, ought to ensure freedom and
security to all religious denominations." [46]

British practice has always been especially sensitive to any form
of ill-treatment of British nationals abroad. It was immaterial whether
the individual involved was of rank and title or of the humblest
station in life.

In the words of Palmerston, in a case of traffic in British slaves in
the West Indies, " it is impossible for Great Britain to permit British
subjects, whatever their colour may be, to be kidnapped into a foreign
country, and there to be held in slavery." [47]

Equally instructive is a Note of Bulwer to the Spanish Foreign
Minister: " You are at liberty to do what you will with any
Englishman who disturbs the public tranquillity; but I must at the
same time warn you that I shall hold the Spanish Government responsible, not only for any murder but for any injury as well as for
any insult committed without provocation upon any subject of Her
Majesty." [48]

Another British envoy to Spain reflected on the same subject in
the course of the Second World War: " On this point Spaniards who
think it worth while to study the English, will note that while it is
impossible to make them prepare for war, and difficult to make them
fight, there was once a ' War of Jenkins' Ear.' [49] Maltreatment of

[46] C. Adler and A. M. Margalith, *With Firmness in the Right. American Diplomatic Action affecting Jews 1840–1945* (1946), p. 106.
[47] Viscount Palmerston to Mr. Villiers (Madrid), December 12, 1835 (24 *British and
Foreign State Papers*, p. 188).
[48] 38 *ibid.*, p. 940.
[49] When Captain Jenkins was examined at the Bar of the House of Commons and
asked by a member what he thought when he found himself in the hands of
the barbarians who had cut off one of his ears, he replied " I recommended my
soul to God and my cause to my country " (T. Smollett, *The History of England
from the Revolution of 1688*, Vol. 6 (1811), Note D to Vol. 3).
    See also Sir Richard Pares, *War and Trade in the West Indies* (1936),
pp. 60-61.

British subjects, however humble, is one of the things the British people will never forgive and never forget." [50]

If subordinate State organs are responsible for any such outrage, it is for the offending State to make full reparation.[51] In the case of crimes committed by individuals, speedy and impartial administration of justice must be expected.[52] British State practice has been firm on compliance with these minimum standards.

At the same time, diplomatic protection was judiciously exercised, and British Foreign Secretaries kept in mind the advice tendered in 1858 in an opinion of a Law Officer of the Crown : " Great Britain can put forward no claim, and can make no demand in this case, which she is not prepared to concede to Naples or to any other recognised Government, however weak or barbarous." [53]

On numerous occasions Britain extended a helping hand to non-British nationals on broad humanitarian grounds. In the course of the Civil War in the Two Sicilies in 1848, Lord Napier suggested to the Neapolitan Foreign Minister a truce and negotiations with the revolutionary government at Palermo under the concerted mediation of France and Great Britain in order to make an end of the cruelties and devastations caused by that war. Palmerston fully approved this course of action.[54]

British envoys were similarly encouraged to maintain unofficial contacts with revolutionary forces and to remind them of the rules of warfare in civilised countries.[55] In these cases, Great Britain limited herself to offering advice to governments which considered themselves entitled to support from Great Britain or, in the case of revolutionary governments, hoped to obtain British recognition. Such special relations appeared to justify to British statesmen advice which might otherwise have been regarded as a " questionable act of propriety and interference," [56] and they simultaneously volunteered offers

---

50 Viscount Templewood, *Ambassador on Special Mission* (1946), p. 201.
   See further *ibid.* on the case of Mr. Apfel who had to suffer two years' imprisonment in " mediaeval conditions."
51 See, for instance, the case of the assault by a Brazilian police guard on three officers of H.M.S. *Forte* (1862–54 *British and Foreign State Papers*, p. 691).
52 See, for instance, the case of the plunder of the wreck of H.M.S. *Prince of Wales* on the coast of Brazil (1861, *ibid.*, pp. 589–590 and 685).
53 Opinion of the Advocate and Solicitor-General to Malmesbury in the case of *The Gagliari*, April 13, 1858 (48 *ibid.*, p. 468).
   See further *Fundamental Principles*, p. 368 *et seq.*
54 Palmerston to Lord Napier, September 22, 1848 (40 *ibid.*, p. 824).
   See also the Queen's speech on the Opening of Parliament, February 1, 1849 (37 *ibid.*, p. 1).
55 See, for instance, Palmerston to Consul-General C. G. Dawkins (Venice), April 5, 1848 (37 *ibid.*, p. 964).
56 H. L. Bulwer to the Spanish Foreign Minister, April 16, 1848 (38 *ibid.*, p. 962).

that, in corresponding circumstances, they would be obliged for reciprocal intervention.[57]

The numerous cases in which British embassies, legations and men-of-war offered shelter to men marked down by their political opponents also deserve to be recalled. Justification for these acts should not primarily be sought on narrow legal grounds but on those of common humanity and decency and in a healthy British reaction to departure by anybody from such standards.[58]

It would equally surpass the scope of this Chapter to give a detailed exposition of the cases of humanitarian intervention in which Great Britain participated. More of these instances than is generally assumed find their legal basis in treaties and unilateral engagements undertaken by Powers against which, in the interest of humanity, intervention was subsequently considered necessary. There remains, however, a residue of cases in which the title to intervention is simply interference in domestic matters contrary to international law.[59]

IV—LESSONS

The remarkable results obtained by British practice in the international protection of human rights on the basis of traditional international law are due to a variety of circumstances.

The example set to the world in the treatment of the individual *inside* the British Empire is probably the foremost point to be stressed. It provided the moral justification for action which sometimes stretched existing international law in the service of Christianity, humanity and civilisation.

Moreover, British statesmen felt justified in insisting on other governments living up to the standards of international law and civilisation because in the period of Britain's greatest strength, they conceived international law not as a static code, but as a living and expanding system.

More important still, they knew their limits. In a world of sovereign States they thought of themselves as standard-bearers of civilisation and human progress, but they did not pretend to exercise influence beyond the reach of British naval and financial power.

---

[57] See, for instance, Palmerston to Bulwer, April 20, 1848 (*ibid.*, pp. 954–955).
[58] See, for instance, Palmerston's Note to the Spanish Minister in London of June 12, 1848 (38 *ibid.*, pp. 1047–1048).
[59] See, for instance, the Protocol of the London Conference on the Greek Question, February 20, 1830 (17 *ibid.*, p. 203) or the dispatch from the Earl of Aberdeen to Sir Stratford Canning (Constantinople), October 4, 1843 (32 *ibid.*, p. 905).

Even within these limits, they succeeded on the whole in exercising their rights judiciously and avoided overplaying their hand by embracing indiscriminately the cases of British nationals who requested interposition by the Foreign Office. At times this policy had to be firmly upheld against powerful pressure groups at home : " Her Majesty's Government have, on every occasion, supported such portions of the complaints preferred by British subjects against sovereign governments, as to them seemed founded in reason and justice," but " it is for Her Majesty's Government, and not for individuals, however respectable, to interpret the Treaty engagements of the Crown,[60] and to determine whether Great Britain is, or is not, entitled to claim redress from foreign governments." [61]

The explanation of this record of achievement probably is that British statesmen felt their way empirically and experimentally towards humanitarian standards compliance with which could be reasonably expected in a largely unorganised international society. In Castlereagh's words, this was done in a spirit of healthy scepticism towards " abstract and speculative principles." [62]

---

[60] Reference is made here to the Anglo-Dutch Treaty of 1824.
[61] Viscount Leveson to the Glasgow East India Association, May 27, 1841 (31 *ibid.*, p. 257).
[62] Confidential State Paper of May 5, 1820 (3 *Cambridge History of British Foreign Policy* (1923), p. 622, at p. 623).

CHAPTER 7

THE IMPACT OF THE EAST-WEST RIFT
ON INTERNATIONAL LAW

FOR an accurate assessment of the impact of the East-West rift on international law, it is essential first to understand the character and significance of this cleavage.

I—THE CHARACTER AND SIGNIFICANCE OF THE EAST-WEST CLEAVAGE

The simplest way of disposing of the issue would be to deny its existence. It would be erroneous to assume that this treatment of the problem was a Western prerogative.

In 1946, Stalin answered questions put to him by the President of the United Press of America as follows [1] : *First Question*: " Do you agree with Secretary Byrnes . . . that there is growing tension between the U.S.S.R. and the United States? " *Answer*: " No." *Second Question*: " If such an increasing tension exists, could you indicate the reason, or reasons, for it, and what are the most essential bases for eliminating it? " *Answer*: " The question does not arise in view of my answer to the preceding question."

If, as was done in a British State paper of the post-1945 period,[2] one side in this conflict is described as the " Slav " group, this is hardly any more illuminating. Actually, such a description is positively misleading. It puts the emphasis on an ethnic or linguistic criterion which, apart from its inaccuracy regarding Yugoslavia since 1948, is at the most of peripheral significance. This explanation— if explanation it is meant to be—fastens on incidentals. It does not give any clue to the mystery why, in comparison to earlier phases, the conflict between the " Slav " and " non-Slav " worlds should have become the overriding struggle in world affairs since the Second World War.

---

[1] J. V. Stalin, *Post-War International Relations* (1947), p. 14.
[2] *Report on the Proceedings of the First Part of the Third Session of the General Assembly of the United Nations* (Cmd. 7630, p. 5).
 Whenever, in this Chapter, for brevity's sake " geographical " terms are used, *Eastern* is meant to be equivalent to being in the power orbit of the Soviet Union and Communist China and *Western* to signify a corresponding position *vis-à-vis* the United States. See also above, pp. 22 and 58–60, below, p. 279, and further 13 *Y.B.W.A.* (1959), p. 236 *et seq.*

146

Any explanation which fails to answer this question condemns itself out of hand. Does the answer lie perhaps in the ideological cleavage between Communism and the values for which the West stands? [3] It would run counter to experience to overestimate this aspect of the matter. The alliances between Francis I, *Rex Christianissimus*, and Sultan Suleyman II, between Richelieu's France and Protestant King Gustavus Adolphus of Sweden, between the Allied Powers and Czarist Russia, or between the Soviet Union and the Western democracies in the Second World War prove the relative insignificance of ideologies in any system of power politics. The position of non-Communist Finland *vis-à-vis* the Soviet Union and, conversely, the defection of Communist-ruled Yugoslavia from the Soviet bloc, lend further support to this assessment.

By a process of elimination, it appears that the answer must be sought in the changes brought about by the Second World War in the structure of international society. Over a prolonged period, the oligarchy of the Greater—and World—Powers has been subject to a continuous process of compression.[4] International society has reached the penultimate stage in its march towards centralisation. It is split into two antagonistic world camps, locked in a nuclear stalemate and uneasily competing for the sympathies and allegiance of, as yet, uncommitted nations.

For purposes of this analysis, it is irrelevant to assign the responsibilities of individual Powers for this development. The question may also be left open whether this trend is attributable to impersonal forces or to errors committed by the leaders of one or the other camp. What matters is the result, and this is hard to contest.

Irrespective of the internal structure and the ideologies prevailing at any moment in the Kremlin or Capitol, the reduction of the international oligarchy to a few giant Powers, each surrounded by junior partners, allies or satellites, imposes a greater strain on international law than it had to bear at any previous stage of its evolution. The fact that this world struggle is accompanied by deep-seated ideological and spiritual dissensions adds further fuel to a situation which in itself is sufficiently explosive. In order to judge fairly the impact of this world struggle on international law, it is advisable to proceed step by step and, in this case, from the roof of the temple downwards to its foundations.

3 See further *Power Politics*, p. 815.
4 See further *ibid.*, p. 113 *et seq.*, above, p. 58, and below, p. 279.

Contemporary international law is best understood if the developments in international law and organisation during the post-1919
and post-1945 periods are recognised as elaborate superstructures,
grafted—chiefly by way of collective treaties—on traditional international law.[5] Awareness of this situation will be some insurance
against the danger of overstatement. It may well be that the East-
West rift has affected merely the superstructure of the United
Nations, but left the basic rules of international law intact. It is,
therefore, proposed to examine first the impact of the East-West
rift on the United Nations and related institutions and, subsequently,
to proceed to the assessment of the effects of this cleavage on the
traditional rules of international customary law.

II—THE EAST-WEST RIFT AND POST-1945 INTERNATIONAL LAW

The United Nations design shows deceptive federal features. In all
the organs of the United Nations, the unanimity principle has
disappeared. The Security Council is endowed with functions of a
true executive body. Under Chapter Seven of the Charter, it disposes
of a formidable array of enforcement measures.

Such apparent advance in international organisation is, however,
more than balanced by the veto of the world Powers. The double
veto extends this right to any question the procedural character of
which is not settled beyond dispute. It is true that if a world Power
is a party to a dispute, the veto does not apply to recommendations
of the Security Council under Chapter Six. If, however, more than
one world Power happens to be on the one or the other side of the
East-West fence, the Power condemned by the Charter to abstention
under Chapter Six may exercise its veto by proxy. The Western
Powers are in this fortunate position and, if Communist China were
admitted to the Security Council, the Soviet bloc would be similarly
placed.

In any case, no such self-denying ordinance applies under Chapter Seven of the Charter. Each one of the permanent members of
the Security Council holds an absolute veto on enforcement measures.
It is immaterial whether it is itself a party to any particular
dispute.

The veto of the world Powers and the simultaneous subjection
of the rest of the members of the international aristocracy to the

---

5 See below, p. 274 *et seq.*

majority principle are telling symptoms of the trend in international society towards the concentration of power.[6]

The antinomy between an effective international organisation for the maintenance of world peace and the veto of the world Powers could be constructively solved on *one* charitable assumption alone : basic agreement between the world Powers. In the British Commentary on the Charter, this major assumption was stated in straightforward language [7] : " It is . . . clear that no enforcement action by the Organisation can be taken against a Great Power itself without a major war. If such a situation arises the United Nations will have failed in its purpose and all members will have to act as seems best in the circumstances. . . . The successful working of the United Nations depends on the unanimity of the Great Powers. . . . If this unanimity is seriously undermined no provision of the Charter is likely to be of much avail."

The draftsmen of Dumbarton Oaks and San Francisco had no choice but to build their edifice on this shaky foundation of the improvised—and always precarious—wartime unity between the world Powers. Years of post-war international " co-operation " between East and West have blown this illusion sky-high and exposed this fundamental weakness of the United Nations.

While the East-West rift lasts, the United Nations may fulfil highly useful functions. It is, however, constitutionally incapable of serving its main purpose, that is to say, the maintenance of world peace against the will of any one of the world Powers.

The East-West rift has affected every one of the major structural and functional features of the United Nations.

Membership

According to Article 4 of the Charter, as interpreted by the International Court of Justice in its Advisory Opinion on the *Competence of the General Assembly regarding Admission to the United Nations* (1950),[8] the General Assembly may decide on the admission of new members only on a positive recommendation by the Security Council. Thus, every candidate for membership depends on the goodwill of each permanent member of the Security Council.

So long as members of the United Nations do not give articulate reasons, their discretion regarding the exercise of their votes is

[6] See above, p. 58, and further *Power Politics*, p. 427 *et seq.*
[7] Cmd. 6666 (1945), p. 16.
[8] *I.C.J. Reports 1950*, p. 4.

unlimited. The reasonableness and good faith postulated by the World Court in its earlier Opinion on *Membership of the United Nations* (1948) [9] must be presumed and are practically unverifiable.

At first, it appeared as if the impact of the East-West rift on admission practice would be to limit the United Nations to the relative universality it had attained from the outset and to transform it into a closed society. Subsequently, however, the trend towards absolute, and even formal, universality reasserted itself,[10] but in a manner profoundly affected by the world cleavage.

In the case of candidates considered committed to one or the other side, admission became a matter of package deals so as not to strengthen gratuitously the voting strength of the other camp. Where, however, new and uncommitted nations were concerned, both sides vied with each other in sponsoring such candidates. Compared with the object of securing the goodwill of these newcomers, the question whether any such State was able to fulfil its obligations under the Charter became a matter of minor consideration. The premature admission of the Congo (Leopoldville) offers the most blatant illustration of these policies of active and competitive co-existence.

The Pacific Settlement of International Disputes

As in the Covenant of the League of Nations, so in the Charter the distinction is adopted between justiciable and non-justiciable disputes, the former to be settled by judicial international institutions, and the latter by procedures of conciliation.

The under-employment of the International Court of Justice is not due primarily to the East-West rift. In their relations with one another, Western States also have proved themselves reluctant in the post-1945 period to bring disputes before this or any other international judicial organ.

Three points are, however, relevant. None of the States in the Soviet-controlled sector of the world is a party to the Optional Clause of the Statute of the International Court of Justice.

The Soviet Union and those of her allies who are parties to the Genocide Convention of 1948 have made a significant reservation.[11] They are not prepared to submit disputes on the interpretation,

[9] *I.C.J. Reports 1948*, p. 10.
[10] See further *Power Politics*, p. 430 *et seq*.
[11] See above, p. 36, and below, p. 203 *et seq*.

application or fulfilment of the Convention to the jurisdiction of the International Court of Justice.

Similarly, in the Antarctica Treaty of 1959, to which the Soviet Union is a party, the only duty incumbent upon Contracting Parties is one of consultation. If a dispute on the interpretation or application of the Treaty cannot be resolved in this way, it can be submitted to the International Court of Justice only " with the consent, in each case, of all parties to the dispute." [12]

To judge by the behaviour of Albania, little appears to be gained by any of these States submitting themselves to the jurisdiction of international courts. In its Judgment in the *Corfu Channel Case* (Assessment of Compensation),[13] the International Court of Justice awarded to the United Kingdom £843,947 by way of compensation. Yet, so far, neither has the Judgment been carried out nor has any announcement been made that the subsequent negotiations between the Parties have reached a successful conclusion.

Such little consolation as there is the United Kingdom may draw from Article 94 of the Charter : " If any party to a case fails to perform the obligations incumbent upon it under a judgment rendered by the Court, the other party may have recourse to the Security Council, which may, if it deems necessary, make recommendations or decide upon measures to be taken to give effect to the judgment." Yet, at least so long as Albania was not guilty of " leftist " aberrations, any action under this Article would merely have produced another Soviet veto.[14]

The reasons why the Eastern States hold back from any international settlement of legal disputes by judicial organs are still substantially the same as those stated by Litvinov at the Hague Conference on the Liquidation of the Russian Debts in 1922 that " it was necessary to face the fact that there was not one world but two —a Soviet world and a non-Soviet world. Because there was no third world to arbitrate, he anticipated difficulties. . . . Only an angel could be unbiased in judging Russian affairs." [15]

The reticence of the Soviet Union and her allies towards international judicial institutions is understandable. How forthcoming would any Western State be in submitting a so-called legal dispute

---

[12] Article XI, Cmnd. 913 (1959), p. 10.
[13] *I.C.J. Reports 1949*, p. 250.
   See further *Vol. I*, p. 653 *et seq.*
[14] See above, p. 59, and below, p. 290.
[15] See also above, p. 58, below, p. 162, and further *Manual*, Vol. 2, pp. 394–395 and 403–404.

to an International Court of Justice, the overwhelming majority of which were composed of members drawn from the People's Democracies? Moreover, do not the excellently argued dissenting opinions in every controversial case that has come before the International Court prove two points? The first is that it is always possible to arrive from an unstated major assumption at any desired conclusion. The second is that the distinction between legal and political disputes is purely subjective. If States desire any international conflict to be settled on the basis of law, it is a legal dispute. If they fear that the decision will go against them or they aim at a modification of existing international law, the dispute is political. The present deep-seated division of the world intensifies the constant tendency in a system of power politics to treat every difference of opinion between greater Powers as a political dispute.

Plenty of evidence exists to sustain this proposition. For years, the Western Powers and the Soviet Union have accused each other of breaches of the Potsdam Agreement of 1945. So far, however, neither side has ventured to challenge the other to take its case before the World Court.

Similarly, the Western Powers base their right of free access to Berlin on international agreements and usage. In identical Notes to the Soviet Union of July 6, 1948, the Governments of the United States, Britain and France stated that they regarded the blockade of Berlin as a " clear violation of existing agreements concerning the administration of Berlin by the four Occupying Powers." [16] Yet, when the issue over Berlin came to a head, where was it raised? In the Security Council. In all likelihood, the Soviet Union would never have consented to the submission of the case to the World Court. An equally significant point is, however, that the Western Powers did not even think it worth suggesting such a solution either then or at any subsequent date.[17]

In her turn, the Soviet Union alleged the incompatibility of the North Atlantic Treaty with the Charter of the United Nations and with her own Treaties of Alliance with the United Kingdom and France. The Western Powers denied these contentions and pointed disapprovingly at the inter-linking system of treaties of mutual assistance among the members of the Eastern bloc. Admittedly, all these

---

[16] Cmd. 7534 (1948), p. 47. See further *Manual*, Vol. 2, pp. 426–427 and 512–513.
[17] See the present writer's letter to the Editor of *The Times*, December 2, 1958.

treaties are political treaties. Yet, like any other type of treaty, political treaties are meant to impose legally binding obligations and, thus, are amenable to interpretation by international judicial organs.

Finally, the Soviet Union considers the use of nuclear weapons to be contrary to the laws and customs of war. So what prevents her from asking the Security Council or the General Assembly of the United Nations to request the Court for an advisory opinion on this issue?

Taking a leaf out of the dispute between the United Kingdom and Albania,[18] the United States,[19] as well as Israel[20] and the United Kingdom itself,[21] made a few attempts to invoke the jurisdiction of the International Court of Justice by way of unilateral submission of cases to the Court, thus daring the Soviet Union and her Eastern European Allies to deny the Court's jurisdiction, which they promptly did. In each of these cases, the Applicants could work on the assumption that in whichever way the other side reacted, they would be bound to score. If the Soviet Union accepted the Court's jurisdiction, it would have to defend weak cases in a probably unsympathetic Court. If she refused to do so, the Applicants would be credited with having shown an exemplary attitude of law-abidingness and, in any case, they would have succeeded in filing their cases with the Court for future reference.

When, however, in 1960, the U-2 and B-47 incidents profoundly disturbed inter-camp relations,[22] neither side thought in terms of submitting the former case to the International Court of Justice or any other judicial or arbitral international organ. In the latter, the United States offered to submit the dispute to a commission of inquiry or to the International Court of Justice. The proposal was not, however, acceptable to the Soviet Union.

---

18 See further 4 *C.L.P.* (1951), p. 23 *et seq.*
19 *Treatment in Hungary of Aircraft of United States of America* (U.S.A. v. Hungary), *I.C.J. Reports 1954,* p. 99 *et seq.*; U.S.A. v. the Soviet Union, *ibid.,* p. 103 *et seq.*, and *Aerial Incident of 27 July, 1955* (U.S.A. and Bulgaria), *ibid. 1957,* p. 186 *et seq.* and *1960,* p. 146 *et seq.*; *Aerial Incident of 4 September, 1954* (U.S.A. v. the Soviet Union), *ibid. 1958,* p. 158 *et seq.* and *Aerial Incident of 7 November, 1954* (U.S.A. v. the Soviet Union), *ibid. 1959,* p. 276 *et seq.*
20 *Aerial Incident of 27 July, 1955* (Israel v. Bulgaria), *ibid. 1957,* p. 182 *et seq.* and *ibid. 1959,* p. 127 *et seq.*
21 *Aerial Incident of 27 July, 1955* (United Kingdom v. Bulgaria), *ibid. 1957,* p. 190 *et seq.*, and *ibid. 1959,* p. 264 *et seq.*
22 See further B. Cheng, *The United Nations and Outer Space,* 14 *C.L.P.* (1961), p. 262 *et seq.*, and F. L. Schuman, *Shadows at the Summit,* 15 *Y.B.W.A.* (1961), p. 5 *et seq.*

Collective Security

According to the scheme of the Charter, the Security Council of the United Nations is the guardian-in-chief of world security. The temporary self-exclusion of the Soviet Union from the Security Council in the early stages of the war in Korea permitted the experiment of action of the United Nations under Chapter Seven of the Charter in circumstances not likely to repeat themselves.[23]

Even so, the Security Council could not act under Article 43 of the Charter ; for the agreements envisaged by this Article had—and have—not been concluded. If they had been in force, it would have made little difference. Whenever a permanent member does not choose to absent itself, but exercises its veto, the Security Council is unable to call on such forces.

For this reason, Vyshinsky's proposal made at the Fifth General Assembly of 1950 for a world police force under the direction of the Security Council does not carry matters any further. In cases which remain unaffected by the East-West rift, unanimity between the world Powers would make it unnecessary to set the force in motion, and in others which arise out of the world's major division, the Security Council would be unable to act.

Nevertheless, it is true that, with the concurrence or acquiescence of the Soviet Union, *ad hoc* United Nations Forces were established in Egypt in the wake of the Suez crisis and in the Congo. In the former case, the two hegemonial Powers tacitly agreed on imposing self-denying ordinances on themselves and on keeping their junior partners and small States in the belt along the world frontier under firm control.[24] In the latter case, both sides agreed, at least initially, to refrain from extending the area of their conflict to this part of Central Africa.[25] The fact that the Soviet Union and her allies refuse to contribute to the United Nations budgets for these Forces underlines, however, the precarious character of these rare instances of limited co-operation between East and West. These efforts are akin to the successful attempts made to ensure Austria's neutrality [26] and neutralise Antarctica.[27]

The substitutes for collective security as envisaged under the

---

[23] See further *Power Politics*, p. 515 *et seq.*
[24] See further 10 *C.L.P.* (1957), p. 284 *et seq.*; 12 *ibid.* (1959), p. 247 *et seq.* and 13 *Y.B.W.A.* (1959), p. 236 *et seq.*
[25] See International Law Association, *Report of the 49th Conference (Hamburg—1960)*, p. 97 *et seq.*
[26] See further *Manual*, Vol. 1, pp. 53 and 207, and 15 *Y.B.W.A.* (1961), p. 233 *et seq.*
[27] See further *Manual*, Vol. 2, pp. 519–520.

Charter of the United Nations were, however, provided in a different form. In building up their antagonistic systems of defensive alliances, both sides relied on the Charter. While, for a time, the Soviet Union favoured Article 107, and the Western Powers chose to rely on Article 51, at a later stage, the Soviet Union and her Allies also came to appreciate the potentialities of the latter Article.[28]

By preparing for the exercise of their " inherent right of self-defence," both sides used Article 51 as an escape clause from the system of collective security under the Charter and returned, with due respect for the verbiage of collective security, to time-honoured defensive alliances and counter-alliances of less sophisticated epochs of power politics.[29]

As early as 1950, a United Kingdom Minister had to confess [30]: " Unfortunately it became clear in the first four years of the life of the United Nations that the conflict between the points of view of the Western Powers and of Soviet Russia and its Eastern European associates went so deep as to make improbable the early achievement on a world-wide basis of the major purposes which the Charter was designed to achieve."

It suffices to refer *en passant* to another victim of East-West tension, the Anglo-Soviet Alliance of 1942. It would be idle to argue retrospectively that one or the other Party had broken the Treaty. The basic assumption was that the wartime unity of the Parties was to be continued into the post-war era. As a matter of fact, each of the parties was lined up on a different side of the world balance of power. Thus, the two parties were unlikely ever to agree in future on the *casus foederis*. If ever a case existed for the application of the *clausula rebus sic stantibus*, it was that of the Anglo-Soviet Alliance, and the same was true of the Franco-Soviet Alliance of 1944.

Other developments contributed even further to undermining faith in the collective system of the United Nations. Forms of aggression which were not entirely unknown in earlier periods of international relations were developed into a fine art : aggression from within and aggression by proxy. So long as a Power avoided being openly implicated in armed intervention against an established Government or in using threats incompatible with Paragraph 4 of

---

[28] See further *Fundamental Principles*, p. 327 *et seq.*, and *Manual*, Vol. 2, pp. 582–583.
[29] See further *Power Politics*, p. 517 *et seq.* and *Manual*, Vol. 2, p. 656 *et seq.*
[30] Cmd. 7883 (1950), p. 3.

Article 2 of the Charter, it apparently remained free to do what it liked to change the world balance in its favour.

The same object could be attained by the use of other Powers, especially non-members of the United Nations.

While the Soviet Union and her allies must bear the responsibility for having started these forms of intervention in Czechoslovakia and Greece,[31] the cases of Guatemala and Cuba prove that the United States of America also employs the pattern of hegemonial intervention at least for the purpose of preventing the erosion from within of Western Hemisphere defence.[32]

A further inevitable result of these forms of aggressive defence is to blur the clear borderline between the state of peace and resort to armed force which it has been the object of the Charter of the United Nations to establish. The states of peace and war are again reduced to their traditional relativity in systems of power politics and power politics in disguise.[33]

International Regulation of Armaments

It needs to be stated merely for the sake of completeness that, in a world so hopelessly split as ours, it proved impossible to devise generally acceptable principles " governing disarmament and the regulation of armaments." [34]

Nonetheless, international lawyers cannot ignore these prolonged and inconclusive discussions in the principal organs and commissions of the United Nations and at the protracted meetings of the Geneva Conference on the banning of nuclear tests.

In an acute form, these exchanges reveal the depth of mutual suspicion and distrust between West and East, a psychological factor of first magnitude which shakes the very foundations of existing international law.[35]

In 1959, the Governments of France, the Soviet Union, the United Kingdom and the United States of America established a ten-nation disarmament committee. Its most significant features were that it was established outside the framework of the United Nations and

---

[31] See further *Power Politics*, p. 529 *et seq.*
[32] See above, p. 154.
[33] See further below, p. 234 *et seq.*
[34] Article 11 of the Charter of the United Nations.
    See further P. Noel-Baker, *The Arms Race* (1958); H. Bull, *The Control of the Arms Race* (1961), and *Power Politics*, p. 534 *et seq.*
[35] See below, pp. 177 and 294 *et seq.*

its membership was based on the assumption of the existence of the two world camps. While Canada, France, Italy, the United Kingdom and the United States represented the one bloc, Bulgaria, Czechoslovakia, Poland, Rumania and the Soviet Union represented the other. In the General Assembly of 1960, the Soviet Union proposed to complete the picture by the addition of five uncommitted States : Ghana, India, Indonesia, Mexico and the United Arab Republic.

The real problem is, however, the one raised before a Senate Foreign Relations Committee, that is to say, whether the Soviet Union can be relied upon to keep an international armaments agreement. While the representative of the United States government felt confident that the Western Powers would keep such an agreement, he was frankly dubious whether " the other fellow would not break it when it was to his advantage." [36]

Doubts such as these are hardly dispelled by pronouncements from leaders of the Russo-Chinese camp such as that made by Khrushchev at a lunch in honour of a foreign State visitor : " Even if all the nations of the world were to take a decision which would not correspond with the interests of the Soviet Union and threatened its security, the Soviet Union would not recognise such a decision and would maintain its right by force. And we have the means to do this." [36a]

At this point, it becomes impossible to resist the temptation of quoting from the Preamble to the Charter of the United Nations: " We the peoples of the United Nations determined to save succeeding generations from the scourge of war . . . have resolved to combine our efforts to accomplish these aims."

[36] Testimony by Mr. Clayton on February 13, 1950 (United States Information Service, *Daily Wireless Bulletin*, February 14, 1950, p. 1).

Bevin expressed himself in a similar vein in the House of Commons (Hansard, House of Commons Debates, March 22, 1950, Vol. 472, Col. 1951) on the chances of an international agreement on the control of atomic energy: " If a country will not open its doors for inspection, what is the use of entering into agreements when you do not know whether they are being kept or not? "

On Stalin's exaggerated faith in the German-Soviet Non-Aggression Pact of August 23, 1939, *cf.* Marshal Yeremenko in *Red Star*, as quoted in *The Times*, June 22, 1961, and further United States Department of State, *Nazi-Soviet Relations 1939–1941* (1948) and A. Seidl, *Die Beziehungen zwischen Deutschland und der Sovietunion 1939–1941* (1949).

[36a] *The Times* newspaper, July 14, 1961.

For a prompt reaction by the leader of the United States Delegation to the Three-Power nuclear Conference at Geneva, in which he accused the Russian Government of bad faith and obstruction, see *ibid.*, July 22, 1961, and further the United States Note of July 15, 1961, to the Soviet Government (*United States Information Service*, July 17, 1961).

Functional International Co-operation

It is not surprising that the basic political division of the world is sharply reflected in the economic field. Economics are a function of politics. The reverse proposition is a dangerous fallacy, refuted time and time again by hard experience.

On a global basis, the Economic and Social Council of the United Nations with its multitude of functional and regional commissions, served by still more sub-commissions, standing committees, *ad hoc* committees and special bodies, reflects an—in the prevailing circumstances—unavoidable discrepancy between intention and attainment. Even so, but primarily on the basis of generous financial assistance by the United States, this body has been able to make constructive use of the competition by the World Powers for developing nations to launch valuable programmes for technical assistance to these countries. That it is advisable to avoid any dogmatism on these matters is shown by the fact that, in the post-Stalin era, the Soviet Union found it impossible to join UNESCO and the International Labour Organisation.

In a more intensive form, international economic co-operation takes place within the precincts of each of the two worlds. Institutions such as the International Monetary Fund, the Bank for International Reconstruction and Development and the International Development Association are open to all. In fact, however, the Eastern States have either never joined these Organisations or have withdrawn from them after short guest performances.

Similarly, institutions such as the General Agreement on Tariffs and Trade, ultimately to be superseded by the Organisation for Trade Co-operation, the Organisation for Economic Co-operation and Development, the European Free Trade Association and the European Economic Community are primarily or exclusively of a sectional character. In the East, Comecon, and multilateral barter agreements are the chief forms of exclusive international economic co-operation and co-ordination.

In such an environment, traditional standards of international economic law tend to change their customary function. Thus, in a multilateral treaty such as the General Agreement on Tariffs and Trade of 1947, the purpose of Article II on general most-favoured-nation treatment is no longer merely to encourage general trade. It is as much to prevent parties to such an agreement from discriminating in favour of outsiders against any of the contracting parties, and to induce outsiders to take part in the work of the Organisation. Thus, one of the purposes of this Article is to ensure that, without the consent of the Organisation, members do not grant preferential treatment to non-member States.[37]

It would be sanguine to assume that the East-West conflict had left untouched the traditional field of international functional co-operation : humanitarian activities. Far from being less pronounced in such matters, the political rift between East and West is aggravated in this sphere by the ideological cleavage between Western democratic and liberal traditions, and the totalitarianism of the Eastern States.

The treatment of the refugee problem in the United Nations is the most pointed, yet by no means the only, example of this experience. In the debates in the General Assembly and the Economic and Social Council which preceded the establishment of the International Refugee Organisation, it was impossible to achieve agreement between West and East on the definition of refugees and displaced persons. In the Eastern view, the Western Powers adopted a pointedly liberal attitude towards what the Eastern States considered to be war criminals and traitors. In Western eyes, the Eastern States equated with these objectionable types anyone who happened to be hostile to their own totalitarian régimes. Consistently, both sides disagreed on the wisdom of the principle of involuntary repatriation and on the categories of persons who should benefit from the activities of the International Refugee Organisation. The Western view prevailed, but the Eastern States refused to take part in the work of the International Refugee Organisation.[38]

In March, 1950, the Soviet Union used the issue of Chinese representation in the Security Council in order to withdraw temporarily even from the United Nations Children's Fund. Similarly, at one stage, the leaders of the Soviet Union must have thought that the World Health Organisation fulfilled functions which were beneficial and unaffected by the East-West conflict ; for the Soviet Union joined this Organisation and actively co-operated in its work. When it became clear, however, that for the proper discharge of its functions, the Organisation would require concrete information, which the Soviet Government was not prepared to supply, and was going to send out field missions to member States, considerations of

---

[37] See below, p. 225 *et seq.*
[38] See further *Manual,* Vol. 2, pp. 436 and 503 *et seq.*, and W. Schätzel and Th. Veiter (eds.), *Handbuch des internationalen Flüchtlingsrechts* (1960).

security and of maintaining a strict isolation of her population from contact with the Western world were treated as overriding. When, however, after Stalin's death, the Soviet leaders considered some relaxation of pressure advisable, the Soviet Union resumed her membership in the World Health Organisation.

Compared with the record of the Soviet Union in the post-1919 period, the establishment of other Communist-ruled States has removed to some extent the sense of isolation from which the Soviet rulers of Russia had previously suffered and has made them even less inclined to join non-Communist States in functional international institutions which entail a substantial curtailment of national sovereignty.[39]

International Protection of Human Rights

The last-minute attempt at the Conference of San Francisco to make the United Nations responsible for the promotion of human rights and fundamental freedoms was a largely nominal success for the protagonists of this policy. It was achieved at the price of not defining these rights and freedoms and leaving the protection, as distinct from the promotion, of these rights with each of the member States. This was the maximum that could be achieved in a heterogeneous international organisation which, from the start, consisted of democratic, authoritarian and totalitarian States and was to be open to all peace-loving States, irrespective of their internal structure.[40]

To assume that a common denominator of human rights could be found between West and East was to ignore the true structure of the People's Democracies. Wartime enthusiasm and propaganda may explain the euphemistic description, then current in the West, of these States as variants of democracy. In fact, the supreme reign of expediency, negation of the rule of law in the Western sense, rightlessness of the individual and unbridled rule of the secret police, accompanied by torture and forced labour camps, are of the essence of these systems.

Thus, the post-war world woke up to the reality of an unparalleled disregard of human rights. Retaliation in kind by the liberated

[39] See further above, p. 148 *et seq.*, and K. W. Davis, *The Soviets at Geneva* (1934) and L. Schapiro, *Soviet Participation in International Institutions*, 3 *Y.B.W.A.* (1949), p. 205 *et seq.*

[40] See further J. N. Hazard, *The Soviet Union and World Bill of Rights*, 47 *Columbia Law Review* (1947), p. 1095 *et seq.*; A. Martin, *Human Rights and World Politics*, 5 *Y.B.W.A.* (1951), p. 37 *et seq.*; H. Lauterpacht, *International Law and Human Rights* (1950), and *Power Politics*, p. 627 *et seq.*

Eastern nations against their German oppressors ; a westward flood of refugees (and war criminals) from the Red Terror ; mass deportations towards the East, and even the wholesale abduction of children ushered in the United Nations era of the international promotion and encouragement of human rights.

Eastern and Western spokesmen in the United Nations used the opportunity of the drafting of an International Bill and Covenant of Human Rights for bitter and futile attacks on each other. In the end, this merely proved the impossibility of eliminating a contradiction in terms, that is to say, leaving untouched the totalitarian structure of States and, at the same time, attempting to make such police States conform with liberal and democratic standards.

As the short-lived Chinese experiment with the " hundred flowers " proved, experiments in socialist legality may be more easily revokable than Western observers appear to conceive possible, and deserve to be watched with sympathetic scepticism over a prolonged period before being accepted at their face-value.[41]

International Trusteeship

In this field, the East-West conflict did not unduly interfere with the working of the United Nations machinery ; for ordinary trusteeship agreements are approved by the General Assembly with a two-thirds majority.

In the one case in which the concurrence of the Soviet Union in the Security Council with the United States draft for the strategic area of her Pacific trust territory was required, the Soviet Union proved to be surprisingly helpful. It is not necessary here to explain this mystery in detail. It suffices to mention the names of the Kurile Islands and of Southern Sakhalin. It is not likely, however, that this miracle will repeat itself.

Similarly, supervision of the administration of the trust territories by the Trusteeship Council proceeds relatively smoothly. Again, the principle of simple majority, which applies in the Trusteeship Council, limits the Soviet sector of the world to making the most of its opportunities for propaganda in the Trusteeship Council as well as in the General Assembly and its Committees concerned with trust territories and other non-self governing territories.

---

[41] See further H. J. Berman, *Justice in Russia* (1950); J. N. Hazard, *Law and Social Change in the U.S.S.R.* (1953), V. Gsovski and K. Grzybowski (eds.), *Government, Law and Courts in the Soviet Union and Eastern Europe* (2 vols. 1959) and D. G. Lavroff, *Les Libertés publiques en Union soviétique* (1960).

Nonetheless, far-reaching differences of opinion between West and East exist. For a variety of reasons—arguable on a strict interpretation of the Charter—the Soviet Union held all the trusteeship agreements to have been vitiated by initial defects and, for a time, refused to take her seat in the Trusteeship Council. Moreover, the Soviet Union and her allies consistently supported the attempts of the " anti-colonial " bloc at reading very much more into Chapter Eleven of the Charter on Non-Self-Governing Territories than had been intended at San Francisco.

In a General Assembly, however, in which former colonies became an increasingly numerous pressure group, and in which the United States of America tended to come down on the anti-colonialist side, the colonial Powers were fighting an unrewarding rearguard action. In this field, the Soviet bloc celebrated its greatest victories by identifying itself—at least in relation to territories controlled by members of the other camp—with the community ideal of an expanding trusteeship.[42]

The Secretariat of the United Nations

The functions of the Secretary-General and the other members of the United Nations Secretariat, as set out in Chapter XV of the Charter of the United Nations, are based on an unstated assumption: the possibility of an international civil service devoted to its international objects without fear or favour of any " authority external to the Organisation." [43]

If, as with the Secretary-General of the United Nations,[44] his responsibilities include political, representative and administrative tasks, member States either accept this major premise or they are likely to clash headlong with the Secretariat and, in particular its head, the Secretary-General.

The Soviet Union and her allies appear to operate from a different starting point. In Khrushchev's words, there are no neutral men.[45] In this view, impartiality can be attained only if, in the absence of a substantial degree of consensus among the member States, the Secretariat refrains from action other than in routine matters. In

42 See further *Power Politics*, p. 660 *et seq.*, and *Manual*, Vol. 2, p. 422 *et seq.*
43 Article 100 (1) of the U.N. Charter.
44 See further *Manual*, Vol. 1, p. 303 *et seq.*, and Vol. 2, pp. 650–651.
45 Interview granted to Walter Lippmann (*New York Herald Tribune*—European ed.—April 17, 1961).
   See also above, p. 151.

a " United " Nations composed of two antagonistic blocs and a shifting third group of uncommitted countries, this means consensus between these three groups.

As both the first and the second Secretary-General of the United Nations refused to see the United Nations in this light, it is not surprising that the Soviet Union and her allies should have come to boycott each of these exponents of a more active type of neutralism. It is equally consistent that, while the Soviet Union favours a transformation of the post of the Secretary-General into a three-headed collective, the Western States categorically resist any attempt at " reforming " the Charter of the United Nations on such lines.

Allied Military Government

Without at least a glance at Allied military government in Germany, Austria, Trieste and Japan, the picture of the superstructure of post-1945 international law would remain incomplete. In spite of diversities, a uniform thread linked all these experiments in international government. They were all profoundly affected by the East-West rift. Each of these territories of former enemy States lay within the vital area of the international frontier between East and West. All of them became security zones of the former Western allies against their former Eastern ally and vice versa. Thus, the original purposes of these ventures in post-war international government were changed beyond recognition. In these circumstances, their legal foundations were shaken to the roots, and the inter-Allied agreements regarding these territories went through a radical process of *de facto* revision.

In Germany, the Four-Power *co-imperium*, which had been established after Germany's *debellatio*, disintegrated on the quadripartite level within little more than two years. Berlin became the symbol of Allied disunity and of the inability of the Four Powers to make the Potsdam Agreement work. Co-operation gave way increasingly to competition for the favours of the defeated enemy.

In this context, problems such as those of dismantling German war industries and disarming Germany assumed a different complexion from that envisaged in prior inter-Allied engagements. Each side established its own German government with claims to represent Germany as a whole. So far, the Soviet Union is the only one of the major Powers which maintains diplomatic relations both with the Federal German Republic and with the German Democratic Republic.

As with the Anglo-Soviet Alliance of 1942, a case can be made by either side for breaches of these engagements by the other side which, in turn, made inevitable its own subesquent breaches of these commitments. On this assumption, the latter breaches can always be justified either on the ground of necessity or reprisal.

It would seem more commensurate to the magnitude of the issue to attempt to see this process of disintegration in a wider perspective. All these agreements were based on the assumption, originally shared by all concerned, of continued unity between the four Occupying Powers. In the case of Germany, the impact of the East-West rift on the legal framework of co-operation between the Western and Eastern Allies was such as to provide apparently another model example for the application of the *clausula rebus sic stantibus*.[46] Owing to the complete change in an underlying political environment, which had been taken for granted by all concerned, these treaties would have come to an end. It is also arguable—and probably corresponds more closely to the expressed intentions of the Parties—that the repeated protestations by each of the Powers concerned of the continued existence of the Potsdam Agreement should be treated as tacit renewals of the Agreement, in spite of all the fundamental changes in basic assumptions that had taken place.

The breakdown, for most purposes, of inter-Allied government in Germany raises the question why quadripartite international government in Austria and, in particular, in Vienna should have survived for so long. In the first place, the Allies treated Austria as a liberated country and allowed her to establish a Government of her own for the whole of the country. Moreover, the functions of Allied Government in Austria were more limited than those exercised in Germany. Thus, the unanimity rule on the quadripartite level hampered, but did not make impossible the conduct of day-to-day government and administration.

Furthermore, the Soviet Union realised that, so long as she was still in a position to delay the conclusion of a peace treaty with Austria, she was in a stronger strategic position and better able to exploit economically the Russian-occupied parts of Austria than after her withdrawal from a country which, in its overwhelming majority, had opted for the West. The Soviet Union was, therefore, willing to respect the *status quo* under the inter-Allied agreements of 1945 on Austria. After prolonged negotiations, this experiment

[46] See above, p. 155.

in post-war co-operation was liquidated by the Austrian State Treaty of 1955 and the adoption by Austria of a status of neutrality.[47]

The fate of the Allied Administration of Trieste is no less revealing. Nominal agreement between West and East was achieved on the provisional and permanent Statutes for the Free Territory of Trieste, and these were incorporated as annexes in the Peace Treaty with Italy of 1947.[48] In January, 1947, the Security Council gave to these annexes the assent required under the Peace Treaty.

One point, however, remained unsettled : the appointment of the Governor, the linch-pin in both the provisional and permanent Statutes. It proved impossible to find a candidate on whom both the Western Powers and the Soviet Union could agree. Thus, Allied military occupation of the Free Territory continued.

Until the defection of Yugoslavia from the Soviet camp, there was continuous friction between the administrations in Zone A, including Trieste and occupied by Anglo-American forces, and in Zone B, occupied by Yugoslav forces. The Soviet Union, deprived of access to the Territory through the desertion of Yugoslavia, limited herself to periodic assertions of alleged breaches of the Peace Treaty by the Western Allies who contented themselves with encouraging in their Zone the *de facto* integration of Trieste in Italy. Finally, by an *inter se* understanding between the two Western Occupying Powers and Yugoslavia, on the one hand, and Italy, on the other, the occupation régime was terminated and the territory of Trieste divided between Italy and Yugoslavia.[49]

Military government in Japan worked, but only at the price of letting the United States pursue her own course. As the other Western Powers were content to acquiesce in this state of affairs, the Soviet Union could be left to please herself. She boycotted the merely consultative Far Eastern Advisory Commission, finding herself in a lonely minority in the Far Eastern Commission, which superseded the Advisory Council, and in the Allied Council for Japan. The latter, being on the spot and, therefore, of potential nuisance value, was soon reduced by the American Pro-consul to a

[47] Cmnd. 214 (1957).
  See also above, p. 154, and further *Manual*, Vol. 1, pp. 53 and 207.
[48] Cmd. 7481 (1948).
[49] Cmd. 9288 (1954). See further *Manual*, Vol. 2, pp. 431 and 552–553.
  On similar difficulties, which arose out of the post-war arrangements regarding Tangier, see *Power Politics*, pp. 406–407, and *Manual*, Vol. 2, pp. 442–443.

mere shadow-existence. Only the complete lack of effective inter-Allied Government in Japan prevented military government there from becoming frustrated by the East-West conflict.

When it came to the conclusion of a Peace Treaty, the Soviet Union found in 1951 at San Francisco that the United States was not prepared to brook either opposition or obstruction. Thus, separate peace treaties offered the most practical form of terminating the state of war between the former Allies and their once common enemy in the Far East.[50]

The conclusions to be drawn from this analysis are necessarily sombre. It would be sheer escapism to put the emphasis either on the relatively harmonious relations between Powers in one and the same camp or on the achievements of the United Nations on the periphery of world power politics. The test of an international order is whether it can cope with the maximum of strain to which it is likely to be subjected. The East-West conflict is in this class. The United Nations is constitutionally incapable of mastering such a situation. If both sides are willing to agree or to impose self-denying ordinances on themselves, or one side temporarily lets matters slide, the machinery can be made to work. In such cases, the imposing superstructure of the United Nations offers meeting-places and techni-cal facilities for reaching agreement which should not be minimised. But, whenever basic agreement between the World Powers is lacking, their freedom of action is, in fact, if not in law, hardly more limited than that of greater Powers in traditional systems of power politics.

The World Powers—and, in the majority of cases, also, the other members of the United Nations—remain free to arm; to con-clude alliances and counter-alliances against one another; to submit or to refuse to submit justiciable disputes to international courts and tribunals; to comply or not to comply with the recommendations of conciliatory agencies in non-justiciable disputes; to obstruct the application of enforcement measures against an aggressor; to keep aloof from functional international co-operation and from any extension of the international trusteeship system, and to protect fundamental rights and human freedoms as much—or as little—as they see fit.

[50] Cmd. 8601 (1952). Russo-Japanese Joint Declaration, October 19, 1956, 1 *Japanese Annual of International Law* (1957), p. 129 *et seq.*; Protocols on the Restoration of Normal Relations between Japan and Poland, February 8, 1957, 2 *ibid.* (1958), p. 208 *et seq.*, and between Japan and Czechoslovakia, February 13, 1957, *ibid.*, p. 209 *et seq.*, Treaty of Peace between Japan and Indonesia, January 20, 1958, 3 *ibid.* (1959), p. 158 *et seq.*

For two reasons, this situation is less apparent than it might be. First, the number of politically sovereign States, that is to say, States which have retained their actual freedom of choice between world peace and world war, has shrunk to a minimum.[51] Secondly the bipolarisation of the world has been accompanied by a considerable intensification of international integration in each of the world's two halves.[52] There is no commensurate integration on the level of East-West relations. The Charter of the United Nations apart, the one common legal bond to which both sides still profess to adhere is the body of the traditional rules of international law.

III—THE EAST-WEST RIFT AND INTERNATIONAL CUSTOMARY LAW

For purposes of this survey, it would be unfair to choose controversial rules of international customary law which are contested even between States in one and the same camp. The question is not whether this or that particular rule is in doubt, but whether broad agreement still exists between East and West on international law as a legally binding set of rules of behaviour. Thus, controversies on issues such as the extent of Soviet territorial waters in the Baltic [53] will be left out of account.

Sovereignty

On the level of international customary law, the rules governing the principle of sovereignty must form the starting point of any inquiry.[54]

In so far as their own rights are concerned, the Eastern States have proved themselves in the United Nations and elsewhere stout and conservative advocates of this principle and, in this respect, they do not differ materially from their Western counterparts.

At the same time, the spy trials on the betrayal of nuclear secrets in Canada, the United Kingdom and the United States,[55] the U-2 incident and the trial of George Blake in the United Kingdom

---

51 See above, pp. 58 and 154, n. 24.
52 See below, p. 274 *et seq.*
53 See further F. de Hartingh, *Les Conceptions Soviétiques du Droit de la Mer* (1960), and Academy of Sciences of the U.S.S.R., *Völkerrecht* (1960).
54 See further *Fundamental Principles*, p. 214 *et seq.*
55 See, for instance, *R.* v. *Woiken* (1946—Canada) 1 C.R. 224, and *R.* v. *Adams* (1946—Canada), O.R. 506, and further M. Cohen, *Espionage and Immunity*, 25 *B.Y.I.L.* (1948), p. 404 *et seq.*

(1961)[56] prove that the practice of Powers on both sides of the world fence is far from being impeccable.

Actually, it is common knowledge that, in systems of power politics and power politics in disguise, most sovereign States make use of this old-fashioned and wasteful means of obtaining information. The general understanding is, however, that, so long as the employers do not identify themselves with their secret agents, they do not become involved, but captor States are free to institute criminal proceedings against such agents. There remain, however, all the subversive activities, directed from Moscow, against the exclusively domestic sphere of other States through Communist outposts in any voluntary movement in other countries which they are able to penetrate.

Recognition

Under international customary law, the subjects of international law are free to use their discretion in deciding on whether to recognise new entities which fulfil the minimum requirements of international personality. Similarly, they are their own judges on whether to recognise the government of any existing subject of international law, and whether they desire to maintain diplomatic relations with it.[57] If any further evidence of the discretionary character of Recognition were required, it has been furnished by the discrepancies in the policies of the Western nations on the recognition of the Communist régime in China.[58]

The East-West conflict has not affected the *positive* aspects of the international law of Recognition. It is more doubtful whether, on occasions, both sides were not overstepping an existing prohibitory rule of international law by the premature recognition of régimes such as the North Korean Viet-Minh Government, and of the French-sponsored Governments of Viet-Nam, Laos and Cambodia in former French Indo-China.

Thus, at a time when France was still actively and effectively engaged in subduing the Communist insurrection in Viet-Nam, the recognition of the Ho Chi-minh régime by the Soviet Union in 1950, followed by similar acts on the part of the other Communist States,

[56] See also above, p. 153.
[57] See further *Fundamental Principles*, p. 228 *et seq.*
[58] See above, p. 76

as the Government of an independent Viet-Nam, amounted to an unwarranted interference with French territorial sovereignty and was, therefore, illegal. The most any third State was entitled to grant at that time was recognition of these rebels as belligerents.

Similarly, recognition by the Western Powers of the Governments of Viet-Nam, the Kingdom of Laos, and the Kingdom of Cambodia followed on the heels of the ratification of the agreements between France and these three States for the devolution of French powers in Indo-China. The United States announcement of recognition of February 8, 1950, referred to the status of these new recruits to international personality as " independent States within the French Union." [59] The British messages to the three Prime Ministers of the same date were couched in more cautious language. The Government in the United Kingdom recognised the three States as associate States within the French Union in accordance with the terms of their agreements with France of 1949 and their Governments as the Governments of these States. This left it open whether these States were dependent or independent States.

As France welcomed these acts of recognition, it is immaterial whether these States were actually dependent or independent States. To the extent to which a suzerain State permits, or even encourages, direct relations between the dependent State and third Powers, recognition of a dependent State is entirely in conformity with international law.

For the same reasons, no rules of the international law of Recognition—as distinct from undertakings to the contrary in the Potsdam Agreement—prevented the Western Allies and the Soviet Union from bestowing such recognition as they cared to grant to the German Governments in their respective zones of occupation, nor were—or are—they under any legal duty to recognise each other's creations.

The East-West conflict has again thrown into sharp relief the discretionary character of Recognition under international customary law and its perennial use in systems of power politics as a means of diplomatic approbation and pressure.

Diplomatic Immunities and Privileges

On the basis of innumerable safe-conducts and long-forgotten treaties, rules of international customary law on the treatment of

---

[59] United States Information Service, *Daily Wireless Bulletin*, February 8, 1950, p. 2. See also L. Kunz, *Critical Remarks on Lauterpacht's " Recognition in International Law,"* 44 *A.J.I.L.* (1950), p. 713 *et seq.*

foreign diplomatic envoys and their missions gradually developed.[60] For good reasons, they were considered to be among the best-honoured rules of international law. Their liberal interpretation and application was equally in the interest of every civilised State, with the *corps diplomatique* in every State jealously and collectively guarding the rights of every one of its members.[61]

Whenever, in the pre-1914 period, international diplomatic law was broken in one of the border zones of civilisation, swift retribution followed. The rise of totalitarian States in the inter-war period put a strain on the established rules ; for each of these States had much to hide. Yet, whether Fascist, Nazi or Communist, they still winced at being branded as barbarians. Mr. Maclean's description of his travels shows how relatively easy it was, before 1939, for a diplomat with private initiative to travel even in forbidden Soviet Asia.[62]

When, in the early 'fifties, East-West relations had reached their lowest ebb, the methods used by some of the East European allies of the Soviet Union to deprive Western diplomats of their traditional rights under international law followed a stereotype pattern : —

First Phase : *Treason Trials.* In order to fortify themselves for the steps to be taken at subsequent stages, treason trials were instituted against nationals of these totalitarian States who were employed by Western diplomatic missions in these countries.

Such trials served several purposes. They were intended to frighten nationals employed by, or in social contact with, Western embassies and legations from maintaining their connections or to induce such nationals to act as agents of the secret police. They enabled the totalitarian Governments concerned to implicate foreign diplomats and consuls, who were either not considered sufficiently " sympathetic " or had acquired too intimate an acquaintance with the country to whose government they were accredited.

Second Phase : *Persona non grata and Closure of Information and Cultural Departments.* Then followed demands for the recall of members of embassies, legations and consulates and for the closure of libraries, and information and cultural services accessible to the public.

In demanding the closure of the British Legation's Information Office, the Rumanian Government did not even take the trouble of fabricating any conspiracy. It made its request to " protect the

---

[60] See above, p. 92 *et seq.*   [61] See above, p. 29 *et seq.*
[62] F. Maclean, *Eastern Approaches* (1949).

national interests " and maintained that the existence of the Information Office was inconsistent with the normal functions of a diplomatic mission.[63]

In a still more summary fashion, the Czechoslovak Government asked that of the United States to reduce the staff of its embassy in Prague and of its consulate at Bratislava by two-thirds within one week.[64] This request was clearly illegal. Yet, by declaring *persona non grata* a corresponding number of United States officials and by refusing to accept any of their successors, the Czechoslovak Government could have attained the same end. Another novelty was the pressure used by the Czechoslovak Government in order to achieve compliance with its request. It intimated that " it would not feel responsible for the safety of the Americans if they were not out of the country by Sunday." [65]

Third Phase : Calculated Insults. Diplomats who survived Phase Two had to be prepared for measures such as the Czechoslovak Government chose to inflict on foreign missions. In Czechoslovakia, cars belonging to diplomats, had to carry yellow identification plates.[66] The choice of the yellow colour was probably not incidental. It was to suggest an association of ideas with the yellow hats which, in medieval days, Jews were obliged to wear and with the yellow star Hitler forced on their descendants.

In addition, considerable restrictions on movement and travel were imposed, thus reducing Western embassies and legations to the position of isolated enclaves. The Soviet Union improved upon these rather primitive means of chicanery. With a peculiar sense of humour, it made foreign diplomats pay increasingly dearly for the privilege of being held *incommunicado*. When, on February 28, 1950, the rouble was given a higher exchange rate, the diplomatic rate in force until then was abolished. As was pointed out in British and United States Notes to the Soviet Government,[67] this measure amounted to an artificial increase in the cost of living of members of foreign

[63] *The Times* newspaper, March 4, 1950.
  On grounds of principle, this assertion was repeatedly contested by the Government of the United States. It maintained that, in modern conditions, such services and activities had become part of the normal activities of diplomatic missions. See, for instance, the Statement made by the Department of State to the Czechoslovak Ambassador in Washington on May 13, 1950 (United States Information Service, *Daily Wireless Bulletin*, May 15, 1950).
[64] United States Information Service, *Daily Wireless Bulletin*, May 1, 1950.
[65] *The Times* newspaper, May 12, 1950.
[66] *Ibid.*, April 22, 1950.
[67] United States Information Service, *Daily Wireless Bulletin*, March 28, 1950, p. 3, and *The Times* newspaper, March 30, 1950.

diplomatic missions. The preferential rate had been adopted by the Soviet Government in 1941 in order to equalise the purchasing power of the rouble with prevailing world prices. As the rouble is not used in international trade, this step was merely calculated to make the life of foreign diplomats in the Soviet Union even more burdensome.

It matters little whether, in some of these instances, the Eastern totalitarian States were formally within their rights in demanding the recall of foreign diplomatic representatives, in restricting their freedom of movement or in making local currency available to them at an arbitrary rate. International diplomatic law has grown on the basis of a liberal application of the principle of reciprocity. Once one group of States sets out to apply this principle restrictively, other States are faced with a dilemma. They can either continue with their own liberal practices and grant customary privileges to those who themselves deny them or they can have recourse to measures of retorsion and reprisals.

After considerable hesitation, though with misgivings and in the mildest form, some of the Western Governments adopted the latter course. Demands for the withdrawal of Western diplomats were countered by corresponding requests to the Eastern States concerned.[68] The closure of Western information and cultural services was also answered in kind.[69] The United States experimented with travel restrictions on the members of Eastern missions whose countries were imposing such restrictions on United States diplomatic personnel.[70] It is apparent why, even on technical grounds, Western democratic States must come off worst in such a competition.

In the end, the real issue was whether it was not better to face such totalitarian States with a choice between scrupulous acceptance

[68] British demand for the withdrawal of a Hungarian attaché in retaliation for declaring two British attachés in Budapest *personae non gratae* (*The Times* newspaper, April 19, 1950); United States request for the closure of the Czechoslovak Consulates at Cleveland and Pittsburgh in retaliation for the reduction in the staffs of the United States Embassy in Prague and the Consulate at Bratislava (United States Information Service, *Daily Wireless Bulletin*, May 15, 1950); Yugoslav expulsion of nine members of the Hungarian Legation in Belgrade in retaliation for the expulsion of ten members of the Yugoslav Legation in Budapest (*The Times* newspaper, September 28, 1949) and corresponding measures against five and eight members of the Czechoslovak and Polish Embassies, respectively, in Belgrade (*ibid.*, October 7, 1949).

[69] British requests to Czechoslovakia for the closure of the Czechoslovak Institute in London and for the termination of the Information Service of the Czechoslovak Embassy in London (*The Times* newspaper, May 16, 1950); for the closure of the Hungarian Cultural Institute in London (*ibid.*, April 20, 1950), and for the closure of the Information Office of the Rumanian Legation in London (*ibid.*, March 17, 1950).

[70] United States Information Service, *Daily Wireless Bulletin*, June 24 and July 7, 1950.

of agreed diplomatic standards and the suspension of diplomatic relations. In the case of Bulgaria, the United States temporarily considered the second alternative to be the only solution.[71]

It may be debatable to what extent the deterioration in the diplomatic standards applied by the members of the Soviet bloc in the closing phase of the Stalinist era was due to their totalitarian character or to the sharpening of the bipolar conflict. The result was, however, evident. In their relations with the West, the matter-of-course acceptance by the Soviet Union and her East European allies of the principles of international diplomatic law and courtesy could no longer be taken for granted. After Stalin's death, the Soviet Union and her Allies indicated that they desired to return to the traditional standards of international diplomatic law and practice. This made it possible for Western States to reciprocate by corresponding relaxations of their own retaliatory counter-measures.

At the Vienna Conference of 1961, the Soviet Union actively cooperated in the collective effort of eighty-one States to put the law

[71] In its Note to the Bulgarian Government of February 22, 1950, the United States Government explained its decision to suspend diplomatic relations with the Bulgarian Government: " Diplomatic relations between the United States and the post-war Government of Bulgaria, since their establishment in September 1947, have not been on a basis which could be called friendly or cordial. Cordiality was scarcely to be expected when Bulgarian officials and the controlled press were constantly denouncing and insulting the United States, and when the Bulgarian Government was violating its peace treaty obligations, ignoring resolutions of the United Nations, and supporting armed action against Greece. It was the hope of the United States Government, however, that relations, if not cordial, at least might be correct. But the treatment accorded to the American Legation in Sofia, including crippling restrictions on the entry and movement of American officials assigned to the Legation and an unprincipled campaign of persecution against the Legation's Bulgarian employees, left no doubt that the Bulgarian Government did not accept even the minimum standards of international practice."

" Despite all these difficulties the United States Government wished to maintain diplomatic contact with Bulgaria because of the sincere desire of the American people to work toward better understanding with the Bulgarian people, with whom ties of friendship have linked them in the past."

" The Government of the United States will continue to maintain its feeling of friendship for the people of Bulgaria and to manifest in every appropriate way its deep interest in their welfare. The Government of the United States, however, is reluctantly compelled to conclude that it is no longer possible, in view of the present attitude of the Bulgarian Government, for the American Minister and his staff to remain in Bulgaria. They have received instructions to leave Bulgaria as soon as possible. At the same time, the Government of the United States requests the recall of the Bulgarian diplomatic mission from the United States." (United States Information Service, *Daily Wireless Bulletin*, February 22, 1950).

During the very same phase of highly strained relations, the Eastern totalitarian States insisted on stretching to the limit their own rights under the accepted canons of international diplomatic law. See, for instance, the *Gubitchev* case (United States Information Service, *Daily Wireless Bulletin*, March 10, 1950).

On mutual charges in the case of M. Nacvalac, a counsellor in the Czechoslovak Mission at the United Nations, see *The Times* newspaper, June 22, 1961, and on the wider aspects of the duties of the United States of America as host to the United Nations, *Power Politics*, p. 749 *et seq.*

on diplomatic relations on a multilateral treaty basis. She and all her European allies who are members of the United Nations became signatories to the Convention on Diplomatic Relations of April 18, 1961.

The emphasis in the Convention on the economic, cultural and scientific functions of diplomatic missions corresponds to a general trend, but also to Russian views on the implications of active and peaceful co-existence. Similarly, the extension of diplomatic immunity to the administrative and technical staff of diplomatic missions may be traced to earlier treaties of a bilateral character concluded between the Soviet Union and other States.

Finally, and most important, under Article 47 of the Convention, the receiving State must not discriminate between States in the application of the Convention. If, however, the receiving State applies any of the provisions of the Convention restrictively because of a restrictive application of that provision to its own mission in the sending State or extends to another State more favourable treatment than is required under the Convention, this is not regarded as discrimination. Thus, the receiving State must ensure to all members of a mission freedom of movement and travel in its territory, but only subject to a reservation which ensures the primacy of the territorial sovereignty of the receiving State. In accordance with Article 26, this right is subject to the laws and regulations concerning " zones entry into which is prohibited or regulated for reasons of national security," but such restrictions must be applied alike to *all* foreign missions.[71a]

The Treatment of Foreigners

In order to avoid exaggeration, topics such as the treatment meted out by the Eastern totalitarian States to persons of dual nationality and the infraction of the property rights of foreigners by the Governments of these States are excluded from discussion.

In the former case, of which the refusal—since temporarily relaxed—of exit-permits to Russian wives of foreign nationals is typical, the Soviet Union could at least make a formal case for being entitled in strict law to her inhuman refusal to grant exit-permits to her own nationals. In the latter, it is arguable that, since the First World War, the minimum standard which States have to observe

71a Cmnd. 1368 (1961).

regarding the property of foreigners has become very blurred, and not in Communist States alone.[72]

No such contention can, however, be put forward to justify the wholesale interferences during the Stalinist era with the personal freedom of foreigners in countries under Russian control and their right to the impartial administration of civil and criminal justice.

It may be that, in the post-Stalinist phase of " socialist legality," such breaches of the minimum standard of civilisation and international law will remain past history.[73] At the same time, considerably fewer legal and meta-legal guarantees exist than in Western democracies against any sudden relapse into totalitarian lawlessness. Thus, while it would be tedious to relate all the major cases under this heading, it still appears salutary to recall at least some of these incidents : the case of Mr. Evans (1948), a British subject who had to undergo strange experiences in the administration of Rumanian civil and criminal justice [74] ; that of Mr. Harrison (1949), who, while under interrogation by the Hungarian secret police, was suddenly shown his fiancée " supported by a man and in a fainting condition " [75] those of the American students (1949), who, without any formal charge ever being made against them, were detained for eight weeks by the Soviet authorities in Germany [76] ; or those of Mr. Sanders and Mr. Vogeler (1950), to whom, while their cases were *sub judice*, the Hungarian Deputy Prime Minister referred in a public speech as leaders of an " important gang of spies and saboteurs." [77]

Irrespective of the question whether any of these British and United States citizens had broken the municipal laws of these Communist States, in each case the minimum standards of justice which apply between civilised States were seriously violated. In the case of Mr. Evans, proceedings which had been finally closed were reopened. Mr. Harrison was the victim of straightforward blackmail.

---

[72] See further 5 *C.L.P.* (1952), p. 295 *et seq.* and 14 *ibid.* (1961), p. 213 *et seq.*

[73] See further *l.c.* above, p. 55 *et seq.*, and the Symposium on *Preventive Detention under Different Legal Systems*, 3 *Journal of the International Commission of Jurists* (1961), p. 69 *et seq.*

[74] British Notes of September 15 and October 4, 1948 to the Rumanian Ministry of Foreign Affairs.

[75] Foreign Office Statement of September 30, 1949, announcing that, as a reprisal, the Hungarian Government had been asked to recall a member of the Hungarian Legation in London (*The Times* newspaper, October 1, 1949).

[76] Protest by the United States to the Soviet Foreign Office, October 6, 1949 (United States Information Service, *Daily Wireless Bulletin*, October 7, 1949).

[77] *The Times* newspaper, February 13, 1950. See further the British Note to the Hungarian Ministry of Foreign Affairs of February 15, 1950, and the Statement of the United States Department of State of February 21, 1950 (United States Information Service, *Daily Wireless Bulletin*, February 22, 1950).

The American students suffered unjustified deprivation of their liberty. In the trials of Mr. Sanders and Mr. Vogeler, the prior " guidance " given to the Court by a prominent member of the Hungarian Government vitiated the subsequent proceedings. In the words of a United States Note to the Soviet Government regarding the two American students, these practices were " in shocking contravention of the most elementary standards of international decency." [78]

In a subsequent Note, the United States Government summarised experiences which did not apply to Hungary alone and drew from this state of affairs some drastic conclusions : " In these circumstances, my Government has given careful consideration to the question whether American citizens are any longer free to transact normal business, or to visit, in Hungary without suffering surveillance, arbitrary arrest, and other intolerable molestations at the hands of the Hungarian police authorities and other infringements of their rights. The conduct of the Hungarian Government over a considerable period of time, and specifically in the present case, compels the conclusion that such freedom is presently denied to Americans in Hungary. The United States Government accordingly is taking immediate steps to prohibit travel by private American citizens to Hungary until further notice." [79]

Shortly afterwards, the Netherlands Ministry of Foreign Affairs issued a similar statement regarding Czechoslovakia : " Since the Netherlands Government is being prevented from giving to Netherlands subjects in Czechoslovakia the normal diplomatic and consular assistance, Netherlands subjects who intend proceeding to Czechoslovakia are earnestly advised to take this into consideration." [80]

For the time being, the treatment of foreigners in the Soviet Union and the People's Democracies appears to have changed for the better. To remain aware, however, of what happened little more than a decade ago is advisable, because such knowledge serves notice of the precarious character of this rapprochement to the standard of civilisation in the sphere of human rights, and these facts constitute a relevant part of the recent history of international law. Even more important, these episodes present object-lessons of the operation of the principle of reciprocity in its positive and negative aspects.[81]

[78] *L.c.* in note 76 above.
[79] Note of December 21, 1949 (United States Information Service, *Daily Wireless Bulletin*, December 21, 1949).
[80] January 10, 1950 (*Netherlands News*, Vol. 16, No. 6—January 13, 1950).
[81] See above, p. 29 *et seq.*

The Observance of Treaties

In a situation in which considerable doubt exists on the attitude of a whole group of States to the rules of international customary law, it is of crucial importance to know whether Russia and her Allies respect at least engagements of a consensual character.

Prior to 1939, the Soviet Union had built up a good record in her standards of treaty observance. In the political field, this achievement was marred only by the breach of the Covenant with Soviet Russia's attack—or her preventive war—against Finland. This cannot, however, count any heavier than the peculiar construction by France of her duties under her Treaty of Mutual Assistance with Czechoslovakia or the interpretation which, during the Appeasement period, most of the League members chose to adopt of the Covenant of the League of Nations.

The Soviet Union was especially careful in the scrupulous fulfilment of her contractual duties in the field of international economic law. The same was true in the post-1945 period. A reservation should, however, be made regarding the non-fulfilment by the Soviet Union and the other Eastern States of their obligations under economic treaties with Yugoslavia. These breaches were disguised as " economic sanctions." Even during the Stalinist era the Western Powers had no corresponding grounds of complaint. In a speech delivered in 1949 the President of the Board of Trade of the United Kingdom commented on the care with which, both regarding quantity and quality of the grain delivered, the Soviet Union had carried out her treaty obligations towards the United Kingdom.[82]

In the political field, the record of the Soviet Union and her satellites was less impressive. Perhaps President Truman exaggerated when he maintained that " the agreement which the Russians made at Yalta to enter the war against Japan was the only one they ever kept out of nearly forty." [83] To see matters in perspective, it is again advisable to ignore the more controversial instances and to concentrate on major cases regarding which less room for disagreement is possible : the breaches of the Bulgarian, Hungarian and Rumanian Peace Treaties of 1947.

Each of these States is bound to " take all measures necessary to secure to all persons under Bulgarian (Hungarian and Rumanian)

[82] Speech made at a meeting of the International Bureau of the Fabian Society (quoted in M. B. Brown, *East-West Trade* (1949), p. 17).
[83] Interview with Mr. Crock of *The New York Times*, February 15, 1950.

jurisdiction, without distinction as to race, sex, language or religion, the enjoyment of human rights and of the fundamental freedoms, including freedom of expression, of press and publication, of religious worship, of political opinion and of public meeting." [84]　In each of these States freedom of political representation, freedom from arbitrary arrest, freedom of religion and freedom of the press were abolished during the Stalinist era, and the extent to which they exist now is difficult to verify. [85]

In the diplomatic exchanges between the United Kingdom and the United States, on the one hand, and the three former satellites of the European Axis, on the other, these States added insult to injury. They suggested that the acts complained of had been carried out in obedience to the Peace Treaties, that is to say, to those clauses which bound them to dissolve all organisations of a Fascist type, and not to permit the existence and activities of anti-democratic organisations. [86]

Each of the three Peace Treaties provides comprehensive machinery for the settlement of disputes relating to their interpretation and execution. If a dispute cannot be settled by direct diplomatic negotiation, it shall be referred to the Heads of the diplomatic Missions of the Soviet Union, the United Kingdom and the United States in the country concerned. [87]

After prolonged and fruitless direct negotiations with the three ex-enemy States, the United Kingdom and the United States adopted this course. The Soviet Union denied, however, that any dispute existed and maintained that these matters fell within the exclusively domestic jurisdiction of these countries. Thus, the first stage of the procedure envisaged by the Peace Treaties was reduced to utter ineffectiveness.

In the Notes of the British and United States Governments of June 30, 1949, the issue of principle was squarely faced. Mr. Bevin pointed out that the " refusal of the Soviet Government to co-operate in putting this procedure into practice is liable to be interpreted as an

84 Article 2 of the Peace Treaty of 1947 with Bulgaria (Cmd. 7483—1948); Para. 1 of Article 2 of the Peace Treaty with Hungary (Cmd. 7485—1948), and Para 1 of Article 3 of the Peace Treaty with Rumania (Cmd. 7486—1948).
85 For factual details, *cf. Official Protests of the United States Government against Communist Policies or Actions, and Related Correspondence* (Supplement II to House Doc. 619 of the 80th United States Congress, 1948) and the British Notes of April 2, 1949, to each of the three ex-enemy States and the informative publications of the International Commission of Jurists.
86 Article 4 of the Peace Treaties with Bulgaria and Hungary and Article 5 of the Peace Treaty with Rumania.
87 Article 36 of the Peace Treaties with Bulgaria and Hungary and Article 40 of the Peace Treaty with Rumania.

attempt on their part (*i.e.*, the Soviet Union) to frustrate one of the provisions of the Peace Treaties. Such refusal, moreover, is in marked contradiction with the regard for treaties frequently expressed by the Soviet Government." [88] The United States Government made the no less pertinent point that the fulfilment of international treaty obligations could never be considered as a purely domestic affair. It added the solemn warning that the " application of such a theory would not only permit the total circumvention of treaty obligations but would destroy the very basis of international law." [89]

As, in these circumstances, the three Heads of Mission could not settle these disputes within the two months granted to them by the Peace Treaties, the United Kingdom and the United States proceeded to the next stage. In accordance with the Peace Treaties of 1947, they asked each of the three ex-enemy States to nominate representatives to the Commissions provided for in these Treaties. The third member remained to be selected by mutual agreement from nationals of a third State or, in the case of failure to reach agreement within one month, by the Secretary-General of the United Nations. The decision of the majority of the members of the Commission was to be definitive and binding. Each of the three ex-enemy States refused, however, to proceed to the nomination of its representative.

In its Advisory Opinion on *Interpretation of Peace Treaties* (1950), the International Court of Justice refuted Soviet contentions that the disputes in question were essentially within the domestic jurisdiction of the three ex-enemy States, and that they were not disputes within the meaning of these Treaties.[90] It also affirmed that each of the three States was bound to " co-operate in constituting the Commission, in particular by appointing its representative." [91]

It was left to the majority of the World Court—with the notable exception of Judges Azevedo and Read—to undo its good work by its subsequent Opinion.[92]

It would be hard to exaggerate the significance of this experience. It may open the eyes of those who still believe in universal bills and covenants of human rights. In these instances, human rights were protected by solemn treaty obligations. Yet what happened? With the connivance of the Soviet Union, these totalitarian States made a

---

[88] *The Times* newspaper, July 1, 1949.
[89] United States Information Service, *Daily Wireless Bulletin*, July 2, 1949, p. 6.
[90] *I.C.J. Reports 1950*, p. 65, at pp. 70 and 74.
[91] *Ibid.*, p. 77.
[92] *Interpretation of Peace Treaties (Second Phase), I.C.J. Reports 1950*, p. 221. See further *Vol. I*, pp. 523–524 and 4 *C.L.P.* (1951), p. 11 *et seq.*

laughing stock not only of the Contracting Parties which attempted to ensure their enforcement but also of international treaties in general. They set a precedent not merely for the breach of internationally guaranteed human rights but, as Mr. Fitzmaurice, as he then was, rightly emphasised in his Oral Statement on behalf of the United Kingdom before the International Court of Justice,[93] for flouting binding obligations in the field of international arbitration.[94]

Once confidence in the pledged word is so severely shaken as it has been in East-West relations, it is hard to build up again a common fund of mutual confidence and trust.[95] This is, however, the foremost task.

It can be approached only from the periphery, that is to say, by tackling jointly minor issues in a constructive spirit and finding that, contrary to expectations, the other side is keeping its promises on these matters. Understandings on topics such as Antarctica and Outer Space are within this category.

Actually, what matters least is the subject-matter of any of these questions. What does matter is to use any of these constructive opportunities as a means to a greater end, that is to say, to foster afresh habits of trust and co-operation. In their absence, it appears well-nigh impossible to break the vicious circle to which, since the end of the Second World War, relations between the two world camps have been confined.

[93] At the Court's sitting on March 2, 1950, *Pleadings*, p. 296 *et seq.*

[94] The reactions provoked at the time by this cavalier attitude to the fulfilment of treaty obligations were succinctly summarised in the *Annual Report of the United States President to Congress on the Work of the United Nations*, 1950: " Our experiences show that agreements with the Soviet Union and her satellites are valid only as and when they record existing situations of fact."

That this statement was the result of mature reflection was borne out by Mr. Acheson's previous statement of February 8, 1950 (United States Information Service, *Daily Wireless Bulletin*, February 9, 1950) in almost the same words: " We have seen also that agreements reached with the Soviet Government are useful when those agreements register facts or a situation which exists and that they are not useful when they are merely agreements which do not register the existing facts."

A similarly pessimistic view was expressed in the joint letter of the three Western Commandants of Berlin to the Soviet Commandant of September 28, 1949 (*The Times* newspaper, September 29, 1949): Recent events " make it impossible for us to retain any confidence in the willingness of the Soviet authorities in Berlin to abide by any agreements reached except when it suits them to do so. Without mutual confidence these quadripartite discussions are valueless. We have therefore been instructed by our High Commissioners to state that we are not prepared to continue with the discussions on the normalisation of life in Berlin until we can be confident that agreements freely negotiated will be honoured in the letter and spirit by the Soviet authorities."

See also above, p. 157.

[95] See below, p. 94 *et seq.*

CHAPTER 8

THE PROBLEM OF AN INTERNATIONAL CRIMINAL LAW

INTERNATIONAL Criminal Law has become one of the *derniers cris* in the post-1945 Doctrine of international law.[1] This movement has received a modicum of hesitant support even in official quarters.[2] It is, therefore, advisable to pause and reflect on the meaning and significance of this term in contemporary international law.

I—THE MEANINGS OF INTERNATIONAL CRIMINAL LAW

The term *International Criminal Law* is used in at least six different meanings in the Doctrine of international law.

International Criminal Law in the Meaning of the Territorial Scope of Municipal Criminal Law

It follows from the rules governing the principle of sovereignty that, to any extent to which subjects of international law are not limited by rules of international law, they are free to determine as they see fit the territorial scope of their municipal criminal laws. They may limit the scope of their criminal laws to acts committed in their own territories and territorial seas, on ships sailing under their own flag or on aeroplanes of their own nationality. They may, however, extend their criminal jurisdiction to acts committed by their own nationals or by foreigners abroad.

In the words of the Permanent Court of International Justice in the *Lotus Case* (1927), " all or nearly all these systems of law extend their action to offences committed outside the territory of the State which adopts them, and they do so in ways which vary from State to

---

[1] See, for instance, S. Glaser, *Introduction à l'étude du droit international pénal* (1954) and *Infraction Internationale* (1957), K. Siegert, *Grundlinien des Völkerstrafprozessrechts* (1953), Oppenheim's *International Law* (ed. H. Lauterpacht—1955) Vol. I, p. 341 *et seq.*, and *Manual*, Vol. 2, pp. 466–467.

[2] See further United Nations, *The Charter and Judgment of the Nuremberg Tribunal* (1949), p. 11 *et seq.*, and *Historical Survey of the Question of International Criminal Jurisdiction* (1949); on the *Draft Code of Offences against the Peace and Security of Mankind*, C. Parry, 3 *I.L.Q.* (1950), p. 208 *et seq.*, and H. Jescheck, *Die Entwicklung des Völkerstrafrechts nach Nürnberg*, 72 *Schweizerische Zeitschrift für Strafrecht* (1957), p. 217 *et seq.*

State."[3]   For our purposes it is unnecessary to attempt to determine the exact point at which the claim of a State to extend the applicability of its own criminal law to acts of foreigners committed abroad amounts to a violation of the rights of other subjects of international law.[3a] What is important is to realise that there is a wide field in which the various systems of municipal criminal law claim concurrent or conflicting jurisdiction.

In practice, the chaos that might result from such concurrent and conflicting claims is reduced to manageable proportions by a prohibitory rule of international customary law.   In principle, the actual exercise of criminal jurisdiction in concrete instances must take place within a State's own territory or in places assimilated to it.[4]

Within these limits it is left to every system of municipal criminal law to determine for itself whether, and to what extent, it applies to crimes with a foreign element, that is to say, to crimes committed abroad.   In this respect, the situation is analogous to that in the field of private international law.   International criminal law in this sense, a terminology widely accepted in nineteenth-century Continental Doctrine,[5] belongs not to international but to municipal law.   As in the case of rules of Private International Law, rules of conflict of

---

[3] Series A, No. 10, p. 20.   See also *Naim Molvan* v. *Attorney-General for Palestine* [1948] A.C. 351.

[3a] Exceptions may be based on special rules of international customary law, as, for instance, in the case of jurisdiction of belligerents regarding war crimes, of criminal jurisdiction over members of armed forces abroad in peace and war, or on treaties, such as capitulation treaties.

Conversely, rules of international law may exclude the exercise of local criminal jurisdiction, as in the case of foreigners enjoying diplomatic immunity.

[4] See further *Vol. I*, p. 184 *et seq.*

In the Commonwealth Act for the Punishment of Crimes committed upon, or beyond the Seas (September 20, 1649), the criminal jurisdiction was established wherever in England an offender was found for, *inter alia*, " all murthers and manslaughters committed by any of the natural leighs of this Nation, upon or against any of the good people of the same in any of the foreign parts wheresoever (upon any matter, cause or occasion originally beginning within this land, during such time as such persons had their abode within the same)."

[5] Already in their *collisio statutorum*, the Glossators and Postglossators dealt with the substance of the problem.

See further H. Donnedieu de Vabres, *Introduction à l'Étude du Droit Pénal International* (1922).   *Cf.* also F. Meili, *Lehrbuch des Internationalen Strafrechts und Strafprozessrechts* (1910), p. 25 *et seq.*, and J. Kohler, *Internationales Strafrecht* (1917), p. 19 *et seq.*

For nineteenth century literature, *cf.* L. von Bar, *Das Internationale Privat- und Strafrecht* (1892); W. von Rohland, *Das Internationale Strafrecht* (1877); F. von Martens, *Völkerrecht* (1883), Vol. 2, p. 358 *et seq.*; J. B. Moore, *Report on Extraterritorial Crime and the Cutting Case* (1887).

Among more recent works in this field, *cf.* M. Travers, *Le Droit Pénal International* (1920–22—5 vols.), H. Donnedieu de Vabres, *Les Principes Modernes du Droit Pénal International* (1928) and the Harvard Research Draft on *Jurisdiction with Respect to Crime*, 29 *A.J.I.L.* (1935), Special Supplement, p. 435 *et seq.*, especially the exhaustive bibliography, p. 447 *et seq.*

criminal laws may, however, be incorporated into a treaty and thus become rules of international conventional law.[6]

International Criminal Law in the Meaning of Internationally Prescribed Municipal Criminal Law

The term " international criminal law " is used in a second meaning when it refers to instances in which a State is bound under international law to visit upon acts of individuals the sanctions of its own municipal criminal law. Obligations of this kind may arise from treaties or from international customary law.

In the late Middle Ages it was customary among the princes of Christendom to bind themselves by reciprocal treaties to prevent and punish piracy or the spoliage of shipwreck.[7] In the course of the nineteenth century, a number of bilateral and multilateral conventions were concluded by which slave-trading was assimilated to piracy.[8] In the same category belong treaties such as the International Phylloxera Convention of September 17, 1878, the International Convention on the Traffic in Women of Full Age of October 11, 1933 and the Convention for the Regulation of Whaling of June 8, 1937.

To the extent to which such conventions impose a duty on States to enact municipal criminal legislation or to punish certain acts committed by their nationals or within their territorial jurisdiction, such conventions may be said to prescribe municipal criminal law. If States fail to live up to their treaty obligations, they themselves do not commit any " international crime." They are, however, responsible for breaches of their treaty obligations.

Similarly, international customary law may prescribe rules of municipal criminal law. Some of the crimes which, in his *Commentaries on the Laws of England,*[9] Blackstone described as offences against the law of nations are relevant instances. Actually, this terminology is of a much earlier date. In a Manifest of the English Parliament against the United Provinces of July 31, 1652, an attack on one of the English ambassadors in The Hague was branded as a crime " *contra omnium Gentium, immo ipsius humanitatis, Jura.*" [10]

---

[6] See, for instance, the Treaty on International Penal Law between Argentina, Bolivia, Paraguay, Peru and Uruguay of January 23, 1889 (18 Martens, *Nouveau Recueil Général des Traités* (2me sér.), p. 432).

[7] See above, p. 104 *et seq.*

[8] See above, pp. 34 and 135 *et seq.*

[9] Book 4, Chap. 5. See also below, p. 187.

[10] J. de Dumont, *Corps Universel Diplomatique du Droit des Gens,* Vol. 6, Part 2, p. 28.

Piracy is listed by Blackstone as the first of these offences. It will be more fully discussed under a subsequent heading.[11] The two other offences against the law of nations enumerated by Blackstone are violation of safe-conducts and infringement of the rights of ambassadors. These offences are not, however, crimes under international law.

The law of nations merely bids States to do everything in their power to ensure the observance of rules of international law such as the inviolability of ambassadors, the immunity of nationals of enemy States under safe-conducts or the treatment of foreigners in accordance with the rule on the minimum standard of international law.

In the case of attacks on foreign envoys or on nationals of other States, a State has fulfilled its own duties under international law when it provides for adequate protection of such foreigners by its police. If, nevertheless, outrages occur, it must do everything in its power to bring the guilty, whether public servants or private citizens, to justice. It may not plead the insufficiency of its own criminal law or the inadequacy of its administration of criminal justice. In this and other respects, international law imposes certain legal duties on subjects of international law.[12] Yet again, when a State fails to comply with these rules, it does not commit an international crime. It becomes responsible for its own breach of rules of international customary law, that is to say, it has committed an international tort. Thus, these offences of individuals against the " law of nations " are not crimes under international law, but offences against rules of internationally postulated municipal criminal law.

To protect the status of a country as a neutral Power, international law does not even require the protection of municipal criminal law. On their own, for their own convenience and in order to demonstrate their international bona fides, some States have enacted such statutes as the British Foreign Enlistment Acts of 1819 and 1870. It is left to each State how to secure most effectively the fulfilment of its own obligations under international law.

The situation is similar when, in the interest of good-neighbourly and peaceful relations with other Powers, States enact criminal legislation against acts likely to discredit the good repute of sovereigns

---

[11] See below, p. 185.
[12] See further *Vol. I*, p. 630 *et seq.*

and other dignitaries of foreign States, because such acts may endanger amicable political and commercial relations with other States.[13] At the most, such municipal criminal law is required by international comity as distinct from international law.

Offences against the law of nations in the meaning of contraventions of municipal criminal law which are postulated by international law or comity, do not constitute evidence for the existence of an international criminal law. States which fail to enact such statutes may, however, be liable for breach of treaty or for the commission of an international tort.

International Criminal Law in the Meaning of Internationally Authorised Municipal Criminal Law

This is the proper place to discuss the examples which, so often, are adduced as evidence *par excellence* of the existence of international criminal law : piracy *jure gentium* and war crimes.

(1) *Piracy jure gentium.* On the basis of a multitude of treaties, two different rules have gradually become incorporated in international customary law.

The first is that every State is under an international obligation to suppress piracy within its own territorial jurisdiction. If a State should fail to do so or should associate itself persistently with piratical ventures, it would certainly violate this rule. It is liable for the commission of an international tort and, in an extreme case, may even forfeit its own international personality and be treated as an international outlaw.[14] To the extent to which, for the purpose of countering piracy, a State requires the assistance of its municipal criminal law, such law may be considered to be internationally prescribed.

In addition, there is the second rule which is summarised by the term piracy *jure gentium.* It means that, in the interest of the freedom of the seas, every State is authorised to assume jurisdiction on the high seas over pirate ships. If it does so it may mete out to pirates any condign punishment, including the death penalty. Yet recognition of acts of piracy as " constituting crimes, and the trial

---

[13] See, for instance, *King* v. *Gordon* (1787—22 State Trials, 213); *King* v. *Vint* (1799—27 *ibid.*, 627); *King* v. *Peltier* (1803—28 How. State Trials, 530), and *Respublica* v. *De Longchamp* (1784) 1 Dal. 3.

[14] See further the present writer's *International Law and Totalitarian Lawlessness* (1943), p. 82 *et seq.*

and punishment of the criminals, are left to the municipal law of each country." [15] The grant to States, under international law, of jurisdiction over pirates is an apparent exception to the principle of the freedom of the seas, according to which, in time of peace, States exercise on the high seas jurisdiction exclusively over ships sailing under their own flag. The exception is, however, only apparent. Pirate ships are not under the protection of any subject of international law, but are *res nullius*, floating chattels which are not allocated to any subject of international law.[16]

(2) *War Crimes*. It is the purpose of the rules of warfare, as developed by the laws and customs of warfare and by international conventions, to draw the dividing line between legal and illegal forms of warfare. Every belligerent State is under an international duty to do everything in its power to ensure respect for the rules of warfare on the part of its armed forces and to punish such infractions as may occur. To this extent the law of war crimes embodies internationally prescribed rules of municipal criminal law.

If individual members of armed forces observe these rules and happen to fall into the enemy's hands, they are merely liable to detention as prisoners of war, but are immune from personal responsibility for hostile acts committed by them prior to capture. If they have transgressed these rules, they are outside the protection granted by international law to ordinary prisoners of war.

Under the impact of the standard of civilisation,[17] rules of international customary law have developed which limit the absolute discretion of enemy States with regard to war criminals. The enemy State may apply to such individuals any punishment, including the death penalty. It must, nevertheless, grant them some form of trial, however summary. Only in this way is it possible to establish whether a breach of the rules of warfare has been committed by the prisoner and, therefore, whether he falls under this extraordinary jurisdiction. Moreover, the trial assists in settling disputed questions of identity.

Belligerents usually comply with this minimum requirement by providing for simplified proceedings in their own military courts and

---

[15] *Re Piracy Jure Gentium* [1934] A.C. 586 at p. 589. See further the Harvard Research Draft on *Piracy*, 26 *A.J.I.L.* (1932), Spec. Suppl., p. 739 *et seq.*
[16] See further *Fundamental Principles*, p. 358 *et seq.*, and Vol. I, p. 338 *et seq.*
[17] See above, p. 70 *et seq.*

under their own municipal laws.[18] The objects of such an internationally authorised extraordinary criminal procedure under municipal law hardly become thereby subjects of international duties, nor do war crimes and espionage constitute evidence of the existence of an international criminal law.

The rules of international law on piracy *jure gentium* and war crimes impose duties upon States to suppress piracy within their own jurisdiction and to exercise proper control over their own armed forces. They also authorise other States to assume an extraordinary criminal jurisdiction under their own municipal law in the cases of piracy *jure gentium* and of war crimes committed by the enemy prior to capture.[19]

International Criminal Law in the Meaning of Municipal Criminal Law Common to Civilised Nations

In the Constitution of the United States the term " offences against the law of nations " is used.[20] It covers acts which international law prescribes, or authorises, to be treated as criminal under the municipal law of the United States,[21] and crimes which, owing to their general noxious character, are punishable in most civilised countries.[22] Again, such crimes can be described only in the loosest sense as offences against the law of nations. They fall into one of two categories.

If a State fails to punish common offences against life, liberty or property, its criminal law falls below the minimum standards of international law and civilisation.[23] In this case the home State of foreigners who suffer from such a state of affairs may hold such a State responsible for the commission of an international tort. Within these limits, a " civilised " type of municipal criminal law is internationally prescribed.[24]

There is a second type of offence, such as the forgery of foreign coins or banknotes. Considerations of international comity, and consciousness of the reciprocity of favours in inter-State relations, may make it advisable for a State to make such acts punishable

---

[18] See further S. Glueck, *War Criminals, Their Prosecution and Punishment* (1944) and *l.c.* above in note 14, p. 57 *et seq.*
[19] See further *Vol. I*, pp. 153 and 346–347.
[20] Article 1, Section 8, Cl. 10.
[21] *Ex parte Quirin et Al.* (1942) 317 U.S. 1.
[22] *United States* v. *Arjona* (1887) 120 U.S. 479.
[23] See above, p. 55 *et seq.*
[24] See above, p. 183.

under its municipal criminal law. International customary law does not, however, impose any obligation on States to take such action. But nothing prevents States from voluntarily limiting their freedom of action by the conclusion of conventions to this effect. This was done, for instance, by the parties to the Convention for the Suppression of Counterfeiting Currency of 1929.[25]

On closer examination, this type of offence against the law of nations dissolves into one of two categories. They either belong to the category of municipal criminal law which is prescribed by international law or they are principles of municipal criminal law which civilised States have *de facto* in common or consider it opportune to assimilate to a common standard by parallel municipal legislation or by means of international conventions.[26]

International Criminal Law in the Meaning of International Co-operation in the Administration of Municipal Criminal Justice

Writers who use the term international criminal law in the meaning of the territorial scope of international criminal law, usually deal under this heading, too, with extradition treaties and other conventions by which States assist each other in the administration of criminal justice.

The *raison d'être* of such treaties is the territorial limitation of national sovereignty. Without international co-operation between States, criminals could defy the municipal criminal laws of most States with relative impunity. Thus, the very purpose of this type of treaty is to strengthen and lengthen, on a basis of reciprocity, the arms of national justice.

Some States do not decide *ex officio* whether a prisoner should or should not be extradited, but leave it to him to raise in a special judicial proceeding any objections he may wish to make against being extradited. Where, as is the case in Great Britain, municipal law permits a prisoner to take such an active part in extradition proceedings, he becomes the means by which it can be conveniently determined whether the demand of another State keeps within the

25 Cmnd. 932 (1960).
26 See, for instance, the Brussels Convention on the Unification of Rules relating to Penal Jurisdiction in matters of Collision, May 10, 1952 (Cmnd. 1128—1960).
   Cf. also the discussions on the Standard Minimum Rules for the Treatment of Prisoners at the First United Nations Congress on the Prevention of Crime and the Treatment of Offenders (1955—U.N.Doc. 1956. IV 4).

reciprocal framework of an extradition treaty, and the limits within which the legislature has permitted the executive to hand over accused or convicted persons to the authorities of another State.

It would, however, be a travesty of the real situation to imagine that States intended any extradition treaty to be a Magna Carta of the criminal profession, or to be based on any principles of international law which prisoners were entitled to invoke in their own right. Thus, according to the Report of the Royal Commission on Extradition of 1878, the typical intention of parties to extradition treaties was to serve, firstly, the common interest of States in the punishment of offences which threaten the wellbeing of society and, secondly, the interest of the State into whose territory the criminal had come that he should not remain at large therein.

Little harm is done if such mutual limitations of the exercise of State jurisdiction by means of treaties are classified as a body of international criminal law.[27] It is necessary, however, to remember that extradition treaties are not concerned with the substance of municipal criminal law, but with the administrative question of foiling the attempt of an accused or convicted person to obstruct by his evasive action the due course of municipal criminal justice.

International Criminal Law in the Material Sense of the Word

It remains to explore whether, beyond municipal criminal law which is prescribed or authorised by international law, international criminal law in a sense comparable to municipal criminal law exists.

In any social group in which a criminal law exists the highest values and interests are protected by rules of criminal law. International crimes would, therefore, be in all likelihood acts of subjects or objects of international law which strike at the very roots of international society.[28] Such rules would have to be of a prohibitory character and would have to be strengthened by punitive sanctions of their own.

Thus, the remaining issue is whether international law knows of rules which would constitute an international criminal law in the true meaning of the term.

---

[27] See further *Vol. I*, p. 256 *et seq.*, and *Manual*, Vol. 2, p. 506 *et seq.*
[28] Similarly, A. N. Trainin, *Hitlerite Responsibility under Criminal Law* (1945), p. 37, and Qu. Wright, *The Law of the Nuremberg Trial*, 41 *A.J.I.L.* (1947), p. 56.

II—THE EVIDENCE FOR THE EXISTENCE
OF AN INTERNATIONAL CRIMINAL LAW

As in other fields of international law, a detached approach to the subject has been made difficult by apodictic and contradictory *a priori* assertions. It was held, for instance, by Politis that as long as international law was a law between sovereign States it could not have a proper penal system.[29]   Similarly, in his *Aspects of Modern International Law*,[30] Sir John Fischer Williams maintained that " in so far as States are the subjects of international law they cannot be the subjects of criminal penalties for misdoing. . . .   In fact the conditions of international life being what they are, it is fair to say that punishment or attempted punishment of a State is itself an offence against international order."

Against this, it has been said : " It is impossible to admit that individuals, by grouping themselves into States and thus increasing immeasurably their potentialities for evil, can confer upon themselves a degree of immunity from criminal liability and its consequences which they do not enjoy when acting in isolation." [31]

Actually, there is no preconceived reason why international law should, or should not, recognise the existence of international crimes. If, on the basis of rules of international customary law or by means of treaties, States have limited their independence by acknowledging the existence of acts of their own or of individuals which other States may treat as international crimes, such a state of affairs is compatible with their sovereignty ; for this only exists within the limits drawn at any time by international law.

Similarly, the group character of the subjects of international law does not decisively militate against the possibility of an international criminal law.   Criminal liability of corporations under municipal law is not an entirely unknown phenomenon.

Finally, the question whether the individual must be regarded as a subject or object of international law is neither here nor there. It is probably correct to hold that, so far, the evidence adduced in

---

29 *Les Nouvelles Tendances du Droit International* (1927), p. 95.
30 (1939), pp. 84 and 88.
    Cf. also the Memorandum by Sir Arnold McNair, as he then was, written in 1944 and quoted in United Nations War Crimes Commission, *History of the United Nations War Crimes Commission and the Development of the Laws of War* (1948), p. 181.
31 Oppenheim's *International Law* (ed. by H. Lauterpacht—1955), Vol. I, p. 357. For Oppenheim's own view, see *ibid.* (1905), p. 201.

favour of the individual as an actual subject of international customary law is rather slender. Yet it would be an unwarranted assumption to hold that only if the international personality of the individual were recognised could the individual be treated as the object of proceedings of an international criminal character. It is possible to imagine a situation in which States mutually agreed on penetrating the monad of the sovereign State and to institute criminal proceedings against such duty-objects of international law. The criminal liability of slaves in Roman law and the criminal proceedings against animals in medieval penal law offer possible analogies.

Whether any subjects or objects of international law are the addressees of rules of international criminal law depends on a simple test : the evidence produced by those asserting the existence of an international criminal law. It is advisable to treat, first, the position under international customary law and, subsequently, to proceed to the examination of relevant treaties.

International Criminal Law as Part of International Customary Law

So-called offences against the law of nations, piracy *jure gentium* and war crimes, can be eliminated from the outset. In these cases international law limits itself to prescribing or authorising the assumption of criminal jurisdiction by States under their own municipal law.[32] If it should be argued that, owing to the primitive state of international law, such a delegation of functions to States does not militate against the description of these rules as being in substance principles of international criminal law, this is only a circuitous way of conceding that international criminal law in any proper sense does not exist.

In the absence of more direct evidence, it is necessary to explore the attitude of relevant elements of law-determining agencies to the problem of international criminal law. In their proper hierarchic order,[33] the decisions of international courts and tribunals, and the practice of individual States, call for examination. As so often happens, the Doctrine of international law, self-contradictory as it is, is of relatively little assistance in determining the issue.

(1) *International Courts and Tribunals.* There is not a single instance in which international judicial institutions, deciding on the basis of international customary law, have classified an act of State

---

[32] See above, p. 183 *et seq.*
[33] See further *Vol. I,* p. 25 *et seq.*

as an international crime. It is hardly convincing to dispose of so
relevant a fact by reference to the voluntary character of international
arbitratio and adjudication. Sufficient cases have been submitted
to international courts and tribunals in which, if they had felt so
inclined, international judicial institutions would have been free to
stigmatise breaches of international customary law as international
crimes instead of treating them as international torts or delicts.

In some cases the award of damages might be considered to be
of punitive character if the tribunals concerned had not taken pains
to point out that such damages had been awarded as moral or
immaterial damages.[34]   Furthermore, a good many of these awards
of damages, especially in cases involving death, contain necessarily
a considerable discretionary element. To imply that this is primarily
of a punitive character is a *petitio principii.* In cases in which
restitutio in integrum is impossible, such damages still partake of
the character of reparation as distinct from that of a penalty.[35]
Against any such inference stand express dicta of international tribunals in which, after full consideration, claims for punitive damages
were rejected outright. These awards derive their especial significance from the fact that, in the opinion of the claimants, limitations
of the arbitration agreement would not have prevented the tribunal
concerned from awarding punitive damages.

In the *Lusitania Cases* (1923) the German-United States Mixed
Claims Commission drew attention to the fact that counsel for the
United States had " failed to point us to any money award by an
international arbitral tribunal where exemplary, punitive, or vindic-
tive damages have been assessed against one sovereign nation in
favour of another presenting a claim on behalf of its nationals." [36]

In spite of the fact that, after the sinking of the *Lusitania,* this act
had been labelled in Allied diplomatic notes and public statements
with all the epithets taken apparently from the vocabulary of an existing international criminal law, and ranging from the description of
this illegal measure of unrestricted submarine warfare as piracy to

---

[34] *Cf.* M. Whiteman, *Damages in International Law,* Vol. 1, 1937, p. 717.
    In the considered view of Miss Whiteman, as expressed in the concluding
third volume (1943) of her exemplary study, " there is an apparent desire on the
part of international tribunals to avoid punitive or exemplary damages. The
assessment of damages is a civil and not a penal act " (p. 1874).
[35] See further *Vol. I,* p. 653 *et seq.*
[36] 7 *R.I.A.A.,* p. 32 at p. 40.

its denunciation as an international crime [37]—it was held by the Commission : " A sufficient reason why such damages cannot be awarded by this Commission is that it is without the power to make such awards under the terms of its charter—the Treaty of Berlin." [38]

In the *Naulilaa Case* (1930) the Special Arbitral Tribunal between Germany and Portugal disallowed the Portuguese claim for punitive damages for the illegal acts committed by Germany against Portugal while the latter was still a neutral power. In the opinion of the Tribunal, it had neither been the intention of the parties to the *compromis* to endow the arbitrators with any " repressive power " nor the intention of the Peace Treaty of Versailles to give such a wide meaning to the Article in question.[39]

If any further evidence were required, it would be furnished by the *Corfu Channel Case* (1949). In the Security Council (February 18, 1947), Sir Alexander Cadogan, as he then was, described Albania's clandestine mining of the Corfu Channel as an " international crime." The Australian member of the Security Council characterised the act as an " international crime of the most serious sort " and as amounting " in substance to something very much of the character of mass murder " (February 24, 1947). The French and United States representatives called it an " offence against humanity."

On March 25, 1947, seven members of the Security Council (Australia, Belgium, Brazil, China, Colombia, France and the United States) voted in favour of a British draft resolution. According to this the laying of mines in peacetime without notification was held to be " unjustified and an offence against humanity." Owing to the exercise of his veto by the Soviet representative, this resolution did not become operative.

In the preceding diplomatic correspondence between Albania and the United Kingdom, the British Government had described the incidents in the Corfu Channel as " deliberate and outrageous " breaches of international law and maritime custom. In its Note of December 9, 1946, the British Government emphasised the general character of the issue. In its opinion it did not only affect the two countries directly concerned, but was a matter of general " safety of life at sea." Albania's action amounted to a " criminal disregard

---

[37] See, for instance, the views expressed by President Wilson in his Address to the Joint Session of the two Houses of Congress of April 2, 1917, 11 *A.J.I.L.* (1917), Supplement, pp. 144 and 150.
[38] *L.c.* in note 36 above, p. 41.
[39] 2 *ibid.*, p. 1035, at pp. 1076–1077.

for the safety of innocent seamen of any nationality lawfully using an international highway."

When, however, these alleged crimes or offences against humanity were subjected to legal scrutiny, the claimant government described the action of the Albanian Government as a " deliberately hostile act," which called for reparation and an assurance from the Albanian Government that there should be no repetition of " this unlawful action." In the United Kingdom Memorial submitted to the International Court of Justice, the Albanian action was classified as an " international delinquency " and, in the special circumstances of the case, as an " offence against humanity which most seriously aggravates the breach of international law and the international delinquency committed by that State."

What was to be the liability which, in the view of the claimant State, attached to such an international delinquency or offence against humanity? According to the British Memorial, " a State found to be delinquent under either (a) or (b) is liable under international law to make reparation for the damage resulting to others from the delinquency." In so far as the measure of reparation or compensation was concerned, the United Kingdom accepted expressly the rules laid down by the Permanent Court of International Justice in the case of the *Factory at Chorzów* (1928), that is to say, the rules which apply in cases of breach of treaties and of international torts.[40]

The Judgment of the International Court of Justice in the *Corfu Channel Case* (*Merits*–1949) followed the same lines. It affirmed Albanian responsibility under international law for the mining of the British men-of-war, and for the damage and loss of human life which resulted from the explosion of the mines. The " crime against humanity " was treated like any other international tort upon which, in the past, international courts and tribunals had adjudicated.[41]

Thus, not in a single case has any international court or tribunal held that a State has committed a crime under international customary law, as distinct from a breach of treaty or from the commission of an international tort, or visited such an act with the sanction of frankly admitted punitive damages. With the exception of international war crimes trials which require separate

[40] See further *Vol. I*, p. 653 *et seq.*
[41] *I.C.J. Reports 1949*, p. 23. *Cf.* also I.C.J., *Pleadings, The Corfu Channel Case*, Vol. 1 (1949).

discussion,[42] the practice of international courts and tribunals cannot be adduced as evidence of the recognition in international customary law of anything even faintly resembling the phenomenon of an international crime or of an international criminal law *stricto sensu*.

(2) *British Practice.* In the present state of research into the practice of individual States it would be presumptuous for anyone to pretend that he is able to speak of State practice as such.[43] All that will be attempted here is to deal with some relevant instances from British practice. Especially in the nineteenth century, British practice has shown in unmistakeable language—and action—its concern with the behaviour of States which public opinion in Great Britain considered to be outrageous, if not criminal.[44]

In 1833 Palmerston was roused to action by a Brazilian law of 1831 and a decree of 1832 by which all negroes, imported or attempted to be imported into Brazil for the purposes of the slave trade, were to be re-exported to Africa. There was good reason to fear that such slaves would be killed by the slavers on the return journey or by African tribes if those slaves were ever to reach their destination. The British Foreign Secretary, therefore, maintained that, irrespective of Brazilian treaty obligations which made such legislation illegal, " on the ground of humanity alone His Majesty's Government feel that they would be justified in pressing this subject upon the consideration of the Brazilian Government." [45] All that Palmerston asked for was a repeal of the obnoxious Brazilian enactments.

Ten years later Stratford Canning protested to the Porte against the revival of the practice of the trial and execution of apostates from Islam. In the particular case in question a Greek youth who had been originally a Christian, had been executed. Canning demanded explanations and an unqualified assurance that in future the recurrence " of such unwise and odious acts " should be avoided.[46]

At the Paris Peace Conference of 1856, Clarendon admitted the rule on the prohibition of intervention in the internal affairs of other

[42] See below, p. 203 *et seq.*
[43] See further 9 *C.L.P.* (1956), p. 244 *et seq.*
[44] See above, pp. 34 and 130 *et seq.*
[45] Palmerston to Fox (Rio de Janeiro), June 5, 1833, 22 *British and Foreign State Papers* (1833–1834), p. 74.
[46] Letter to M. Pisani (Dragoman), Constantinople, December 16, 1843, 32 (1843–1844) *ibid.*, p. 914. *Cf.* also Aberdeen's Dispatches to Canning of January 16, 1844, *ibid.*, p. 915 and of March 19, 1844, *ibid.*, p. 924. See also above, p. 134.

sovereign States, but affirmed that there were cases where the exception to this rule became equally the right and duty of foreign Powers. The particular case before the Conference was the misrule in Naples which was lending fervour to the revolutionary nationalist and democratic movement. Clarendon asked the Conference to demand from the Government of the Two Sicilies an improvement in its system of government and an amnesty in favour of those condemned or detained for political offences without judgment.[47]

The atrocities perpetrated a few years later against the Christian population in Syria led to collective action by the Powers, based on a convention with the Porte for the pacification of Syria.[48] The Ottoman officials and Druses responsible for these pogroms were tried before a tribunal established by the Porte at the request of the European Powers, and a commission, composed of all the Treaty Powers, supervised the trials.[49]

With the passive assistance of the Chinese Government, the Boxer Movement committed crimes which shocked public opinion abroad. The German minister was murdered. The German Legation was attacked and kept in a state of siege. The Chancellor of the Japanese Legation was murdered. Foreign civilians were killed and tortured, and foreign cemeteries were desecrated. These deeds led to the intervention of the European Powers, the United States and Japan.

In their joint Note of December 24, 1900, the Powers listed these "crimes unprecedented in human history, crimes against the law of nations and against civilisation . . . committed under peculiarly odious circumstances" and demanded expiation and guarantees against their repetition.

China accepted responsibility and, by way of reparation, agreed to the dispatch to Berlin of an extraordinary mission, headed by an imperial prince, to express regret ; the creation of a monument on the place where the murder of the German minister had been committed, with an inscription expressing the Emperor's regret for the murder ; the severest punishment of the persons listed by the Powers and repeated in an imperial decree ; the suspension for five years of official examinations in all towns where foreigners had been ill-treated or massacred ; the erection of monuments in the foreign cemeteries

[47] Protocol No. 22 of the Peace Conference of Paris, April 8, 1856, 46 (1855–1856) *ibid.*, p. 127.
[48] Convention of September 5, 1860, 50 (1859–1860) *ibid.*, p. 6.
[49] Protocol of the 21st Meeting of the Conference between the Representatives of the five European Powers and the Ottoman Porte, January 29, 1861, 51 (1860–1861), p. 414.

which had been defiled ; the right of each Power to maintain a permanent guard over its legation and to put the legation quarter in a defensible position, Chinese being prohibited to reside in such quarters and, finally, equitable indemnities to all the Powers.[50]

In other cases, international disapprobation of reprehensible acts of States took forms other than those of diplomatic remonstrance or of intervention. Refusal of Recognition and the rupture of diplomatic relations offered means which, in the eyes of British Statesmen, provided a suitable reply to outrageous behaviour on the part of foreign Powers.[51]

What are the essential features of this practice?

First, it appears that States are not necessarily indifferent to acts which are incompatible with the most elementary dictates of humanity and civilisation.

Secondly, in defence of such values, States do not appear to appeal to any alleged international criminal law.

Thirdly, they do not appear to be aware of the existence of any specific international criminal procedure, but apply general devices which they use equally for the defence of their own rights and interests. In doing so without distinction between rights accruing to them from breach of treaty, from the commission of an international tort or from an " international crime," they acknowledge the fact that international customary law has not yet led to that specialisation which permits a distinction to be drawn between international " civil " and " criminal " law. The degree of reprobation is not expressed by reference to rules of international law of any special character, but in the strength of the diplomatic language used and in the severity of otherwise unwarranted interference with a right sacrosanct in time of peace : the territorial integrity of sovereign States.

Thus, the analysis of two elements of law-determining agencies of high evidential value does not appear to offer any evidence for the existence of either the concept of international crime or for rules of a specifically penal character in the body of international customary law. The position is still, as it was summed up by the Committee on the Permanent Court of International Justice of the

---

[50] United States, *Foreign Relations* (1900), p. 244, and 1901, App., p. 306.
[51] See above, p. 137 *et seq.*

First Assembly of the League of Nations in 1920 : " There is not yet any international penal law recognised by all nations." [52]

International Criminal Law as Part of Treaty Law

In their mutual relations States are free to develop international customary law. Nothing prevents them from establishing on a treaty basis new branches of international law with principles and standards of their own.[53] If they desire to do so they may evolve rules of an international criminal law which apply to themselves, to any of their own organs or to any individual under their jurisdiction. The only question which arises *de lege lata*, is whether they have actually done so.

Piracy by treaty, the criminal jurisdiction of international institutions, the Convention against Terrorism of May, 1937, and pertinent developments of international law within the framework of the United Nations call for examination.

(1) *Piracy by Treaty.* An early instance of the assimilation to piracy of acts of foreigners which, otherwise, would have been beyond the cognisance of municipal criminal law, and whose unilateral punishment might have led to international complications, is offered by the Jay Treaty between Great Britain and the United States of November 19, 1794. By its Article 21, Great Britain was permitted to treat as pirates citizens of the United States who had taken commissions as French privateers.

The most celebrated case, however, is the gradual assimilation by means of bilateral and multilateral treaties of slave trading to piracy *jure gentium*, a policy steadfastly pursued by Great Britain since the beginning of the nineteenth century as part of her campaign to outlaw this peculiar form of free enterprise.[54]

The transformation in this case of a moral principle into a rule of international treaty law is of more than historical significance. The respect shown by British statesmen and courts [55] to the international rights of other States is impressive.

In a Declaration of February 8, 1815, the Congress of Vienna

League of Nations, Records of the First Assembly. Meetings of the Committees, Vol. 1 (1920), p. 589.
    Cf. also the penetrating remarks on this subject in H. Kelsen, *Law and Peace* (1942), p. 103 *et seq.*

[53] See further below, p. 215 *et seq.*, and 9 *C.L.P.* (1956), p. 247 *et seq.*

[54] See above, pp. 34 and 135 *et seq.*

[55] *Cf. The Le Louis* (1817) 2 Dodson 210. See also *The Antelope* (1825) 10 Wheat. 66.

had denounced the Slave Trade as being " repugnant to the principles of humanity and universal morality." The Conference of Aix-la-Chapelle of 1818 solemnly declared that " the negro slave trade was an odious crime, the disgrace of civilised nations, and that it was a matter of urgency to put an end for ever to this scourge which had so long desolated Africa, degraded Europe and afflicted humanity." The plenipotentiaries of the five European Powers reiterated their condemnation of these " criminal operations " in a Resolution of the Congress of Verona of November 28, 1822.[56]

Neither statesmen nor writers dreamt, however, of asserting that a change in the existing position under international customary law had been achieved by these declarations. They realised that such modifications of international law as were required depended on the free consent of every sovereign State concerned.

Great Britain bought the limitation, and subsequent total prohibition, of the Spanish slave trade at the price of considerable financial sacrifice. In the same way she obtained the Portuguese renunciation of slave-trading north of the Equator.

In some of the bilateral treaties concluded by Great Britain, the African slave trade was stigmatised as piracy. In others Great Britain was content to secure the co-operation of contracting parties without any formal denunciation.

When treaties in this field provided for adjudication of suspect vessels, the mixed tribunals were merely authorised to adjudicate on the ships involved and, in appropriate cases, to set free the slaves found in such vessels. The tribunals did not exercise any criminal jurisdiction over the owners and crews of these ships. This task was left to the municipal courts of the flag-States concerned.

Under the multilateral Treaty of December 20, 1841, by which the slave trade was declared piracy, detained vessels and their crews were handed over to the flag-States to be dealt with by them in accordance with the municipal criminal laws of the contracting parties.

Not even this justly celebrated venture in international legislation by means of bilateral and multilateral treaties led to the creation of international crimes in the strict sense of the word. All that the Powers attempted to do was to establish an exceptional jurisdiction for the visit and search of suspected ships ; in the case of some of the bilateral treaties, to decide on an international level on the

---

[56] See above, pp. 34 and 135 *et seq.*

character of the vessels as slave traders, and to apply to slave-traders relatively uniform rules of municipal criminal law, prescribed in some cases by international treaties.

In the light of more recent over-statements in which actions of foreign governments are too readily decried as " crimes against humanity," the most remarkable feature of this collective effort made a century ago is the clearheadedness and intellectual honesty with which these reformers went about their task. They were aware of their limitations under international law and used persistently the most straightforward way of overcoming these obstacles.

At a time when the British Government and its Minister in Washington were doing everything in their power to induce the United States to conclude a treaty with Great Britain as a further link in the chain of Britain's bilateral treaties for the suppression of the African slave trade, Stratford Canning wrote to his namesake in the Foreign Office : " There is no denying that the general concurrence of Maritime Powers is necessary to constitute slave trade piracy as part of international law, but it is also evident that before that general consent be obtained it is competent to any two Powers to carry the principle by mutual agreement into practice, as far as they are themselves concerned, and to apply it reciprocally with all its consequences to their respective subjects." [57] Even after the conclusion of the multilateral Treaty of 1841, Great Britain did not ascribe to it any mythical legislative effects on non-parties.[58] In relation, for instance, to the Ottoman Porte, it was bluntly admitted that, " in the absence of a treaty with the Porte it would be illegal to issue orders to British naval forces in the Black Sea to detain Turkish vessels conveying slaves from Georgia and Circasia." [59]

The salutary effect of this law-abiding practice was that States were induced to set an example by raising their own standards of conduct in concord with like-minded States or in co-operation with States which, for other reasons, considered it worth while to live up to the standards expected by the world's leading Powers. Although the anti-slavery treaties failed to make any notable contribution to the development of international criminal law, they are an object lesson on how to achieve real advances in the law of nations.

[57] Letter of April 22, 1823, 11 *British and Foreign State Papers* (1823–1824), p. 409, at p. 410.
[58] See further *Vol. I*, p. 458 *et seq.*
[59] The Secretary to the Admiralty to Lord Wodehouse (Foreign Office), December 2, 1854, 45 *ibid.* (1854–1855), p. 1145. See also the Note from Lord Aberdeen to M. Lisboa (Brazil) of August 6, 1845, 34 *ibid.* (1845–1846), p. 711.

The attempts made in the post-1919 period to develop piracy by way of analogy bore little fruit. The effort to assimilate illegal submarine warfare to piracy proved abortive. The reasons for this failure were unconnected with Article 3 of the unratified Washington Treaty, relating to the use of submarines and noxious gases in warfare, of February 6, 1922. Yet even the draft, as it stood, merely provided for the optional trial of any such " as if " pirate " before the civil or military authorities of any Power within the jurisdiction of which he may be found." [60] In the Preamble of the Nyon Agreement of September 14, 1937, the submarine attacks on merchant ships of other than the conflicting Spanish parties are described as measures " which should be justly treated as acts of piracy." This, however, merely provided the background and justification for the collective and repressive measures on which the Parties had agreed. Neither of these Treaties constituted any further development towards the creation of an international criminal law.

(2) *The Criminal Jurisdiction of International Institutions.* On a limited scale, developments towards an international criminal law may be detected in the case of some international institutions.

International river commissions, such as the European Danube Commission, the Central Commission of the Rhine and the International Commission of the Elbe had some powers of punishing contraventions of their regulations for river police. In the case of the Rhine and Elbe Commissions, appeal from the court of first instance could alternatively be made to the Commission or to local courts.[61] In all three cases, these rights of jurisdiction were in substance police powers and, at the most, nominally of a penal character.

The Mixed Courts in Egypt and Tangier are of little interest ; for they merely substituted abstractions from European criminal codes and procedures for local criminal laws and administrations which were not considered to give sufficient guarantees of fair treatment to nationals of Western States.[62] In any case, they are matters of the past. The chief value the penal practice of these Courts may

---

60 See further *l.c.* in note 14 above, pp. 96–97.
61 See, for instance, Article 44 of the Elbe Convention of February 22, 1922 (M. O. Hudson, *International Legislation*, Vol. 2 (1931), pp. 851–852).
62 The standard work is still J. Y. Brinton, *The Mixed Courts of Egypt*, 1930. See further the Montreux Convention for the Abolition of Capitulations in Egypt of May 8, 1937 (Treaty Series, 1937, No. 55); the authoritative anonymous article on the Convention in 19 *British Year Book of International Law* (1938), p. 161 *et seq.*; A. McDougall, *The Termination of the Egyptian Mixed Courts* (25 *ibid.*, 1948, p. 386 *et seq.*); the Declaration of the International Conference of Tangier, October 29, 1956 (Cmnd. 60—1957), and G. H. Stuart, *The International City of Tangier*, 1955.

still claim lies in the material which they provide for the comparative study of Western criminal laws and procedures as applied in a Near Eastern setting.

The Courts of the Inter-Allied Rhineland Commission, the Courts of the Governing Commission of the Saar Basin, the Plebiscite Courts in Upper Silesia of 1921 and in the Saar of 1935, the Control Commission and Restoration Courts in post-1945 Germany contribute little more to the elucidation of our subject. They either applied *ad hoc* statutes and orders, replaced the local criminal law by that of the respective Occupying Powers, or themselves administered the local law. Their function did not consist in the evolution of an international criminal law. It was their task to apply an internationally agreed, or their own, municipal criminal law in cases in which the foreign Powers concerned were not prepared to entrust such jurisdiction to the ordinary organs of local criminal justice.[63] Like the Mixed Courts, these instances are exceptional cases of the temporary substitution of one municipal criminal law by that of other Powers. They are freaks which confirm the general rule.

Some play has also been made of the, in part, penal character of Article 16 of the Covenant of the League of Nations. Actually this Article stated very clearly the legal consequences of a disregard by a member State of its obligations under Article 12, 13 or 15 of the Covenant. A pact-breaker " shall *ipso facto* be deemed to have committed an act of war against all other members of the League " —but not an international crime.

It has been suggested that this transformation was achieved by the Resolution of the Eighth Assembly of the League of Nations, by which aggressive war was branded as an " international crime." Yet, whatever the legal significance of this Resolution may have been, the members of the League showed by their actual policies towards Japanese aggression in China and by the farce of their sanctions experiment against Italy that, at the most, they regarded

---

63 See further P. Huguet, *Le Droit Pénal de la Rhénanie Occupée* (1923); E. Fraenkel, *Military Occupation and the Rule of Law* (1944), p. 171 *et seq.*; F. L. Carsten, *The British Summary Court at Wiesbaden, 1926–1929* (7 *Modern Law Review* (1944), p. 215 *et seq.*); Ordinance No. 2 (1945) on Military Government Courts of the Military Government for Germany (*Military Government Gazette*, 1945, p. 7) and the British Ordinance No. 68 on Control Commission Courts of January 1, 1947, *ibid.* 1947, p. 437 *et seq.*; S. Wambaugh, *Plebiscites Since the World War*, Vol. 2 (1933), p. 218 and *The Saar Plebiscite* (1940), pp. 228 *et seq.* and 401 *et seq.*, and Convention on the Settlement of Matters arising out of the War and the Occupation between the four former Occupation Powers and the Federal Republic of Germany, May 26, 1952, as amended October 23, 1954 (Cmnd. 656—1959).

these breaches of the Covenant in the same light as any other breach of treaty obligations. To hold differently now would appear to be a manifest case of *venire contra factum proprium* on the part of any State which, during the Appeasement Period, even granted *de jure* recognition to the fruits of Italy's aggressive war against Ethiopia.

(3) *The Convention against Terrorism.* The Convention for the Prevention and Punishment of Terrorism of November 16, 1937, contained an engagement on the part of the Contracting Parties to make acts of terrorism of an international character, that is to say, committed on the territory of another contracting party, punishable under municipal criminal law. It also extended the scope of traditional extradition in the case of political crimes and provided for police co-operation between the signatories against terrorists.

A Supplementary Convention of the same date, which never came into operation, provided for an auxiliary type of an international criminal court. Its jurisdiction was to be limited to cases in which a party to the main convention refused to try a terrorist in its own courts or to extradite him to another Contracting Party.

Again, the Convention against Terrorism merely extended the scope of crimes which, by treaty, were made punishable offences under municipal law, and the customary range of extradition treaties.

(4) *International Criminal Law within the Framework of the United Nations.* Has this situation been in any way changed since the creation of the United Nations?

In its Resolution on the Extradition and Punishment of War Criminals of February 13, 1946, the General Assembly recommended to members and non-member States the extradition of war criminals to the countries where they had committed their crimes for the—twice stated—purpose of " trial and punishment *according to the laws of these countries.*"

The trials of the major German and Japanese war criminals before international military courts have, however, been hailed as major departures from traditional patterns. The legal standards of the Tokyo Trial were perhaps unusual. Criticism such as has been advanced of the Tokyo Trial [64] cannot, however, be levelled against

---

[64] See further Lord Hankey, *Politics, Trials and Errors* (1950), p. 80 *et seq.*, and G. Ireland, *Uncommon Law in Martial Tokyo*, 4 *Year Book of World Affairs* (1950), p. 54 *et seq.*

the judges of Nuremberg. The proceedings were conducted with scrupulous regard for the rights of the Defence.

In form, the law applied by the tribunal was international law : international customary law, in so far as war crimes in the technical sense were concerned, and newly established treaty law regarding crimes against peace and humanity.[65]

It emerges from the British Aide-Mémoire of April 23, 1945, how dubious the British Government felt about these war crimes in the wider sense. In so far as crimes against peace were concerned, it was not at all clear to the British Government whether they could "properly be described as crimes under international law." [66] In a further memorandum of May 28, 1945, and in an Aide-Mémoire of June 3, 1945, these doubts were laid at rest.[67] In a different form, however, they came to the surface again at the meeting of the Four-Power Conference of June 29, 1945. Sir David Maxwell Fyfe, as he then was, pointed out that one thing was essential : " What we want to abolish at the trial is a discussion as to whether the acts are violations of international law or not. We declare what the international law is so that there won't be any discussion on whether it is international law or not." [68]

Nevertheless, the four Powers were fully entitled to take the action on which they had decided regarding both German and Japanese war criminals. As was pointed out in the Nuremberg Judgment, the Parties to the Charter of the Tribunal merely did jointly what each of them, if in sole control of Germany, could have done alone. In the exercise of their *co-imperium* over Germany, the Occupying Powers were not limited to the application to Germany of the customary law of warfare, but were free to agree on any additional legal principles which they cared to apply. Similarly, the unconditional surrender of Japan provided a sufficient legal basis for trying the Japanese war criminals in accordance with legal principles which went beyond the scope of international customary law. For these very reasons, however, both these international military tribunals were in substance more akin to municipal war crime courts than to truly international tribunals.

By a Resolution of December 11, 1946, the General Assembly

---

[65] See further 2 *Y.B.W.A.* (1948), p. 94 *et seq.*
[66] United States, Department of State, *International Conference on Military Trials, London, 1945* (1949), p. 19.
[67] *Ibid.*, pp. 39 and 41.
[68] *Ibid.*, p. 99.

affirmed the principles of international law recognised by the Charter and Judgment of the Nuremberg Tribunal. The maximum of legal significance that can be attributed to this Resolution is that, in future, any member of the United Nations will be estopped from contesting the validity of these principles as rules of international law. Thus, in any future war, the extraordinary jurisdiction of belligerents regarding war crimes in the technical sense will be extended to crimes against peace and humanity committed in connection with such wars. The effect of this innovation is that the sphere of extraordinary State jurisdiction under municipal criminal law has been vastly enlarged, and still tighter ropes have been drawn in advance round the necks of the losers in any other major war.

Another effort of the United Nations which calls for comment is the Convention on the Prevention and Punishment of the Crime of Genocide of December 9, 1948. The term was first proposed by Dr. Lemkin in the course of the war [69] and incorporated in the United States Indictment of the Major German War Criminals.

Genocide is described in the Convention as a " crime under international law " and includes a number of acts committed " with intent to destroy, in whole or in part, a national, ethnical, racial or religious group, as such." The Contracting Parties undertake to enact the necessary legislation to provide effective punishment for persons guilty of the offences enumerated in the Convention. The Convention applies to any persons committing genocide, " whether they are constitutionally responsible rulers, public officials or private individuals." Persons charged with genocide are to be tried by the courts of the State in the territory of which the act was committed or by an international penal tribunal " as may have jurisdiction with respect to these contracting parties which shall have accepted its jurisdiction."

In order to appreciate the value of this Convention it may be permissible to look at the reality of the situation.

The worst offender in this field in recent times was Germany under Hitler. The Occupying Powers and the other United Nations had plenty of opportunity to bring these criminals to justice. The same was true of any crime of this character which, in China and elsewhere, the Japanese had committed.

Similarly, in the case of the forcible deportations of Germans from Czechoslovakia, Eastern Germany and Poland, the inhumanity with which many of these deportations were carried out is undeniable.

[69] *Axis Rule in Occupied Europe* (1944), p. 79 *et seq.*

There would be, however, hardly sufficient evidence to prove intent of committing genocide on the part of those who were responsible for these acts.

In the case of the mass deportations of Baltic nationals by the Soviet Union, the intention of those responsible for these deportations was probably primarily strategic. Finally, Pakistan and India, as well as Israel and the Arab States, accused each other of the commission of this crime.

If the Convention were applied to any of these cases, it would be for Czechoslovak, Indian, Iraqi, Israeli, Pakistani, Polish, Russian and Jordan courts to find on the acts committed by their own governments. Hardly any of these alleged crimes were committed spontaneously by irresponsible individuals.

The Convention is, however, based on the assumption of virtuous governments and criminal individuals, a complete reversal of the truth in proportion to the degree of totalitarianism and nationalism practised in any country. In any event, even if this assumption were correct, the criminal law of every civilised State provides sufficiently against any act of the type enumerated in the Convention. As Sir Hartley Shawcross, as he then was, once put it, murder remains murder whether committed against one or a million. In either case a criminal can be hanged only once.

Thus, the Convention is unnecessary where it can be applied and inapplicable where it may be necessary. It is an insult to the intelligence and dangerous, because it may be argued *a contrario* by brazen upholders of an unlimited *raison d'Etat* that acts enumerated in the Convention, but not committed with the *intent* of destroying groups of a people " as such " are legal.

The Convention—like the Universal Declaration of Human Rights —is, as Brierly formulated it,[70] symptomatic of a " tendency to seek a sort of compensation for all that is so terribly discouraging in the international outlook of today by dissipating energies to achieve results which prove on examination to mark no real advance."

(5) *International Criminal Law in the European Communities.* The Treaties concerning the three European Communities contain a number of provisions of a penal character.[71] These experiments in

---

The Genocide Convention, The Listener (1949), p. 401.
        Cf. also H. von Weber, *Die strafrechtliche Bedeutung der europäischen Menschenrechtskonvention*, 65 *Zeitschrift für die gesamte Strafrechtswissenschaft* (1953), p. 334 *et seq.*, *Vol. I*, p. 271 *et seq.*, and above p. 36.
[71] See, for instance, Articles 36, 47, 50, 54, 58, 59, 64–66 and 68 of the Treaty on the European Coal and Steel Community, April 18, 1951, 1 *European Y.B.* (1955),

supranationalism or functional federalism aim at attaining so high a degree of political and economic integration through the functional backdoor that, in the *inter se* relations between the members of these Communities, international law tends to approximate to municipal law. It is, therefore, not surprising that these Treaties should embody the beginnings of an—intrinsically federal—type of criminal law.[72]

III—THE PROBLEM OF INTERNATIONAL CRIMINAL LAW
de lege ferenda

International law prescribes municipal criminal law in circumstances in which, without such limitations of unrestricted State sovereignty, municipal criminal law might fall below internationally accepted minimum standards. It authorises the exercise of criminal jurisdiction under municipal law in circumstances in which, otherwise, such jurisdiction might be lacking or remain controversial. But international law has not yet evolved a branch of criminal law of its own.

To anybody who does not conceive of law in a vacuum, but is aware of the interrelationship between law and its specific social background, such a result will not be surprising; for international society still lacks any of the conditions on which the rise of criminal law depends.[73]

The origin of criminal law in primitive communities is still controversial.[74] It is, therefore, advisable to avoid over-generalisation.

For some primitive communities, the sacral origin of criminal law is a plausible hypothesis. Yet even in such communities, serious breaches of military discipline were branded as criminal. Other offences, however, may well have been treated as crimes because this was thought to be the only means of averting the vengeance of the gods on the whole tribe. Awe of the gods, and fear of the priests, who ministered to them, provided a substitute for the lack as yet of a strong central power, the firm foundation of criminal law in a subsequent phase of its evolution. Unfortunately, world society has no

p. 359 *et seq.*; Articles 87 and 192 of the Treaty on the European Economic Community, March 25, 1957, 4 *ibid.* (1958), p. 413 *et seq.*, and Articles 83, 144, 145 and 164 of the Treaty on the European Atomic Energy Community, March 25, 1957, 5 *ibid.* (1959), p. 453 *et seq.*

72 See further below, p. 280, and *Manual*, Vol. 1, p. 343 *et seq.*, and Vol. 2, pp. 660–661.

73 See further B. Malinowski, *Crime and Custom in Savage Society* (1932); J. Lambert, *La Vengeance Privée* (1936) and A. S. Diamond, *Primitive Law* (1950).

74 See also above, p. 17.

common gods, and the high priests of international law do not inspire
the holy terror of the magicians of old.

In other primitive communities, criminal law owed its origin to
more rational considerations. In such social groups, acts which, from
the point of view of the community, were considered most reprehensible and dangerous were treated as crimes, that is to say, as acts
which could not be left to be settled by way of blood feud or compo-
sition. Yet, for a long time, such communities did not consider
themselves strong enough to insist on punishment proper. They first
chose outlawry instead of, or as an alternative to, punishment.[75] In
the formulation of Pollock and Maitland, early English law " could
not measure its blows; he who defied it was outside its sphere; he was
outlaw. He who breaks the law has gone to war with the community; the community goes to war with him." [76]

International outlawry as a means of retaliation by subjects of
international law against persistent lawlessness on the part of other
States is at least a feasible proposition. Doubts which at the present
stage of the evolution of world society arise on the wisdom of applying this device in inter-State relations are primarily connected with
the present division of the world into two diametrically opposed
camps.[77] Each of the antipodes is likely to hold its protecting shield
over the black sheep within its own fold, and little would be gained
were the two camps ever to outlaw each other.

The rise of the contemporary type of State has also a lesson to
tell. After the princes of Europe had established their absolute power
within territorially defined States, they firmly held in their hands both
the swords of war and of justice, and both swords were " annexed to
the Sovereign Power." [78] In the words of the old English forms of
indictment, crimes were committed " against the peace of our Lord,
the King, his Crown and Dignity."

Here lies the explanation why, in the present state of world society,
international criminal law in any true sense does not exist.

In the Nuclear Age, most of the " sovereign and equal " members
of the United Nations have lost their political, as distinct from their
legal, sovereignty and know their place in the international
hierarchy.[79] In form, they all are subject to the Charter of the United

---

[75] See further *l.c.* in note 14 above, p. 85 *et seq.*
[76] Sir Frederick Pollock and F. W. Maitland, *The History of English Law*, Vol. 2
(1923), p. 449.
[77] See above, p. 146 *et seq.*
[78] Hobbes, *De Corpore Politico* (1684), Part 2, Chap. 1, 8.
[79] See above, pp. 58 and 154, note 24.

Nations, and its Chapter Seven, which, like Article 16 of the Covenant of the League of Nations, embodies provisions that, in part, may be thought to be of a penal character. There are, however, some Powers which are not only in fact immune to the application of collective enforcement measures, but also, in law, are in a privileged position. By the reservation of their veto power, they have made sure that merely paper swords of war and justice can be wielded against them by the international quasi-authorities of the United Nations.[80] They are fully conscious of the fact that the real swords of war and justice are still " annexed to the Sovereign Power."

In such a situation an international criminal law that is meant to be applied to the world Powers [81] is a contradiction in terms. It presupposes an international authority superior to these States. Actually, any attempt to enforce an international criminal code against either the Soviet Union or the United States would be war under another name. Thus, proposals for a universal international criminal law fall into the category of the one-way pattern for the reorganisation of international society.[82]

With other schemes of this type they share the deficiency of taking for granted an essential condition of their realisation, a *sine qua non* which cannot easily be attained : the transformation of the present system of world power politics in disguise into at least a world federation.[83] If, and when, the swords of war are taken from their present guardians, then, and only then, will the international community be strong enough to wield the sword of universal criminal justice.

---

[80] See above, pp. 58 and 150 *et seq.*, and below, p. 300 *et seq.*

[81] See, for instance, V. Pella, *La Criminalité Collective des Etats et le Droit Pénal de l'Avenir* (1926). For further references to proposals *de lege ferenda*, see H. von Weber, *Internationale Strafgerichtsbarkeit* (1934); G. Weis, *International Criminal Justice in Time of Peace,* 28 *Transactions of the Grotius Society* (1943), p. 38 *et seq.*; M. A. Caloyanni, *Les Criminels de Guerre et le Nouveau Droit Pénal International*; F. B. Schick, *International Criminal Law—Facts and Illusions,* 11 *M.L.R.* (1948), p. 290 *et seq.*, and United Nations, International Law Commission, *Historical Survey of the Question of International Criminal Jurisdiction* (1949).

[82] See further *Manual*, Vol. I, p. 359 *et seq.*

A more promising, though less ambitious, line of development might be the creation of international criminal law within each of the two halves of present-day international society. If either side were content to look not primarily at the international " crimes " committed by the other, but set to work to remedy the deficiencies inside its own world, then proposals for an international criminal law might lose some of their less attractive ideological features and even claim a certain educational value. International criminal law might then contribute to the articulate formulation of the positive values for which the Western and Eastern worlds stand.

[83] It is to Lorimer's credit that, more than half a century ago, this lonely figure perceived clearly the intrinsic connection between schemes for an international criminal law *stricto sensu* and for an international government. *Cf.* his *Institutes of the Law of Nations,* Vol. 2 (1884), p. 279 *et seq.*

CHAPTER 9

THE PRINCIPLES AND STANDARDS
OF INTERNATIONAL ECONOMIC LAW

INTERNATIONAL economic relations [1] are front page news. Economic
assistance to developing countries, trade relations between " Free
Enterprise " and " Communist " States, revaluation and devaluation
of currencies, the safety of investments abroad, the budgetary aspects
of United Nations Forces, and new international institutions, such as
the European Economic Community, the European Free Trade Association, the Organisation for Economic Co-operation and Development, the International Development Association and the Latin
American Free Trade Association are but a few items selected at
random. Each of these problems has intricate legal aspects, and they
all are within the province of Public International Law. It may not be
out of place, therefore, to inquire whether the Doctrine and practice
of international law are properly equipped to deal with this host of
topical issues.

I—THE CHALLENGE OF AN EXPANDING FIELD

The answer to this question can hardly be an unqualified affirmative.
In this respect, matters were considerably simpler in the liberal era
between 1815 and 1914. On both national and international levels,
economic transactions were primarily within the sphere of private
initiative. The gold standard, and other standards related to it,
operated automatically. All that States were expected, and required,
to do was to keep the ring for industry and commerce by the conclusion of uncomplicated treaties of commerce. Their purpose was to
ensure the maximum of freedom for commerce and navigation.

This object could be achieved by means of a few straightforward
legal devices, such as treaty clauses providing for most-favoured-
nation or national treatment or for minimum standards regarding the
life, liberty and property of foreign nationals. There were minor

---

[1] The terms *international economic relations* and *international economic law* are
used in this chapter as including, and applying to, international financial and
monetary transactions.

210

controversies such as the argument between Great Britain and Russia on the compatibility of export bounties for sugar with most-favoured-nation treatment or the dispute between Britain and the United States of America regarding the Panama Canal tolls.[2] These, and other differences of a similar character, could be adequately settled within the traditional framework of international law.

Imperialism, as it developed from the nineties of the last century, forecast the shape of things to come. The true turning point was, however, the First World War. In the post-1919 period, the picture rapidly changed. The disequilibrium caused by the war, the problems of reparations and inter-Allied debts, the growth of economic nationalism and protectionism and last, but not least, the general trend towards control by the State of activities formerly reserved to the individual deeply affected both national and international economies. On the national level, this avalanche of changes brought with it a marked shift in emphasis from private to public law. It also led to a vast expansion of the traditional frontiers of international law. It was not surprising that in this changing environment the lawyer should temporarily lose his bearings and look suspiciously like a relic of old and bygone days.

A glance at the textbooks of the post-1919 period and at the syllabuses in international law of the law schools of the leading universities all over the world will indicate how the challenge was met. It is probably no exaggeration to say that it was done largely by ignoring the problem.

One of the reasons for this negative attitude was that there were—and still are—too few teaching posts in the field of international law. The few scholars and practitioners specialising in the subject were overburdened with ordinary day-to-day commitments. Thus, the tasks awaiting treatment were mainly left undone. To put matters in this way is not to be lacking in appreciation to the few exceptions to the general rule, to men such as Fischer Williams, Jèze and Lippert, but rather to emphasise the debt of gratitude which international lawyers owe to these scholars. It was not accidental that each of these distinguished specialists either had come out of government service or was in exceptionally close touch with government departments concerned with economic matters. The legal advisers to foreign offices and trade departments were the only reliable repositories of knowledge in this field.

[2] See further 22 *B.Y.I.L.* (1945), p. 96 *et seq.*

To be fair to academic international lawyers, it is necessary to add that, simultaneously, international law was expanding in many other directions. International institutions developed and opened out a wide vista in the field of the law of international institutions.[3] The emergence of the aeroplane provided the opportunity for another new branch of international law : international air law.[4]

The hesitation of international lawyers to embark on these new fields was strengthened by their growing awareness of a more fundamental problem. Their traditional exposition of international law was the result of accumulated wisdom, derived largely from deductive speculation and the use of rather questionable eclectic methods. This attitude did scant justice to the vast amount of evidence of a much higher intrinsic value, such as the decisions of international and national courts and the practice of States. Thus there was an equal—if not more pressing—need for the overhaul of the whole system of traditional international law and its re-evaluation by means of an inductive approach.[5]

It is necessary to draw attention to the whole of this chaotic picture in order to understand that the problem of international economic law is merely one facet of a much wider question. The Doctrine of international law is confronted with an issue which has been faced long ago by every mature and self-respecting system of municipal law. Every system of municipal law requires the type of treatment which one may expect to find in a standard book or course on Jurisprudence or English Legal System. Side by side, however, with these general topics, there are the various branches of municipal law. They are recognised as proper subjects for separate and technical treatment. An English lawyer would not expect to find a detailed picture of the laws of Contract, Tort, Evidence, Commercial Law or Conflict of Laws in a bird's-eye view of English law. Yet this is still largely the amorphous state of international law. Writers and teachers attempt as best they can to cope in general treatises and lecture courses both with the general and particular aspects of their subject.

The time appears to have come for the establishment of separate branches of international law, supplementing treatises on, and teaching in, the general principles of international law. Such specialisation will not only result in providing more adequate knowledge in the

---

3 See further below, p. 274 *et seq.*
4 See also below, p. 214.
5 See further *Vol. I*, p. 4 *et seq.*, and I.C.L.P. (1956), p. 240 *et seq.*

narrower fields, but is likely to enrich insight into the nature, functions and principles of the law of nations as such.[6]

II—Defining International Economic Law

International Economic Law may be defined as the branch of Public International Law concerned with the ownership and exploitation of natural resources; the production and distribution of goods; currency and finance; related services as well as the status and organisation of those dealing therewith.

The primary value of such a descriptive definition lies in what it excludes rather than in what it includes. International Economic Law is concerned only with such aspects of economic phenomena as come within the purview of *Public* International Law.

The reasons for this self-limitation are not of a metaphysical nature. Nor can they be determined by reference to what, in a neo-naturalist terminology, it has become fashionable to term the "nature" of things; for this considerably varies according to their "society" or "community" environment.[7] These reasons are, partly, doctrinal and, partly, pragmatic. Some of the topics excluded are adequately covered by established branches of municipal law such as Private International Law and the Law of International Commerce. While the former is concerned with all matters of private law containing a foreign element, private commercial relations with a foreign element are the concern of the latter.

A certain measure of overlapping between both these branches of municipal law and International Economic Law is unavoidable and can do little harm. Thus, the Treaties of 1930 and 1931 on the legal régime of bills of exchange and cheques may be claimed as their own by specialists in each of these three fields. None of them can entirely ignore material of this character. The international economic lawyer would, however, be the first to concede that any branch of municipal law which has become "international" primarily for the purpose of obtaining a measure of uniformity should not for this reason alone be removed from the branch of municipal law initially involved.

Is there not much to be said for including in International Economic Law everything that affects businessmen and, at one phase or another, is characterised by an international element? If the

[6] See I.C.L.P. (1956), p. 247 *et seq.*
[7] See above, p. 9 *et seq.*

relevant problems are primarily seen as they arise in a solicitor's office, a barrister's chambers or the board-room of an international combine, International Economic Law would perhaps be more useful if it were conceived primarily in terms of International Business Law.

The price of such a treatment of the subject would, however, be high. International Economic Law would be in serious danger of losing its legal unity. One concession to this treatment appears, however, feasible. The more we move from lower to higher levels of international economic integration the less need exists for any rigid distinction between international and municipal law; for, at this stage, international law increasingly approximates to municipal law. Thus, for instance, on the subject of economic activities inside the European Communities, International Economic Law becomes indistinguishable from International Business Law, and scope for a European Business Law, as distinct from an International Business Law on a worldwide scale, exists.

Similarly, some services and transactions are of an economic character in the wider sense, but are excluded from International Economic Law for pragmatic considerations of a different kind. They are sufficiently coherent and wide in scope to form specialised branches of international law of their own. In particular, this applies to International Labour Law, International Social Law, International Transport Law as well as the Law of International Copyright and Industrial Designs.

It remains to explore whether it is possible to substantiate the claim by which International Economic Law as a special branch of International Law stands and falls, that is to say that it can call its own the requisite minimum of legal rules and principles. On the surface, this claim appears to be belied by the predominance of economic treaties as compared with relevant rules of international customary law and general principles of law recognised by civilised nations. Like other treaties, economic treaties are limited in their legal effects to the contracting parties. Is it not, therefore, self-evident that such treaties can hardly aspire to being regarded as the vehicles of generally applicable rules and principles of international economic law?

Reasoning on these lines ignores one of the most important functions fulfilled by treaties in the evolution of international law: the establishment in this way of optional legal principles and standards. Standards in this context mean subsidiary legal rules by reference to which the scope of the optional legal principle laid down in a treaty is determined as, for instance, freedom of navigation on the footing of most-favoured-nation or national treatment.

III—COMPULSORY AND OPTIONAL RULES OF INTERNATIONAL LAW

The growth of international law cannot be adequately understood if it is seen through the mirror of the history of the Doctrine of international law. Since the early days of the Middle Ages, the practice of the European law of nations has shown a remarkable continuity.[8] Within and outside the Holy Roman Empire there was a sufficient number of *de facto* and *de jure* sovereign princes who found it advisable to fill by treaties the void of lawlessness then prevailing in inter-State relations.[9]

To give an idea of the importance of treaties at that early stage, there exist at least twenty-one treaties of a truly international character which were concluded by the kings of England with foreign princes during the twelfth century.[10] What is today called the Law of Peace was a state of international relations which entirely depended on treaties establishing such a foundation for peaceful intercourse between nations. The precariousness of this status was underlined by time limits during which it applied, and still more by the greater frequency of treaties which were content merely to provide for a state of truce. In the absence of such treaties, any foreign prince or merchant was an enemy and, as such, liable to suffer any form of arbitrariness and violence.[11]

The principle of reciprocity mitigated unrestricted indulgence in licentiousness. Magna Carta offers evidence of the reality of the operation of this principle. Subject to the reservation of the ancient liberties and customs of the English boroughs, the Charter granted personal freedom and security to foreign merchants during their stay in England. In Article 41, it was enacted that they were not even to be disturbed in case of war, provided that English merchants were treated abroad in the same manner. Yet freedom of commerce could be established on a safer basis by treaties creating mutual legal obligations than by unilateral promises under municipal

---

8 See above, p. 43 *et seq.*
9 For early English practice, see above, p. 85 *et seq.* On the practice of the Italian City States which had acquired a state of *de facto*, if not *de jure* sovereignty approximating to that of international persons, *cf.* A. P. Sereni, *The Italian Conception of International Law* (1943), p. 10 *et seq.*
10 See above, p. 86 *et seq.*
11 See above, pp. 59 and 96 *et seq.*

law. It was also found convenient to enlarge the scope of such freedoms on a footing of mutuality.

The treaties concluded in this field, as in others, by the kings of England with other sovereigns, developed on varied lines. While some of these were quickly discarded, others were regarded as being so useful that they were repeatedly applied between the same Powers and copied in other treaties. In numerous treaties the rights of foreign merchants were set out in considerable detail. Treaty clauses provided for the safety of their persons, dwellings and business houses. Their right of access to court in matters civil and criminal, as well as their right of exit with their property and exemption from obnoxious taxation, were expressly stipulated.

A time came, however, when it was no longer considered necessary to proceed in so cautious a manner. It was to the advantage of every prince that his subjects should enjoy abroad such considerate treatment. Thus it was gradually taken for granted that foreigners would be treated in this manner. From this, it was but one further step to the view that the home State of a foreigner could expect as of right such treatment of its subjects abroad. Similar developments took place in the fields of denial of justice, the law of wreck and the limitation of lawful reprisals.[12]

What is the significance of these treaties for the growth of international law? A comparison will make this apparent. Both the treaties establishing minimum rights of foreigners under international law and the rules on this subject as they now exist under international customary law provide legal rules of conduct. Once, however, rules have become embodied in universal or general international customary law, they are automatically applicable and compulsory for all subjects of international law. If the rule rests on a treaty basis, it is optional in the sense that any State is free to enter, or not to enter, into such a commitment.

By means of treaties, subjects of international law are able to circumscribe precisely the operation of a legal principle or standard, and limit it by exceptions in favour of other principles or standards.

Thus, the most-favoured-nation standard comes into operation exclusively on a consensual basis. Contracting parties may, for instance, exclude contingencies in which reasons of national or international public policy may make the application of differential treatment advisable. Or, in certain cases, the most-favoured-nation

---

[12] See above, p. 123 *et seq.*

standard may have to give way to the standard of preferential treatment as it is enjoyed by the members of the British Commonwealth under the Ottawa Agreements of 1932.[13]

Contracting parties have as a rule various patterns at their disposal. There is no limit to their initiative and imagination. They may wish to adopt well-known types of clauses; they may venture into the unknown, and experiment with variants of old patterns, or they may attempt to evolve new principles and standards.

Thus treaties provide a fascinating field of pioneer work. Some of the clauses may prove so ingenious and attractive—as happened in the case of the most-favoured-nation standard—that they came to provide prototypes for innumerable draftsmen following in the footsteps of their predecessors. In the course of time, others may become so commonplace that they sink back into the body of international customary law. Others again may be most suitable for relations between States desiring to establish highly integrated relations with one another, as, for instance, clauses usually only to be found in treaties on customs unions. Finally, some standards are more suited for relations between States with radically different ways of life, such as the Soviet Union and the United States of America. Thus, optional principles and standards are a means of elastic and experimental legislation in the realm of international law, and treaties are the instruments by which, *inter partes*, they are transformed into temporary or permanent rules of international law.

Recognition of the fact that treaties fulfil the function of transforming optional into compulsory rules of conduct at the choice of the contracting parties may assist in overcoming the habit of underestimating their importance in international law. In order to explore effectively this multitude of optional patterns evolved by nations in the period of more than eight hundred years during which contemporary international law has developed, it is necessary to group together treaties which fulfil the same or similar social functions. Fulfilment of this task is the ultimate justification for separate branches of international law based primarily on treaties and held together by the unifying bond of the same social purpose. The real test, therefore, of the need for recognising international economic law as a separate branch of international law is whether international economic law can call its own a sufficient number of legal principles and standards.

[13] See further *l.c.* in note 2 above, pp. 109 and 118.

IV—THE PRINCIPLES
OF CLASSICAL INTERNATIONAL ECONOMIC LAW

Optional principles of international law differ from those of a compulsory character not only in being binding exclusively on the parties to treaties in which they are embodied, but also in a further respect. The principles of international customary law are merely abstractions from relevant legal rules of international customary law.[14] By way of contrast, optional principles can be embodied in treaties in a form which gives them the character of immediately applicable legal rules of considerable scope.

If two States agree without further qualification to grant to each other and their nationals complete freedom and equality of commerce and navigation, the principles of freedom and equality of commerce and navigation are stipulated in absolute terms and entitle the contracting parties to the immediate and full enjoyment of these rights.

Only in cases in which parties desire to " relativise " the grant of such rights on a footing of, for instance, inland or foreign parity does any need exist to define these rights in more concrete terms. This can be achieved with the assistance of the standards of international economic law.

The legal principles and standards embodied in treaties of an economic character have crystallised in the course of an evolution extending over centuries. As they proved themselves in the course of long experience, the system of international economic law consisting of these principles and standards may be termed classical.

The chief principles of classical international economic law are freedom of commerce—a notion considerably wider than freedom of trade, which is merely one of its several forms—and various freedoms of communications on land as well as at sea, such as freedom of access to a territory or to the high seas, freedom of transit and freedom of inland navigation.

The only one of these principles which has outgrown its treaty basis and primary connection with international economic law is that abstracted from the rules governing the freedom of the seas. It has become part of the body of general international customary law.[15]

What all these freedoms have in common is their predominantly negative character. They aim at monopoly, preferential treatment or

[14] See *Fundamental Principles*, p. 200 *et seq.* or *Manual*, Vol. I, p. 37 *et seq.*
[15] See further *Fundamental Principles*, p. 358 *et seq.*

equality of treatment by means of stipulated duties of non-interference on the part of the other contracting party.

Occasionally, prohibitory rules in such a treaty nexus fulfil an additional function. They aim at the limitation of a freedom under international customary law or treaty law for the purpose of making possible the realisation of an overriding common objective. The prohibition of the slave trade is an illustration in point. In this way, a formerly legitimate form of free enterprise was outlawed and made criminal [16] and, by means of bilateral and multilateral treaties, the beginnings of an international economic quasi-order were laid.[17]

V—THE STANDARDS
OF CLASSICAL INTERNATIONAL ECONOMIC LAW

If, as was the rule, the freedoms of classical international economic law were granted subject to reservations, the standards of international economic law provided the requisite legal techniques.

Seven of these standards are of primary significance :

The *Minimum Standard* deserves first place among the standards of international economic law ; for, so far, it is the only standard in this field which has grown into a rule of general international customary law. As already mentioned, it began its career by being incorporated in innumerable treaties in order to secure to foreign merchants a modicum of security for their persons and property. In the fullness of time, the standard developed into a rule of international customary law and its applicability was widened so as to apply to all foreign nationals. Thus, the rule on the minimum standard offers an example *par excellence* of the contribution made by this special branch of international law to the growth of general international law, in this case the law of international torts.

The *Standard of Identical Treatment* also can claim a long pedigree. Princes promised each other that they would grant identical treatment to each other's merchants. As in the case of the law of diplomatic immunity, such reciprocal treatment could be applied in a narrow or a liberal spirit. It was in the mutual interest of princes to interpret extensively the scope of diplomatic immunity, and this led to generously wide rules in favour of foreign diplomatic envoys.[18]

---

[16] See above, pp. 34, 135 and 198 *et seq.*
[17] See further *Manual*, Vol. I, pp. 60 and 138 *et seq.*, *Vol. I*, p. 425 *et seq.*, and *Fundamental Principles*, p. 376 *et seq.*
[18] See above, pp. 29, 92 and 169 *et seq.*

Similarly, the interests of both mercantilist and liberal economies operated as a rule in favour of an extensive application of the principle of identical treatment in the economic field.

In the case of countries of similar structure and complementary interests, the *Standard of National Treatment* is appropriate. This standard provides for inland parity, that is to say, equality of treatment between nationals and foreigners.

Another standard which has proved to be of particular usefulness is that of *Most-Favoured-Nation Treatment*.[19] In accordance with this standard, States undertake to grant each other the same rights or favours as they have granted, or may grant, to any third State. The great merit of this standard in its unconditional form is that it generalises automatically among contracting parties the advantages *ejusdem generis* granted by any of them to any third State.

The egalitarian function of this standard corresponds to one of the permanent interests of sovereign States. It is applicable irrespective of the internal political, social or economic structure of the contracting States. This explains both the historical continuity in the application of the most-favoured-nation standard and the wide use made of the standard. It provides a common meeting ground for primitive and developed countries, agricultural and industrial communities and, within limits, free-enterprise and planned economies. In exceptional cases, it has been applied outside its original context of international economic relations. It is, however, in this field that the standard has primarily proved its usefulness.

As the criterion of equality of treatment is the treatment accorded to third States, the most-favoured-nation standard is compatible with discrimination between foreigners and nationals. Thus, in protectionist and nationalist periods, it is not exposed to the objections which may militate against the standard of national treatment.

Related to the Most-Favoured-Nation Standard is the *Standard of the Open Door*. Both aim at the same object : equality of opportunity for foreign States and their subjects. Yet in the case of the standard of the open door, the *tertium comparationis* is not primarily, or not only, third States, but any one of the contracting parties who are beneficiaries. The standard was a typical product of an imperialist era, in which Powers jealous of one another imposed self-denying ordinances on themselves and their competitors in a nominally sovereign State which is also a contracting party.

19 See further *l.c.* in note 2 above.

The *Standard of Preferential Treatment* stands in sharp contrast to all these standards aiming at some kind of equality. In an international system consisting merely of three States, the standards of preferential and most-favoured-nation treatment could be envisaged as compatible with each other. Yet in any wider inter-State system, the two standards are mutually exclusive in the sense that they cannot be applied simultaneously and can be only formally harmonised with each other as, for instance, by way of an exception to most-favoured-nation treatment in favour of neighbouring States or members of a customs union.

The last standard which can claim to be of general interest in this field is the *Standard of Equitable Treatment*. Its importance lies in spheres affected by an increase in State planning. It also provides the only solution in cases in which currency disequilibrium or changes in the structure of national economies force States to adopt measures of quantitative restriction of imports or allocation of foreign currencies. In such a situation, this standard provides the only means of operating effectively the most-favoured-nation standard and of achieving an at least proportionate equality between foreign States.

VI—THE FUNCTIONS OF THE PRINCIPLES AND STANDARDS OF INTERNATIONAL ECONOMIC LAW

It is a legitimate object of industry and commerce to attain the maximum freedom of commerce. In periods of mercantilism, political considerations call for the encouragement of certain types of exports, and the discouragement of others. In an era of economic liberalism, freedom of commerce tends to become a shibboleth. In State-controlled economies, a revival of the mercantilist approach to the problem is taking place on a higher plane.

Naturalist writers on international law tended to construe freedom of commerce as a natural right. In doing so, they interpreted this alleged natural right rather narrowly or subjected it to important exceptions. In the main, however, they were content to treat it as an imperfect right. In practice, this meant that questions of freedom of commerce and communications were considered to be matters within the unfettered domestic jurisdiction of States. Thus, there was only one way in which these ideals could be realised, that is to say, by the conclusion of treaties to this effect.

In exceptional circumstances a weak State may be forced to agree to a unilateral grant of freedom of commerce or navigation. More frequently, defeated nations have to accept for an interim period unilateral limitations of their economic sovereignty which are explicable only on grounds of their inferior power. Also, in a fair number of cases, the reciprocal application of any of the principles and standards of international economic law is merely of a formal character, disguising but thinly the reality of the situation : the economic domination of one country by another. Yet when all this is said, there still remains the great bulk of commercial treaties by which, on a footing of reciprocity and mutuality, a considerable measure of freedom of commerce or communications is achieved.

Each of the principles and standards of international economic law can assist in attaining this object. Six of the standards have the feature in common that, through them, the freedoms of commerce and communications are achieved on a footing of equality. But the standard of national treatment alone secures absolute inland parity. The minimum standard, the standard of most-favoured-nation treatment and the standard of the open door aim primarily at foreign parity. Their *raison d'être* is the exclusion of discrimination as compared with other foreign competitors.

It would be a mistake to think of the standards as operating in isolation from one another. If, for instance, the most-favoured-nation standard is coupled in a treaty with that of national treatment, it may well secure treatment to foreigners which is privileged as compared with that of the nationals of one of the contracting parties. Thus, a treaty of commerce may provide for national and most-favoured-nation treatment. If it should then happen that one of the contracting parties concluded a treaty with a third State exempting each other's nationals from military service, the State enjoying most-favoured-nation and national treatment may claim for its subjects exemptions which are not available to the nationals of the other State.

A similar situation may arise when there is a discrepancy between the standard of national treatment and the minimum standard of international law. The presumption then is that, in concluding the treaty, the parties intended to add to, but not detract from, their rights under international customary law.

The principles and standards of international economic law offer to contracting parties a number of methods for achieving, in any given circumstances, the freedoms of classical international economic law. It is the merit of these optional principles and standards that their geographical, temporal and functional scope can be determined by the parties at will. States may vary as they wish the clauses embodying these principles and standards. It would mean, however, not seeing the wood for the trees to concentrate on the multitude of accidental treaty clauses and to ignore the basic principles and standards and their enduring significance.

VII—THE STANDARDS OF INTERNATIONAL ECONOMIC LAW WITHIN THE FRAMEWORK OF THE UNITED NATIONS

So long as the economic mechanisms of international trade were allowed to operate in a more or less automatic manner, it was sufficient to frame the principles and standards of international economic law on a bilateral level.

This was no longer the case in the post-1919 period. Yet as generals are prone to prepare for past wars, so statesmen tend to save the peace of a previous generation. The Covenant of the League of Nations was true to pattern. Though the era of free trade had gone for good, the Peace Settlements of 1919 were based on the unstated major premise of a liberal international economy.

Article 23 (e), the only Article of the Covenant dealing with international trade, was the outward symbol of this mentality. It was left to the Permanent Court of International Justice in the case of *Railway Traffic between Lithuania and Poland* (1931) to reveal the precarious character of the legal obligations undertaken by League members under this Article.

The Atlantic Charter, Article 7 of the Anglo-American Lease-Lend Agreement of 1942, the Bretton Woods Agreements, and the Charter of the United Nations breathe a fresh spirit. They have three relevant features in common.

First, the objectives of international economic policy are considerably widened. The classical freedoms are no longer the only— or even the main—reason for State concern with this field. Matters such as higher standards of living, full employment, economic and social progress and development are proclaimed as legitimate topics of joint international action.

Secondly, these objects are to be pursued in accordance with general principles laid down in multilateral treaties.

Thirdly, international economic institutions on a scale unknown in the past have been called into being as substitutes for the vanished automatic mechanisms of multilateral international trade.

The outstanding example of this type of international institution is the International Monetary Fund. Its purpose is to secure the maintenance of the gold exchange standard and the prevention of competitive depreciation of exchanges. If it were not for the weaknesses inherent in the political superstructure of the United Nations, this development might well be described as the establishment of an economic international public order.

An important step towards a corresponding Specialised Agency in the field of international trade has been taken with GATT, the General Agreement on Tariffs and Trade, ultimately to be replaced by the Organisation for Trade Co-operation.[20] Over forty States are full members of GATT. Nine others have provisionally acceded to the Agreement or are linked with it by special arrangements, and seventeen more States apply the Agreement *de facto*. If the Organisation for Trade Co-operation should come into existence, its function will be, *inter alia*, to administer the General Agreement.[21] Thus, the Agreement, although limited in scope to questions of customs tariffs and international trade, is of more than transient interest. The analysis of the Agreement will be limited to its effects on the principles and standards of international economic law.

The General Agreement and the International Economic Quasi-Order

The General Agreement operates within the wider international framework of the United Nations. The play of the principles and standards embodied in the Agreement is, therefore, limited by the overriding requirements of this international economic quasi-order.[22] The technical devices used to achieve this purpose are reservations formulated by way of exceptions. Thus, the contracting parties remain free to take any action in pursuance of their obligations under the United Nations Charter for the maintenance of international peace and security (Article XXI (c)). Similarly, care has been taken to co-ordinate the Agreement with the obligations of the

---

20 Unless otherwise stated, references are to the revised text (1955) of the GATT Agreement.
21 *Ibid.*, p. 1 *et seq.*
22 For the distinction between international order and quasi-order, see *Manual*, Vol. I, pp. 141, 152, 171–172 and 178–179.

signatories towards the International Monetary Fund (Articles III (6) (a) ; VII (4) and XV).

The General Agreement and the Most-Favoured-Nation Standard

In accordance with Article II of the Agreement, the most-favoured-nation standard in its unconditional form applies to customs duties, charges imposed in connection with the importation and exportation of goods or on the international transfer of payments for imports or exports, and to methods and formalities in connection with importation and exportation. In a subsidiary way, the most-favoured-nation standard is used in connection with matters of internal taxation and regulations (Articles II and IV), freedom of transit (Article V (5)), marks of origin (Article IX (1)), and the administration of quantitative import and export restrictions (Article XIII (1)). The most-favoured-nation treatment under Article II is subject to important reservations in favour of the standard of preferential treatment. In addition, all standards are subject to general exceptions in the interest of national public policy and the security of the contracting parties (Articles XX and XXI).

In interpreting the general most-favoured-nation clause of Article II (1) of the GATT Agreement, it is essential to bear in mind that the general agreement represents a transitional stage between bilateralism and multilateralism in international economic relations. Thus, any advantage in the categories mentioned above that an individual member of GATT grants to any other State—members of GATT and non-member States—accrues immediately and unconditionally to all other members of GATT.

Moreover, in the central field of GATT activities, that is to say, customs duties and other charges imposed on imports, individual contracting parties negotiate with each other on a bilateral basis, but at the same time and in the same place at a Session of the Contracting Parties.

The results of these negotiations are embodied in Schedules forming an integral part of the GATT Agreement (Article III (7)). Thus, each contracting party remains free to determine for itself the scope of the concessions it is willing to make. Subject, however, to reservations regarding the withholding and withdrawal of concessions (Article XXVII), action in emergencies (Article XIX) or in the case of nullification or impairment of concessions (Article XXIII) and the modification of Schedules (Article XXVIII), these

Schedules provide the level of foreign parity regarding tariffs between the parties to the General Agreement (Article III (1) (a)) : " Each contracting party shall accord to the commerce of the other contracting parties treatment no less favourable than that provided for in the appropriate Part of the appropriate Schedule annexed to this Agreement."

Doubtful points in the evolution of the standards of international economic law are expressly settled. The limits within which anti-dumping and countervailing duties are considered compatible with the principle of non-discrimination are clearly defined (Article VI). The principle of non-discriminatory treatment applies to State-trading enterprises (Article XVII). Neighbouring States and members of a customs union may grant to one another special advantages for the facilitation of frontier traffic (Article XXIV). The problem of export subsidies is tackled in Article XVI.

In order to encourage the expansion of multilateral trade, the contracting parties undertake to eliminate quantitative restrictions on import and export trade (Article XI (1)). This rule is, however, subject to important exceptions in scope (Article XI (2)) and in the interest of the balance of payments (Articles XII–XV).

The General Agreement and the Standard of Equitable Treatment

So long as some currencies remain scarce, other States may have to maintain policies of quantitative restrictions of imports. Equality of treatment can then only be achieved on a footing of proportional equality. Here the standard of equitable treatment comes into its own. In principle, quotas fixed by a party to the Agreement must be allotted by reference to the share of other contracting parties in any particular trade during a representative base-period (Article XIII (2) (d)). The standard is equally applicable where, for other reasons, such as the protection of home agriculture or fisheries or owing to a shortage of supplies, State control and regulation in any field become imperative (Articles XI (2) and XX).

The General Agreement and the Standard of National Treatment

In any case in which, under a bilateral treaty, a party to the General Agreement should grant national treatment to any non-contracting State, the general most-favoured-nation clause of Article II would automatically make any party to the Agreement eligible to share in such advantages. The General Agreement provides, however, expressly for national treatment of contracting parties as regards internal taxation and regulation (Article IV). In this case, the standard of national treatment fulfils an auxiliary function in the interest of the equality of treatment postulated under Article III (1) (a). Discriminatory internal taxes might frustrate the effects of the concessions made under the tariff schedules. The standard of national treatment is equally implied in the provision for freedom of transit (Article V).

The General Agreement and the Minimum Standard

In matters concerned with freedom of transit, the draftsmen of the General Agreement could build on the foundations laid in the Barcelona Convention and Statute of 1921 on Freedom of Transit. They were similarly helped in laying down a code of international commercial conduct by earlier multilateral treaties such as the Convention for the Publication of Customs Tariffs of 1890, the Convention for the Simplification of Customs Formalities of 1923 and the Agreement on False Indications of Origin on Goods of 1925. The essential features of the provisions on valuation for customs purposes (Article VII), customs formalities (Article VIII), marks of origin (Article IX) and publication and administration of trade regulations (Article X) are certainty, publicity, good faith and reasonableness.

One of these clauses (Article X (3)) deserves special comment. The parties undertake to maintain or institute as soon as practicable, judicial, arbitral or administrative tribunals or procedures for the prompt review and correction of administrative action relating to customs matters. By this is meant provision for objective and impartial review of administrative action, even though such procedures may not be fully or formally independent of the agencies entrusted with administrative enforcement. Thus, as in the wider field of the minimum standard of international law, it is again a treaty which, in the first instance, makes it incumbent on States to grant a certain minimum of justice and judicial protection to foreign nationals and companies in matters in which they would otherwise be completely at the mercy of other States. The function of the minimum standard of international economic conduct as formulated in the Agreement is to assist in the application of the Agreement in accordance with the intentions of the contracting parties and to prevent a circumvention of the other standards through petty administrative discrimination.

The General Agreement and the Standard of Preferential Treatment

Forms of preferential treatment are permitted in the General Agreement only by way of exception. Within the limits laid down in the Annexes to the Agreement, tariff preferences and arrangements in force within the British Commonwealth, between territories of the French Union, between the Benelux countries, between the United States and the Philippines, between Chile and her neighbours, and between Uruguay and Paraguay may be maintained.

It should, however, be remembered that, in connection with the negotiations of the schedules of tariff concessions, some of the preferential margins were substantially reduced and others completely eliminated. Furthermore, the Agreement contains a ceiling for margins of preference (Article II (4)).

It is impossible for parties to create new areas of preferential treatment by way of a customs union or a free-trade area on terms less favourable to other parties than they enjoyed in the constituent territories prior to such closer integration. Even then only a complete customs union may be envisaged, that is to say, a customs union which amounts to the substitution of a single customs territory for two or more customs territories. Similarly, in the case of a free-trade area, the elimination of substantially all the duties and other restrictive regulations of commerce between the members must be the ultimate objective. Any other new arrangement of a preferential character falling short of a complete customs union or free-trade area is compatible with the Agreement only if it can be considered as an interim arrangement leading within a reasonable time to a full customs union or free-trade area as defined in Article XXIV of the General Agreement.

The General Agreement and the Standard of Economic Good Neighbourliness

Article 74 of the Charter of the United Nations, which forms part of the Chapter on Non-Self-Governing Territories, embodies a principle which is not limited to the colonial sphere : Members of the United Nations agree that " their policy in respect of the territories to which this Chapter applies, *no less than in respect of their metropolitan areas,* must be based on the general principle of good neighbourliness, due account being taken of the interests and well-being of the rest of the world, in social, economic and commercial matters."

The General Agreement proves that, in international relations, the principle of good neighbourliness can be more than a Platonic declaration. The draftsmen of the General Agreement have widely applied the principle and transformed it into a new standard of international economic law : the standard of economic good neighbourliness. They have achieved this object by a number of devices which form a constructive alternative to mere agreement to disagree on issues not susceptible of any hard-and-fast ruling.

Unilateral action on the part of contracting parties has been limited in cases in which it would amount to wanton use—or rather abuse—of sovereign discretion and, without any corresponding benefit to the party applying such measures, merely harm other States. Thus, anti-dumping or countervailing duties are permissible only if foreign dumping or subsidies are likely to cause material injury to an established industry in the country contemplating such counter-measures or will retard materially the establishment of a domestic industry (Article VI (6) (a)). Similarly, restrictions authorised under the Agreement in the interest of safeguarding the national balance of payments must be really necessary in order to maintain reasonable monetary reserves, and be applied in such a way as to avoid unnecessary damage to the interests of other contracting parties (Article XII). Under Article XIV (2), some departures from the rule of non-discrimination are permissible, but only with the consent of the Contracting Parties in respect of a small portion of its external trade, when the benefits to the contracting party concerned " substantially outweigh " any injury which may result to the trade of other contracting parties.

In order to give concrete meaning to the standard of economic good neighbourliness, the General Agreement provides for co-operation between parties on two different levels. Primarily, contracting parties are under a legal obligation to consult with others who are most directly affected by any unilateral action on their part. In addition, the contracting parties acting jointly and described in the Agreement as the Contracting Parties—in capital letters (Article XXV (1)) [23]—are endowed under the Agreement with far-reaching functions.

[23] In the transitional version (*l.c.* in note 20 above, p. 65).

The general principle of consultation with other contracting parties in all matters affecting the operation of the Agreement is laid down in Article XXII. More specific duties are undertaken by the contracting parties in a number of provisions. They may be summarised under four headings :

First, to give information to other interested contracting parties (Article XIII (3) (a) and (c)).

Secondly, to review the operation of internal laws at the request of other interested contracting parties (Articles VIII (2) ; IX (6) and XXIII (1)).

Thirdly, to consult with other interested contracting parties (Articles III (5) ; XVI (1) and XXII).

Fourthly, to negotiate with other interested contracting parties (Articles III (5) and IV (d)).

In cases in which diverging interests of members cannot be adjusted by means of direct settlement, collective action by the Contracting Parties—ultimately to be replaced by the Assembly of the Organisation for Trade Co-operation—comes into play. The contracting parties are to meet from time to time in conference. It is the purpose of these meetings to facilitate the operation and to further the objectives of the Agreement, and to give effect to the provisions of the Agreement which involve joint action. Each contracting party has one vote and, normally, decisions are taken by a majority of the votes cast. A waiver of obligations of contracting parties, which is not specifically provided for elsewhere in the Agreement, requires a two-thirds majority of the votes cast, and such majority must include more than half of the contracting parties (Article XXV [24]).

The functions of the Contracting Parties are mainly those of a co-ordinating and supervisory body.

Under the heading of co-ordination should be mentioned the duties of contracting parties to report on measures contemplated or taken which are likely to affect other contracting parties (Articles VII (1) ; X (3) (c) and XVI) and to consult and negotiate with the Contracting Parties (Articles XII (4) ; XIII (4) ; XVI (i) and XIX (2)). The right of the Contracting Parties to initiate discussions between contracting parties (Article XII (5)) also falls into this category.

---

[24] In the transitional version (*l.c.* in note 20 above, pp. 65–66).

Still more important are the supervisory tasks of the Contracting Parties. They extend from supervision of the observance of the main principles of the Agreement (Articles VII (4) (c) ; XVI (5) ; XVIII (6) ; XIX (3) and XX (j)) *via* the right of granting the waiver of specified obligations—and in exceptional circumstances, of any obligation—undertaken by contracting parties (Articles VI (6) ; XII (4) ; XXIII (2) [25] and XXV (5)),[26] to revisory functions in the interest of orderly economic change (Articles XVIII and XXIV) and the adaptation of the General Agreement to changed conditions (Article XXX).

The General Agreement represents an important step in the evolution of the principles and standards of international economic law. It marks the transition from bilateralism to the establishment of a multilateral economic framework. The effect of the Agreement is to limit—however slightly—economic sovereignty by the silken cords of *pacta de contrahendo* ; to give guidance to the contracting parties jointly and severally by means of legally binding standards, and to strengthen the machinery of international economic institutions by the creation of an international economic organ not condemned merely to study, report and recommend, but authorised to act and decide.

VIII—THE PRINCIPLES AND STANDARDS OF INTERNATIONAL ECONOMIC LAW ON LEVELS OF HIGHER INTEGRATION

On levels of even closer international economic co-operation, such as the Organisation for Economic Co-operation and Development (OECD) [27]—the successor to the Organisation for European Economic Co-operation—an even more remarkable transformation of the principles and standards of classical international economic law will be observed. They are replaced by apparently vague formulations of common goals of economic policy which the members agree, both individually and jointly, to pursue.

The aims of OECD are to promote policies designed to achieve three objects :

First, to attain the maximum of economic development, full employment and rise in the standards of living, without impairing financial stability in the member countries ;

[25] In the transitional version (*l.c.* in note 20 above, p. 65).
[26] In the transitional version (*ibid.*, p. 66).
[27] Cmnd. 1257 (1960).

Secondly, to contribute to sound economic expansion both in
member and non-member countries, and

Thirdly, to assist in the expansion of world trade on a multilateral and non-discriminatory basis in accordance with the
international obligations undertaken by the member States.

In the pursuit of these aims, the governments of the member States
have undertaken that, both individually and jointly, they will promote
the efficient use of their economic, scientific and technological
resources ; pursue policies designed to achieve both economic growth
and financial stability, external as well as internal, and to avoid
developments which might endanger their economies or those of
other countries; and reduce or abolish existing obstacles to international trade and the movements of capital, especially to countries
requiring technical assistance and expanding export markets.

These objectives are considerably more ambitious than those
aimed at in the bilateral treaties of earlier phases of international
economic co-operation ; they directly concern every individual
citizen.   They are not, however, intended to be attained by the
creation of immediately enforceable and clear-cut legal obligations.
They are to be pursued jointly in an atmosphere of growing habits
of close and regular contact between the governmental and administrative representatives of the members of the Organisation, tactfully
served and guided by a select body of international civil servants
and experts.   The stage of principles and standards of a predominantly negative character is here left behind and replaced by broad
objectives and elastic standards of joint endeavour.

In judging the value of legal commitments of so vague a
character, three points should be kept in mind. *First,* prolonged
experience with the Organisation for European Economic Co-
operation has proved how much can be attained in such an intimate
environment provided the will to co-operate exists. *Secondly,* for
the very reason that the objectives aimed at so closely affect internal
economies, the operative driving force cannot be any grudgingly
accepted legal commitment but only consciousness of the complete
identity of national self-interest and the international interests jointly
pursued. *Thirdly,* if governments share such a basic attitude, but
are not either able or willing to press the integration of their
economies beyond co-operation on the confederate level, the less
common action they are compelled to take the better it is. Such a
situation is a constant reminder that spontaneous co-operation

between them is as much in their own individual interest as in that of all other members.

To maintain indefinitely such a state of free and willing co-operation is difficult and, at times, may prove impossible. If, therefore, exceptional conditions exist such as those which have made possible the creation of the supra-national communities of Western Europe,[28] it is possible to aim at the realisation of objectives similar to those pursued by OECD in an environment even more remote than this from that of classical international economic law.

At this stage, principles and standards of conduct, but of a more intimate and exacting character, come into their own again. The co-ordination and supervision of their application is, however, entrusted to organs which are typical of the pattern of functional federalism.[29] Until the point of no return is reached in such a process of gradually increasing amalgamation, the obligations undertaken by member States remain international in character. From then onwards, however, the law applied in such communities—principles and standards alike—tends to become increasingly akin to national economic law.

Then, the circle closes again. What began as a movement towards international co-operation ends with the creation of bigger units wielding greater economic sovereignty than the entities they have replaced. But in the relations *between* these new super-Leviathans, the need for international co-operation on the level of traditional forms of international economic law is greater than it was ever before.

---

[28] See below, pp. 280 and 285.
[29] See further also above, pp. 206–207, and below, p. 312.

CHAPTER 10

JUS PACIS AC BELLI?

THE traditional system of international law is based on the distinction between the law of peace and the law of war. In the formative period of international law, thinkers were fully aware of the problems hidden behind this classification. Positivist writers took over these conceptions, framed against the background of a philosophical vista of society. Yet in their hands these terms lost their original significance.

I—THE NATURALIST BASIS OF THE DICHOTOMY

Conceptions such as peace and war are intimately linked up with opinions on the structure of international society and the motive powers behind it. Naturalist writers have indicated their attitudes towards these problems in their abstractions from political reality, and, as in our own time, the *is* and *ought* are not always neatly separated from each other. Reality and Utopia often are amalgamated in the picture of the state of nature drawn by these thinkers.

Whether the " natural condition of mankind " is depicted in darker or brighter colours depends on the pessimistic or optimistic, or, if it were preferred, on the " realist " or " idealist " outlook of each individual philosopher. Correspondingly, the emphasis changes from war, as the natural state of relations between States, to peace as " the state most highly agreeable to human nature." [1]

Hobbes and Pufendorf are typical representatives of the two schools of thought. A passage in Hobbes' *Elements of Law* gives the quintessence of his view :

> Seeing then to the offensiveness of man's nature one to another, there is added a right of every man to everything, whereby one man invadeth with right, and another with right resisteth ; and men live thereby in perpetual diffidence, and study how to preoccupate each other ; the estate of men in this natural liberty is the estate of war. For war is nothing else but that time wherein the will and intention of contending by force is either by words or actions sufficiently declared ; and the time which is not war, is peace.[2]

[1] Pufendorf, *De Jure Naturae et Gentium Libri Octo* (1688), Bk. VIII, Ch. VI, 2.
[2] Pt. I, Ch. 14, II ; similarly in his *Leviathan*, Ch. 13. See also Plato, *The Laws*, Bk. I, 2 ; Pierino Belli, *De Re Militari et Bello Tractatus* (1563), Pt. I, Ch. I, I ;

The opposite thesis finds equally firm upholders and may be illustrated by a quotation from Pufendorf's *De Jure Naturae et Gentium Libri Octo* :

> Now it is one of the first principles of natural law that no one unjustly do another hurt or damage, as well as that men should perform for each other the duties of humanity, and show especial zeal to fulfil the matters upon which they have entered into particular agreements. When men observe these duties in their relations one with another, it is called peace, which is a state most highly agreeable to human nature and fitted to preserve it, the creation and preservation of which constitutes one of the chief reasons for the law of nature being placed in the hearts of men.[3]

It was not accidental that the earlier naturalists were more impressed by the reality of *bellum omnium contra omnes* than by the Utopia of *civitas maxima*. In the formative period of absolutism, the Leviathans found themselves involved in a continuous struggle for survival both on the internal and external fronts. The absolutist States were not yet strong enough for the grand strategy which required the compact units of greater Powers, backed by mercantilist systems of economics and taxation as well as by standing armies of considerable size. They were yet too weak to rely on big and decisive strokes.

The undefined medley of war in peace provided the congenial atmosphere for the young absolutist State in its fight for survival and preponderance.[4] It was, therefore, only logical that Grotius should have entitled his main work *De Jure Belli ac Pacis Libri Tres*; for war appeared to him the all-inclusive and overriding phenomenon : " There is no controversy which may not give rise to war." [5]

Thus, war occupies the central position in the systems of the early naturalists. This statement is open to the challenge that it unduly

---

Spinoza, *Tractatus Politicus* (1677), Ch. 2, § 14 and Ch. 3, § 13; Wolff, *Jus Gentium* (1764), Ch. VIII, Para. 959.

This concept also underlies the distinction in Muslim law between the " World of Islam " and the " World of War." *Cf.* M. Khadduri, *The Law of War and Peace in Islam* (1955), p. 51 *et seq.*

On *dharma*, an Indian notion of law, see All-Indian Seminar, 1960, on *Indian Traditions and the Rule of Law among Nations.*

[3] *Loc. cit.* above, p. 11. See also *ibid.*, Bk. II, Ch. II, 7 or his *De Officio Hominis et Civis juxta Legem Naturalem Libri Duo* (1673), Bk. II, Ch. XVI, I.

Cf. also the dictum in *Miller* v. *The Resolution*, U.S. Court of Appeals (1781), 2 Dallas 1 : " As the state of nature was a state of peace, and not a state of war, the natural state of nations is a state of peace and society."

[4] *Cf.* F. Meinecke's masterly description of the political background of this period in *Die Idee der Staatsraison in der neueren Geschichte* (1929), p. 514 *et seq.*

[5] Bk. I, Ch. I, I.

For other appreciations and interpretations of the place of the naturalists in the history of the Doctrine of international law, see *Manual*, Vol. 2, p. 392 *et seq.*, and further 9 *C.L.P.* (1956), p. 235 *et seq.* See also above, pp. 9 and 65.

minimises the intentions of these writers. As is commonly accepted, their aim was to limit the horrors of war, and, as appears to follow from their doctrines of *bellum justum*, to limit the resort to war. The requirement of a *justa causa* appears to suggest that the normal state of affairs between States is one of peace, departure from which is merely permissible in clearly defined cases.

In so far as the intent of any writer is concerned, it is hard to furnish convincing proof for any thesis. It is, however, relevant to bear in mind that most international lawyers of that period did not have a merely academic interest in international law nor were they the equivalent of modern pacifists. They were men of the world, and a good many of these writers were actively engaged in diplomacy or held honourable and honoured posts as legal advisers to the very princes whom they were supposed to subject to the rule of law. Furthermore, all of them alike were anxious to see their legal propositions accepted by State practice. It would, therefore, have presupposed a childlike naïvety or a saintly character on their part to assume that they were completely unaware either of the power reality surrounding them or of the concessions which had to be made to make their systems acceptable to the powers that be.

Such considerations can and should not do more than neutralise the current story-book version of the early history of international law. Quite apart from the laudable or deplorable intentions of their creators, doctrines must be judged on their own merits and by the functions which they fulfil in the reality of society. Once they have been propounded, they live a life of their own, and the uses to which they are put depend on social forces beyond the control of their authors.

II—The Ideology of Bellum Justum

The two main problems around which naturalist thinking on war centres are well brought out in Gentili's definition of war as *publicorum armorum justa contentio*.[6]

The concept of war as a *public* contest merely put into legal form the overriding objects of absolutist policy, that is to say, to achieve and hold the monopoly of legitimate physical force. The memory of the Middle Ages when vassals waged their private wars against their overlords, and the central authority merely attempted to limit these feuds, was still fresh in the early days of the absolutist State. It

---

[6] *De Jure Belli Libri Tres* (1589), Bk. I, Ch. II.

therefore could not be asserted too often that any form of civil war was essentially different from the wars waged between sovereign princes and, in Bacon's words, was " like the heat of a fever." [7]

The intellectual support rendered to the cause of absolutism could only recommend the doctrine of *bellum publicum* to absolutist rulers. In this light, the insistence of naturalist writers on the need for a declaration of war acquires a new meaning.

Sovereigns did not so much consider the prerequisite of a just war as a burdensome limitation of their freedom of action, but as a golden opportunity of transforming their *de facto* monopoly of physical force into a *de jure* monopoly. The duty of the prince to guard the community against the danger of illegal war was bound to strengthen his claim to undisputed and exclusive authority in matters of peace and war. Duty implies competence, and competence has a tendency towards exclusiveness. This aspect of the matter is strongly stressed by Vitoria : " Such a State, then, or the prince thereof, has authority to declare war, and no one else." [8]

Once the absolute State was firmly established, other considerations induced sovereigns to forget about the solemn obligation for a declaration of war and this requirement fell into general disuse.[9] State practice could, however, accept without reservation the plea of the naturalists for the outlawry of private war.

Rulers were still supposed to consult " the good and the wise " [10] on the prerequisites of *bellum justum*. What advice had the fathers of international law to offer? It is proposed to limit this examination to Gentili, for, with insignificant exceptions, his catalogue of *causae justae* is typical of the naturalist approach to this problem.[11] It appears only fair to select this distinguished Oxford professor of Italian extraction as he is claimed to be the first to place the subject of war on a non-theological basis,[12] and his grasp of the doctrine

---

[7] In his essay *Of the Greatnesse of Kingdomes and Estates* (1597), XXIX.

[8] *De Indis et de Jure Belli Relectiones* (1541), *Relectio Secunda*, No. 7 (1625). See also Grotius, *De Jure Belli ac Pacis Libri Tres*, Bk. III, Ch. 3, II, and, on the origins of his *De Jure Praedae Commentarius* (1604), see 1 (N.S.) *S.P.T.L.J.* (1951), pp. 494–495.

[9] *Cf.* Sir Travers Twiss, *The Law of Nations* (1875), Vol. II, p. 65.

[10] Vitoria, quoting from Terence, *op. cit.*, No. 21.

[11] Useful surveys of this doctrine are contained in R. Regout, *La Doctrine de la Guerre Juste* (1935), W. Ballis, *The Legal Position of War* (1937), J. von Elbe, *The Evolution of the Concept of the Just War in International Law*, 33 *A.J.I.L.* (1939), p. 665 *et seq.* and E. Reibstein, *Völkerrecht*, Vol. I (1958), pp. 121 *et seq.* and 621. See further *Manual*, Vol. 2, p. 584 *et seq.*

[12] T. E. Holland, *Studies in International Law* (1898), p. 58.

of *bellum justum* is said to have been even firmer than that of Grotius.[13]

According to Gentili, the first group of just wars is provided by defensive wars. They include what he charitably terms wars waged for reasons of expedient defence : " A defence is just which anticipates dangers that are already meditated and prepared, and also those which are not meditated, but are probable and possible." [14]

This all-embracing formula was wide enough to satisfy the most extreme adherent of the reason of State. Yet, obligingly, Gentili does not stop at this point. He proceeds to elaborate the grounds which justify even offensive wars and classifies them under the headings of honour, necessity and expediency.[15]   In the case of an alliance, a prince is justified in coming to the assistance of his ally as long as he is convinced of the justice of his ally's cause. If treaty obligations should prove to be incompatible with each other and both cases happened to be equally just, " preference should be given to the one who has priority." [16]

Should his disciples still feel any qualms of conscience as to the " justice " of their contemplated war, Gentili provides further arguments which even the most scrupulous or least gifted adept of power politics could hardly fail to grasp.   These considerations are derived from concepts of subjective and relative justice. A sovereign may be engaged in an unjust war, but he may be wrongly under the impression that his cause is just. This Gentili considers enough to exonerate a prince, although the unfortunate consequence of such liberalism may be that " in nearly every kind of dispute neither of the two disputants is unjust." [17]

Finally, a State may have a cause which, relatively, is less just than that of its opponent. But in this case it must be remembered that " one man does not cease to be in the right because his opponent has a juster cause." [18]   Thus, " invincible ignorance," as Vitoria has called this state of mind,[19] is the best keeper of a king's conscience, if he wishes to rule in accordance with the precepts so ably set out by Machiavelli but equally feels bound to engage exclusively in " just " wars of a " defensive " or " offensive " character.

[13] C. Phillipson, Introduction to Gentili's *De Jure Belli Libri Tres* (Carnegie Endowment translation, 1933), Vol. II, p. 33a.
[14] Gentili, *ibid.*, Bk. I, Ch. XIV.
[15] *Ibid.*, Chs. XV, XVII, and XVIII.
[16] *Ibid.*, Bk. III, Ch. XVIII.
[17] *Ibid.*, Bk. I, Ch. VI.
[18] *Ibid.*, Bk. I, Ch. VI.
[19] *Loc. cit.*, No. 32.

In these circumstances, a naturalist may be forgiven for not always bearing in mind his own subtle distinctions and for bluntly stating that " by the consent of nations a rule has been introduced that all wars, conducted on both sides by authority of the sovereign power, are to be held just wars." [20]

It appears that there is little substance in the time-honoured assertion that the naturalists have subjected war to law, and that cynical disregard of these norms by State practice merely amounts to regrettable breaches of clearly defined standards. It would amount to special pleading to retort that, at least in form, sovereigns paid their respect to these rules when they attempted to justify their wars in terms of the doctrine of *bellum justum*. In effect, this did not mean that war was subordinated to natural law, but that natural law was made subservient to the reason of State.

In an international society in which the ruler of a State is responsible only to his own conscience, a doctrine with as many loopholes as that of *bellum justum* was bound to degenerate into an ideology serving the interests which it was supposed to control.

Had the naturalists insisted on more rigid standards, their teachings would have been ignored or interpreted out of existence. In accordance with their " realist " outlook, they were prepared to come to terms with the powers that be. Thus their theories could be turned to useful purposes.

As Machiavelli reflects, " the people will complain of a war made without reason." [21] Consequently, rulers are well advised not to ignore their home front, and this is the more necessary the wider awake public opinion and conscience happen to be. It is equally necessary to break the spirit of the enemy and to mobilise opinion in neutral countries. What can better serve this purpose than a foolproof case regarding the justice of one's own cause? In the field of intellectual warfare, which is not a twentieth-century invention, the authority of a Vitoria, Gentili or Grotius is worth a good many battalions, and, as has been shown, it was easy enough to apply their doctrines in accordance with the requirements of power politics.

The implications of these theories, however, were even more far-reaching. The naturalists conveniently lent their authority to the thesis that some rather disconcerting passages in the Gospel on war

---

[20] Grotius, *loc. cit.*, Bk. II, Ch. 17, S. 19.
[21] See further *The Prince* (1513), Ch. XVIII

were not to be taken too literally, and that war, provided that it was just, was authorised both by divine and natural law.[22]

Seemingly, the naturalists consider war as an exceptional remedy. They do so, however, in a manner which does not actually hamper the supremacy of force in international society, and they provide statesmen with an ideological cover, highly appreciated in ages characterised by glaring gaps between the religious and ethical standards of individual morality and the requirements of power politics.[23]

The conclusions reached so far may be summarised as follows :

First, naturalists derive their concepts of peace and war from their vistas of the structure of international society either by abstractions from reality or by wishful speculations on human nature.

Secondly, for the " realist " school of naturalists, war is the overriding phenomenon, and peace must be defined negatively by reference to war. The object of the " idealist " school of naturalists to limit war to an exceptional remedy is frustrated by their own casuistry. It deprives the doctrine of *bellum justum* of any objective criteria by which to distinguish between just and unjust wars and invites subjectivism and abuse by State practice. Thus, their doctrines degenerate into mere ideologies of power politics.

Thirdly, the insistence of naturalist writers on the element of *bellum publicum* in their definitions of war corresponds to the interests of rising absolutism, as does their postulate of a declaration of war. Therefore, during the period of early absolutism this part of their doctrines meets with full approval in State practice.

III—PEACE AND WAR IN TRADITIONALIST DOCTRINE AND IN THE PRACTICE OF INTERNATIONAL LAW

The traditionalist approach to the problem of peace and war is a medley of doctrines and assumptions. They may be discussed under three headings : The doctrine of the normalcy of peace, the doctrine of the alternative character of peace and war, and the doctrine of war as a status and objective phenomenon.

The Doctrine of the Normalcy of Peace and the Functions of War

In the leading treatises on international law the order of things, as it appeared to the naturalists, is reversed. *Jus Belli ac Pacis* is boldly transformed into *Jus Pacis ac Belli*.

---

[22] *e.g.*, Vitoria, *loc. cit.*, Introd. Compare, however, with this approach, Brand's *Stultifera Navis* (1497), and Erasmus's *Stultitiae Laus* (1508) and *Querela Pacis* (1517).　　　　　　　　[23] See further *Power Politics*, p. 218 *et seq.*

It is mostly taken for granted that peace is the normal state in international relations. Only exceptionally a writer condescends to state in so many words this " self-evident " assumption. Phillimore, in his *Commentaries upon International Law*, does so with commendable clarity [24] : " We have hitherto considered States in their normal, that is, their pacific relations to each other. . . . We have now to consider the abnormal state of things which ensues upon a disturbance of these normal relations, when these rights have been invaded and these obligations not fulfilled."

Actually, any such assertion implies views and judgments on the nature and functions of war which are far from being self-explanatory. The naturalists found their solutions of these problems by means of abstractions from reality or deductions from human nature. Writers who enjoyed the deceptive security of a relatively stable balance of power system as it existed between 1815 and 1914, might have held with some justice that they, too, had drawn the obvious conclusions from their era of peace. For a generation which has witnessed two World Wars in its lifetime, the assumption of peace as the normal state of international relations is more problematic.

In systems of power politics and power politics in disguise, war is not an unhappy incident or an incalculable catastrophe, but the culminating point in a rising scale of pressure, the last resort of power politics when diplomacy fails to achieve its objects by the threat of force or the application of less drastic forms of pressure.[25] Thus, the doctrine of the normalcy of peace is founded on a complete misinterpretation of the functions of war in international society.

A good many writers have tried to avoid the real issue by remarkable feats of escapism. Over and over it has been repeated that war is an event,[26] a question of fact,[27] or " an international fact in the first degree." [28] If this meant that war were legally irrelevant, it would prove too much ; for it would imply that international law was not capable of dealing with legal problems arising out of war. Rightly, international lawyers do not draw so defeatist a conclusion from any

[24] Vol. III (1885), p. I. See also C. Phillipson, *The Effect of War on Contracts* (1909), p. 25; Anonymous, *The League of Nations and the Laws of War*, 1 *B.Y.I.L.* (1920–1921), p. 109 *et seq.*; A. P. Higgins, *The Law of Peace*, 4 *ibid.*, (1923–1924), p. 153 *et seq.*; Sir John Fischer Williams, *Chapters on Current International Law and the League of Nations* (1929), p. 73 *et seq.*
[25] See further *Power Politics*, p. 191 *et seq.*
[26] *Cf.* Q. Wright, *Changes in the Conception of War*, 18 *A.J.I.L.* (1924), p. 756.
[27] See G. J. Webber, *Effect of War on Contract* (1940), p. I. See also the 2nd edition (1946), p. 17 *et seq.*
[28] The Permanent Court of Arbitration in the case of the Russian Indemnities (1912), I. Scott, *Hague Court Reports*, p. 297, at p. 301.

of the above mentioned premises. This classification of war may also mean that war entails legal consequences, but is not capable of legal control.[29] To prove this is the avowed or implied object of those who interpret war as akin to revolution or as an emergency agency of change. How could a legal system attempt to control revolution or effect far-reaching changes without elaborate legislative organs in which international law is so utterly lacking? As, however, the need for revolution or sweeping changes is apparent only in exceptional circumstances, peace may still be considered to be the state of normalcy in the inter-State system.

Others arrive at similar results by way of different reasoning. They assert that war is not at all incompatible with international law, but comparable to legal institutions such as self-help or a right of action and is a sanction of international law by means of which the law of peace is enforced.[30]

It may be true that, in certain circumstances, war is an agency of self-help and the means of violently adapting international society to fundamentally changed conditions. It would, however, be highly unrealistic to maintain that these are the only or the main functions of war. They are as manifold as the objects of power politics.

It appears that neither the self-denying classification of war as a fact nor any *ad hoc* sociology of international lawyers can furnish proof for the thesis that peace is the normal state in international law and relations. In the idealist variety of naturalist Doctrine, the primacy of peace was logically assured by the concept of *bellum justum*. If traditionalist Doctrine were consistent, it would have to derive its assertions regarding the normal or exceptional character of peace and war from detached observation of the reality of international relations. The actual fluctuations between periods of peace and war do not appear to justify a theory of the normalcy of peace.[31] This assumption is but a lingering relic of naturalist philosophising on the nature of man.

The Doctrine of the Alternative Character of Peace and War and the Reality of State Practice

In systems of naturalist writers, this doctrine is perfectly understandable. As they keep reprisals within narrow limits, and war

---

[29] Wright, *loc. cit.* in note 26 above.
[30] For a more detailed examination of these and other theories on war, see *Power Politics* (1st ed.—1941), p. 129 *et seq.*
[31] *Cf.* Q. Wright, *The Causes of War and the Conditions of Peace* (1935), p. 21 *et seq.*, and *A Study of War* (1942), Vol. I, p. 653.

depends on a *justa causa*, " war and peace are correlatively opposite, and what is said affirmatively of the one is said negatively of the other." [32]   Thus, Grotius can quote Cicero with approval : " *Inter bellum et pacem nihil est medium.*" [33]

It should not, however, be forgotten that even among naturalists this doctrine was not upheld with unanimity. In the words of Pufendorf,[34] " some states more expressly denote a relation toward other men than do others, since they signify distinctly the mode in which men mutually transact their business. The most outstanding of these are peace and war."

In view of the fact that traditionalist Doctrine does not and cannot insist on a just cause as a condition of legal war, and State practice has made extensive use of military reprisals, pacific blockades and similar devices, the proposition of the alternative character of peace and war as part of existing international law [35] requires to be proved to be believed. It may claim to be in accordance with the practice of English Courts.[36] Their view may be summarised in the words of Lord Macnaghten in *Janson* v. *Driefontein Consolidated Mines, Ltd.*[37] : " The law recognises a state of peace and a state of war, but . . . it knows nothing of an intermediate state which is neither the one thing nor the other—neither peace nor war."

This statement must, however, be read in its context which indicates the reason for the rigid adherence of English Courts to the doctrine of the complementary character of peace and war. It follows from the general attitude taken by English Courts regarding vital issues of foreign affairs affecting their country. These matters are within the prerogative of the Crown, and " it must be for the supreme power, whatever it is, to determine the policy of the community in regard to peace and war. . . . If and so long as the Government of

---

[32] Gentili, *loc. cit.*, Bk. III, Ch. XXIV.
[33] *Op. cit.*, Bk. III, Ch. XXI, I, I, and Cicero, *Philippica*, VII.
[34] *Op. cit.*, Bk. I, Ch. I, 8.
   See further *Manual*, Vol. 2, p. 579 *et seq.*
[35] *Cf.* A. D. McNair, *The Legal Meaning of War*, 11 *Grotius Society Transactions* (1926), p. 33, and J. L. Brierly, *International Law and Resort to Armed Force*, 4 *Cambridge Law Journal* (1932), p. 314.
   For corroborative studies such as those by Grob and others, and further evidence in favour of a *status mixtus* or a state of intermediacy between peace and war, see above, p. 4, n. 19.
[36] On the attitude of United States Courts which have a similar tendency to leave such " political " decisions in the hands of the Executive, see Q. Wright, *The Control of American Foreign Relations* (1922), p. 172 *et seq.*, W. J. Ronan, *English and American Courts and the Definition of War*, 31 *A.J.I.L.* (1937), p. 650, and *Manual*, Vol. 2, pp. 915 and 579 *et seq.*
[37] [1902] A.C. 484, at p. 497.

the State abstains from declaring or making war or accepting a hostile challenge there is peace—peace with all attendant consequences—for all its subjects." [38]

English judicial practice is not derived from the scrutiny of international law, but is based on a division of functions between the judiciary and the executive, considered desirable for purposes of English law. In particular, this doctrine gives expression to the legitimate concern of Courts for the certainty of their municipal law. It is, however, impossible to derive from this practice any conclusions on the validity of the doctrine of the alternative character of peace and war as a doctrine of international law.

As in the case of the doctrine of the normalcy of peace, this doctrine must derive such justification as it can claim from State practice. Actually, the foreign relations of all great Powers contain frequent instances of resort to armed force short of war or, as they are sometimes called, " pre-belligerent acts." [39] Military interventions and reprisals, material guarantees and pacific blockades have become household terms of power diplomacy and treatises on international law.[40] It, therefore, suffices merely to refer to them in order to indicate the problematic character of the alternative between peace and war.

It can hardly be doubted that these measures are " tinged with a hostile character." It is admitted that they are " often but the trail which awaits only a spark to be kindled into the full blaze of open war." Yet it is still asserted that they are " not in themselves inconsistent with the maintenance of peace." [41]

In some instances, arguments to the effect that such measures merely constitute an abuse of force and amount to war in disguise

---

[38] [1902] A.C. 484, at pp. 497–498.
   Cf. also Sir Arnold McNair, *Legal Effects of War* (1948), p. 1 *et seq.*
[39] F. E. Smith, *International Law* (1903), p. 90.
[40] *Cf.* T. E. Holland, *op. cit.*, p. 130 *et seq.*; A. E. Hogan, *Pacific Blockade* (1908); J. Westlake, *Collected Papers* (1914), p. 572 *et seq.*; E. C. Stowell, *Intervention in International Law* (1921); C. C. Hyde, *International Law* (1922), Vol. II, p. 192 and (1945), Vol. 2, p. 1654 *et seq.*; P. H. Winfield, *The History of Intervention in International Law*, 3 *B.Y.I.L.*, 1922–1923, p. 130 *et seq.*; *The Grounds of Intervention in International Law*, 5 *ibid.*, 1924, p. 149 *et seq.*; S. Maccoby, *Reprisals as a Measure of Redress Short of War*, 2 *Cambridge Law Journal* (1926), p. 60 *et seq.*; A. E. Hindmarsh, *Force in Peace* (1933); H. Rumpf, *Is a Definition of War Necessary?* 18 *Boston University Law Review* (1938), p. 705 *et seq.* and L. C. Green, *Armed conflict, War and Self-Defence*, 6 *Archiv für Völkerrecht* (1957), p. 387 *et seq.*
[41] Sir Robert Phillimore, *op. cit.*, Vol. III, p. 16.

may be appropriate.[42] They do not, however, offer a satisfactory explanation of all or even the greater majority of these cases.

It is difficult to see how the limited application of force can amount to war if not only third States but also the State against which these measures are taken insist on the continuation of peaceful relations with the State resorting to a limited use of armed force. The current explanation that, by international customary law, these measures have been incorporated in the law of peace is correct if it means that resort to armed force short of war may be lawful in certain circumstances. Yet how can writers who take this line square with their contention the attitude of third States in those cases in which they insist on the application of the laws of neutrality to their own relations with the contending States, while the latter insist on the continuance of a state of peace between themselves? [43]

This view leads to the paradoxical concept of neutrality in time of peace, not a very pleasant constellation for followers of the doctrine of the alternative character of peace and war. This doctrine and the reality of measures short of war can be reconciled only at the price of depriving the state of peace of all positive criteria and reducing it to a purely negative status.[44]

To see peace and war in their proper perspective, it is necessary to analyse these states against the background of the reality of power politics, the overriding phenomenon in international affairs.[45] Powers are in a state of peace with each other when they are prepared to

---

[42] A. G. Heffter, *Le Droit International de l'Europe* (edited by F. H. Geffken—Paris, 1883), p. 246; Th. Baty, *The Canons of International Law* (1930), p. 110; C. Parry, *Some Nineteenth Century Pacific Blockades*, 8 *Zeitschrift für ausländisches öffentliches Recht und Völkerrecht* (1938), p. 672 *et seq.*

[43] On the blockade by France of Formosa (1884), see Hall-Higgins, *A Treatise on International Law* (1924), pp. 439–440; on the British-German-Italian blockade of Venezuela, J. Basdevant, *L'Action Coercitive Anglo-Germano-Italienne contre le Vénézuéla*, 11 *R.G.D.I.P.* (1904), p. 422 *et seq.*, and Westlake, *op. cit.*, p. 585.

[44] The inability of traditionalist Doctrine, based on the assumption of the alternative of peace and war, adequately to deal with the use of force in " peace," may be illustrated by a few examples: H. Wheaton, *History of the Law of Nations in Europe and America* (1845), p. 759: " It remains . . . an undefined and undefinable exception to the mutual independence of nations "; Hall-Higgins, *op. cit.*, p. 434: " Reprisals are acts of war in fact, though not in intention "; E. M. Borchard, *" War " and " Peace,"* 27 *A.J.I.L.* (1933), pp. 115–116: " It must be conceded that *de facto* war, with or without a full state of war, is one of the commonest of phenomena, and . . . it cannot be reconciled with a state of peace "; Oppenheim's *International Law* (edited by H. Lauterpacht—London, 1940), Vol. II, p. 107: " Compulsive means are in theory and practice considered peaceable, although not amicable means of settling international differences " (deleted in the subsequent edition of 1952, p. 132); H. Lauterpacht, *" Règles Générales du Droit de la Paix,"* 62 *Hague Recueil* (1937), p. 191: *" Le droit international conçu comme un ensemble de règles réglant la paix* (ou, ce qui revient au même, interdisant la violence)."

[45] Cf. *Power Politics*, p. 13 *et seq.*

apply to their mutual relations the extensive system of legal rules
which is characterised, *e.g.*, by respect for territorial sovereignty, the
freedom of the seas and the exclusion of the use of armed force. In
effect, this means a state of relations in which States are willing to
limit themselves to the application of political and economic power.[46]
Powers are in a state of war with each other and of neutrality towards
third States, if, subject to the limitations of international customary
and treaty law, they choose to apply against each other power to the
utmost, *i.e.*, military as well as political and economic power.

State practice has merely drawn its own conclusions from the
complete breakdown of the doctrine of *bellum justum* when Powers
consider themselves free not only to change over at will from a state
of peace to a state of war, but also entitled to the liberal use of
limited force.[47]

It is characteristic of this state of affairs that it does not necessarily lead to the comprehensive use of power, as in the case of war.
Whether the state of peace continues with the State against which
limited force is applied or not, depends on the latter's decision.
Similarly, it is left to third States to decide for themselves whether,
in their relations with the contending States, they prefer the laws of
peace or neutrality.

Even if all States directly and indirectly concerned acquiesced in
the limited use of force, it would be a misnomer to call such a *pax
bellicosa* by the name of peace. It would be equally unwarranted to
call war a state in which both contending States insist on the continuation of their peaceful relations, merely because third States wish to
apply the law of neutrality during such a *bellum pacificum*. All these
constellations are incompatible with the states of peace and war ; they
constitute a state of their own : a *status mixtus*.

State practice showed equally scant respect for the concept of

---

46 See, on the different forms of power, B. Russell, *Power* (1938) and, further,
Power Politics, p. 13 *et seq.*
47 See on the unlimited right to war in modern international law, Hall-Higgins,
op. cit., p. 82, and on the attitude of British practice, the note of Mr. Christie
to the Marquis of Abrantes (Dec. 30, 1862) and the dispatch of Lord Russell to
Mr. Lettsom (Dec. 24, 1864), *Fontes Juris Gentium*, Series B, Sectio I, Tomus I,
Part II (1856–1871), Nos. 2398 and 2375. The measures applied by France and
Great Britain against the Netherlands in order to achieve the separation of Belgium
in 1832–1833 (Hogan, *op. cit.*, p. 80 *et seq.*) and similar measures of " international
police " (Hall-Higgins, *op. cit.*, p. 441) show that State practice interprets liberally
the conditions assumed by Doctrine to limit the use of force in " peace." As
Brierly observes, " all these writers seem conscious of a certain unreality in the
profession of the law to regulate reprisals " (*loc. cit.*, p. 309). See also C.
Eagleton, *The Form and Function of the Declaration of War*, 32 A.J.I.L. (1938)
p. 19 *et seq.*

bellum publicum. Since the beginning of the nineteenth century [48] States have insisted on their right, at their discretion, to recognise revolutionaries as belligerents, and, on less firm ground,[49] as insurgents if the insurrection amounted to a civil war. Again, State practice has found it necessary to build a half-way house, this time between the unreserved application of the rule of non-intervention in the domestic affairs of other States and recognition of an insurgent government as the government of a sovereign State, a measure considered illegal while a civil war lasts.

If the government against which the revolutionary movement is directed itself recognises the belligerency of the insurgents, third States are usually inclined to accept the position of neutrals in the contest.[50] If, however, that government is unwilling to do so, it is left to third States to decide for themselves whether they wish to ignore the civil war or elevate it into war proper by recognising the insurgents as belligerents.

Thus, we are confronted with other typical instances of the *status mixtus* : at their discretion, States may consider one and the same phenomenon as a domestic affair, compatible with a state of peace, or as war.

The conclusion seems unavoidable that, as in the case of the doctrine of the normalcy of peace, the doctrine of the alternative character of peace and war cannot stand the test of confrontation with State practice. It should be discarded as an uncritically accepted

---

[48] A. Rougier, *Les Guerres Civiles et le Droit des Gens* (1903); Resolution adopted by the *Institut de Droit International*, 1900, in Carnegie Endowment, *Resolutions of the Institute of International Law* (1916), pp. 157–159; H. A. Smith, *Great Britain and the Law of Nations* (1932), Vol. I, p. 261 *et seq.*, particularly also the opinion quoted there of Dr. Lushington (May 29, 1823, p. 293): " To apply the strict principles of the Law of Nations to a state of things so anomalous, would, I apprehend, tend only to mislead the parties interested, for these questions are always mixed up with political considerations, and the practice will in some degree differ from the theory. Of this we have many instances in regard to Spanish South America, the British Government having endeavoured to carry on its intercourse on equitable and beneficial principles, rather than adhere to the letter of the Law of Nations." See also Lord Russell's dispatch to Lord Lyons (Washington), Oct. 3, 1861, *Fontes Juris Gentium, loc. cit.*, No. 2431. In the view of Smith, " the true doctrine is that the recognition of the insurgent government is the necessary and logical consequence of recognising the fact of war." (*Some Problems of the Spanish Civil War*, 18 *B.Y.I.L.* (1937), p. 18.) See further *Fundamental Principles*, p. 230 *et seq.*

[49] See G. G. Wilson, *Insurgency and International Maritime Law*, 1 *A.J.I.L.* (1907), p. 46 *et seq.*; Hall-Higgins, *op. cit.*, pp. 46–47; A. D. McNair, *The Law relating to the Civil War in Spain*, 53 *L.Q.R.* (1937), p. 484 *et seq.* (particularly on the quasi-blockades established by insurgents); H. Lauterpacht, *Recognition in International Law* (1947), p. 270 *et seq.* and T. C. Chen, *The International Law of Recognition* (1951), p. 398 *et seq.*

[50] *Cf.* Hall-Higgins, *op. cit.*, pp. 36–37.

remnant of a now merely historically relevant naturalist approach to the problem of peace and war.

The Doctrine of War as a Status and Objective Phenomenon

Attempts at defining war in traditionalist Doctrine are dominated by Grotius' definition of war as a status or condition : " War is the condition of those contending by force, viewed simply as such." [51] The emphasis on the status of war as the alternative to that of peace is congenial to medieval thinking. It finds its legal expression in *diffidatio*, the message of defiance which severs the tie of faith between him who sends it and him who receives it.[52] This concept of war as a status equally fits into the naturalist scheme, as naturalist writers consider peace incompatible with the use of armed force between States.

Special treaty obligations apart, Doctrine cannot rely on the certainty of a declaration of war as an equivalent to the old *diffidatio*, and, in the face of considerable State practice to the contrary,[53] cannot assert a rule of international customary law requiring a declaration of war. Whether, in these circumstances, insistence on war as a status means anything, depends on Doctrine being able to find an objective criterion defining war as distinct from peace and the *status mixtus*.

If writers were consistent, they would have to remember in their definitions of war their own assumptions of peace as the normal state and of the alternative character of peace and war. Such consideration for their own doctrines would necessarily lead them to a definition of war by reference to peace. Yet this would be too much to expect. The best of which traditionalist Doctrine seems capable in relating war to peace, is contained—albeit only in the index—in a leading textbook: " Peace: see Termination of War." [54]

Commonly, war is defined as a contention of States through their armed forces for the purpose of overpowering each other.[55] At first sight, the element of the definition, *contention of States through their*

---

[51] *Op. cit.*, Bk. I, Ch. I, S. 2, I: " *Status per vim certantium qua tales sunt.*" See J. Westlake, *International Law*, Vol. II (1913), p. I, and A. D. McNair, *loc. cit.*, p. 33.

[52] Westlake, *ibid.*, p. 8. This form of declaration of war was used for the last time in 1657 when Sweden declared war against Denmark by a herald-at-arms sent to Copenhagen (Sir Travers Twiss, *op. cit.*, p. 62).

[53] T. J. Lawrence, *War and Neutrality in the Far East* (1904), p. 26 *et seq.*

[54] Hall-Higgins, *op. cit.*, p. 941.

[55] *Cf.* Westlake, *op. cit.*, p. 1; Oppenheim's *International Law*, Vol. II, Section 57, p. 168; and C. Eagleton, *The Attempt to Define War, International Conciliation* (1933), p. 259 *et seq.*

armed forces, appears to offer an objective criterion of distinction between the states of peace and war.

Even if this were so, this definition could not be regarded as adequate ; for it does not cover two types of war. States, geographically widely separated, may declare war on each other and apply the laws of war (*e.g.*, confiscation of property belonging to the enemy State and internment of enemy aliens) in their mutual relations without being able to bring about a contention between their armed forces. Or, a State which is at war may deem it prudent to withdraw its armed forces in such a way that, again, there is no opportunity for the required contention between the armed forces to occur.

Instances of the first class of war are provided by the relations between South and Central American States and the Central Powers in the First World War and by corresponding situations in the Second World War. An example of the second type is offered by the Bulgarian withdrawal before the Rumanian troops in the Second Balkan War.

A still more serious flaw in this definition is in its inability to indicate objectively the borderline between war and a *status mixtus*. States may contend through their armed forces, but, as in the case of the extensive battles in 1938 and 1939 between Russian and Japanese troops on the frontier between the Soviet Union and Manchukuo, may be unwilling to consider such acts as a state of war. Thus, this definition either amounts to the assertion that States are at war with each other against their own will, or these cases have to be distinguished from war by the introduction into the definition of a subjective element such as *animus belligerendi*.[56]

Traditionalist Doctrine usually chooses this latter alternative as the lesser evil. This means that not much is left of the assumption of the alternative character of peace and war and of the apparently objective criterion of the contention of States through their armed forces. The acceptance of *animus belligerendi* reduces the traditionalist definition of war to the truism that States contending with one another through their armed forces are at war with each other if

---

[56] *Cf.* Westlake, *ibid.*, pp. 1–2; McNair, *loc. cit.*, p. 45; Oppenheim, *ibid.*, p. 241. See also the pertinent comment by Sir Wilfrid Greene, M.R., in *Kawasaki Kisen Kabushiki of Kobe* v. *Bantham S.S. Co., Ltd.*: " What *animus belligerendi* meant was again a matter of obscurity, and to define war by relation to it came near to define war by itself " [1939] 2 K.B. 544, at pp. 557–558, and the observations of Sir John Fischer Williams, *The Covenant of the League of Nations and War*, 5 *Cambridge Law Journal* (1933), p. 8 *et seq.*

they want to be at war with one another. If one of the contending
States unmistakably expresses its will, the status of war is created.
If, however, belligerents fail to do so, third States are free to interpret
at their own discretion the legal significance of " a contention of States
through their armed forces."

This failure of traditionalist Doctrine is not the fault of individual
writers. It is due to the impossibility of achieving what they attempt
to do. In a system of international law which admits the limited use
of force to its law of peace, or in which there are more than two
states of legal relations, it is impossible to find an objective criterion
which distinguishes the status of war both from the status of peace
and from that of *status mixtus*.

In these circumstances, all that can be said is this :

Declared war creates a status of war between the States directly
concerned and in relation to third States.

Measures taken in a *status mixtus* and undeclared war automatically create a state of war between the States directly concerned,
and of neutrality in relation to third States, only if the State
against which these measures are directed or undeclared war is waged,
chooses to consider such action as amounting to war. In the absence
of an unequivocal declaration to this effect, third States are free to
decide for themselves whether they wish to regulate their relations
with the contending States in accordance with the law of peace or the
law of war.

It appears that, when faced with the concrete task of defining war,
traditionalist Doctrine has to disregard its own assumptions of peace
as the normal state and of the alternative character of peace and
war. The current definition of war is incomplete and only seemingly
objective. The express or implied inclusion in this definition of
animus belligerendi either amounts to the implicit admission of the
existence of a *status mixtus* which is determined by intentions rather
than acts, or to the unavoidable acceptance of a *continuum* between
peace and war which reduces peace to a purely negative status.

If the laws of neutrality are applied in a state which the " belligerents " consider to be peace, or those of warfare in a state which
third States regard as peace, no intrinsic difference between the states
of peace and war exists. The application of the laws of peace and
war becomes a question of consensus amongst the States directly and

indirectly concerned.[57] Doctrine based on State practice does not and cannot provide objective tests regarding the circumstances in which either the one or the other set of rules is to be applied, and the practice of power diplomacy is not a promising field in which to look for initiative in the precise separation of measures the choice of which is essentially a question of expediency.

Thus, none of the assertions of the traditionalist Doctrines on peace and war can be upheld.

The doctrine of the normalcy of peace is merely a survival of naturalist thought, but is incompatible with the real functions of war in international society.

The doctrine of the alternative character of peace and war, of the same naturalist origin, minimises or ignores the reality of State practice which has created rules pertaining to neither a state of peace nor a state of war, but constituting a *status mixtus*.

The doctrine of war as a status and objective phenomenon breaks down over the reality of the *status mixtus*. This status is not separated from those of peace and war by any objective tests. States contend by power in peace and war. In a state of peace, they are limited to the use of political and economic power. In a *status mixtus*, they supplement these forms of power by the use of military power. In a state of war, they use all available forms of power. It betrays an over-estimation of the differences between political and economic power as compared with military power, to imagine that, in a system of power politics, any qualitative difference between the states of peace and war exists.

The traditional division of international law into the law of peace and the law of war may be expedient for didactic purposes. The unavoidable subjectivity of the available criteria of distinction between the two, or better three, states of typical legal relations between States deprives this classification of any claim to scientific sacrosanctity.

IV—THE DISTINCTION BETWEEN PEACE AND WAR
IN INTERNATIONAL CONVENTIONS

It remains to examine whether the conclusions reached so far are affected by relevant international conventions. If States had desired

---

[57] Thus, States may slip as informally from war into peace as from peace into war. *Cf.* Hyde, *op. cit.*, Vol. 3 (1945), p. 2386; T. C. Transill, *Termination of War by Mere Cessation of Hostilities*, 38 L.Q.R. (1922), p. 26 *et seq.*; W. E. Beckett, *The Right to Trade and the Right to Sue*, 39 *ibid.* (1923), p. 89 *et seq.*

to create a clear borderline between peace and war, they could have achieved this object only at the price of renouncing their claim to the use of force in time of " peace." Then war and the use of armed force would have become identical, and a clearly discernible criterion of war would have become available.

This truly objective test was used by the Second Hague Convention of 1907 in the Convention on the Limitation of the Employment of Force for the Recovery of Contract Debts. Nevertheless, the Powers represented at the Second Hague Peace Conference were not prepared to abolish the *status mixtus* as such.

This became embarrassingly evident in the discussions of the second sub-committee of the Second Commission when the Chinese military delegate analysed the proposed Convention on Compulsory Declaration of War in the light of the then recent Boxer expedition, and suggested a clear definition of war.[58]

In the words of a contemporary writer, " no one replied to these embarrassing questions. Governments are not loath to have the definition of what constitutes war shrouded in mystery ; for in the greater number of States possessing a parliamentary form of government the decision to make war is hedged about with formalities and special constitutional requirements, and governments have in the past and are likely in the future to find it convenient for reasons of domestic and foreign policy to resort to measures of war while maintaining that no war exists." [59]

Thus, again, the term " hostilities " used in this convention really means acts of armed force carried out with the intent of war, and the door is kept wide open for undeclared war developing out of measures taken within the scope or under the cover of the *status mixtus*.[60]

The attempts made in the post-1919 period to distinguish between legal and illegal wars are equally instructive. In the Covenant of the League of Nations, terms such as war, threat of war, resort to war and acts of war are freely used. This question has received so much

---

[58] Carnegie Endowment, *The Proceedings of the Hague Peace Conferences* (1921), Vol. III, p. 169. See also above, pp. 196–197.

In the view of the German Supreme Court, " although the Chinese expedition of 1900–1901 did not conduct a war in the sense of international law, and no declaration of war was made on China, it found itself nevertheless in a situation similar to that of war " (*Reichsgericht, Zivilsachen*, 58, p. 328).

[59] E. C. Stowell, *Convention Relative to the Opening of Hostilities*, 2 *A.J.I.L.* (1908), p. 55.

[60] See Westlake, *Collected Papers, supra*, pp. 591–592.

attention [61] that it will suffice to emphasise merely the aspects particularly relevant to our discussion.

President Wilson's drafts make it obvious that he was fully aware of the dangers threatening his scheme if the *status mixtus* should be allowed to survive. Article VII of his various drafts runs as follows :

> If any Power shall declare war or begin hostilities, or take any hostile step short of war, against another Power before submitting the dispute involved to arbitrators as herein provided, or shall declare war or begin hostilities, or take any hostile step short of war, in regard to any dispute which has been decided adversely to it by arbitrators chosen and empowered as herein provided, the contracting parties hereby bind themselves not only to cease all commerce and intercourse with that Power but also to unite in blockading and closing the frontiers of that Power to commerce or intercourse with any part of the world and to use any force that may be necessary to accomplish that object.

In the course of the drafting of the Covenant of the League of Nations, Wilson's attempt seriously to curb power politics was quietly undone, and his formulations were replaced in a matter-of-course way and in the traditional terminology : " minor changes . . . of an entirely trivial character." [62]

Further support for the view that war in the meaning of the Covenant was limited to war in the technical sense, was given by the equivocal treatment of the Corfu incident in League quarters and, particularly, by the sibylline report of the Committee of Jurists on this matter.[63]

The evasive attitude taken by the members of the League towards the war between Bolivia and Paraguay,[64] and still more so towards the " war in disguise " [65] in Manchukuo, led to a situation in which illegal war under the Covenant came to be limited to cases in which the members of the League were prepared to say so.[66]

Similarly, the use of the term " war " in the Kellogg Pact enables States to exercise their full discretion in deciding whether the use of armed force by a State or even contentions of States through their

[61] *Cf.* Eagleton, *Attempt to Define War, loc. cit.,* pp. 250 and 259 *et seq.*
[62] D. H. Miller, *The Drafting of the Covenant* (1928), Vol. I, pp. 59, 213, 214 and 222, and Vol. II, pp. 12, 81–84, 101, 138 and 149.
[63] See *Power Politics,* p. 479.
[64] *Cf.* R. M. Cooper, *American Consultation in World Affairs* (1934), p. 114 *et seq.*
[65] Lytton Report, p. 138.
[66] *Cf.* J. L. Brierly, *Sanctions,* 17 *Grotius Society Transactions* (1932), p. 79: " It seems clear that the action of Japan has not constituted a ' resort to war ' in breach of her obligations under the Covenant "; Q. Wright, *When Does War Exist?,* 26 *A.J.I.L.* (1932), p. 367; H. Lauterpacht, *" Resort to War " and the Interpretation of the Covenant during the Manchurian Dispute,* 28 *ibid.* (1934), pp. 48 and 52. See, however, Eagleton, *ibid.,* p. 250.

The Expanding Field

armed forces are to be considered as wars within the meaning of the Pact.[67]   Furthermore, the United States Secretary of State himself thought it necessary to affirm in the correspondence preceding the conclusion of the pact that each Party alone would be " competent to decide whether circumstances require recourse to war in self-defence." [68]   Thus, again, illegal war was limited to armed contentions between States which the Parties cared to consider as such.

State practice in the post-1919 period went still further in obliterating the few distinguishing marks that were left between peace, *status mixtus* and war.   If, in the case of a measure taken within the *status mixtus*, a State is free under international customary law to consider such a step as an act of war, it is also free to sign away its discretion to exchange the *status mixtus* for that of war.   Thus, it was stipulated in the Peace Treaty of Versailles [69] that measures which might include military reprisals [70] should not be regarded by Germany as acts of war.

A similar clause is contained in the Hague Agreements of 1930.[71] In the Declarations exchanged on January 20, 1930, Germany acknowledges that, in case of an intentional default, " it is legitimate that, in order to ensure the fulfilment of the obligations of the debtor Power resulting from the New Plan, the creditor Power or Powers should resume their full liberty of action."

Yet even this use of the rules underlying the principle of consent was surpassed by the self-contradictions of the Appeasement Period. On the one hand, the Powers assembled at Nyon upheld the fiction that the Spanish War was not an international war, and most of those States refused to grant to the insurgents recognition as belligerents. On the other hand, they did not base the Nyon Agreement on the obvious inadmissibility of sinking foreign merchantmen in time of peace.   In order to enable the totalitarian aggressors to save face, they assimilated these acts of illegal intervention to piratical acts by submarines and aircraft of " unknown " Powers and arraigned the " pirates " for their violations of Part IV of the Treaty of London

---

[67] *Cf.* Borchard, *loc. cit.*, p. 116, and Eagleton, *ibid.*, p. 284 *et seq.*

[68] Text of the Note of June 23, 1928, in 22 *A.J.I.L.* (1928), Supplement, p. 109. See further *Fundamental Principles*, p. 327 *et seq.*, and *Manual*, Vol. 2, p. 581 *et seq.*

[69] Part VIII, Sec. I, Annex II, § 18, 13 *A.J.I.L.* (1919), Supplement, p. 264.

[70] *Cf.* A. D. McNair, 5 *B.Y.I.L.* (1924), p. 182, and on *The Legality of the Occupation of the Ruhr, ibid.*, p. 17 *et seq.*

[71] Exchange of Declarations between the Government of Germany and the Belgian, British, French, Italian and Japanese Governments of Jan. 20, 1930, 24 *A.J.I.L.* (1930), Supplement, p. 271.

of 1930, *i.e.*, rules applicable in time of war between sovereign States.[72]

Thus, the multilateral agreements concluded in pre-1914 days and during the post-1919 era have contributed little if anything to the establishment of more solid criteria of distinction between peace and war. They have probably increased the tendencies, inherent in the position of the states of peace and war under international customary law, towards subjectivism and an unscrupulous abuse of terms.[73]

---

[72] Preamble to the Nyon Agreement regarding Submarines, para. 2: " Whereas these attacks are violations of the rules of international law referred to in Part IV of the Treaty of London of April 22, 1930, with regard to the sinking of merchant ships and constitute acts contrary to the most elementary dictates of humanity which should justly be treated as acts of piracy." 19 *B.Y.I.L.* (1938), p. 205. See also the Additional Agreement concerning Surface Vessels and Aircraft (*ibid.*, p. 206).

[73] On the position under the Charter of the United Nations, see above, pp. 59 and 146, below, pp. 279, 301 and 311, and further *Fundamental Principles*, p. 327 *et seq.*, and *Manual*, Vol. 1, p. 170 *et seq.*, and Vol. 2, p. 579 *et seq.*

CHAPTER 11

FUNCTIONS AND FOUNDATIONS
OF THE LAW OF WAR

AN air of paradox surrounds the law of warfare. War is the alternative tactic to negotiation on the international scene, and its function is to impose by force the will of one group on another.[1] Within limits—admittedly more reassuring on paper than in reality— even the law of the United Nations cannot help accepting this intrusion of the rule of force into organised world society.[2] At the same time, international law purports to control the modalities of warfare, legal and illegal alike.[3] A functional analysis of the law of war, corresponding to that of war itself, may assist in understanding the bewildering nexus between the rule of law and the rule of force in a state of war.

I—FUNCTIONS OF THE RULES OF WARFARE

The Declaration of St. Petersburg of December 11, 1868—one of the earliest multilateral treaties on the conduct of hostilities [4]—offers a valuable clue to the functions of the rules of warfare. In its concluding Paragraph, it refers to the need, " in view of future improvements which science may effect in the armament of troops, for further consultation between the Powers in order to maintain the principle which they had established in the Declaration " and to " conciliate the necessities of war with the laws of humanity." [5] In the Preambles to the Hague Conventions on Land Warfare of 1899 and 1907,[6] the " interests of humanity " are linked even more directly

---

[1] See above, p. 21 et seq., and further Power Politics, p. 191 et seq.
[2] See further Fundamental Principles, p. 327 et seq., and Manual, Vol. 1, p. 170 et seq., and Vol. 2, p. 579 et seq.
[3] See further International Law Association, Report of the New York Conference (1958), p. 563 et seq., and Verdross Festschrift (1960), p. 243 et seq.
[4] It was preceded by the Declaration of Paris on Maritime Law, April 16, 1856 (Martens, 15 N.R.G., p. 767), and the Geneva Convention on the Amelioration of the Condition of the Wounded of Armies in the Field, August 22, 1864 (Martens, 18 N.R.G., p. 607).
[5] Martens, 18 N.R.G., p. 474.
[6] J. B. Scott, The Hague Conventions and Declarations of 1899 and 1901 (1915), pp. 100 and 102.

with the ultimate *ratio juris in bello*: the " ever progressive needs of civilisation." [7]

It is no service to international law—and, in any case, constantly refuted by the realities of warfare—to pretend that the rules of warfare seriously restrain the supremacy of force in time of war. The laws of war are based on the assumption of war as an extreme, but not necessarily remote contingency in international relations. As is stated in the Preamble to the Hague Convention on Land Warfare of 1907, it is necessary for the Parties to " bear in mind the case where the appeal to arms has been brought about by events which their care was unable to avert." [8]

Resort to force in any form is a step back in an ever continuing civilising process.[9] If indulged in by organised social groups, it depends on the relative size and number of the contestants and the potency of the means of destruction at their disposal whether their armed conflicts seriously endanger the material bases of civilisation and the values for which it stands. Once the chain reaction of negative reciprocity is set in motion, the risk of a relapse into pristine savagery is greatly increased.

It is the function of the rules of warfare to attempt to impose some barriers, however ineffective, against this return to complete anarchy by the imposition of minimum standards on the conduct of war.

The test of these rules comes when, as it is put in the St. Petersburg Declaration of 1868, the duties towards civilisation conflict with the necessities of war. These are synonymous with the tactical and strategic requirements of war, and both serve to attain the overriding object of war: the imposition of the victor's will on the defeated.

If the rules of warfare are viewed in the light of the functions of war, four types of such rules emerge. The first type can serve its purpose without coming into conflict with the necessities of war.[10] Sadistic acts of cruelty, which do not even purport to have terrorisation as their object, or wanton acts of destruction of property which

---

[7] See above, p. 78 *et seq.*

[8] *L.c.* in note 6 above, p. 100. Similarly, the Preamble to the Geneva Prisoners of War Convention of 1929 speaks of the " extreme event of a war " (Cmd. 3794—1931, p. 41).

[9] See further above, p. 67 *et seq.*

[10] Similarly in Article 6 (b) of the Charter of the International Military Tribunal of Nuremberg (Cmd. 6668 (1945), p. 5), war crimes in the technical sense were limited, *inter alia*, to " devastation not justified by military necessity." See below, p. 264.

cannot even claim to form part of a " scorched earth " policy belong to this category. They have received attention by the International Military Tribunals of Nuremberg and Tokyo. In situations of this kind, the rules of warfare are most effective: for they can operate on the line of least resistance from the authorities of belligerents.

The second type of rule sets limitations to warfare in cases in which considerations of civilisation demand priority over military interests. The prohibition of the use of poison and poisoned weapons illustrates this type of rule.[11]

The third type attains a true compromise between the requirements of civilisation and the necessities of war. Thus, in the St. Petersburg Declaration of 1868, explosive or inflammable projectiles below 400 grammes in weight are prohibited. The Parties to the Declaration decided that, in the case of weapons below this weight, the " necessities of war ought to yield to the requirements of humanity." If, however, owing to greater weight, these weapons were more likely to attain their appointed object of disabling or killing the " greatest possible number " of the military forces of the enemy, their use did not run counter to the " laws of humanity " as enunciated in the Declaration. Rules on the prohibition of the destruction of cultural property which is not actually in enemy use offer further examples of this type of law.[12]

The fourth type of rule is merely a formal compromise between the standard of civilisation and the necessities of war. Here, in fact, the rule of force is supreme. Rules which expressly proclaim the necessities of war as an overriding constituent element or are emasculated by an " as far as possible " clause illustrate this slightly hypocritical variant of the rules of warfare.[13] Its function is not to safeguard the minimum standard of civilisation. It is to cover up the inability or unwillingness to achieve this object. Thus, the function of this fourth, and purely admonitory, type, like that of any other ideology,[14] is, if not to deceive, to disguise the failure of constructive achievement.

As, in a different, but comparable context, the late Judge Lauterpacht held in a forthright Separate Opinion, commitments of this type are in law " illusory " because the reservations are hardly verifiable. It is " irrelevant for this purpose that, having regard to

---

11 See further the present writer's *Legality of Nuclear Weapons* (1958), p. 26 *et seq.*
12 See, for instance, the Hague Convention on the Protection of Cultural Property in the Event of Armed Conflict of May 14, 1954 (Cmd. 9837—1956).
13 See below, p. 259.
14 See above, pp. 11 and 25 *et seq.*, and further *Power Politics*, pp. 730–731.

public opinion, an enlightened State is not likely to invoke any such reservation capriciously, unjustifiably, and in bad faith." [15] Reservations of this kind reduce allegedly legal rules to purely moral prescripts.

The four types of the rules of warfare, and their functions, can be illustrated by a simple diagram :

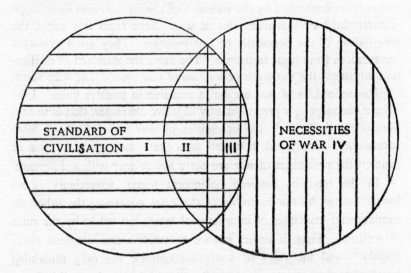

Only the second and third types of the rules of warfare, that is to say, those putting the requirements of civilisation before the necessities of war or constituting a real compromise between these conflicting considerations create the paradox posed in the introductory paragraph of this Chapter.

In the reality of State practice, the apparent self-contradiction of the situation tends to vanish. Whenever the two requirements clash, States make at most marginal concessions to the standard of civilisation. Moreover, the working principle of reciprocity assures that the self-denial of any weapon or opportunity also means its denial to the enemy.[16]

Finally, breaches of any of these or other rules of warfare by one side give the other a right of reprisal and, in fact, a hardly limited freedom of action. The self-limitation and relative insignificance of the rules of war in fields which are dominated by the necessities of war explain the mystery of the co-existence of law and force in a state of war. *De minimis non curat Mars.*

[15] *Norwegian Loans* case, *I.C.J. Reports 1957*, pp. 50, 52 and 54.
[16] See above, pp. 15 and 29 *et seq.*

Both the standard of civilisation and the necessities of war are rationalisations of conflicting social forces in international society. On the legal level, these formative agencies assume complementary functions. That of the former is positive and regulative, and that of the latter either limiting or purely negative. Thus, to any extent to which the laws of warfare are truly prohibitory rules, their actual contents are controlled by the standard of civilisation, and their scope is determined by the necessities of war. Seen from this angle, the true nature of the necessities of war emerges. They are a synonym for freedom from legal restraints.[17] The more the standard of civilisation advances, the more the necessities of war recede, and vice versa.

The necessities of war are but a negative in positive guise. Like another concept of a predominantly negative character, that is to say, domestic jurisdiction,[18] the necessities of war are a facet of State sovereignty. Compared, however, with State sovereignty in time of peace,[19] the necessities of war are State sovereignty with a difference.

In the relations between belligerent States, sovereignty is no longer limited by the ensemble of the rules governing the other six fundamental principles of international law,[20] but solely by the rules of warfare. Thus, it comes nearest to pristine and pre-legal sovereignty,[21] and the rules of warfare constitute the only remaining barrier left against sovereignty in its most violent and anarchic form. This, by the way, also explains why observance of the rules of warfare is ensured by exceptionally strong sanctions. Until peace is re-established, and breaches of the rules of warfare can be treated again as international torts calling for reparation, any violation of these rules may be punished by the enemy as a war crime.

Thus, it is advisable to be fully aware of the place allocated in the scheme of the law of war both to the laws of humanity and to the necessities of war or military necessities. The laws of humanity are *pars pro toto* for the standard of civilisation, and the necessities of war stand for wartime sovereignty. They should neither be mistaken for necessity in the meaning of impossibility of performance of an

---

[17] See further *Vol. II*, Chap. 10 or *Mélanges Séfériadès* (1961), Vol. 1, p. 13 *et seq.*
[18] See further *Vol. I*, p. 116 *et seq.*
[19] See further *l.c.* note 18 above and *Fundamental Principles*, p. 214 *et seq.*
[20] See further *Vol. I*, p. 9 *et seq.* and *Fundamental Principles*, p. 195 *et seq.*
   On the survival, within limits, in a state of war of the duties incumbent on belligerent States in relation to enemy nationals under the minimum standard of international law, see *Vol. II*, Chap. 5.
[21] See further 10 *C.L.P.* (1957), p. 264 *et seq.*

international obligation [22] nor, as the term *military* necessity may suggest, be limited to the law of land warfare.

II—LEGAL FOUNDATIONS OF THE RULES OF WARFARE

In the absence of convincing evidence to the contrary, it must be assumed that the rules of warfare owe their existence to the same law-creating processes as any other rules of international law. They must be rules of international customary law, treaty law or general principles of law recognised by civilised nations.[23] The exclusive character of the three law-creating processes does not prevent the reception of any of the multitude of non-legal motive powers and rules of conduct into international law.[24] Canons of natural law, the laws of humanity, requirements of civilisation, the conscience of mankind and even the somewhat mythical *conscience juridique* are as eligible as any other relevant social phenomena for transformation into rules of international law. One condition, however, must be fulfilled: evidence that the rule complies with the hall-marks of at least one of the three law-creating processes.[25]

In relation to the laws of war, insistence on the exclusiveness of the three law-creating processes may be challenged on superficially attractive grounds. Thus, a number of multilateral treaties contain express references to the laws of humanity, the dictates of public conscience and the general opinion of the civilised world.[26] The International Military Tribunal of Nuremburg appears to have relied on the " elementary dictates of humanity," [27] and even the World Court has found occasion to invoke " elementary considerations of humanity." [28] Thus, it appears advisable to sift carefully the available evidence and, in particular, the governing treaties and pertinent *dicta* of international courts and tribunals.[29]

---

[22] See further *Vol. I*, p. 641 *et seq.*
[23] See *ibid.*, p. 25 *et seq.*
[24] See *ibid.*, p. 49 *et seq.*
[25] For the applicable tests, see *ibid.*, pp. 27 and 59 *et seq.*
[26] See below, p. 265 *et seq.*
[27] Cmd. 6964 (1946), p. 45. See below, p. 269 *et seq.*
[28] *I.C.J. Reports 1949*, p. 22. See below, p. 269 *et seq.*
[29] In a chapter of necessarily limited size, it would be impossible to sift the whole available evidence. If, therefore, a choice has to be made, it is in favour of international judicial and treaty practice rather than the pronouncements of individual States or views expressed in the Doctrine of international law. The reasons for such selectiveness are not primarily of a pragmatic character. They are based on views of the hierarchical order of the elements of law-determining agencies which have been fully explained elsewhere. *Vol. I*, p. 28 *et seq.* and 11 *C.L.P.* (1956), p. 235 *et seq.*

The Laws and Customs of War

The "laws and general customs of war" or the "general laws and customs of war," as they are termed in the Preambles to the Hague Conventions of 1899 and 1907 on the Laws and Customs of War on Land,[30] illustrate a typical form of the growth of international customary law.

One form of this process is the gradual transformation of treaty law into international customary law.[31] Another form which, in the laws of peace and neutrality, plays a more subordinate role,[32] is very prominent in the evolution of the laws of war. The origin of this type of rule of international customary law lies in municipal enactments passed by leading nations as standards of conduct for their own armed forces.

If such municipal legislation follows roughly parallel lines, or States, which themselves have not passed legislation of a similar character, find these codifications acceptable, rules embodied in municipal statutes tend to be interpreted as giving expression to generally accepted usages. Subsequently, such usages may come to be accepted as law. Finally, it may happen that these rules of international customary law receive even greater precision and are further developed by way of multilateral treaties.

One of the earliest relevant regulations on the conduct of hostilities appears to have been the Ordinance for the Government of the Army published in 1386 by Richard II of England. On pain of death, he prohibited any acts of violence against women and unarmed priests, the burning of houses and the desecration of churches and other sacred places.[33] Similar provisions were embodied in the Articles of War, issued by Emperor Maximilian in 1508. They

---

[30] Scott, *The Hague Conventions*, p. 100.

[31] See further *Vol. I*, pp. 52, 191 and 197–198.

[32] International maritime law offers a number of illustrations of an analogous development. The rules on the avoidance of collisions at sea, published in 1840 by Trinity House; the British Code of Signals of 1857, and legislation passed in 1862 on the prevention of collisions at sea set examples which, first, were followed in the national legislation of other maritime nations, and—probably before they had grown into rules of international customary law—were transposed into multilateral treaties. See further Colombos, *The International Law of the Sea* (1959), p. 291 *et seq.*

[33] Sir Nicholas Harris Nicolas, *History of the Battle of Agincourt* (1827), Appendix p. 107 *et seq.* The Proclamation on the same subject made by Henry V, probably in 1415, but possibly later (*ibid.* (1832), pp. 52–53 and Appendix, p. 31 *et seq.*) is clearly based on that of 1386. For even earlier illustrations of these prohibitions, see *Black Book of the Admiralty*, Vol. I (1871), pp. 24 and 34.

A possible link exists between such proclamations and earlier penitential Church discipline. *Cf.* I. A. D. Draper, *Penitential Discipline and Public Wars in the Middle Ages*, 43 *International Review of the Red Cross* (1961), p. 1 *et seq.*

exempt, however, from protection holy places in enemy use.[34] From then onwards, princes inside and outside the Holy Roman Empire vied with one another in publishing articles of war and *règlements* on similar lines until, by the eighteenth century, every self-respecting army in Europe had equipped itself in this fashion.[35]

The next stage was initiated by the United States Field Instructions of 1863, the work of Francis Lieber. Following this lead, other governments also set out in greater detail their own views of the law of land warfare. It became necessary to do this in the form of manuals for the guidance of the armed forces. The first British *Manual of Military Law* was published in 1884.[36]

The difference between the Articles of War and Manual phases in the evolution of the rules of land warfare is marked. While the one constitutes the formative period of the customs of war (*usus in bello*), in the other a good many of these customs have hardened into rules of international customary law or become codified in multilateral conventions.

Contemporary editions of these manuals are even likely to be issued in compliance with treaty obligations to this effect.[37] Thus, subject to express reservations made by some of the issuing authorities regarding the unofficial character of their Manuals, they offer valuable evidence of the views taken by individual Powers of the laws and customs of war.[38]

The Charters and Judgments of the International Military Tribunals of Nuremberg and Tokyo assist further in obtaining a clear picture of generally accepted rules of international customary law in this field. While in the Charter of the Tokyo Tribunal " conventional " war crimes, that is to say, war crimes under international customary law, are described merely in general terms as " violations

---

[34] Article XIII, *Corpus Juris Militaris* (1724), Part One, Col. 4.

[35] For a comprehensive collection of texts, see *l.c.* above, note 34.

   Cf. also Pappus von Tratzberg, *Holländisch Kriegs-Recht und Articulus-Brieff* (1644).

[36] This Manual is now in its 9th edition (Parts I and II: 1956, Part III: 1958). *Cf.* also the United States Field Manual on *The Law of Land Warfare* (1956), and Sections 28–31 of Article 193 of the Disciplinary Code of the Armed Forces of the Soviet Union (1950) in H. J. Berman and M. Kerner, *Documents on Soviet Military Law and Administration* (1955), pp. 94–95. On the history of these Manuals, see J. W. Garner, *International Law and the World War*, Vol. I (1920), p. 2 *et seq.*

[37] See, for instance, Article 1 of the Conventions on Land Warfare of 1899 and 1907 and the Articles on the Dissemination of the Geneva Conventions of 1949 (I: Article 47; II: Article 127; and IV: Article 144).

[38] On the purposes of the British Manual, *cf.* Part I (1956), p. 1, and, on those of the U.S. Manual, *l.c.*, note 36 above, p. 3.

of the laws or customs of war," [39] these crimes are enumerated more specifically in the Charter of the Nuremberg Tribunal. They include, but are not limited to " murder, ill-treatment or deportation to slave labour or for any other purpose of civilian population of or in occupied territory, murder, or ill-treatment of prisoners of war or persons on the seas, killing of hostages, plunder of public or private property, wanton destruction of cities, towns or villages or devastation not justified by military necessity." [40]

On war crimes in these categories, the Nuremberg Tribunal made a number of directly relevant observations. In particular, it held that prisoners of war had been " ill-treated, tortured and murdered, not only in defiance of the well-established rules of international law, but in complete disregard of the elementary dictates of humanity." [41]

Rules of international customary law and multilateral treaties, prohibiting misdeeds of the kind which the Tribunal castigated, exist in abundance. Thus, there was no real need for the Tribunal to pray in aid any additional law-creating process. In all probability, the concluding words of this dictum were no more than a psychologically understandable pleonasm, for it would be hard to break any of the laws of warfare for the protection of individuals without disregarding some elementary dictates of humanity.

In practice, it is likely to make little difference which way the proposition is formulated. It would, however, mean stepping outside *lex lata* to reverse the statement that every breach of rules of warfare of this type amounts to a breach of considerations of humanity, and to suggest that every disregard of elementary dictates of humanity was not only immoral, which it is, but also automatically a breach of a rule of international customary law, which it is not.

In another passage of the Nuremberg Judgment, it was made fairly clear that the Tribunal did not consider the laws of humanity as an independent law-creating process. It held that the law of war was to be " found not only in treaties, but in the customs and practices of States which gradually obtained universal recognition, and from the general principles of justice applied by jurists and practised by military courts." [42]

[39] United States Department of State, *Occupation of Japan* (1946), p. 149.
[40] Article 6 (b)—Cmd. 6668 (1945), p. 5.
     Article 6 (b) of the Charter of London of 1945 telescopes basic provisions of the Hague Regulations of 1907 on Land Warfare, which themselves are declaratory of international customary law. See further the *Nuremberg Judgment*, Cmd. 6964 (1946), at p. 48.
[41] Cmd. 6964 (1946), p. 45.
[42] *Ibid.*, p. 40.

The Judgment of the Tokyo International Military Tribunal (1948), which, on basic issues, is closely modelled on that of the Nuremberg Tribunal, further clarifies the passage on prisoners of war in the Judgment of Nuremberg. In the view of the Tokyo Tribunal, the reasons why acts of inhumanity against prisoners of war are illegal are not in doubt. They are "forbidden by the customary law of nations as well as by conventions." [43]

On closer examination, the Judgment of the World Court in the *Corfu Channel* (*Merits*) *Case* (1949) bears out as little as that of Nuremberg the thesis that dictates of humanity constitute a fourth law-creating process. The Court speaks of "elementary considerations of humanity, even more exacting in peace than in war." [44] Yet, in relation to times other than war, the Court was careful to fortify its position in the very same Paragraph of its Judgment by two well-established rules of international customary law. They comfortably carry the Judgment. [45]

Actually, the *obiter dictum* on the position in time of war positively precludes the construction that the Court recognised considerations of humanity as an independent law-creating process. The World Court identified obedience to elementary considerations of humanity in a comparable situation but one in which the parties were in a state of war, with application of Hague Convention VIII of 1907. [46] This Convention on the Laying of Automatic Submarine Contact Mines, to which Albania was not a party, is a model illustration of Type Four of the rules of warfare. [47] It is a masterpiece of the art of drafting non-imperative rules of semi-legal semblance. [48] What, therefore, the World Court established in effect was that, in a wartime situation corresponding to that before it, a State would have moral, but not legal, obligations towards its enemy.

Conventions on Land Warfare

Like any other type of treaty, [49] conventions on any aspect of warfare may be law-making and, thus, binding merely on the parties. Alternatively, they may be declaratory either of international customary law or of general principles of law recognised by civilised nations.

---

43 *Judgment* (1948), Part A, Chapter II, p. 11. 44 *I.C.J. Reports 1949*, p. 22.
45 See further *Vol. I*, pp. 51, 195 and 340.
46 Scott, *The Hague Conventions*, p. 151 *et seq.*
47 See above, p. 258.
48 See *l.c.* note 11 above, p. 8. 49 See *Vol. I*, p. 421 *et seq.*

To establish accurately the declaratory or constitutive character of a treaty clause is of more than theoretical interest. A declaratory treaty, even if not in force, still constitutes a reliable codification of international customary law or general principles of law. Similarly, the distinction between declaratory and constitutive treaties assumes major importance in the case of treaties which, like the Hague Conventions of 1899 and 1907, contain general participation clauses.

This means that if but one of a number of belligerent States is not bound by such a convention, any of the other parties may treat the convention as inapplicable to the conflict in question. If, however, any particular clause of the treaty is merely declaratory of international customary law or general principles of law, belligerent States remain bound to comply with these obligations stemming from international customary law. Moreover, it would be mistaken to take too static a view of the declaratory or constitutive character of rules of treaty law. What, at one time, may have been a constitutive rule may subsequently become so generally accepted as law, irrespective of embodiment in any treaty, as to assume a declaratory character.

The Judgments of both International Military Tribunals bear witness to these propositions. In the view of the Nuremberg Tribunal, the rules laid down in Hague Convention IV of 1907 on Land Warfare and the annexed Rules of Land Warfare represented an " advance over existing international law at the time of their adoption." Yet, " by 1939, these rules laid down in the Convention were recognised by all civilised nations, and were regarded as being declaratory of the laws and customs of war." [50]

The Tokyo Tribunal was less inclined to play down the declaratory character at the time of their adoption of the Hague Conventions of 1899 and 1907 and of the Geneva Conventions on Prisoners of War of 1906 and 1929. It held that these Conventions " consisted less in the addition of new rules to the existing body of international law than in a restatement in more precise form of the rules of customary law and practice already recognised as established." [51]

The Tribunal proceeded to discuss the implications of this finding for the Hague Conventions of 1907 and Geneva Red Cross Conventions of 1929: " These Agreements not only impose direct treaty obligations upon the Contracting Powers, but also delineate more

---

[50] Cmd. 6964 (1946), p. 65.
[51] *Judgment* (1948), Part A, Chapter III, p. 17. See also *ibid.*, p. 31.

precisely the customary law. The effectiveness of some of the Conventions signed at The Hague on 18 October 1927 as direct treaty obligations was considerably impaired by the incorporation of a so-called 'general participation clause' in them, providing that the Convention would be binding only if all the belligerents were parties to it. The effect of this clause is, in strict law, to deprive some of the Conventions of their binding force as direct treaty obligations, either from the very beginning of a war or in the course of it as soon as a non-signatory Power, however insignificant, joins the ranks of the belligerents. Although the obligation to observe the provisions of the Convention as a binding treaty may be swept away by operation of the 'general participation clause' or otherwise, the Convention remains as good evidence of the customary law of nations, to be considered by the Tribunal along with all other available evidence in determining the customary law to be applied in any given situation." [52]

In the Geneva Red Cross Conventions of 1929, the general participation clause, prone as it is to set in motion a snowball process of negative reciprocity, was reduced to a simple reciprocity clause. It was provided that if one of several belligerent States was not a party to one of the Conventions of 1929 on the Amelioration of the Condition of the Wounded and Sick in Armies in the Field [53] or on the Treatment of Prisoners of War,[54] the Convention should, nevertheless, remain binding between those belligerent States which were parties thereto. In the Red Cross Conventions of 1949, this clause was amplified so as to make the principle of reciprocity work in favour of a wider application of these treaties. If one of the Powers in conflict which is not a party to one of these Conventions accepts and applies it, the parties to the Conventions are under a duty to observe it in relation to the accepting Power.[55]

The Hague and Geneva Conventions are attempts to develop the rules on land warfare and the treatment of persons in the captivity of an enemy State beyond the requirements of the minimum standard

---

[52] *Ibid.*, pp. 29–30. See also *ibid.*, pp. 31 and 37.
[53] Article 25. Cmd. 3940 (1931), p. 38.
[54] Article 82 (2). Cmd. 3794 (1931), p. 67.
[55] Article 2 (3) of Conventions I–IV.

It is for the Parties to decide in good faith whether the non-party fulfils these conditions. In the case of denunciation, it is expressly provided that the denunciation shall have effect only in respect of the denouncing " Power " (Convention I: Article 63; Convention II: Article 62; Convention III: Article 142, and Convention IV: Article 158).

See also below, p. 269.

of civilisation as these are prescribed by relevant rules of international customary law and general principles of law recognised by civilised nations. At the same time, the draftsmen of these Conventions were fully cognisant of the fact that none of these codifications could aspire to be exhaustive. Thus, they were anxious to avoid the interpretation that any issue not covered by the codified Rules of Land Warfare was no longer governed by either international customary law or applicable general principles of law, and they denounced any such misinterpretation of their intentions.

In the Preamble to Hague Convention IV of 1907, an attempt was made to forestall any such interpretation by means of the so-called de Martens Clause [56]: "Until a more complete code of the laws of war has been issued, the High Contracting Parties deem it expedient to declare that, in cases not included in the Regulations adopted by them, the inhabitants and the belligerents remain under the protection and the rule of the principles of the law of nations, as they result from the usages established among civilised peoples, from the laws of humanity, and the dictates of the public conscience."

The Tokyo Tribunal firmly relied on the de Martens Clause.[57] It held that the Convention on the Treatment of Prisoners of War of 1929 was the " more complete code of the laws of war " which had been envisaged in the Preamble of Hague Convention IV.[58] In support of this view, the Tribunal relied on Article 89 of the 1929 Convention, according to which, in the relations between the parties, the Convention was to complete Chapter II of Section One of the Hague Regulations. The Tribunal refrained, however, from drawing from this finding the conclusion that, by 1929, the subject had been so comprehensively codified as to dispense with rules based on the other two law-creating processes. In any case, so rigid a view could hardly have been squared with the recommendations of the Geneva Conference of 1929 itself in which the Conference pointed to a number of considerable tasks then still unperformed.[59]

Like the Geneva Red Cross Conventions of 1929, those of 1949 on Prisoners of War [60] and the Protection of Civilians [61] are declared complementary to the corresponding sections of the Hague Regulations on Land Warfare of 1907. Moreover, between Contracting

---

[56] See further *l.c.* in note 11 above, p. 10.
[57] *Judgment* (1948), Part A, Chapter III, p. 32.
[58] *Ibid.*, p. 34.
[59] Final Act, July 27, 1929 (Cmd. 3795—1931), pp. 25–26.
[60] Article 135 of Convention III.
[61] Article 154 of Convention IV.

Parties, the Geneva Conventions I to III of 1949 replace earlier Conventions on the same subjects.[62]

In each of the Geneva Conventions of 1949 it is expressly provided that, even when a denunciation has taken effect, there shall not be any legal vacuum. If made in time of peace, a denunciation takes effect one year after notification to the Swiss Federal Council and, if made during a conflict, only when peace has been established and all obligations towards protected persons have been fulfilled. The denunciation " shall in no way impair the obligations which the Parties to the conflict shall remain bound to fulfil by virtue of the principles of the law of nations, as they result from the usages established among civilised peoples, from the laws of humanity and the dictates of the public conscience." [63]

These clauses, like the identical formulation in Hague Convention IV of 1907,[64] illustrate a further function fulfilled by these treaties. They serve as vehicles for the transformation of moral motive powers, tenets and aspirations into legal duties. While the incorporation of such notions in treaties amounts to a reception of otherwise non-legal rules, this treaty habitat hardly enhances the evidential value of these phrases in favour of the existence of a fourth and independent law-creating process.

The General Principles of Law Recognised by Civilised Nations

It is possible to consider the *dicta* on elementary considerations of humanity in the Judgment of *Nuremberg* (1946) and the *Corfu Channel (Merits) Case* (1949) relevant also from the point of view of the general principles of law.

Some values of a humanitarian character are acknowledged by civilised nations, and this distinguishes them from both savage and barbarian societies.[65] From this premise, it is arguable that the legal systems of all civilised communities protect these values, and it is, therefore, legitimate to abstract from the pertinent rules of municipal law applicable general principles of law.

Yet, for centuries, civilised nations have also considered themselves entitled to wage war with one another. It would, therefore, still have to be determined at which point the necessities of war had

---

[62] Convention I: Article 59; Convention II: Article 58, and Convention III: Article 134.
[63] See *l.c.* in Paragraph 2 of note 55 above.
[64] Similarly, in the Geneva Protocol of 1925 on Gas Warfare (Cmd. 3604—1930, p. 2) reliance is placed on the " general opinion of the civilised world."
[65] See above, p. 65.

to give way to general principles of law and vice versa. The reference in the *Corfu Channel (Merits)* Judgment to Hague Convention VIII does not suggest undue confidence in the regulative effect of such general principles of law.[66]

The application of these general principles of law would be least open to challenge where they would be most expendable, that is to say, in the fields covered by the first of the four types of the laws of war.[67] Even so, they would not be completely redundant. In exceptional situations in which the necessities of war do not call for the infliction of pain, death or destruction, it may be doubtful whether a prohibitory rule of international customary or treaty law exists. In such an eventuality, the general principles of law could be invoked to fulfil their accustomed subsidiary function of closing any real or imaginary gap in the rules of international law.[68]

The Judgment of the International Military Tribunal of Nuremberg contains other *dicta* which are potentially relevant from the point of view of the general principles of law recognised by civilised nations. In a passage concerned with waging aggressive war, the Tribunal contrasted the " general principles of law " laid down in the Kellogg Pact with mere " administrative matters of procedure." [69] In this instance, the Tribunal did not use the term " general principles of law " as referring to the third of the three law-creating processes of international law. It merely emphasised in this way the broad and sweeping character of the rules laid down in the Kellogg Pact and the significance of this feature of the Treaty for its interpretation.

In the following sentence, the Tribunal mentioned all three law-creating processes. Somewhat surprisingly, however, it described the last of these as the general principles of *justice*.[70] This unusual formulation may have been due to a conscious identification of law and justice. It is, however, more likely that there is another explanation for this, on the surface, overt reliance on natural law.

The Defence had urged on the Tribunal that a fundamental principle of law excluded the classification of an act as a crime and its punishment in the absence of a pre-existing law : *Nullum crimen sine lege, nulla poena sine lege.* It was submitted that *ex post facto* punishment was abhorrent to the law of all civilised nations ; that no

---

66 See above, p. 265.
67 See above, p. 257.
68 See *Vol. I,* p. 43 *et seq.*
69 Cmd. 6964 (1946), p. 40.
70 See above, p. 264.

sovereign Power had made aggressive war a crime at the time the alleged criminal acts were committed ; that aggressive war had remained undefined ; that no penalty had been fixed for its commission, nor any court created to try and punish offenders.[71]

The Tribunal disposed of these arguments primarily by reference to its Charter. Irrespective of whether the law of the Charter was retrospective, it was binding on the Tribunal.[72] The Tribunal did not, however, leave matters at this. It dealt with the substance of the submissions made by the Defence and held that the maxim *nullum crimen sine lege* was " not a limitation of sovereignty but . . . in general a principle of justice." [73]

Actually, the first of these propositions is too sweeping, and the two propositions are not mutually exclusive. If the prohibition of *ex post facto* legislation were a general principle of law recognised by civilised nations, it would constitute a limitation of sovereignty at least in relation to foreigners who are protected by the minimum standard of international law.[74] It would not, however, limit the exercise of jurisdiction over individuals who, by *debellatio*, had come under the *co-imperium* of enemy States.[75] Moreover, limitations of sovereignty and principles of justice may well march together and hardly call for an unqualified contrast as incompatibles.

If the Tribunal had wished to consider the argument of *ex post facto* law on its merits, it might have been expected to tackle the issue from the angle of comparative law. It would probably have found that, while liberal and individualistic systems of municipal law view with disfavour the retroactivity of penal laws, even they have not always been able to dispense entirely with this device.

The Tribunal might well have reached one of two conclusions. It might have held that the maxims *Nullum crimen sine lege, nulla poena sine lege* did not epitomise a general principle of law recognised by civilised nations. It might also have found that the prohibition of retroactive criminal responsibility was a general principle of law recognised by civilised nations, but that, as in municipal law, so in international law, exceptional circumstances justified departures from this principle.[76]

---

71 Cmd. 6994 (1946), p. 38.
72 *Ibid.*, p. 38.
73 *Ibid.*, p. 39.
74 See *Vol. I*, p. 200 *et seq.*
75 See further, *ibid.*, pp. 297–298. *Cf.* also Cmd. 6964 (1946), p. 38.
76 For an instructive discussion in the context of the Danzig Constitution of the self-neutralising maxims *Nullum crimen sine lege* and *nullum crimen sine poena*,

Instead, the Tribunal proceeded by way of a remarkable *tour de force*. It disposed of the objection to the retroactivity of criminal responsibility by a reasoning which is hardly convincing and derived the criminality of aggressive war from a somewhat spurious law-creating process : the general principles of " justice." The Tribunal held that, in attacking neighbouring States without warning, the attacker knew that he was doing " wrong." Therefore, " so far from it being unjust to punish him, it would be unjust if his wrong were allowed to go unpunished." [77]

One thing is certain. This reasoning is not based on the general principles of law recognised by civilised nations. At the same time, it is not necessary to harp on the relapse of the Nuremberg Tribunal into law-making by reference to natural law, for, in view of the clear provisions of the Charters of London and Tokyo, the efforts of the Tribunal in this respect were completely supererogatory. More likely than not, the Tribunals invoked the general principles of justice to cover their own uneasiness over the departures of their Charters from a strong Western legal tradition in creating retrospectively the war crimes against peace and humanity.[78]

In dealing with the defence of superior orders, the Nuremberg Tribunal came nearest to relying on the last of the three law-creating processes. Without saying in so many words that the irrelevance of superior orders in cases in which a moral choice existed was a general

see A/B 65, p. 54 *et seq.*, and *Vol. I*, p. 109 *et seq. Cf.* also J. Hall, *General Principles of Criminal Law* (1947), p. 19 *et seq.*; H. A. Smith, *The Crisis in the Law of Nations* (1947), p. 46 *et seq.*, G. Ireland, *Ex post facto from Rome to Tokyo*, 21 *Temple Law Quarterly* (1947), p. 27 *et seq.*, and J. T. Woodhouse, *The Principle of Retroactivity in International Law*, 41 *Grotius Transactions* (1955), p. 69 *et seq.*
[77] Cmd. 6964 (1946), p. 39.
The Tokyo Tribunal associated itself expressly with this finding (*Judgment* (1948), Part A, Chapter II, p. 10). See also 15 *Law Reports of Trials of War Criminals*, p. 166 *et seq.*
A strong reassertion of the prohibition of the retroactivity of penal laws will be found in Article 99 of Geneva Convention III of 1949. In Article 99, which includes jurisdiction of the Detaining Power to proceed against prisoners of war accused of war crimes, it is expressly provided that " no prisoner of war may be tried or sentenced for an act which is not forbidden by the law of the Detaining Power or by international law, in force at the time the said act was committed."
In Paragraph 2 of Article 68 of Geneva Convention IV of 1949 the principle of *Nulla poena sine lege* is applied in a still more extreme form. In the cases in which, in principle, the Occupying Power is authorised to impose the death penalty on protected persons, one of the further conditions to be fulfilled is that " such offences were punishable by death under the law of occupied territory in force before the occupation began." On reservations made by, *inter alia*, the United States of America and the United Kingdom to this Clause, see Pictet's *Official Commentary*, Vol. IV, (1956), p. 370, and, for the text of these reservations *cf.* Cmnd. 550 (1958), pp. 334 and 348.
[78] See further 2 *Y.B.W.A.* (1948), p. 94 *et seq.*

principle of law, the Nuremberg Tribunal held that this was a rule " in conformity with the law of all nations." [79]

The fact of the change in the British and United States military law in the course of the Second World War from the view of superior orders constituting a defence to its very opposite suffices to prove the precarious character of the Tribunal's exercise in comparative criminal law.[80]

Nonetheless, the Tribunal correctly stated that, in cases such as killing or torture in violation of international law, the defence of superior orders was never recognised.[81] The explanation for this is not, however, any uniform rule of municipal law to this effect, but authority under a well-established rule of international customary law to disregard this defence.[82] Moreover, both International Military Tribunals could rely on express provisions in their Charters, in accordance with which superior orders did not exempt any accused from criminal responsibility, but could be taken into account in mitigation of punishment. It is significant that, in the case of the accused Jodl, the Nuremberg Tribunal did not content itself with its comparative law argument. It thought it advisable to fall back on the express exclusion of the defence of superior orders by Article 8 of the Charter of London.[83]

Thus, international judicial practice confirms that the rules of warfare, like the rest of the rules of international law, must be shown to be the product of one of the three primary law-creating processes —international customary law, treaties and the general principles of law recognised by civilised nations—or that they have come into existence through the agency of secondary law-creating processes, such as Recognition or Consent.

---

[79] Cmd. 6964 (1946), p. 42.
[80] See further the present writer's *International Law and Totalitarian Lawlessness* (1943), pp. 62–63, and 60 *Harvard Law Review* (1947), p. 545 *et seq.*
   The Tokyo Tribunal expressly associated itself also with this passage (*Judgment* (1948), Part A, Chapter II, p. 10). *Cf.* also Paragraph 347 of the 1940 ed. of the United States *Basic Field Manual* on the *Rules of Land Warfare*, pp. 86–87, with Paragraph 509 of the 1956 ed. of *The Law of Land Warfare*, pp. 182–183, and Article 6 of the *Disciplinary Code of the Armed Forces of the U.S.S.R.*, June 1, 1946, re-issued in 1950 (Berman and Kerner, *l.c.* note 36 above, p. 50).
[81] Cmd. 6964 (1946), p. 42.
[82] See *l.c.* in notes 78 and 80 above.
[83] Cmd. 6964 (1946), p. 118.

CHAPTER 12

REFLECTIONS ON THE LAW
OF INTERNATIONAL INSTITUTIONS

THE Law of International Institutions is not a synonym for the descriptive treatment or the structural analysis of international institutions. The term has come to stand for a specialised, and largely autonomous, branch of International Law.

As a distinct academic discipline and separate teaching subject, the Law of International Institutions probably came into existence in the University of London in the closing years of the Second World War and has since been introduced in a number of other British and foreign universities. Thus, after an interval of one and a half decades, it is perhaps timely to review the experiment.[1]

I—THE STUDY OF INTERNATIONAL INSTITUTIONS

The present-day study of international institutions in its legal and non-legal aspects is greatly indebted to a considerable number and variety of earlier experiments. To provide in this Chapter a consecutive history of the gradual evolution of the subject is neither possible nor necessary.[2] It may, however, be helpful to abstract from the abundant material the most significant patterns of treatment which international institutions have received before the Second World War. They can be summarised under six heads:

(1) The opening stage was characterised by an *unreflective* description of individual international institutions or groups of such institutions. In the nature of things, those which received attention before any others—actually since the seventeenth century—were congresses and conferences. If writers employed any method beyond putting to best use such common sense, humour or wit as they could muster,

---

[1] In Chaps. 9–11 of the *Manual* an attempt has been made to give an exposition of the Law of International Institutions in accordance with the system and the comparative method outlined in this chapter. See also below, p. 288 *et seq.*, and 4 *I.L.Q.* (1951), p. 299 *et seq.*

[2] See, in particular, J. ter Meulen, *L'Evolution de l'Idée de l'Organisation Internationale* (1917–1940); C. Lange, *Histoire de l'Internationalisme* (1910–1954), and H. Wehberg, *L'idée de l'Organisation Internationale à l'époque des Conférences de la Haye*, in *Études Scelles* (1950), Vol. II, p. 633 *et seq.*

it was the historical technique of the age, interlaced with refreshingly saucy observations.

De St. Disdier's *Histoire des Négociations de Nimegue* (1680), the *Works* of Sir William Temple (1720), the reports and letters by Sir Leoline Jenkins (1724) and the anonymous *Histoire des Traités de Paix et autres Négociations du dix-septième Siècle* (1725) are some outstanding illustrations of this *genre*.

(2) From here it was but one step to an *historical* treatment of international institutions with the full technical and critical apparatus at the disposal of the trained historian.

The best that can be attained by this method—and its limitations —is exemplified by works such as (in the chronological order of their subjects) Webster's *Congress of Vienna* (1934), Bourquin's *Histoire de la Sainte Alliance* (1954), Dupuis' *Principe d'Équilibre et le Concert Européen* (1909), Crowe's *Berlin West African Conference, 1884–1885* (1942) and Temperley's *Peace Conference of Paris* (1920–1924).

(3) In the *legal* field, classical works such as Lammasch's *Lehre von der Schiedsgerichtsbarkeit* (1914), Schücking's *Werk vom Haag* (1912–17) or Hudson's *Permanent Court of International Justice* (1943) have set exemplary standards for the monographic treatment of the subject. Also a good many dissertations on the highest post-graduate level of the pre-1914 and inter-war periods deserve to be kept in mind as quarries for material in need of re-examination and re-analysis. Yet, the law of international institutions is probably most indebted to some of the textbook writers on international law, for they had to face most consciously the problem of fitting into their own systems the growing number and variety of international institutions.

In retrospect, probably the most perceptive treatment international institutions received in their early days from international lawyers was that given to them by Friedrich von Martens.[3] He was of sufficient stature to view the then nascent international institutions in the light of the international realities and needs of his time. Thus, while not ignoring the fact that international institutions are neces-sarily the products of the autonomous will of participating States, he did not allow himself to be overwhelmed by this knowledge. He, for one, was not content with merely classifying international institutions together with other " important " types of treaty relations. His

[3] First published in Russian in 1882–1883 (German translation by Bergbohm, Vol. I (1883) and Vol. II (1886)).

special merit lay in recognising the functions of the international institutions of his time as organs of international society.

This approach provides a remarkably elastic framework. All that is needed, as time goes on, is to adjust this scheme so as to let it reflect continuously the needs of an international society moving from an unorganised state to one of more conscious, but not necessarily more harmonious, organisation. It was left to the penetrating mind of Alfred Verdross to make the distinction between international law in unorganised and organised international society one of the cornerstones of his own presentation of international law.[4]

(4) Frequently allied with the legal treatment of international institutions was a *radical* and *pacifist* approach to the subject *de lege ferenda*. Even leaving aside the authors of earlier schemes for permanent peace,[5] blueprints such as those of Jeremy Bentham, William Ladd, Sartorius, Parieu, Lorimer, Bluntschli and, last, but not least, the Emperor of Brazil belong to this category. These projects have in common that their authors regard international institutions as the primary means of approximating international relations to the rule of law within civilised States.[6]

(5) It is necessary to distinguish from the pattern of the self-revealed reformer that of the undisclosed *evangelist* who prefers to leave unstated his major teleological assumptions, but purports to speak *ex cathedra* as lawyer or social scientist. "Faith" in international organisation, a "progressive" attitude towards controversial issues and affirmation of the need for "dedicated" research are some of the signs by which representatives of this approach to the subject can be readily identified.

Coupled with a critical view of existing international institutions, this treatment could do but little harm. In fact, however, it tends to go hand in hand with an *apologetic* attitude towards present-day international institutions. At this point, "*gradualism*," as this treatment has also been termed, is liable to degenerate into an ideology of existing international institutions and their deficiencies.

(6) Finally, the study of International Relations as the branch of Sociology concerned with international society has made its impact on research in the field of international institutions. It has made it

---

[4] Cf. *Die Verfassung der Völkerrechtsgemeinschaft* (1926) and the successive editions of *Völkerrecht* (first published in 1937). See also below, p. 279 *et seq.*

[5] For a helpful, recent collection, see H.-J. Schlochauer, *Die Idee des ewigen Friedens* (1953).

[6] See further *Jeremy Bentham and the Law* (1948—eds. G. W. Keeton and the present writer), p. 173 *et seq.*

possible to supplement essentially descriptive accounts of international institutions by more penetrating forms of *sociological* analysis of their structure and functions.

II—THE LAWYER'S CONCERN

On the surface, there is all the difference between the interest of the practitioner and the academic lawyer in international institutions. Each appears to move on a different plane.

The typical concern of the practitioner, including legal advisers to foreign offices and international institutions, is to construe controversial texts ; to steer presiding officers of the organs and committees of particular institutions safely through the shoals of procedural troubles or to instruct delegates in how most effectively to create them ; to advise the executives of international institutions on the limits of their discretionary powers and those of member States on the scope of matters still essentially within their domestic jurisdiction ; to assist in the harmonious—or imperialist—solution of conflicts of jurisdiction between international institutions and to prepare drafts for new, or the amendment of existing, constitutions.

While the academic lawyer, too, may be expected to be able to perform competently at least the more constructive of these tasks, his own specific work begins where that of the practitioner ends. Beyond exposition and systematisation, his distinct task is to assess critically the impact made on existing international law by individual international institutions, groups of such institutions and the ensemble of international institutions, and to judge the significance of these superstructures in the ever-continuing struggle between the Rule of Force and the Rule of Law in international relations.[7]

Even if a practitioner is not preoccupied with more immediate problems, he is severely handicapped in coping publicly with these wider issues of evaluation, and the same applies to academic lawyers with self-imposed commitments of a similar character. It would not

---

[7] If the Rule of Law in international relations is to be no more than a meaningless synonym for existing international law, but a standard of measurement *de lege ferenda*, it must apply stricter tests than those required for international law on the level of auto-interpretation by its subjects. This does not necessarily imply that the Rule of Law in international relations must be identical with the meaning of this term within national communities (see, for instance, the meaning attached to it by the International Commission of Jurists, 2 *Journal of the I.C.J.* (1959), p. 3, n. 2). It must, however, postulate at least a state in which subjects of international law are automatically accountable to one another before international judicial organs for alleged breaches of international law, and are no longer free to contract at will out of the prevailing international order into the anarchy of the Rule of Force. See also below, pp. 288 and 297 *et seq*.

only be tactically unwise, but also of questionable taste to represent vested interests—in this respect, international institutions have become as much vested interests as any national or other " establishment "— and, at the same time, use this inside knowledge for the vivisection of one's charges or professional contacts. If lawyers finding themselves in this position are not prepared to accept an apparently no longer self-understood implication of their commitments—that is to say, to withdraw into dignified silence, they are perforce limited to concerning themselves in public with the brighter side of these topics. Worse still, they may even be tempted to paint their pictures in brighter colours than the subject actually warrants.

The treatment of the judicial practice of the World Court in the literature of international law offers an easily verifiable illustration of this proposition. This thesis at least explains why informed criticism of fallible judgments and opinions remains so much the exception and, in the analysis of this judicial material, exegesis and apologetics are found to be safe and, therefore, favoured techniques.

To make articulate the difficulties which are bound to arise if these functional incompatibilities are ignored is not to propose a rigid separation of theory from practice, but to underline their complementary character. There are sufficient other opportunities for the academic lawyer to keep in touch with practice without jeopardising either his independence or integrity. This is as much a necessity for him as it is in the practitioner's interest to keep abreast with the latest theoretical advances. If nothing else, the practitioner can gain from this contact short cuts to insights which, otherwise, he may have to acquire by the painful process—painful, if not for him, then at least for his clients—of trial and error. The issues which have given rise to the Advisory Opinion of the International Court of Justice on the *Constitution of the Maritime Safety Committee of the Inter-Governmental Maritime Consultative Organisation*,[8] elected in January 1959, vividly illustrate this point.

III—The Place of Studies on International Institutions in the Context of International Law

Agreement in the abstract on the test for determining the place of international institutions in the system of international law can be

---

[8] *I.C.J. Reports 1960*, p. 150 *et seq.*
    To judge by available evidence, an informed and frank study of the deficiencies in the drafting of the constitutions of post-1945 international institutions would be likely to be rewarding.

reached without much difficulty. It is to find a presentation of the subject which reflects faithfully the decisive realities of contemporary international society.[9] Yet, the attempt to settle in less abstract form the nature of these realities is likely to lead to the parting of the ways.

Overriding Realities

Seven aspects of international relations appear to determine more decisively than others the structure of contemporary world society :

(1) Present-day world society is bipolarised in two world camps. Centrifugal trends inside each of these camps assist in mitigating temporarily this fundamental cleavage.

(2) In each of the world camps, power tends to become increasingly concentrated in one or a few hegemonial Powers.

(3) The post-1945 armaments race has led to a point of relative saturation. The leading Powers in both camps realise that the price of nuclear warfare is co-extermination of the chief centres of civilisation on either side. So long as this phase of nuclear stalemate lasts, the political weight of uncommitted States is considerably larger than their *potentiel de guerre* in terms of pre-nuclear calculations.

(4) The United Nations is constitutionally incapable of providing more than an international quasi-order. It stands and falls with the willingness of the world Powers not to contract out of it by the use of the escape clauses of Articles 27, 51 and 107 of the Charter.

(5) Such modicum of security as exists in a divided world is a reflection of the nuclear stalemate reached between the world camps and the temporary balance between the sectional and antagonistic quasi-orders provided by the world camps.

(6) To obtain an accurate estimate of the significance of functional international institutions as, for instance, the specialised agencies of the United Nations, the limitations of the powers of these institutions appear more significant than the deceptively wide scope of their jurisdiction. Institutions of this type offer improved techniques of international co-operation. Even in relation to members, these activities remain largely optional and, as yet, hardly indicate any general movement towards international government on a world scale.

---

[9] See, for instance, C. W. Jenks, *The Common Law of Mankind* (1958), p. 23, and C. Rousseau, *Principes de Droit International Public*, 93 *Hague Recueil* (1958), p. 374.

(7) Supra-national institutions, such as the three Communities of
" Little Europe," represent the highest form of international integration so far reached. Yet, like territorial federations, this functional
variant of federalism is a constitutional experience which reflects the
needs of but limited sectors of contemporary world society.[10]

Guiding Principles

If, by and large, this analysis of the decisive realities of contemporary world society is correct, it suggests three guiding principles
for the treatment of international institutions in the context of mid-
twentieth century international law :

(1) So long as the international quasi-order of the United Nations
remains as precarious as, so far, it has proved to be, the rules
governing the fundamental principles of international customary law
must remain both the starting-point and focus of any realistic system
of international law. Compared with more ambitious and ephemeral
superstructures of the past on a consensual basis, the rules of international customary law have shown a remarkable degree of stability
and elasticity.

(2) The differences in the degree of international integration
attained inside, and between, the world camps make it necessary to
search for a presentation of the subject which will give a fair picture
of international law as applied on each of these levels.

One of the consequences and attractions of such a presentation
of the subject is that it brings out the relativity of truth in a whole
collection of fashionable, but somewhat sweeping, assertions, Several
come immediately to mind : independence having been replaced by
interdependence ; hegemony having given way to " sovereign
equality " ; the individual having been transformed from an object
into a subject of international law ; hypotheses such as the prohibition of the abuse of rights or *ex injuria jus non oritur* having become
integral parts of international law at large.

(3) The systematic arrangement of the law of international
institutions must, above all else, be free of teleological value-
judgments which are rationally unverifiable. It may be that international society is on the march towards a world in which States
organise themselves increasingly by means of institutions to meet
individual and social needs or that it is on the move towards the

---

10 For further discussion of these and other controversial points, *cf. loc. cit.* in
note 1, above.

Rule of Law. Yet, it may also be *en route* towards some other, and less auspicious, destination. However inspiring some of these objectives may be, it would reduce international law to a vehicle of wishful thinking, if not propaganda by way of insinuation, to let these highly impressionist and subjective vistas affect the systematic exposition of international law in general and of the law of international institutions in particular.

Substitution, Amalgamation or Consolidation?

Two, at first sight, attractive possibilities must be mentioned. The one would be for all practical purposes to *substitute* international law on the level of international institutions for international law at large. The other would be to *amalgamate* the presentation of international law on the institutional level with that of international law.

At most, these patterns of substitution and amalgamation reflect the decisive realities inside and on the fringes of, but not between, the world camps. In a world society, the degree of integration reached inside, and on the periphery of, the great blocs is hardly the decisive criterion. What matters is the relative strength and weakness of the law that links the potentially hostile factions.[11]

Considerations of this nature appear to rule out both the patterns of substitution and amalgamation. They do not, however, exclude the possibility of finding an adequate place for the legal aspects of international organisation in a mid-twentieth century system of international law. Yet, this must be done in a manner which does not sacrifice the decisive realities outlined above to the temptations of wishful thinking and escapism.

In this context, two constitutional aspects of contemporary international organisation are pointers to a commensurate solution of the quandary : the elements of both remarkable unity and diversity in the constitutions of international institutions.

International institutions can claim a double unity. Albeit on a merely consensual basis, they represent what there is of a world quasi-order as well as of competitive orders of a more limited character.[12] Thus, they provide semi-constitutional international frameworks and in this lies their functional unity.

[11] See above, p. 146 *et seq.*
[12] For searching observations on these fragmentary orders, *cf.* M. S. McDougal and H. P. Lasswell, *The Identification and Appraisal of Diverse Systems of Public Order,* 53 *A.J.I.L.* (1959), p. 1 *et seq.*

Beyond this, they share three presumptions in favour of their jurisdiction. Each of these has received judicial recognition by the World Court. These presumptions are first, in favour of the competence of international institutions of any description to determine the scope of their own jurisdiction ; secondly, in favour of the exclusive jurisdiction of international institutions in matters entrusted to them ; and, thirdly, in favour of granting to international institutions such implied powers as are indispensable to the proper fulfilment of their functions.

It would probably be overshooting the mark to read more into these propositions than that they are the result of the judicial interpretation of the typical intentions of parties to treaties by which international institutions are constituted. Yet, in the absence of express stipulations to the contrary, members of international institutions must expect international judicial organs to apply these presumptions. Such a state of affairs differs, however, merely in degree from one in which these rebuttable presumptions are regarded as part of the body of international customary law ; for the rules of international customary law also prevail only in the absence of treaty stipulations to the contrary.

At the same time, the growth of international institutions since the First World War has led to a considerable variety in these consensual superstructures. In addition to the traditional types of comprehensive institutions (confederations such as the League of Nations and United Nations) as well as non-comprehensive international institutions (judicial, administrative and quasi-legislative), a growing number of hybrids between these basic institutional forms have come into existence. They represent new types of international institutions of a universal, regional and sectional character.

This double feature of a remarkable unity and diversity suggests the appropriate place for international institutions in the system of international law. They form a sufficiently distinctive and wide field of studies to make them eligible for treatment as a special branch of international law : the Law of International Institutions. Both in its unity and diversity, this branch of international law is comparable to others which have come to be accepted on a similar footing : international economic law, the law of the sea, and international air law.

The existence of such special branches not only does justice to important and constructive developments in international law, but also fulfils a protective function. It acts as a necessary, although not always effective, brake against the danger of over-specialisation within any of these fields.

Whatever the shortcomings of this treatment, it may probably claim three points in its favour. It emphasises the continuity in the evolution of international law and, thus, provides some immunity against over-estimating the significance of international institutions. At the same time, it allows for any new developments to be tested without disturbing in any way the exposition of the established portions of international law. Finally, once such a new branch of international law has proved itself, it can easily be consolidated within the system of international law.

IV—THE SYSTEM AND METHODS OF THE LAW OF INTERNATIONAL INSTITUTIONS

It remains to. deal with the system and methods of the Law of International Institutions. As in other fields, these, at first glance dreary subjects cover the most fundamental decisions of scholarship. This perhaps accounts for the strong inhibitions against removing these issues from their habitat in the realm of inarticulate and frequently subconscious major premises of legal thinking.[13]

The explanation of the riddle of such resistance may well be that a specialist's conspectus of his field consists largely of intuitive and impressionist images which, on closer acquaintance with the subject, he tends to regard as axiomatic. If he himself remains largely unconscious of these irrational conditioning factors of his scientific work, he necessarily communicates, as a teacher and writer, these hidden thought-pictures in a form which is as effective as it is unscientific. He conveys his unspoken assumptions by way of insinuation and implication, that is to say, in a manner which secures acceptance without reflection.[14]

Awareness of the irrational aspects of these problems makes it easier to understand the often instinctively strong reaction to the

[13] For a timely survey of some significant trends in the contemporary Doctrine of International Law, *cf.* J. L. Kunz, *El Sistema de derecho internacional,* in *Estudios Trelles* (1958), p. 87 *et seq.,* or *The Systematic Problem of the Science of International Law,* 53 *A.J.I.L.* (1959), p. 379 *et seq.* See further 9 *C.L.P.* (1956), p. 235 *et seq.*

[14] The systematic analysis of the literature of international law from this point of view would be more than an enjoyable piece of detective work. It would constitute an essential contribution to a new discipline concerned with *Irrationalia Juris Gentium.*

rational discussion of issues of system and methods : a deep-seated anxiety not to be disturbed by conscious thought on these hidden thought-pictures. Whatever the limitation of this interpretation may be, it serves to encourage self-criticism and a resolve to disclose at least one's own relevant major premises.

Systematic Premises

If a conscious attempt is made to lay bare the major premises on which the present writer's system of the Law of International Institutions is based, they add up to a seven-point programme :

(1) In the systematic presentation of the law of international institutions, it is necessary to bring out the long lineage of *ad hoc* international institutions, in particular, conferences and arbitration tribunals, in the evolution of international law. This is an effective way of counteracting current illusions on the " novelty " of the subject.

(2) It is necessary to emphasise the limited variety and significance from the point of view of the Rule of Law of the traditional non-comprehensive institutions : judicial, administrative and quasi-legislative.

(3) It ought to be duly explained that the comprehensive international institutions on the confederate level of the post-1919 and post-1945 eras are little more than attempts to combine under one head the three types of non-comprehensive institutions. To drive home this point, comparisons with earlier experiments on the confederate level and the exposition of their constitutional shortcomings are helpful.[15]

(4) Discussion of the scope of the jurisdiction of international institutions must be balanced by due emphasis on the limitations of their powers so as to do full justice to the realities of international institutional life.

(5) It ought to be shown that apparently novel institutions other than supra-national institutions [16] are little more than hybrids between the traditional forms of comprehensive and non-comprehensive international institutions.

These institutions call for classification in a manner that clarifies both the differences in their geographical radius of operation and

[15] The classical works on this subject are still Pufendorf's *Gründliche Untersuchung von der Art und Eigenschaft eines irregulären Staats* (Appendix to *Gründlicher Bericht von dem Zustande des H. R. Reiches Teutscher Nation* (2nd ed., 1715)), p. 715 *et seq.*, and *The Federalist* (Hamilton, Madison and Jay, 1787–1788).
[16] See below, p. 285, under (6).

their real functions. Thus, hybrid international institutions may be conveniently divided into *universal* institutions, *universalist* institutions (*i.e.*, institutions which fall short of, but aim at, universality), *regional* institutions and *sectional* institutions.

Regional institutions, such as the International Commission for the Northwest Atlantic Fisheries or the Commission for Technical Co-operation in Africa south of the Sahara, are predominantly functional and, therefore, open to all States in the area. Others, however, even if apparently regional in a geographical sense, are sectional because, in fact if not in law, they are directed against identifiable non-member States. This applies as much to the North Atlantic Treaty Organisation as to the Warsaw Treaty Organisation or, in the microcosm of the Near East, to the Arab League.

(6) The particular characteristics of supra-national institutions, in particular their essentially federal character, must be adequately explained.[17]

(7) Finally, room must be found for the exposition of the potentialities which, *de lege ferenda*, international institutions hold out in a world prepared to transform itself from a power-ridden society into an international community inspired by the ideal of the good neighbour.

Methods

If we dig in the garden, we use a spade. If we search for oil, we employ a rock-drill. In other words, the choice of tools depends on the depth to which we intend to probe. Thus, there is scope for the application of a number of methods side by side with one another. The *historical* and *analytical* methods do not call for any special comment in their application to the Law of International Institutions. A few remarks may, however, be advisable on the application in this field of the remaining four techniques : the descriptive, comparative, critical and relativist methods.

For the exposition of the essentials of an individual institution, the use of the *descriptive* method is frequently sufficient, especially for introductory purposes. If a fair picture of the objects, membership, organisation, scope of jurisdiction and powers of an international institution, its intended duration and the possibilities for the revision of its constitution is provided, this is at least something, although hardly more than any intelligent reader may be expected

[17] See further *l.c.* in note 1, above.

to achieve himself by attentively perusing the text of the constitution in question. If, however, one institution after another is treated in this manner, the tediousness of this technique and the boredom it produces become painfully apparent.

From this point of view, the *comparative* method, although more demanding, is probably preferable. If, for this purpose, international institutions of all types are indiscriminately lumped together, this is likely to produce a comparable state of exhaustion. If, however, these institutions are sufficiently broken down from a functional point of view, the comparative method becomes both instructive and stimulating. It throws into relief the typical legal patterns and their variations in relation to each of the main aspects of international institutions. Thus, if the comparative treatment is limited to related institutions, it provides categories of thinking and criticism which are equally indispensable for purposes of analysis and drafting, and are not otherwise obtainable.

Like any other branch of law, the Law of International Institutions does not exist in a vacuum. It provides normative frameworks for entities which make their own impact on social life and themselves are conditioned by it. Thus, this branch of international law must itself also fulfil social functions of both an active and passive character.

If, for instance, the question of the significance of international institutions from the point of view of the Rule of Law in international relations is raised,[18] the international lawyer tends to take one of three typical attitudes. He may refuse to commit himself in any way by taking refuge in the metalegal character of the question. Another not uncommon reaction is to acclaim uncritically any addition to the number and powers of international institutions as constituting an approximation to this goal. Finally, in a manner less escapist than the first, and less emotional than the second approach, a serious effort may be made to find a rationally verifiable answer.

At this point, the *critical* method comes into its own. As in relation to other problems of evaluation in the field of international law, the inter-disciplinary treatment of international institutions provides the appropriate technique. This means employing for purposes of evaluation the findings of related disciplines, in particular those offered by the discipline of International Relations.[19]

---

[18] See note 7 above.
[19] See further, 9 *C.L.P.* (1956), p. 250 *et seq.*

Proposals *de lege ferenda* for the development of international institutions in the style of the nineteenth-century reformers [20] have exposed the Doctrine of international law to the not always unjustified criticism of meddling with politics. To avoid this charge, it is not necessary to withdraw behind the safety curtain of *lex lata*. It is, however, advisable to treat issues of legal planning in a manner less exposed to charges of political partisanship.

In this context, it must be recalled that more than one solution exists for any social problem. In other words, the social engineer or planner is well advised to apply a *relativist* method and be prepared, within reason, to elaborate side by side as many relevant patterns of reform as he is able to conceive.[21] Yet, however creative the legal planner may be, in the end he will find that all his patterns are merely variations of one theme: the limitation of State sovereignty, and they will vary chiefly according to the degree to which it is assumed that such restrictions are acceptable to potential member States.

But this formulation, so generally used, hides rather than reveals what in any such case is meant to happen. Any limitation of the jurisdiction of one entity in favour of another means an extension of the latter's jurisdiction. Thus, any limitation, including the undertaking to renounce the exercise of a particular jurisdiction, involves a transfer of jurisdiction. In the last-mentioned case, this is the right to command the non-exercise of the jurisdiction in question. Therefore, whenever jurisdiction is transferred, it is transferred from one person or group of persons to another person or group of persons.[22] Extension of the scope of international institutions means the transfer of jurisdiction from national " élites " and civil services to their international and supra-national counterparts. This explains why it is so easy to engender ardent enthusiasm in the abstract for the extension of the Rule of Law in international relations and further international integration, but why, otherwise than on regional or sectional levels, words tend to outrun deeds.

20 See above, p. 276.
21 See below, p. 288 *et seq.*, and further, *Power Politics* (1951), Part Three, and, for the application of this method to international institutions, *l.c.*, note 1, above, Chap. 12.
22 See further, 10 *C.L.P.* (1957), p. 264 *et seq.*

CHAPTER 13

SCOPE AND LIMITS OF INTERNATIONAL LEGISLATION

INTERNATIONAL law-making by means of treaties has assumed such a scale as to make necessary not only the creation of an international legislative drafting bureau,[1] but also of another new branch of international law : that of international legislation. One of the chief tasks of this branch might be to concern itself with the factors which, at any time in the evolution of international law, determine the functional frontiers of the law of nations. As it is, these determinants remain somewhat inarticulate. The unavoidable consequence is that, more often than not, international law-makers either stray—or are led against their better instincts—beyond the functional optimum frontiers of their time or fail to make the fullest possible use of their opportunities.

The factors which condition the functional scope of international law may be called field-determining agencies. Three of these agencies may claim to be of special significance : the degree of integration of international society or any of its segments, the measure of structural uniformity of States, and the value of their ethical common denominator.

Some instances of international law-making since 1945 will provide suitable illustrations of both wisdom and folly in international legislation.

I—THE INTEGRATION OF INTERNATIONAL SOCIETY

In view of the central place of the Charter of the United Nations in present-day international organisation, this " new international order "[2] deserves pride of place in any such examination.

In an age of world powers and world wars, the whole world forms necessarily one single activity area of international power politics. Objectively, therefore, the integration of international society has reached a point which makes world peace the only

---

[1] C. W. Jenks, *The Need for an International Legislative Drafting Bureau*, 39 *A.J.I.L.* (1945), p. 163 *et seq.* and *The Common Law of Mankind* (1958), p. 408 *et seq.*

[2] *Report of the International Law Commission Covering its First Session* (1949— U.N. Doc. A/1/925), p. 8. See further, *Power Politics*, p. 427 *et seq.*

alternative to world chaos. The only question that remains is whether, subjectively, integration has kept pace with the objective integration of international society into one world society for purposes of peace and war.

In the Preamble to the Charter of the United Nations, its members have asserted their resolve to meet the chief challenge to our age in a constructive spirit. They have proclaimed the determination of the peoples of the United Nations to "save succeeding generations from the scourge of war, which twice in our lifetime has brought untold sorrow to mankind." In Article 1 of the Charter, they have made the maintenance of international peace and security the prime purpose of the United Nations.

When the means by which this objective is to be attained are examined, they appear to be as sensible as might be expected in any confederation of States. They show a reasonable balance between emphasis on the peaceful settlement of international disputes and on collective security. A reservation is perhaps advisable regarding the lack of interest which the draftsmen of the Charter showed in problems of peaceful change and the regulation of national armaments. These, however, are minor flaws in a system which is foolproof so long as one condition is fulfilled : concord between the permanent members of the Security Council. If the draftsmen of the Charter were mistaken in this basic assumption, and experience has proved that they were, the United Nations is constitutionally incapable of fulfilling its appointed task of maintaining international peace.[3]

Does this imply that the signatories of the Charter did not mean what they so solemnly proclaimed in the Preamble and Article 1 of the Charter of the United Nations? It may be taken for granted that they all wanted peace and that, even now, this is still true. The world Powers cherished, however, and continue to cherish, another good even more than the agreed common good of world peace : their freedom of action. It is of little consequence whether this is described as sovereignty or one's own cherished way of life. The fact remains that each of the world Powers made its acceptance of the Charter dependent on acquiescence by the other members of the United Nations in its privileged position in the "new world order."[4]

This situation presented the draftsmen of the United Nations

[3] See above, p. 146 *et seq.*
[4] See further *Power Politics*, p. 443 *et seq.*, and 10 *C.L.P.* (1957), p. 264 *et seq.*

with a dilemma. Were they to confess failure to the peace-hungry nations or to attempt to square the circle? In accordance with the age-old motto of opportunism that half a loaf is better than no bread at all, they provided a questionable substitute for a true international order and tried their best to convince themselves and the world at large that the result of their labours had all the appearances of at least half a loaf of bread.

The devices which served to give legal shape to this new system of power politics in disguise were simple. Each of the permanent members of the Security Council had been granted the right of veto in all but procedural matters.[5] While a member which is a party to a dispute may not vote in proceedings under Chapter Six of the Charter, it is free to do so when it comes to the application of enforcement measures under Chapter Seven. The veto applies to other important activities of the United Nations, such as the admission of new members and the revision of the Charter. In the General Assembly the majority principle applies, but primary responsibility for maintaining world peace rests with the Security Council. If, however, the General Assembly should concern itself with such matters, it is limited to the function of making mere recommendations. Finally, the architects of post-1945 peace built into the Charter the escape clauses of Articles 51 and 107. On these rest the defensive alliances which the world camps have concluded against each other with growing speed and intensity of effort.[6]

The reasons for the impotence of the United Nations in the East-West cleavage are no mystery. At Dumbarton Oaks, Yalta and San Francisco, the United Nations attempted to have the best of both worlds : power politics and a world community. Even in the relations between the wartime allies, subjective integration had not reached a degree which would have permitted the transformation of their society relations into those of a true international community. The result was what might have been expected: another system of power politics in disguise.[7]

Counter-examples to the United Nations which have taken into account this field-determining agency are provided by the political, economic and military integration—inside each of the world camps. In each of these one of the super-Powers occupies a hegemonial

[5] See also above, p. 59 *et seq.*
[6] See above, p. 154 *et seq.*
[7] See further *Power Politics*, p. 695 *et seq.*

position.[8]   Political and military co-operation under the North
Atlantic Treaty and international economic co-operation inside the
Western camp are paralleled by corresponding co-ordination in all
three fields within the Eastern bloc.   This sectional integration is
not, however, accompanied by comparable efforts on the universal
level of the United Nations.[9]

II—Structural Uniformity

Classical international law could largely ignore the internal structure
of the subjects of international law ; for its functional scope only
touched the fringes of the problem.   It was limited to the protection
of foreigners who might be affected by the low standards of government in any particular country.[10]   Exceptional instances of humanitarian intervention were based more often than not on the consent
of the Power directly concerned, usually the Ottoman Empire.[11]
At times, changes in the internal structure of States put a temporary
strain on accepted principles of international law.   Thus, the increase
at a different pace in the scope of economic State activities in various
countries raised the question whether such State enterprises were
entitled to the immunities freely granted to more traditional forms
of State activity abroad.   Yet even in these instances, a broad reciprocity of rights and duties under international law remained
unimpaired ; for, corresponding to the expansion of the sphere of
State immunity, the sphere of direct State responsibility for such
economic activities automatically extended.[12]

In attempts at bringing to life the rather vague references to the
protection of human rights in the Charter of the United Nations,[13]
the field-determining agency of structural uniformity of the members
of the United Nations cannot, however, be ignored.

The first question that arises is whether States which, in principle,
are willing to safeguard human rights are prepared to protect them
not only by their own municipal law, but also to undertake treaty
obligations to this effect towards all other members of the United
Nations.   To this extent, the problem is one of the subjective conditions of international integration.   There remains, however, the

---

8 See further 10 *C.L.P.* (1957), p. 264 *et seq.* and 13 *Y.B.W.A.* (1959), p. 236 *et seq.*
9 See below, p. 300 *et seq.*
10 See above, pp. 55 and 130 *et seq.*
11 See above, p. 141 *et seq.*
12 See above, p. 32 *et seq.*
13 See further *Power Politics*, p. 613 *et seq.*

distinct issue of the minimum of objective structural uniformity of
parties to such a treaty.

During the Second World War and in its aftermath, international
lawyers and the public at large have been treated to learned comparative studies in the world's constitutions. From these it apparently
emerges that there may be some minor differences in emphasis in
Western as compared with Eastern, and in democratic as compared
with authoritarian and totalitarian constitutions. Nevertheless, we
are told, these discrepancies are smaller than might be expected.
Thus, the Soviet Constitution of 1936 (as well as its 1947 version)
has a whole chapter on fundamental rights and duties of citizens.
These rights include inviolability of person and home, privacy of
correspondence and freedom of speech, of the press, of assembly
and demonstration. The catalogue of rights and duties of citizens
in the Czechoslovak Constitution of 1948 is still more elaborate. It
is only equalled by the generous provisions of the Charter of the
Spanish People of 1945, in itself a significant date.

Such argument ignores but one minor point : the real structure,
as distinct from the democratic façade, of totalitarian States. Their
constitutions are made primarily for export. Suppression of the
individual and denial of human rights whenever it suits the powers
that be can hardly be regarded as regrettable exceptions and excesses
in any of these States. Personal insecurity and constant fear harboured
by the subjects of totalitarian States, omnipotence of the secret police,
ill-treatment and torture of innocent and suspect alike as well as of
their families, forced labour and concentration camps, and refusal
of passports to those who have no greater desire than to escape
from this particular brand of " democracy," are of the essence of
such systems. Such changes as have been made in the post-Stalinist
phase of socialist legality are, as yet, too recent to be taken at their
face value.[14]

Would it have been too much to expect from those responsible
for the activities of the United Nations that they should have drawn
the obvious conclusion from the fundamental heterogeneity in
structure of the member States of the United Nations, and that they
should have adjourned *ad Calendas Graecas* all proposals for universal covenants of human rights? On the contrary, they approached
this task with a remarkable sense of urgency, displaying considerable

[14] See above, p. 175 *et seq.*

originality in developing novel techniques of escapism from a disagreeable reality.

On December 10, 1948, the General Assembly approved a Declaration of Human Rights, embodying twenty-eight fundamental rights and one article on the duties of the individual. Some of the articles of the Declaration are in the best traditions of Liberalism and social democracy and are hardly-disguised attacks on totalitarianism. Others have been duly censored as being " couched in language which is calculated to mislead and which is vividly reminiscent of international instruments in which an ingenious form of words serves the purpose of concealing the determination of States to retain full freedom of action." [15] The novelty value of the Declaration lies, however, in its self-confessed lack of legally binding force. It is meant to be a " common standard of achievement for all peoples and all nations." [16] In the debates which preceded the adoption of the Declaration, the non-committal character of the Declaration was duly stressed by the speakers of most delegations. In fairness, it must be added that, at the same time, they fervently emphasised the distinct moral value of this epoch-making event.

The Declaration may be regarded as being only an interim measure. In due course, it is to be strengthened by a Covenant on Human Rights, with the drafting of which the Human Rights Commission and the General Assembly of the United Nations have been occupied for years. Yet is it not sufficient indication of what will be in store for this draft Covenant to remember that nine States abstained from voting even on the Declaration? These included the Soviet Union, Czechoslovakia, and the Union of South Africa, all States in which, to say the least, the protection of human rights is somewhat problematic. Is it expected that these States will become parties to a legally binding instrument such as a Covenant on Human Rights? Even if they did, would they be likely to agree to the submission to an international body of controversies regarding the interpretation and application of the Covenant? Assuming that this miracle, too, could be performed, how is the evidence for alleged breaches of the Covenant to be obtained from any of the totalitarian States? Finally, how is such a Covenant to be enforced

[15] H. Lauterpacht, *The Universal Declaration of Human Rights,* 25 *B.Y.I.L.* (1948), p. 373.
[16] On such constructive effects as can possibly be claimed for the Declaration, see E. Schwelb, *The Influence of the Universal Declaration of Human Rights on International and National Law, Proceedings of the American Society of International Law* (1959), p. 217 *et seq.*

unless by war or by the self-elimination of such totalitarian States? Thus, a universal Declaration and Covenant may provide admirable programmes for another world crusade, but they strain present-day international law well beyond its functional optimum.

The lessons which had to be learned to avoid such dissipation of energy might have been derived from the non-implementation of the Articles on human rights in the Peace Treaties of 1947 with Bulgaria, Hungary and Rumania. These Treaties impose stringent obligations on the ex-satellites of the European Axis to secure to all persons under their jurisdiction, " without distinction as to race, sex, language or religion the enjoyment of human rights and of the fundamental freedoms, including freedom of expression, of press and publication, of religious worship, of political opinion and of public meeting." The treaties further provide for an arbitration procedure which is to apply in the case of disputes concerning their interpretation or execution. Yet all these clauses are continuously flouted by these ex-enemy States with the exception of Finland ; for they know that they can rely on approval of their policies from the Kremlin.[17]

If States, which basically believe in the rule of law in the Western sense and in the freedom of the individual, covenant with one another for the international protection of human rights, the position is entirely different ; for such a treaty is primarily of a declaratory character. It serves to create a common denominator and to ensure the maintenance of these standards in the exceptional cases in which the municipal law of one of the parties falls below the generally agreed minimum or fails to be adequately enforced. The European Convention on Human Rights offers an illustration of the constructive possibilities, and the limits, of the effective international protection of human rights in a more congenial environment than that of world society. All the States actively participating in this experiment [18] are broadly similar in their democratic structure. Beyond this, they may even claim that they share an extensive fund of common spiritual and ethical values.

III—THE ETHICAL COMMON DENOMINATOR

In the Preamble of the Statute of the Council of Europe it is asserted —with truth for most, but not for all, of its members— that they share " spiritual and moral values which are the common heritage

[17] See above, p. 177 *et seq.*
[18] See above, p. 74.

of their peoples and the true source of individual freedom, political liberty and the rule of law, principles which form the basis of all genuine democracy." For an official document, this passage shows remarkable insight. One is only left wondering why the same Powers do not consider the reverse proposition to be equally true when they sit down together with representatives of totalitarian States to draft universal declarations and covenants on human rights or on the freedom of the press.

Be this as it may, there is an ethical minimum on which, at any time, the functional scope of international law depends as much as on any of the other field-determining agencies. The least that even in so rudimentary a legal system as that of international law every State must expect from every other State is that it will carry out in good faith its obligations under international customary law and treaties to which it is a party.[19] The more ambitious international law-makers are, the more heavily they tax such faith in the pledged word.

In the relations inside each of the world camps, the hegemonial position of each of the super-Powers, common ideologies and fear of the intentions of the other bloc forge bonds likely to stand considerable pressure. In the relations between the two worlds, the value of their ethical common denominator becomes of overriding importance; for, ultimately, there is merely one sanction with which either side can visit the other's bad faith: war. Short of this extreme step,[20] even satellite States can make a laughing stock of solemnly concluded peace treaties, or, as in the case of Albania, ignore jauntily a judgment of the World Court.[21]

It is unnecessary to reiterate the evidence for the low level of the ethical fund still shared between the two world camps.[22] If further proof were required it would be furnished by the slow motion picture of the Geneva Conference on the ban of further nuclear tests.

In these circumstances, to think of a treaty between the nuclear Powers on the international control of nuclear energy appears somewhat unrealistic. The distrust of the Western Powers in the good faith of the Soviet Union is such that a treaty of this kind would require a degree of interference with internal affairs to which the Soviet Union could not be expected to agree. Nothing less, however,

---

[19] See above, pp. 33 and 177, and further *Fundamental Principles*, p. 290 *et seq.*
[20] See above, p. 148 *et seq.*
[21] See above, pp. 151 and 177 *et seq.*
[22] See above, p. 146 *et seq.*

could induce the United States to discontinue the production of nuclear weapons or to destroy her own stocks of such weapons. In any case, such a treaty would not cover all the other means of mass destruction such as those of chemical and biological warfare. Thus, an agreement on the international control of nuclear energy would still leave unsolved problems as big as it might settle. To control all these preparations for war would mean to subject to international control whole branches of theoretical and applied research and of national industries. States which are not even willing to establish an international order on the level postulated by the purposes and principles of the United Nations are not likely to pay so high a price for peace.

When such an impasse is reached, international law can do little to assist in breaking the vicious circle. At all times it can merely give legal expression to such unity of purpose as exists. It must leave the major issues of co-existence in a divided world to the wisdom and self-restraint of those in whose power it is to unleash the storm of a Third World War, and to the stabilising elements in this precarious equipoise of agglomerations of power.

By assisting in the growing integration of the non-Communist world, Western international lawyers can help to make sure that, at least, this equilibrium will be maintained.[23] Thus, the East-West cleavage need not stand in the way of further extension of the functional frontiers of international law within the Western world. If anything, the common danger may give additional impetus to such trends.

CHAPTER 14

THE PROSPECTS FOR INTERNATIONAL LAW

INTERNATIONAL law has survived astonishingly well the host of ingenious horoscopes cast regarding its future by magi in many lands.[1] Some have been prophets of gloom and have prognosticated its impending breakdown. Others have purported to see a constellation of circumstances which promises an unexpectedly bright future for the weakling in the laws family.

When, at times, such astrologers appear in groups, it is not sufficient to explain their emergence in terms of individual psychology; for, like the phenomenon which they analyse, they themselves are very much the product of their environment. Allowing for exceptions, they fall into two categories which are fairly closely related to the cycles of pre- and post-war periods. For the sake of brevity, and without disrespect, they may be named the " pre-war " and " post-war " schools.

Whenever an existing balance of power system tends to decline, the Powers bent on its overthrow direct some of their preliminary and diversionist attacks against its legal superstructure. Their propagandists—and, not infrequently, bona fide students of international law—tend to explain, and excuse, breaches of cumbersome treaties and promises with profound reflections on the weakness of international law in general and more or less ingenious arguments which provide a quasi-sociological ideology for acts of sheer international lawlessness.[2]

This type of situation is the normal background for the usually destructive reasoning of the " pre-war " school of thought. During the subsequent upheaval of a major war, belligerents charge one another—and neutrals charge both the warring camps—with alleged and real infractions of the rules of warfare and neutrality.[3]

---

[1] To enable readers to judge for themselves this evaluation, and the methods on which it is based, in the light of their own assessments of the evolution of international law since the Second World War, the text of this Chapter has been left in substance as it had been written in November, 1945.
See also above, p. 5.

[2] See further the present writer's *International Law and Totalitarian Lawlessness* (1943), p. 13 *et seq.*

[3] See *ibid.*, p. 30 *et seq.*

Unless, as happened in the case of the totalitarian aggressors, one side itself confesses its open disdain for the standards of civilisation and the very notion of international law, belligerents are usually very forthright in making liberal promises regarding the reign of law they intend to establish once victory has been achieved. This situation provides a starting-off point for the " post-war " school. Taking such official manifestos too literally—or too seriously—the disciples of this school have a tendency to sin as much on the side of unrestrained day-dreaming as the " pre-war " school sins by trading in unmitigated gloom.

If there were no alternative to a choice between these two schools, the " post-war " idealists would probably be the lesser evil. As they do not challenge the reality of international law, they do less harm to the object of their inquiry than the " pre-war " fraternity. The overstatements of the " pre-war " school are not limited to the vulnerable parts of international law—the law of power which merely serves as an ideological cover for the requirements of international political strategy [4]—but are directed against the fabric of the law of nations as a whole. By way of contrast, followers of the " post-war " school habitually make it their business to acclaim in optimistic anticipation, as an alternative to power politics, legal superstructures such as the League of Nations which, seen in retrospect, are little more than rather thin disguises of the rule of force.[5] They might have fared better if they had adopted an attitude of waiting, seeing, and judging by results rather than by the good intentions displayed in pious resolutions and patient charters.

In spite of their diametrically differing conclusions, both schools have in common a feature which explains one of their deficiencies in method : neither pays sufficient attention to the social realities underlying international law, that is to say, international society, and they fail to take into proper account the peculiarities of the driving forces in it and its specific structure.[6] While the " pre-war " school underestimates the possibilities left even in a system of power politics to international law, the " post-war " school ignores the inherent limitations imposed by power politics on international law. Any prognosis of the course which international law is likely to take in the years to come must try to avoid equally the " realism " of the one, and the " idealism " of the other, school.

[4] See above, pp. 11 and 25 *et seq.*
[5] See above, pp. 24 and 251 *et seq.*
[6] See above, p. 21 *et seq.*

The pattern on which international law is most likely to develop in the post-war years to come is conditioned by the world order—or rather quasi-world order—represented by the United Nations. As, in kind, the United Nations does not differ from the League of Nations, it appears unnecessary formally to distinguish this type of international law from that of the League period. Yet in order to bring out its specific features it may be helpful first to sketch the pattern of pre-1914 international law and, finally, to consider whether there are any other patterns of order and law which can assist in the further integration of international society.

I—THE PRE-1914 PATTERN OF INTERNATIONAL LAW

International law, as it developed between the Napoleonic wars and the First World War, is distinguished by two salient features :

The first is the *Principle of National Sovereignty.* To the extent to which the absolute freedom of a State is not limited by rules of international law, a State remains free to do what it likes, and all matters with regard to which its freedom of action is not restricted remain within its exclusive jurisdiction.[7]

The second is the *Principle of Consent.* Unless it can be shown that a legal rule is universally or generally recognised as forming part of the body of international customary law, it is not binding on a State that has not given its express or tacit consent.[8]

An individualistic legal system of this kind may be adequate in an exceptionally static social environment or between groups which only rarely come into contact with each other. While the second assumption applied only in the beginnings of contemporary international society,[9] the first would be a singularly misleading description of the expansion of the original European State system into present-day world society.[10]

In so dynamic an environment, a system of international law, in which changes were subject to a veto reminiscent of the ancient Polish Diet, could be expected to work only on the condition of all concerned showing continuously superhuman restraint. Was a State that had made what it considered to be a reasonable request to leave it at that, if the other party refused to comply with its demand?

7 See above, p. 25, and further *Fundamental Principles*, p. 214 *et seq.*
8 See above, p. 36, and further *Fundamental Principles*, p. 262 *et seq.*
9 See above, p. 43 *et seq.*
10 See above, p. 51 *et seq.*

Or was it to be expected that a State should make concessions merely in order to appease a persistent and embarrassing member of international society?

Provided that States had a certain modicum of strength, they were spared having to ponder over such difficult issues of international morality. If they wanted anything badly enough and felt strong enough to take it, they did so, and if a State felt confident that it might successfully resist the demands of an aggressor, it would stand up for its rights. Thus, the question whether any existing equilibrium was to be disturbed depended ultimately on the issue whether any particular State was prepared to throw its whole existence into the scales.

Admittedly, naturalist writers on international law attempted to distinguish between just and unjust wars. Yet there hardly ever was a war which, according to their rather elastic criteria, could not somehow be justified.[11] Even the pretence of such a distinction was subsequently abandoned, and States had no longer to find quasi-legal excuses for doing what, in any case, they had decided to do.[12] Thus, pre-1914 international law was either subservient to international politics—a typical example of the Law of Power [13]—or limited to fields which, from the point of view of the rule of force, were irrelevant. Here there was a certain scope for the assertion of the two other types of law, the Law of Reciprocity [14] and, in embryo, the Law of Co-ordination.[15] If, over prolonged periods, this international anarchy was not quite as obvious as might have been expected, this was due to the international quasi-order represented by the Concert of Europe.[16] As long as the Greater Powers were in general agreement, there was a semblance of order, but the alternative to unanimity was chaos.

II—INTERNATIONAL LAW
WITHIN THE FRAMEWORK OF THE UNITED NATIONS

The crucial issue of comprehensive international institutions such as the League of Nations or the United Nations is not necessarily whether they form an alternative to power politics. It would be no

11 See above, p. 236 *et seq.*
12 See above, p. 240 *et seq.*
13 See above, pp. 11 and 25 *et seq.*
14 See above, pp. 15 and 29 *et seq.*
15 See above, pp. 13 and 34 *et seq.*
16 See further *Power Politics*, p. 178 *et seq*

small thing if their existence reversed the traditional relations between the rule of force and international law, that is to say, limited power politics to forms of pressure short of the application of physical force. With reservations, which created dangerous loop-holes, the draftsmen of the League Covenant and of the Kellogg Pact attempted to achieve this result and failed.[17] Now again the Parties to the new collective system voice their determination to " save succeeding generations from the scourge of war, which twice in our lifetime has brought untold sorrow to mankind " ; they define as the primary purpose of the United Nations the maintenance of international peace and security and enunciate the principle that " all members shall refrain in their international relations from the threat or use of force against the territorial integrity or political independence of any State, or in any other manner inconsistent with the purpose of the United Nations."

Experience has shown that most States at most times keep their international obligations. The negative implication of this statement makes it necessary, however, to scrutinise the other side of the picture. As long as none of the permanent members of the Security Council becomes guilty of infractions of the Charter of the United Nations, the coercive machinery of the Organisation appears perfectly satisfactory. Yet in so far as these five Powers are concerned, they are able by their veto to exempt themselves from the sanctions of the law they may contravene. Thus, in fact, they are as much above the law as any sovereign State was in the pre-1914 period.

If evidence were required to prove the reality of this contention, it is furnished by the fact that some of these Powers, at present, have the monopoly of the atomic bomb and—to use the words of the Atomic Charter [18]—other methods of warfare, " which may constitute as great a threat to civilisation as the military use of atomic energy." It may be hoped that the present state of affairs is merely of a temporary character until the United Nations Commission has made its recommendations. It remains, however, to be seen whether the Powers will take the recommendations of this Commission more seriously than their predecessors took those of the various disarmament conferences during the interval between the First and Second World Wars.[19]

---

[17] See further *Fundamental Principles*, p. 327 *et seq.*, and *Vol. II*, Chaps. 1 and 2.
[18] Statement issued on November 15, 1945, by the President of the United States, the Prime Minister of the United Kingdom, and the Prime Minister of Canada. *The Times* newspaper, November 16, 1945.
[19] See further *Power Politics*, p. 534 *et seq.*

As long as, in fact, the monopoly in weapons of such destructive force exists, it amounts to the emergence of a new type of super-Leviathan which is incomparably more powerful than other States which formerly called themselves sovereign States. From a realistic point of view, the attribute of sovereignty can be applied today only to States which either have at their disposal weapons of cosmic warfare or are able to minimise the effects of the application of such weapons against themselves.[20]

The main difference which, therefore, exists between the post-1945 and the pre-1914 systems of international organisation is the amazing reduction in the number of *de facto* sovereign States.[21] Believers in the *laissez-faire* principle in international affairs may deduce from this development that the dialectics of world society will ultimately bring about the completion of this trend towards world centralisation, provided that what is left will be considered worth organising into a world State.

In so far as the small hierarchy of world Powers is concerned, their position is more analogous to the position of sovereign States under pre-1914 international law than to that of smaller States under the Charter of the United Nations.

The position is not very different if we inquire whether, in the Charter of the United Nations, an alternative has been evolved to the principle of consent, the other corner-stone of classical international law. Again, if allowance is made for the exceptional position of the permanent members of the Security Council, the United Nations Charter makes provision both for the maintenance of collective security and for peaceful change, the two concomitants of international order. The competences granted to the Security Council regarding the settlements of disputes which are likely to endanger international peace and security are more than ample to deal with conflicts between lesser States. Even a member of the Security Council must abstain from voting if it is itself a party to a dispute. Whether this means what it purports to mean, only the future can tell.

A member of the Security Council may take a detached attitude towards a dispute with one of the parties which happens to belong to its " security zone " or it may regard any adverse opinion not only as directed against that State, but also as impairing its own

---

20 See further above, p. 279, and 10 *C.L.P.* (1957), p. 264 *et seq.*
21 See further above, p. 58 *et seq.*, and *Power Politics*, p. 113 *et seq.*

prestige. Should one of the permanent members of the Council be a party to a dispute and be forced to abstain from voting, this self-denying ordinance does not extend to the all-important Chapter Seven of the Charter: " Action with respect to Threats to the Peace, Breaches of the Peace, and Acts of Aggression." Thus it appears that in this field also things have not changed so very much in so far as the great ones of this earth are concerned.

There is still no proper international order on which international law may securely rest. The Concert of Europe, balance of power systems, or the principle of the unanimity of the world Powers are at the best substitutes with two world wars on their debit side. If the relations between the members of the Security Council were such as to make war between them unthinkable, the formal survival of veto powers might not be very significant.

It cannot be denied that between the United States of America and the Soviet Union, the two foremost power units in our atomic age, there are no actual or potential conflicts of interest on which a peaceful compromise should not be possible. Equally, more than ever today, the interests of the British Commonwealth are identical with those of world order and peace. It may also be assumed that the other members of the Security Council—world Powers by courtesy rather than otherwise—will not themselves willingly initiate another major conflagration.

Yet, it must not be overlooked that, as compared with the nine-teenth century, our age suffers from a new cleavage, the split of the world into two, if not three, ideological camps. The United States of America has become identified with all the positive and negative feelings which are associated with private enterprise, monopoly capitalism, and economic conservatism. The Soviet Union appears to stand for State socialism and social planning, even at the price of serious restrictions of personal freedom. The United Kingdom and the Continent of Europe are in the midst of working out a synthesis which will allow them to combine the positive features of both ways of life, that is to say, the dignity of the individual with social security. This means that the conception of national sovereignty now protects values which, whether actual or fictitious, mean something to millions all over the world.

It may be hoped that each of the world Powers looks in a spirit of toleration at the social pattern practised by the others and rather wishes to learn from them than to spread its own brand of temporary happiness. It would, however, be unsafe to assume, that, once the memory of the common struggle against the enemies of world civilisation recedes into the background, the world Powers will not again take an eristic view of these ideological differences. Thus, any prognosis of the prospects of international law has to be made with the reservation that the foundations of international law are as dubious as they ever were, unless comfort is derived from the decreasing number of really sovereign States or from the increase in the destructive powers wielded by the super-Leviathans.

The Charter of the United Nations envisages, and provides scope for, a variety of techniques which may contribute to the further development of international law.

Codification

The General Assembly is expressly charged with the duties of initiating studies and making recommendations for the progressive development of international law and its codification. To judge by the experiences of the attempted codification of subjects such as the law of territorial waters, responsibility of States, or neutrality under the auspices of the League of Nations or of the results of the Hague Codification Conference of 1930, not too much should be expected from this direct approach to the problem. The results of fifty years' efforts might be expected to have dampened the enthusiasm of those who tended to overestimate the significance of codifications of municipal law and the applicability of this technique to international law.[22]

As happened during the Hague Conferences of 1899 and 1907, frequently the price of formal agreement on a controversial issue was a vagueness that perpetuated the possibilities of conflicting interpretations. Or, as may be seen from the official replies to the various League questionnaires, *ex abundanti cautela*, Foreign Offices added so many qualifications to what had been considered perfectly straightforward rules of international customary law that the attempts at codification merely compromised formerly unchallenged principles of international customary law. Yet, as happens so often in the case of ill-judged progressive moves, their by-products are so much more valuable than the efforts themselves; and, in this case, these were the private and official studies which had been prepared for purposes of documentation.

22 See further *Manual*, Vol. 1, p. 367 *et seq.*

International Case Law

The International Court of Justice has the same scope as the Permanent Court of International Justice had within the framework of the League of Nations. As under the Statute of the Permanent Court of International Justice, States remain their own masters whether they desire to submit legal disputes to the World Court. Yet, in future, the Court will have more opportunities to give guidance by means of advisory opinions than were open to the Permanent Court of International Justice.

While the League Court was authorised to render advisory opinions at the request of the Assembly or Council of the League of Nations alone, the General Assembly of the United Nations may authorise other organs of the United Nations and specialised agencies to request advisory opinions of the Court on legal questions arising within the scope of their activities.

If it is recalled that, in the past, not even the International Labour Organisation had direct access to the Permanent Court of International Justice, the progress made is considerable, provided that the General Assembly confers the privilege on all suitable institutions. Such a policy would enable the International Court of Justice to make a still greater contribution than was made by the Permanent Court of International Justice to the law of international institutions, one of the most constructive and most neglected branches of international law.[23]

To judge by the work of the Permanent Court of International Justice, the most significant aspect of the new Court will not be its achievement of actual settlements—the mere fact that States classify a particular dispute as legal is an indication of its relative insignificance[24]—but the body of case law that may be expected from the practice of the Court.

The Statute of the International Court of Justice reaffirms the Article of the Statute of the Permanent Court of International Justice that the decisions of the Court have no binding force except between the parties and in respect of that particular case. In the case of an advisory opinion, there are no parties, and, therefore, such opinions have no legally binding force whatsoever. Yet the persuasive authority of a well-reasoned decision or advisory opinion, given by a bench composed of the world's leading international lawyers, is greater than

[23] See above, p. 274 *et seq.*
[24] See above, p. 150 *et seq.*

that of the most illuminating views held on any subject in this field by individual writers.

Although no miracles should be expected, a slow but sure enrichment of international law by the practice of the International Court may be taken for granted as long as States do their part, that is to say, submit a sufficient number of disputes to the Court, and thus keep the mills of justice grinding.[25]

Institutional Integration

Corresponding to the widening scope and growing intensity of international relations, the need for international collaboration in matters as diverse as economic, financial, social, cultural and educational relations is likely to call for an expansion in existing international institutions and the creation of new agencies. Yet it should not be overlooked that, in these spheres, underlying differences in outlook and social organisations may in some cases make the creation of a universal international institution inadvisable and may call for closer collaboration between States of a similar type or on a regional basis. Nevertheless, inter-Allied wartime institutions have proved to what extent even States organised as differently as the United States and the Soviet Union can work together in international institutions, provided that there is an overriding object, and they are determined to make the experiment a success.

Further development along the road of functional international integration may benefit from two lessons of the past.

First, international institutions are likely to achieve the maximum of efficiency in inverse proportion to their dependence on Foreign Offices. A comparison between the achievements of the Universal Postal Union and the International Telegraphic Union [26] will explain the reason. Until Foreign Offices have disabused their minds of thinking in terms of power politics first and foremost—which, in a system of power politics, they can hardly be expected to do—it is hard for them to consider any issue in terms of the intrinsic merits of this or that solution, and functional integration depends upon an attitude of mind which springs from intimate knowledge and professional enthusiasm.

Secondly, there is no surer way of killing initiative than to reduce such institutions to the sterility of mere deliberative and resolution-

---

25 See above, p. 150, and further *Vols. I* and *II*, and 4 *C.L.P.* (1951), p. 1 *et seq.*
26 Transformed in 1934 into the International Telecommunication Union.

producing bodies. Even a cursory perusal of the International Labour Code, published by the International Labour Office, shows how much useful work was done in vain. There is no reason why conventions adopted by the International Labour Conference with the required qualified majority should not become automatically binding on member States.[27]

Progress in the institutional sphere is not only likely to contribute to the further stabilisation of international society, but also to the growth of entirely new branches of international law. In fields such as international economic, financial, and labour law, promising beginnings have been made, although they have hardly yet received sufficient attention from the academic international lawyer.[28] Apart from the fact that these subjects are practically important, they are valuable from the point of view of the teacher; for they help to weigh the balance within the system of international law still further against the Law of Power, and in favour of the Law of Reciprocity. While the former is but an embarrassment and handmaid of the rule of force, the latter derives its validity from the reciprocal interests of the members of international society in its observance, and restrains any potential transgressor by the threat of exclusion from the benefits accruing from such reciprocal relation.[29]

Functional integration of world society need not be conceived on exclusively universal lines. Links between some States may allow for more intensified co-ordination of efforts than, at the present stage, may be called for on a world-wide scale. This may either be due to affinities, as they exist between the members of the British Commonwealth, or to geographic considerations, as they apply among States situated in America or in other regions of the world.[30] As long as such closer unions are not planned with any antagonistic objects in mind,[31] but for a common purpose, they may fulfil a special function which follows from their experimental and pioneering character. If they are a success, they invite repetition on a larger scale. Thus, the post-1919 experiment in the organisation of European air transport or the co-operation of the American States in the Pan-American Union[32] offer material that is taken from actual life and, for this reason, is superior to any, however perfect, blue-print.

[27] See further *Manual*, Vol. 1, p. 260 *et seq.*
[28] See above, p. 210 *et seq.*
[29] See above, pp. 9 and 21 *et seq.*
[30] See above, p. 223, and *Manual*, Vol. 1, p. 329 *et seq.*
[31] See above, p. 285, and *Manual*, Vol. 1, p. 355 *et seq.*
[32] Incorporated in 1948 in the Organisation of American States.

Apart from the danger that regional or sectional international institutions may become vehicles of centrifugal tendencies, the fact that the benefits to be derived from such efforts may be primarily limited to one region does not necessarily speak against the desirability of a universal international institution. The reconstruction of devastated areas, the establishment of an international administration for the Danube on the lines of the Tennessee Valley Authority, and the work of UNRRA in Europe and the Far East are all tasks the principal benefits of which will not accrue to the United States of America or to the British Commonwealth. Yet, without their full support, no such scheme could hope to be a success.

It is the privilege of a world Power to be associated with everything of significance that happens anywhere in the world. This explains why, even without apparent reciprocity, support for such schemes may be expected from such Powers. The fact that world Powers themselves take such a line—a recent instance was provided by the Conference regarding the re-establishment of the International Régime in Tangier [32a]—in itself suggests that it would be wise to tread cautiously in so far as any apparently exclusive development of international law and institutions is concerned.

Fundamental Rights and Freedoms

It is a healthy reaction against the rigid positivism of a bygone period that attention is increasingly paid both to the moral and spiritual bases of international law as well as to the individual as the basic unit on which, ultimately, both national communities and international society rest.[33] When, during the age of imperialist expansion, international law ceased to be the public law of the European Christian States, it jettisoned its Christian basis in favour of rather vague standards applicable to all civilised nations, and an even more disastrous phase of international law commenced when every sovereign State as such was considered eligible to become a subject of international law. Had it not been for this lack of discrimination, the world might have noticed earlier than it did the anomaly of treating nations ruled by fascist gangsters as the equals of civilised communities.

It is thus perfectly understandable that the founders of the United Nations resolved to make the Organisation responsible for promoting

32a See further *Manual*, Vol. 1, p. 249, and Vol. 2, 442–443 and 456–458.
33 See above, pp. 65 and 130 *et seq.*

" respect for human rights and for fundamental freedoms for all without distinction as to race, sex, language, or religion." It is not, however, so easy to see how the compliance of the members with these principles is to be secured.[34]

In the Charter, all members have pledged themselves to take " joint and separate action " with the Organisation for the achievement of this purpose. Ultimate responsibility for the discharge of these functions will rest with the General Assembly and, under its authority, with the Economic and Social Council.

It is possible to imagine that the Economic and Social Council will draw up recommendations and draft conventions on the lines of constitutional and international precedents of bills and declarations of human rights. Yet what would happen if the General Assembly or the Security Council were asked to address themselves to an alleged breach of such standards as laid down in such resolutions or conventions?

Would the highest or lowest standard of achievement among the members of the United Nations have to be taken as the measuring rod? Are only such freedoms and rights as are recognised by all or the majority of the United Nations considered fundamental? Is the United Nations to concern itself with the question whether a member State secures such rights to its citizens both in law and in fact? Would any such investigation be outside the competence of the Organisation, as it would constitute an interference with " matters which are essentially within the domestic jurisdiction of any State "? Matters become still more complicated if the question is raised how, if at all, members could be compelled to remedy deficiencies in their government and administration, amounting to breaches of fundamental rights and freedoms.[35]

It may be replied that such principles are merely intended to give expression to the conscience of the world and that they share their weakness—and greatness—with other catalogues of moral precepts. Yet in a world which has applied international morality primarily as a useful means of propaganda,[36] a serious danger exists that such vague and undefined principles may be used as cloaks of

[34] See above, pp. 160 and 177.
[35] See further *Power Politics*, p. 627 *et seq.*
[36] See further *ibid.*, pp. 166 and 218 *et seq.*

intervention and as excuses for impairing the universal character of the Organisation.

This criticism is not meant to propose a wholesale abandonment of any attempt at realising this object of the United Nations. It is merely due to anxiety lest here—as in the field of international law in general—the use of speculative thinking leads to results not necessarily contemplated by the sponsors of these standards. It is, therefore, suggested that, in the initial stages, these principles should be applied empirically [37] as, for instance, in United Nations trust territories.

The promotion of these rights and freedoms has been expressly proclaimed as one of the chief objectives of the trusteeship system. As the Trusteeship Council includes all the permanent members of the Security Council and will probably contain a fair cross-section of the other members of the United Nations, this body may provide a useful testing ground for the more concrete formulation of principles which appear acceptable at least to a majority of the members of the Council with respect to territories under the sovereignty of the United Nations.[38] Similarly, on the precedent of the Philadelphia Charter adopted by the International Labour Organisation,[39] specialised international agencies might be encouraged to elaborate similar professional charters.

Or, in connection with the settlement of concrete political disputes, the Security Council or other organs, exercising quasi-legislative functions under agreements between the parties concerned, might make it a practice to pay attention to the adequate protection of fundamental human rights and freedoms. In this respect, the Minorities Treaties of 1919 and the German-Polish Convention regarding Upper Silesia of 1922 may be recalled.[40]

While the abstract approach chosen in the Charter of the United Nations is too vivid a reminder of eighteenth-century mentalities and ideologies, more concrete and realistic attempts to deal with individual issues within the competence of the United Nations in the spirit of the Charter might prepare the ground for more ambitious plans at a later stage.

[37] See above, p. 130 *et seq.*
[38] See further *Power Politics*, p. 648 *et seq.*
[39] May 10, 1944. See further *Power Politics*, pp. 323 and 587.
[40] See above, p. 31.

The Outlook for International Law on the Level of the United Nations

Subject to the reservation that international law still rests on the basis of a mere quasi-order,[41] the prospects for international law within the framework of the United Nations are not unpromising.

In principle, resort to armed force is outlawed. Compared with the Covenant of the League of Nations or the Kellogg Pact, the improvement is obvious. It is now a matter of complete indifference —if it was not so already in the past—whether a State merely resorts to the use of armed force or whether it means to resort to war in the full meaning of the term. Any threat or use of force, including reprisals and other coercive measures which involve the use of force, has been declared illegal.[42]

The " inherent right of individual or collective self-defence " has been subjected to the scrutiny of the Security Council and to its over-riding jurisdiction.[43] Between members of the United Nations neutrality has been replaced by collective responsibility : " All members shall give the United Nations every assistance in any action it takes in accordance with the present Charter, and shall refrain from giving assistance to any State against which the United Nations is taking preventive or enforcement action." [44]

If members are willing to settle their differences by means of their own choice, the United Nations provides ample machinery for the adjustment of legal and political disputes.[45] The International Court of Justice will do well if it only maintains the traditions and the prestige acquired by the Permanent Court of International Justice.

Should the miracle happen and, over a prolonged period, the members of the Security Council behave as guardians of world peace rather than advocates of their own interests, they would not only greatly contribute to the cause of order in international society, but they might elaborate in their practice a set of quasi-legislative principles, a body of international equity rules which might be applicable in similar cases.

While any picture of this kind may be dismissed as speculation coming dangerously near the statements of the " post-war " school, the case law to be expected from the International Court of Justice

---

[41] See above, pp. 24, 59, 146 and 209.
[42] See above, pp. 154 and 301.
[43] See above, pp. 155 and 279.
[44] See further above, p. 154, and *Power Politics*, p. 492 *et seq.*
[45] See further above, p. 150 *et seq.*, and *Power Politics*, p. 458 *et seq.*

and institutional integration of the international society on universal, regional and functional lines will probably form the most constructive aspects of the international law to come.

III—THE ASSIMILATION OF INTERNATIONAL TO MUNICIPAL LAW

To hold that power politics and war are inevitable consequences of the organisation of international society on the basis of sovereign States and empires, which, being sovereign, insist on their freedom of armaments, tends to become a commonplace. Yet, it appears to have required the advent of the atom bomb to induce statesmen to make declarations such as that " every succeeding discovery makes greater nonsense of old-time conceptions of sovereignty." [46] The problem is whether there is any practical means of removing the question-mark behind the United Nations pattern of international law.

At this point a parallel between international and municipal law may be helpful. In spite of Kelsen's identification of law and the State, it remains sociologically true that they are separate phenomena. Ultimately, the State is a power organisation, and law rests securely on this basis ; for the State insists on its monopoly of legitimate force, puts its overwhelming strength behind the law and, if necessary, forestalls revolution by additional machinery for the adaptation of the law to changing requirements. It does not appear that international order can be bought at a lesser price.

Even if nothing but the monopoly of armed force—or of weapons of cosmic warfare—were to be transferred from the State to world society, this would mean establishing a limited form of world government with a legally defined jurisdiction of its own. Every time sovereign States agreed to change a confederation into a federation, such a transformation of relations under international law into relations under municipal law took place.

So long as the central government is to be granted merely limited authority, and the residual powers remain with the member States of the union, the federal pattern compares favourably with any other. While it leaves open the possibility of further integration, it ensures to the constituent States the maximum of freedom in spheres which do not yet call for uniform regulation and an overriding central authority.[47]

[46] See further *Power Politics*, p. 551 *et seq.*
[47] See further *ibid.*, p. 804 *et seq.* and, on the functional variant of federation in the shape of supra-national institutions, above, pp. 206, 280 and 284, and further *Manual*, Vol. 1. p. 343 *et seq.*

Bearing in mind the vested political and economic interests bound up with the survival of sovereign States and empires, the emotional forces sustaining them and the lack of any comparable world loyalties, such a possibility may be dismissed as Utopian. Considered, however, in terms of the magnitude of the challenge which the occurrence of two world wars in one generation and the invention of unprecedented means of destruction present to world civilisation, a federal framework for world society and world law may provide a commensurate answer to a problem that the world may ignore at its peril.

INDEX

314

The London Institute of World Affairs

Founded 1934

c/o THE FACULTY OF LAWS, UNIVERSITY COLLEGE LONDON
GOWER STREET, LONDON, W.C.1

(i)

THE LONDON INSTITUTE OF WORLD AFFAIRS

Founded 1934

OBJECTS

The LONDON INSTITUTE OF WORLD AFFAIRS is a self-governing, independent research and teaching organisation for the study of world affairs.

The Institute seeks to achieve this object by the promotion of conferences, lectures, discussion groups and research upon the main problems of world affairs, and by its various publications. It is an unofficial body committed to no particular party and no particular ideology.

The membership of the Institute is international, and its activities are financed by the subscriptions and donations of its members, and by income from its various activities.

The minimum subscription is £2 2s. 0d. *per calendar year*.

Members receive the *Year Book of World Affairs* free of charge and post free, and are entitled to purchase volumes in the Library of World Affairs at a reduction of twenty-five *per cent.* below the published price, provided that such copies are ordered from the Secretary of the Institute.

The Institute is responsible for the full teaching programme in connection with the University of London Diploma in International Affairs (full time course), which extends over two years, and awards a Diploma in International and Comparative Air Law on the basis of an approved course of study.

THE INSTITUTE'S TEACHING PROGRAMME

DIPLOMA IN INTERNATIONAL AFFAIRS

This is a Diploma in the Humanities of the Extramural Department of the University of London, and the lectures for the full-time (day) course are the responsibility of the London Institute of World Affairs.

The Diploma course extends over two years, the subjects for the first year being:

> Modern International History
>
> International Law
>
> International Economics.

In the second year the subjects studied are:

> International Relations
>
> International Institutions
>
> International Economic Law.

The fees for the course are sixteen guineas each year.

Candidates for the Diploma are required to attend twenty-four lectures and discussion classes in each subject, and are expected to do such written work as will be prescribed. At the end of each year students are required to take an examination in each of the prescribed subjects, and on the results of these examinations the Diploma is awarded.

THE INSTITUTE'S TEACHING PROGRAMME

DIPLOMA IN INTERNATIONAL AND COMPARATIVE AIR LAW

This is a Diploma awarded by the London Institute of World Affairs on the basis of examinations held annually by the Institute. The examination is divided into two Parts, which may be taken separately:

Part I: General Principles of International and Comparative Air Law.

Part II: Selected Problems of International and Comparative Air Law.

Candidates for the Diploma must have pursued a recognised course of study in order to qualify for admission to the examination.

Full details and application forms for both Diplomas may be obtained from:

The *Organising Tutor*,
The London Institute of World Affairs,
c/o The Faculty of Laws,
University College London,
Gower Street, London, W.C.1.

PUBLICATIONS OF THE INSTITUTE

Editors: George W. Keeton and Georg Schwarzenberger

THE YEAR BOOK OF WORLD AFFAIRS

The *Year Book* contains research articles of permanent interest on important aspects of world affairs. Copies of Vol. 14 (1960) are available at £2 15s. each and Vol. 15 (1961) at £3 3s. each. Limited numbers of previous volumes are also available, at £2 5s. each.

CONTENTS FOR 1962

REPORTS ON WORLD AFFAIRS

£3 3s. net

THE LIBRARY OF WORLD AFFAIRS

(All books in the Library are supplied post free in the United Kingdom)

1. *Making International Law Work.* By George W. Keeton and Georg Schwarzenberger. Second Edition. *(Out of print.)*

2. *China Moulded by Confucius: The Chinese Way in Western Light.* By His Excellency Dr. F. T. Cheng. Illustrated. 25s.

3. *A Manual of International Law.* By Georg Schwarzenberger. Fourth Edition. 2 Vols. £4 10s.

4. *The Crisis in the Law of Nations.* By H. A. Smith. *(Out of print.)*

5. *Great Britain, the United States and the Future.* By J. E. Tyler. 12s. 6d.

6. *China, The Far East and the Future.* By George W. Keeton. Second Edition. *(Out of print.)*

7. *Czechoslovakia between East and West.* By W. Diamond. 18s. 6d.

8. *The Allied Military Government of Germany.* By W. Friedmann. *(Out of print.)*

9. *The Law and Custom of the Sea.* By H. A. Smith. Third Edition. 23s. 6d.

10. *The Charter of the United Nations.* By L. M. Goodrich and E. Hambro. Third Edition. *(Out of print.)*

11. *The Law of the United Nations: A Critical Analysis of its Fundamental Problems.* By Hans Kelsen. Second Edition by Salo Engel. *(In preparation.)*

12. *The North Atlantic Treaty, the Brussels Treaty and the United Nations Charter.* By Sir W. Eric Beckett. *(Out of print.)*

13. *Finland: The Adventures of a Small Power.* By Hugh Shearman. With maps. *(Out of print.)*

14. *The World of the Slavs.* By A. Mousset. 18s. 6d.

15. *Russia and the United States.* By P. A. Sorokin. Second Edition. *(Out of print.)*

16. *The International Law of Recognition.* By T. C. Chen. *(Out of print.)*

17. *International Law through the Cases.* By L. C. Green. Second Edition. £4

18. *Power Politics: A Study of International Society.* By G. Schwarzenberger. Second Edition (revised). £3

19. *International Economic Organizations.* By C. H. Alexandrowicz. *(Out of print.)*

20. *Expropriation in International Law.* By S. Friedman. *(Out of print.)*

21. *The General Principles of Law as applied by International Courts and Tribunals.* By Bin Cheng. £4 10s.

22. *The Law of Nations: Cases, Documents and Notes.* By H. W. Briggs. Second Edition. £3 17s. 6d.

23. *Law and Social Change in the U.S.S.R.* By J. N. Hazard. 30s.

24. *The British Commonwealth in International Law.* By J. E. S. Fawcett. *(In preparation.)*

25. *International Relations: The World Community in Transition.* By N. D. Palmer and H. C. Perkins. Second Edition. £2 15s.

26. *The Communist Theory of Law.* By Hans Kelsen. 37s. 6d.

27. *Organising for Peace: International Organisation in World Affairs.* By D. S. Cheever and H. Field Haviland, Jr. £3

28. *Nationality and Statelessness in International Law.* By P. Weis. *(Out of print.)*

29. *Germany and the North Atlantic Community: A Legal Survey.* By M. Bathurst and J. L. Simpson. 38s. 6d.

30. *Law and Structures of Social Action.* By K. S. Carlston. 38s. 6d.

THE LIBRARY OF WORLD AFFAIRS

(All books in the Library are supplied post free in the United Kingdom)

Members of the Institute who wish to obtain publications in the Library at the special reduced price (25% less than the published prices) should order them from *the Secretary of the Institute.*

Non-Members should address orders to Messrs. Stevens & Sons Limited, the official publishers of the Institute.

(Addresses are on the Order form overleaf.)

APPLICATION FOR MEMBERSHIP

TO THE SECRETARY,

THE LONDON INSTITUTE OF WORLD AFFAIRS
C/O THE FACULTY OF LAWS, UNIVERSITY COLLEGE LONDON,
GOWER STREET, LONDON, W.C.1.

I enclose £............................. * as membership subscription to

THE LONDON INSTITUTE OF WORLD AFFAIRS for the year

19......

BLOCK
CAPITALS
PLEASE
{
Name ....

Address ....

....

Date ....

* Minimum Annual Subscription £2 2s. ($6.30).

ORDER FOR PUBLICATIONS *

MEMBERS	NON-MEMBERS
TO THE SECRETARY, THE LONDON INSTITUTE OF WORLD AFFAIRS, c/o THE FACULTY OF LAWS, UNIVERSITY COLLEGE LONDON, GOWER STREET, LONDON, W.C.1.	TO STEVENS & SONS, LTD., 11 NEW FETTER LANE, LONDON, E.C.4. *[Telephone: Fleet Street 7102 Cables: RHODRONS, London.]*

(Please delete address which does not apply)

Please send the following books in the Library of World Affairs

Nos. ....

....

BLOCK
CAPITALS
PLEASE
{
Name ....

Address ....

....

Date ....

Overseas postage, packing and insurance is charged at the following rates:

Orders of value up to £1: . . . 1s. 6d. postage.
Orders in excess of £1:
first £1: . . . 1s. 6d. postage.
each additional £1: . . . 8d. extra.

☐ Remittance enclosed   ☐ Charge to account

* See note on page vii.

January 1962   THE EASTERN PRESS, LTD.